CALIFORNIA REAL ESTATE APPRAISAL
Residential Properties

Fourth Edition

George H. Miller, C.G. R.E.A., P.C.A., R.E.C.I.
*Chairman, Real Estate Department, West Valley College
and Real Estate Appraiser, Saratoga*

Katy R. Gallagher, P.R.A., C.R.E.A.
Certified Residential Real Estate Appraiser, Lake Tahoe

H. Glenn Mercer
Emeritus, City College of San Francisco

Kenneth W. Gilbeau, M.A.I.
Real Estate Appraiser, San Jose

Prentice Hall, Englewood Cliffs, New Jersey 07632

Library of Congress Cataloging-in-Publication Data

California real estate appraisal : residential properties / George H.
Miller . . . [et al.].—4th ed.
    p. cm.
    Rev. ed. of: California real estate appraisal / George H. Miller,
H. Glen Mercer, Kenneth W. Gilbeau. 3rd ed. c1987.
    Includes index.
    ISBN 0–13–312067–8
    1. Dwellings—Valuation—California. 2. Real property—Valuation—
California. 3. Dwellings—Valuation. 4. Real property—Valuation.
I. Miller, George H.   California real estate appraisal.
HD266.C22C24   1995
333.33′82′09794—dc20
                             94–40190
                                CIP

Copyright © 1995, 1987, 1977, 1972 by Prentice-Hall, Inc.
A Simon & Schuster Company
Englewood Cliffs, New Jersey 07632

Printed in the United States of America

10 9 8 7 6 5 4 3 2 1

Cover design: Marianne Frasco
Manufacturing buyer: Ilene Sanford

ISBN 0-13-312067-8
ISBN 0-13-378829-6 (Special Edition)

Prentice-Hall International (UK) Limited, *London*
Prentice-Hall of Australia Pty. Limited, *Sydney*
Prentice-Hall Canada Inc., *Toronto*
Prentice-Hall Hispanoamericana, S.A., *Mexico*
Prentice-Hall of India Private Limited, *New Delhi*
Prentice-Hall of Japan, Inc., *Tokyo*
Prentice-Hall of Southeast Asia Pte. Ltd., *Singapore*
Editora Prentice-Hall do Brasil Ltda., *Rio de Janeiro*

This book is dedicated to appraisal and
real estate students and professionals
who strive for excellence.

GEORGE H. MILLER
KATY R. GALLAGHER

To be conscious that you are ignorant
is a great step to knowledge.

BENJAMIN DISRAELI

CONTENTS

ILLUSTRATIONS, *xiii*

PREFACE, *xv*

1   **IMPORTANCE AND PURPOSES OF APPRAISALS, 1**

Importance of Appraisals, *2*
What Is an Appraisal?, *3*
Types of Appraisals, *4*
Purposes of Appraisals, *6*
Summary, *12*
Discussion Questions, *12*
Multiple-Choice Questions, *13*

2   **NATURE AND CHARACTERISTICS OF PROPERTY AND VALUE, 14**

Influences on Real Estate Value*
Legal Considerations in Real Estate
Types of Value

What Is Property?, *14*
What Is Real Property?, *14*
What Is Personal Property?, *15*
What Is Value?, *16*
What Is Market Value?, *18*
Other Common Value Terms and Definitions, *19*
Forces Affecting the Value of Real Property, *20*
Basic Powers of Government against Private Real Estate, *22*
Other Possible Restrictions Against Private Real Property, *24*
Summary, *24*
Discussion Questions, *24*
Multiple-Choice Questions, *25*

*Note: The bold, italicized items under certain chapter heading indicate the specific topics required for California State licensing, comprising the "Body of Knowledge."

3   PRINCIPLES CONTROLLING REAL ESTATE VALUE, 27

Economic Principles
Highest and Best-Use Analysis

Principle of Highest and Best Use, *27*
Principle of Supply and Demand, *28*
Principle of Substitution, *29*
Principle of Anticipation, *29*
Principle of Change, *30*
Principle of Conformity, *31*
Principle of Contribution, *32*
Principle of Competition, *32*
Principle of Consistent Use, *32*
Principle of Increasing and Decreasing Returns, *33*
Concept of Agents in Production, *34*
Concept of Opportunity Cost, *35*
Summary, *35*
Discussion Questions, *35*
Multiple-Choice Questions, *36*

4   ECONOMIC ANALYSIS, 38

Real Estate Market and Analysis
Influences on Real Estate Value

International Real Estate Activity, *38*
Economic Analysis, *41*
National Economy, *41*
Regional Analysis, *44*
City Analysis, *49*
Neighborhood Analysis, *51*
Summary, *59*
Discussion Questions, *60*
Multiple-Choice Questions, *61*

5   THE APPRAISAL PROCESS, 62

Valuation Process

Defining the Problem—Clarifying the Assignment, *63*
Collection and Analyses of Data—Gathering and Interpreting
    Information, *71*
Highest and Best-Use Analysis, *72*
Performing the Three Approaches, *72*
Reconciliation of the Three Approaches and the Final Estimate
    of Value, *74*
Communicating the Results of the Appraisal, *75*
Summary, *75*

Discussion Questions, *76*
Multiple-Choice Questions, *76*

6   CONSIDERATIONS IN SITE ANALYSIS, 78

Property Description

Type of Lot, *80*
Size, *85*
Shape, *86*
Slope, *86*
Drainage, *92*
Soil Composition, *93*
Trees, *93*
Exposure to Sun and Weather, *95*
View, *95*
Access, *96*
Availability of Utilities, *96*
Off-Site Improvements, *100*
Deed Restrictions, Easements, and Rights-of-Way, *101*
Availability of Public Transportation, *101*
Proximity to Earthquake Fault Zones and Flood Hazard
    Areas, *101*
Proximity to Nuclear Facilities or Hazardous Waste Sites, *102*
Proximity to Electric and Electromagnetic Fields (EMF), *102*
Summary, *102*
Discussion Questions, *103*
Multiple-Choice Questions, *103*

7   FUNDAMENTALS OF SITE EVALUATION, 106

Site Value
The Sales Comparison, or Market Data, Approach, *106*
The Allocation Approach—The Ratio of Total Value
    to Site Value, *111*
The Abstractive or Extraction, Approach, *112*
The Land Development Approach, *112*
The Land-Residual Approach, *113*
Plottage, or Assemblage, *115*
Ground Rent Capitalization, *115*
Summary, *116*
Discussion Questions, *116*
Multiple-Choice Questions, *116*

8   CONSTRUCTION METHODS AND MATERIALS, 119

Property Description—Basic Construction and Design

Climate and Available Materials, *120*

Analysis of the Structure, *121*
Equipment in the Building, *141*
Yard Equipment and Materials, *153*
Factors in Analysis of High-Quality Residences, *157*
Factors in Analysis of Fair-Quality Residences, *160*
Summary, *162*
Discussion Questions, *162*
Multiple-Choice Questions, *163*

9 ARCHITECTURAL STYLES AND UTILITY, 167

Consumer Acceptance of Styles, *167*
Esthetic Appeal of Materials, *169*
Roof Styles, *175*
Window Styles, *177*
Multiple-Family Residential Styles, *181*
Functional Utility in Single-Family and Multiple-Family
    Residences, *181*
Undesirable Style and Functional Utility Factors, *195*
Two-Story versus Single-Story Residences, *195*
Summary, *197*
Discussion Questions, *197*
Multiple-Choice Questions, *197*

10 COST APPROACH: ESTIMATING COSTS, 200

Reproduction versus Replacement Cost

Reproduction Cost and Replacement Cost, *201*
Methods of Estimating Costs, *201*
Sources of Cost Data, *208*
Site or Yard Improvements, *211*
Indirect Costs, *212*
Discussion Questions, *214*
Multiple-Choice Questions, *214*

11 COST APPROACH: ACCRUED DEPRECIATION ANALYSIS, 216

Accrued Depreciation
Methods of Estimating Depreciation

Physical Deterioration, *217*
Functional Obsolescence, *217*
Economic Obsolescence—External Obsolescence, *218*
Measurement of Accrued Depreciation, *219*
Limitations of the Cost Approach, *226*
Summary, *227*

Discussion Questions, *228*
Multiple-Choice Questions, *229*

12   SALES COMPARISON, OR MARKET DATA, APPROACH, 231

Sales Comparison Approach

Collection of Sales Data, *232*
Processing Sales Data, *236*
Analysis of Sales Data, *240*
Comparison Between Sales and Subject Property, *240*
Correlation of Market Data Sales, *246*
Limitations of the Market Data Approach, *246*
Summary, *247*
Discussion Questions, *247*
Multiple-Choice Questions, *248*

13   INCOME APPROACH: INCOME AND EXPENSE ANALYSIS, 250

Estimation of Income and Expenses
Operating Expense Ratio

Gross Income, *251*
Vacancy and Rent Loss, *252*
Expenses, *253*
Broker's Net, *256*
Reconstructed Operating Statement, *257*
Discussion Questions, *257*
Multiple-Choice Questions, *258*

14   INCOME APPROACH: CAPITALIZATION THEORY
AND TECHNIQUES, 261

Direct Capitalization
Gross Rent Multiplier Analysis

Capitalization Rates, *263*
Selection of Capitalization Rates, *265*
Capitalization Techniques, *271*
Gross Rent Mulitplier, *274*
Limitations of the Income Approach, *275*
Summary, *276*
Discussion Questions, *277*
Multiple-Choice Questions, *277*

15 RECONCILIATION AND FINAL VALUE ESTIMATE, 280

Valuation Process—Reconciliation and Final Value Estimate Appraisal Statistical Concepts

Type of Property Appraised, *281*
Final Value Estimate, *285*
Statistical Concepts, *286*
Summary, *287*
Discussion Questions, *287*
Multiple-Choice Questions, *288*

16 WRITING THE REPORT, 289

Report Writing

Types of Reports, *289*
Essential Elements of an Appraisal Report, *291*
Types of Appraisal Reports, *292*
Form Report, *293*
Letter Report, *306*
Narrative Report, *306*
Report Elements, *310*
Oral Reports, *318*
Summary, *319*
Discussion Questions, *319*
Multiple-Choice Questions, *319*

17 COMPUTERIZATION OF THE APPRAISAL PROCESS, 321

Hardware Considerations, *321*
Information and Data Resources Services, *324*
Software Programs, *326*
State-of-the-Art Technology, *327*
Summary, *331*

18 CONSIDERATIONS IN APPRAISING OTHER TYPES OF SINGLE-FAMILY RESIDENCES, 332

Legal Considerations in Appraisal—Forms of Property Ownership

Mobile Homes, *333*
Nonmobile Homes, *335*
Townhouses, Rowhouses, Condominiums, Cooperative Apartments, Community Apartment Projects, and Cluster Homes, *337*
Modular, Manufactured, and Kit Homes (Factory Built), *345*

Patio Homes and Duets (Zero Lot Line), *347*
Compact Homes, *348*
Planned Unit Development (PUD), *350*
Time Shares, *351*
Summary, *351*
Discussion Questions, *352*
Multiple-Choice Questions, *352*

19   *SPECIAL-PURPOSE APPRAISING, 355*

Valuation of Partial Intersets

Lease Interests, *355*
Easements, *356*
Air Rights, *357*
Solar Rights, *358*
Plottage, or Assemblage, *358*
The Part Take, *359*
Severance Damage, *361*
Access Rights, *361*
Considerations in Appraising Single-Family Residential Properties
    Close to Public Facilities, *362*
Summary, *366*
Discussion Questions, *366*
Multiple-Choice Questions, *366*

**20   *PROFESSIONAL OPPORTUNITIES IN REAL ESTATE
       APPRAISING, 368***

Salaried Opportunities, *369*
Nonsalaried Opportunities (Independent), *373*
Professional Organizations, *375*
The Future of Appraising as a Profession, *378*
Responsibilities of the Appraiser, *379*
Liabilities of the Appraiser, *379*
Summary, *380*
Discussion Questions, *380*

**21 *LICENSE AND STATE EXAMINATION REQUIREMENTS, LENDER
      APPRAISAL GUIDELINES, AND COMMON ERRORS
      AND OMISSIONS, 381***

State Licensing, *382*
Lender Appraisal Guidelines for Single-Family Residences, *384*
Common Errors and Omissions by Appraisers and How
    to Avoid Them, *385*

APPENDIX I
TITLE IX-FEDERAL INSTITUTIONS REFORM, RECOVERY,
AND ENFORCEMENT ACT (FIRREA), 392

APPENDIX II
UNIFORM STANDARDS OF PROFESSIONAL APPRAISAL
PRACTICE (USPAP), 402

APPENDIX III
BODY OF KNOWLEDGE, 411

APPENDIX IV
ANSWERS TO CHAPTER QUESTIONS, 418

APPENDIX V
GLOSSARY OF RESIDENTIAL APPRAISAL TERMINOLOGY, 441

INDEX, 501

ILLUSTRATIONS

2–1 Extent of land ownership, 15

5–1 California government survey lines, 65

5–2 Township breakdown, 66

5–3 Metes and bounds description, 67

5–4 Example of lot and block (recorded tract), 68

6–1 Lot types, 80

6–2 Residence situated on an uphill lot, 87

6–3 Residence situated on a downhill lot, 88

6–4 Residence situated on a sidehill lot, 90

6–5 Residence situated on a top-of-hill lot, 91

6–6 Facilities in a developed residential lot, 94

6–7 Septic tank installation, 99

7–1 Land-residual approach, 115

8–1 Construction details of a house, 121

8–2 Residential floor plans with identical square footage, 122

8–3 Construction details of a low-quality California ranch house, 124

8–4 Construction details of a very good quality California ranch house, 124

8–5 Construction details of a good quality masonry house, 125

8–6 Most common roof coverings, 126

8–7 California ranch, low-cost (minimum quality) construction, 130

8–8 California ranch, fair (just below average) construction, 131

8–9 California ranch, average construction, 132

8–10 California ranch, good construction, 133

8–11 California ranch, very good construction, 134

8–12 California ranch, excellent construction, 135

8–13 Contemporary, fair construction, 136

8–14 Contemporary, good construction, 137

8–15 Comtemporary, excellent construction, 137

8–16 Mountain cabin, low-quality construction, 138

8–17 Mountain cabin, good construction, 139

8–18 The major types of residential gas heating systems, 144

8–19 A residential solar energy system that provides heating and cooling of space and heating of water, 147

8–20 Solar heating a swimming pool, 148

8–21 Functional floor plan for use of solar energy, 149

8–22 Energy-efficient home, 150

8–23 Dead bolt lock, 152

9–1 California ranch, single story, 168

9–2 California ranch, split level, 169

9–3 California ranch, two story, 170

9–4 California ranch–Cape Cod combination, 171

9–5 Comtemporary, 171

9–6   Traditional French provincial, 172

9–7   Conventional French provincial, 172

9–8   Contemporary French provincial, 173

9–9   Normandy French, 173

9–10   Country French, 174

9–11   Dutch colonial, 174

9–12   Victorian, 175

9–13   English Tudor, 176

9–14   English half-timber (Elizabethan), 176

9–15   English cottage, 177

9–16   Traditional Italian, 178

9–17   Spanish, 178

9–18   Conventional Mediterranean, 179

9–19   Contemporary Mediterranean, 179

9–20   International modern, 180

9–21   New England colonial, 180

9–22   Contemporary colonial, 181

9–23   Traditional colonial, 182

9–24   Southern colonial, 183

9–25   California Monterey, 184

9–26   Cape Cod, 184

9–27   Contemporary architectural design or Pacific Island hut roof, 185

9–28   Modified gambrel roof, 185

9–29   Geodesic dome, 186

9–30   Modern mansard, single story, 186

9–31   Contemporary mountain chalet, 187

9–32   Classic A-frame mountain cabin, 187

9–33   Log cabin, 188

9–34   Contemporary shed roof, 188

9–35   Pyramid, 189

9–36   Modern mansard, two story, 189

9–37   Roof styles, 190

9–38   The cupola, 191

9–39   Window styles, 191

9–40   Poor floor plan, 192

9–41   Good floor plan, 192

10–1   Measurement of living area, porches, and garage of single-story home, 203

12–1   Sample sales history—DataQuick, 233

12–2   Multiple listing—closed sale transaction, 235

12–3   Flood zone determination, 236

12–4   Plat map, 237

14–1   Six functions of one dollar—8% annual interest, 262

16–1   Uniform Residential Appraisal Report, 295

17–1   Sample sketch addendum: 2-story, trilevel home with 3-car garage and in-law quarters in basement, 328

17–2   Location map addendum, 330

18–1   Mobile home park with standard side yards, 335

18–2   Mobile homes with zero lot line placement, 336

18–3   Nonmobile home, 336

18–4   Overhead view of beach townhouse development, 338

18–5   Typical townhouse elevations, 339

18–6   A mountain townhouse, 339

18–7   Floor plan of townhouse, 340

18–8   Overhead view of rowhouses, 341

18–9   San Francisco rowhouse elevations, 342

18–10   Eastern rowhouse elevations, 342

18–11   Condominium ownership, 343

18–12   Overhead view of large development of cluster homes, 345

18–13   Overhead view of cluster homes of small development, 346

18–14   Modular home, average quality, 347

18–15   Patio homes or garden homes (zero lot line), 348

18–16   Floor plan of patio home (zero lot line), 349

18–17   Planned unit development, 350

19–1   Plottage, 359

19–2   Part take for expressway, 360

PREFACE

Sweeping and historic changes have occurred in the real estate industry since the third edition of *California Real Estate Appraisal: Residential Properties* was published. As a direct result of the savings and loan debacle, which caused hundreds of banks, thrifts, and other lending institutions to close their doors due to real estate losses amounting to billions of dollars, the federal government instituted the Financial Institutions Reform and Recovery Act in 1989, known as FIRREA. This act imposed strict and binding regulations on the real estate sales and appraisal industries. These industries had been largely self-regulated, and while on a state level, real estate sales and brokerage firms were beginning to experience more stringent licensing requirements, including extensive educational requirements, the impact of FIRREA was to superimpose national standards, demanding that each state create a regulatory department to ensure compliance with the new laws.

The appraisal industry had been self-regulated by a group of trade organizations, which conferred degrees of expertise according to various professional criteria established by each organization. The new federal regulations required that standardized licensing be instituted, so the major organizations joined forces with the Congressional Subcommittee to create the Uniform Standards of Appraisal Practice, known as USPAP. This body of standards and rules applies to most federally related real estate transactions and contains specific guidelines for practical appraising, including the definition of appraisal parameters, appraisal ethics, and appraisal practice procedures.

The rigid regulations initially imposed on the appraisal industry were effective across the wide spectrum of commercial and residential properties. It has been recently recognized at the federal level that the major source of the savings and loan crisis problems resulted from commercial transactions and that some residential transactions may require a lesser degree of regulation. The Appraisal Standards Board is beginning to allow significant changes to the departure provisions of USPAP, which in effect begin to "deregulate" some of the transactions. The "de minimis," or threshold level for lenders to require full appraisals has been raised, and the impact of this allowance for a "less than full appraisal" is yet to be determined. As with many new regulatory endeavors, the pendulum generally swings widely at first, from strong enforcement under stringent rules, to "un-doing" some of the tenants that cause business to be too restrictive, and eventually, a middle ground is reached.

This fourth edition of *California Real Estate Appraisal* is designed specifically to address the changes in the appraisal industry, their impact on real estate transactions, and their practical application for appraisers, real estate professionals, lenders, and consumers. We have included the pertinent FIRREA and USPAP texts, and the California licensing requirements. A complete set of residential appraisal forms, including the 1993 Uniform Residential Appraisal Report (URAR), the Condominium form, the 2-4 Small Income form, the Land form, the Limited Appraisal Report form (limited scope) developed for the "less than full" appraisal, and a narrative report are included in a student and teacher supplement to this textbook. We have expanded our text to include the impact of the computerization of the appraisal industry and discuss current and future appraisal business trends. We have updated and enhanced our glossary of appraisal terms, as well. This material is designed to comply with the State of California licensing requirements, and provide the necessary information and study guide material to assist appraisers in preparation for the state examination.

The appraisal concepts, standards, and practical constructs presented in this book are intended to provide a current and continuing, relevant resource for understanding and practicing the appraisal profession.

Acknowledgments

We wish to acknowledge the following appraisal professionals who have contributed to our fourth edition:

Marty Carrick, Canada College appraisal instructor, San Mateo

Nolan B. Cavey, appraiser in the Sacramento area

Jane Chiavacchi, appraiser in Saratoga

Barry R. Cleverdon, Sierra College appraisal instructor and appraiser in the Sacramento area

Gary R. Fisher, appraisal instructor at Beale Air Force Base

Glenn Frizzel, Foothill College appraisal instructor, Palo Alto

Donna Grogan, MBA, El Camino Community College instructor in Torrance

Robert R. Keeling, appraiser in the Sacramento area

Neil Lefman, MAI, appraiser in the San Jose area

Dr. Charles B. Mayfield, Los Angeles Southwest College, real estate coordinator

Dave Morrison, MAI, appraiser in the San Jose area

Susumu Nakazato, appraisal instructor in the Sacramento area

Joan Robinson, Santa Clara County Assessor's Office, and De Anza College appraisal instructor

Greg E. Stephens, appraiser in the San Jose area

Gretchen A. Walsh, appraiser and partner, George H. Miller Associates, Saratoga

Dave Zaches, MAI, appraiser in the Saratoga area

Patricia Steinfurth, apprentice appraiser, Saratoga

We also wish to acknowledge The Appraisal Foundation, whose dedication to promotion of appraisal standards continues to enhance the professionalism of the appraisal industry. The Appraisal Foundation has given us permission to publish excerpts of the Uniform Standards of Professional Appraisal Practice (USPAP) in this book. Note that the excerpts are only portions of the USPAP text, and complete annual and updated editions are available for purchase from The Appraisal Foundation, 1029 Vermont Avenue, NW, Suite 900, Washington, DC 20005.

In addition, we wish to thank Shelley Silvas, Sacramento Regional Sales Manager, her entire staff, and all of the people at DataQuick, a nationwide real estate information service, for their assistance in preparation of the computerized data resource material used in our fourth edition.

Finally, we extend a special thanks to Bradford and Robbins, producer of computerized appraisal forms for both *Microsoft Windows* and *Macintosh* users, for their assistance with production of the appraisal forms and matching sketches used in this text book. We used *Clickforms,* the *Windows* version of the forms and sketch program for IBM-compatible personal computers. An introductory version of the *Clickforms* Uniform Residential Appraisal Report (URAR) form program software is an option with the purchase of this text book, providing a means of producing a complete appraisal report for course credit purposes. The Windows software may be exchanged for the *MacAppraiser* Macintosh version, if the platform is an Apple Macintosh computer.

Chapter 1

IMPORTANCE AND PURPOSES OF APPRAISALS

The need to possess their own land is strongly developed among people in many cultures. This feeling is intensified as increasing world population threatens to deprive more and more people of land and as the distribution of land continues to be, for the most part, driven by wealth. California, once glamorized as the land of opportunity, is now considered by many to be overcrowded, and for the first time, some people are actually leaving the state for less populated areas of the country.

The rise in land values is almost directly proportional to the increase in population. *In our increasingly credit-stimulated, profit-motivated, government-controlled, tax-oriented, space-deprived, pollution-threatened, inflation-prone real estate economy, the appraisal of real estate becomes a more and more complex and sophisticated procedure.*

Property values in California reached an all-time high in the late 1980s due to an unprecedented combination of events that conspired to artificially inflate property prices. The deregulation of the lending industry under the Reagan Administration allowed lenders to make loans without consistent guidelines and without appraisers conforming to accountable standards. In addition, lending rules were diluted, allowing speculative loans to be made with very little supporting data. Major commercial properties were the primary target for these "loose" transactions, but a significant number of residential properties were also involved. This inflation resulted in a fiscal crisis for banks, thrifts, and other lending institutions when many of the transactions were examined, and the values found excessive. The result was the savings and loan scandal, climaxing in 1989, when the federal government announced that the real estate losses amounted to more than $200 billion.

In response to the crisis, which caused hundreds of lending institutions to close their doors, the federal government passed the Financial Institutions Reform and Recovery and Enforcement Act (FIRREA), which established new regulations affecting the entire real estate industry, but most significantly the appraisal business. Title XI (Sec. 1101) of the FIRREA, entitled Real Estate Appraisal Reform Amendments, defines the purpose, as follows:

> The purpose of this title is to provide that Federal financial and public policy interests in real estate related transactions will be protected by requiring that

real estate appraisals utilized in connection with federally related transactions are performed in writing, in accordance with uniform standards, by individuals whose competency has been demonstrated and whose professional conduct will be subject to effective supervision.

The most significant result of FIRREA was the requirement, effective January 1, 1993, that *all* "federally related real estate appraisals" be performed *only* by appraisers that were licensed or certified by the state in which the real estate was located.

A Congressional Appraisal Subcommittee was created to monitor all appraisal-related activities, standards, and regulations and to oversee the establishment of uniform appraisal standards for each state. The subcommittee recognized that the Uniform Standards of Professional Appraisal Practice (USPAP), generated by an ad hoc committee comprised of nine appraisal organizations, originally published in 1986, were a good platform to work from, and with some revisions, USPAP was adopted for federal use.

USPAP is interpreted and amended, from time to time, by the Appraisal Standards Board of the Appraisal Foundation, subject to confirmation by the Appraisal Subcommittee. The original ad hoc committee was formed by the various appraisal organizations so that appraisers could participate in the regulatory process, and this group formed the nucleus of the Appraisal Standards Board.

USPAP sets forth standards and guidelines for appraisers, governing appraisal practice and ethics. The USPAP text is contained in Appendix II.

Typically, when the initial regulations were drafted, they were very restrictive. Since the initial standards were issued, many changes have been made, allowing more flexibility for appraisals and radically reducing certain appraisal criteria. The impact of these "deregulating" changes are yet to be determined, and regulations will continue to evolve. The roll of appraisers remains an integral part of the real estate and lending industries, and the importance of professional, reliable appraisals remains paramount.

IMPORTANCE OF APPRAISALS

By industry convention in the past, and now by legislative directive, no real estate venture of any significant investment can take place without the aid of an appraisal or opinion of value. Appraising is the basis of the entire real estate industry. Thousands of appraisals, to determine everything from property taxes to loans, have a great economic effect on California business. There is a continuing need for well-trained real estate appraisers.

For many California families, the most important investment is their home. Here they live and prosper. The land on which they live is the only land many can call their own. For this reason alone, knowledge of the fundamentals of real estate appraisal is of prime importance for selection of the home most suitable to the family's or the individual's needs. Because of the constantly changing economy and environment, continued study of appraising is necessary to keep abreast of this dynamic field.

WHAT IS AN APPRAISAL?

Webster's Dictionary[1] defines appraisal as "an estimated value set upon property."

FIRREA dictates that an appraisal must be "a written statement used in connection with a federally related transaction that is independently and impartially prepared by a licensed or certified appraiser setting forth an opinion of defined value of an adequately described property as of a specific date, supported by presentation and analysis of relevant market information."

USPAP defines *appraisal* as follows: "(noun) the act or process of estimating value; an estimate of value. (adjective) of or pertaining to appraising and related functions; e.g., appraisal practice, appraisal services."

We must keep in mind the words *estimated* and *opinion*. An appraisal is only an estimate, or opinion, although it is often a reasonably sophisticated one. The reliability of an appraisal is limited to data available and the ability and objectivity of the appraiser. In trying to form a realistic opinion of the value of a property, most people have difficulty being completely objective. An appraiser's primary concern is to consider impersonally all available facts to arrive at a realistic estimate of value.

Subjective opinions of value vary widely. A property owner may consider a tax assessor's appraisal much too high or a lender's appraisal too low. Many real estate brokers seeking realistic listing prices (asking prices) from homeowners are painfully aware that people who own and live in their homes may not be the best judges of the market value of their property. It is understandably difficult for the prospective seller to be completely objective.

Generally, in single-family residential appraising, the same real estate parcel appraised by two competent, objective appraisers should show no more than a 5 percent difference. Of course, there are exceptions. For example, a one design, custom-constructed home suited to unusual tastes would allow a greater range of possible values because of its unusual aspects. Or an overbuilt home, an example of *superadequacy,* constructed to unusually rigid owner specifications—having a basement in an area where basements are seldom found, for example, or a backyard greenhouse that is glass enclosed and air-conditioned—might have cost several thousand dollars more than most buyers would be willing to pay for such improvements.

Real estate appraising is not an exact science but an opinion of

---

[1]Terms throughout this book are from *Webster's New Collegiate Dictionary.*

value. Different people's opinions can certainly vary; we must use judgment in balancing the variables to form an intelligent opinion of value. Where enough similar properties exist and a sufficient number of recent sales have occurred, any two knowledgeable and objective appraisers should arrive independently at similar values for the same property.

TYPES OF APPRAISALS

Appraisals assume different forms for different purposes.

Visual Comparison

Most buyers of single-family residences, whether they know it or not, have made an appraisal—that of visual comparison. Before they buy, almost all buyers compare many available properties for style, number of rooms, quality of construction, and neighborhood. Only after making these comparisons do they settle on the house of their choice. They have actually performed an appraisal using a simple market data, or comparison, approach.

Comparative Market Analysis (CMA)

This is a term often used by real estate brokers in preparing a report for prospective sellers and buyers, indicating market trends in various neighborhoods, based on computer statistics generated from multiple-listing service data. Generally, these analyses are used for clients to determine a listing price for the sale of a home or for buyers to determine if a list price is reasonable for a given location. These reports are a form of appraisal and can be misleading if used to determine the value of an individual property. These reports are not prepared by professional appraisers and do not take into account all of the factors that affect the value of an individual property, nor are they regulated by the reporting standards of professional appraisers.

Licensed and certified appraisers are bound by the FIRREA and USPAP regulations. USPAP Standard 2 dictates the content and form of the report that communicates the results of an appraisal to a client or any party for whom the appraiser performs a service, for federally related transactions. There are two basic forms of report governed by this standard—written, which is the only form recognized for federally related transactions, and oral, allowed under USPAP for other transactions. The full text of Standard 2 is provided in Appendix II; however, an overview is summarized, as follows:

Standards Rule 2–1 dictates that each written or oral appraisal report must:

1. Be set forth in a manner that will not be misleading.

2. Contain sufficient data so that the person reading it can understand it.

3. Disclose any extraordinary assumption or limiting condition affecting the appraisal and its impact on value.

There are three basic types of written appraisals: form reports, letter reports, and narrative reports.

Standards Rule 2–2 defines the elements that must be included in any written report, summarized as follows:

1. Identify and describe the property.

2. Identify the interest being appraised.

3. State the purpose of the appraisal.

4. Define the value to be estimated.

5. State the effective date and the date of the report.

6. Describe the process of collecting, confirming, and reporting data.

7. State assumptions and limiting conditions.

8. State information analyzed, procedures used, and reasoning methodology to support analysis, opinion, and conclusion.

9. Indicate highest and best use.

10. Explain exclusion of any of usual approaches, if excluded.

11. Provide information indicating compliance or departure from standards.

12. Include the appropriate certification.

Standards Rule 2–4 declares that the rules for oral reports are the same as for written reports, to the extent possible.

Form Report

Form reports, now largely computerized, are generally used by organizations and government agencies that process a great many appraisals of the same type of property. A form report is a checklist of various important aspects of a property and its improvements: total number of rooms, number of bedrooms and baths, type of roof, square footage, condition, age, and other salient features. The form includes a simple market analysis. An estimate of value is inserted at the bottom of the report.

The most widely used version of a form report is the Uniform Residential Appraisal Report (URAR), created as an industry standard format for use by Fannie Mae and Freddie Mac, the nation's two largest mortgage holders. This simple report generally requires several hours to prepare once the field work has been done.

Letter Report

A letter report states an opinion of value that is generally supported by comparable sales and other data compiled by the appraiser but not submitted with the letter. Backup material, accumulated by the appraiser in the course of his or her work, is retained in office files; if necessary, it can be assembled into a more complete written report. A professional appraiser knowledgeable in the area in which the property is located can usually prepare this type of report in less than half a day. A client who is familiar with the appraiser's work and who respects his or her opinion might call for a letter report when a quick estimate of value is needed.

Narrative Report

A narrative report, rarely used for residential appraisal since the advent of computerized form reports, is a complete appraisal in volume form, from 40 to 50 typewritten pages up to as many as 80 pages or more. It includes most of the pertinent data gathered by the appraiser during many hours, and even days, of collecting and assimilating facts. The narrative report can best support the appraiser's opinion of value. If the report is clearly and objectively written, a knowledgeable, objective reader can follow the logical steps and arrive at an opinion of value similar to the opinion of the appraiser.

The selection of the form of the report usually depends on the purpose the appraisal will serve. A narrative report calls for the most complete appraisal, while the form report is the most commonly used.

PURPOSES OF APPRAISALS

The purpose of an appraisal depends on the need of those seeking the estimate of value. Appraisals are most commonly used for the purposes of lending, insurance, inheritance tax, property tax assessment, real estate brokerage, selling, buying, living trusts, leases, eminent domain, financial statements, or divorce settlements.

Appraising for Lending

All successful lending institutions that deal in single-family residential loans make some sort of appraisal of the property that will be security for the loan, in order to protect their investment. Most lenders appraise both the property and the person requesting the loan. A credit check determines whether the borrower is responsible and can fulfill the payment requirements. If the borrower fails to fulfill obligations, the lender is protected by an appraisal that reflects a realistic value that can be translated, if necessary, into enough money to reimburse the lender.

Most lending institutions, such as banks, savings and loan associations, life insurance companies, and individuals, make loans based on a percentage of value. For example, on a $200,000 home, many might lend 80 percent of appraised value, or $160,000. An extra margin of safety is therefore built in, since conventional loans are rarely extended for the full amount of the sales price of the home.

Generally, appraisals for lending purposes for single-family residences consist of either a form report or a letter report. Seldom does the lender require or wish a full narrative report.

Appraising for Insurance

In the case of a single-family residence, most lenders insist that a fire insurance policy be taken out on the house itself, generally for no less than the amount of the loan. This protects the lender in the event that a fire destroys the house. The lender is named first in the loss-payable clause of the policy.

The appraisal for insurance purposes represents the amount of money required to replace the building at today's construction costs. Land is not insured against fire damage; only the replacement cost of the structure is insured. Some insurance policies, however, do not allow for building code upgrades that are often required for reconstruction after a fire.

Appraising for Inheritance Tax

The state of California requires that all real property subject to inheritance taxes be appraised by a state inheritance tax referee (formerly inheritance tax appraiser). This includes single-family residences as well as other types of real estate. The referee's fee is a small percentage of the total estimated value of the property.

The inheritance tax referee's report of the present market value of the property is usually submitted to the proper authority in the form of a letter. The estimate is generally supported by records of several comparable sales, a personal inspection of the property, and an analysis of recent sales activity in the area.

Appraising for Local Property Tax Assessment

As a result of the passage of Proposition 13 by California voters in June 1978, appraising for property tax assessment purposes has changed. Before that time, state law required that all private real estate in the state, with the exception of some tax-exempt properties, be appraised each year to determine their market value. These appraisals were made by the various county assessor's offices throughout the state. Local taxes were then assessed against the property based on a percentage of market value (usually 25 percent) by applying local tax rates including the cost of local city, county, and school district services. These taxes of so many dollars per $100 of assessed value were then applied to determine the annual property taxes. This was a fairly complicated procedure that caused confusion for most property owners. Added to this were the unprecedented price increases that occurred in California single-family residential real estate, especially in the urban areas in 1977. These increases were caused by a combination of the dramatic influx of industry and people into the urban areas of California for a variety of reasons and the availability of relatively *low-cost, fixed-rate* financing. With this unprecedented increase in home prices (40 percent within the year in some urban areas), property taxes skyrocketed. Because taxes were being assessed at an equivalent rate of 3 percent of the market value each year on many properties, this especially threatened many retired homeowners and those on fixed incomes who could not afford these rising tax payments. The result was the passage of Proposition 13, which reduced all local property taxes to no more than 1–1.25 percent of the market value and rolled back the date of value to March 1, 1975, on those properties that had not sold between March 1, 1975, and June 6, 1978. If they had sold between those dates, the value was the market value (usually represented by the selling price) as of the date of the sale.

Since June 1978, all properties are appraised and reassessed only as of the time of a sale or of transfer of any property rights. Also, any major improvements or additions, such as a swimming pool or an additional room, are cause for a reassessment of the property to include the value increment (usually the cost) of such improvements. All other properties are automatically taxed at an annual increment of no more than 2 percent—for example, if property taxes were $2,000 for a given year and there had been no major improvements or property transfer during that year, then the maximum property tax increment the following year would be $40 (2 percent of $2,000).

The effect of this voter-dictated change has been that those owners who purchased their homes at an earlier date enjoy a lower local property tax than those who purchased at a later date. It is quite possible for two adjoining homeowners, one who purchased a home in 1970 and one who purchased a similar home next door 25 years later, in 1995, to have a difference of 300 percent in their annual property taxes, even though both homes have essentially the same market value and enjoy the same local governmental services. Because of this property tax change, some homeowners who might have considered buying a newer or larger home under the pre-Proposition 13 tax plan might delay buying or withdraw completely as potential buyers of another home because of the tax obligation under the post-Proposition 13 property tax plan. The effect has been that buyers generally tend to stay longer in homes. Another effect has been the shifting of the major local property tax burden from industrial and commercial properties to residential properties because commercial and industrial properties tend to sell at longer intervals (20 to 30 years) than single-family residential properties, which sell on an average of every 5 to 10 years. If this continues, the major local property tax burden will inevitably fall upon residential property owners.

For now, as far as the student appraiser is concerned, annual local property taxes will be approximately between 1 and 1.25 percent of the market value (usually the selling price) of any new property transfer or between 1 and 1.25 percent of the cost of any new improvements or additions to the property. The student appraiser or licensee, however, is cautioned to investigate any areas that might have special sewer, street, or other public improvements or assessments, including Mello-Roos and other special assessments that might affect local property taxes in that particular area, possibly causing a tax burden of more than 1.25 percent of the market value of the property.

Appraising for Selling

Before an owner can sell property, its market value must be determined. Because most owners of single-family residences have inflated ideas of their properties' values, the professional real estate agent must be careful to recommend an asking or listing price that is not ridiculously high. On the other hand, recommending too low a figure can discourage the owner from selling. Policy varies with each office and appraiser; however, the listing price should be as close to market value as possible. Most property is sold at about a 5 percent reduction from the realistic listing price.

Most appraisals of homes to be sold are based on prices brought by similar properties. Many real estate sales offices keep a record of recent sales either through a multiple-listing service or in their own index of sales activity. These records are invaluable for comparing similar properties when an asking price must be placed on a particular property. This data is used to generate comparative market analysis (CMA) reports.

Another effective appraisal method for listing or selling purposes is the cost approach. An appraiser knowledgeable in the given area can usually make a simple cost analysis by estimating the lot value and the present value of the improvements, measuring the structure, and applying a unit cost factor less depreciation to arrive at a total maximum listing price.

Appraising for Buying

Most purchase appraisals for single-family residences are made by the prospective buyer. These appraisals take the form of the market approach, a review of homes offered for sale that fit the pocketbook of the potential buyer. The buyer compares the important features and prices of many properties and then makes a selection, usually by visual comparison.

Appraising for Living Trust

One way to avoid probate is to leave property under either a revocable or irrevocable trust. Many people who want to leave real estate and other property can do so by having an attorney prepare a living trust. Appraisals are needed to estimate the value of the real estate being left under the trust.

Appraising for Leases

If a property owner needs to know the value of a lease, which may be for a 5-, 10-, or 30-year term, to a tenant, an appraiser knowledgeable in the appraisal of leasehold interests and estates is required.

Appraising for Eminent Domain

Eminent domain is the right of a public body to take private property for public purposes. The public body exercises this right under *condemnation*—a term not to be confused with condemnation of a building because it is unsafe or does not meet health standards. To exercise the right of eminent domain, the public body must show the greatest public need commensurate with the least private damage. The other stipulation is that a fair price be paid for the property. The state and federal constitutions protect the individual against deprivation of private real property without just compensation, which has been interpreted by the courts as market value. To determine market value, the public body has the needed property appraised either by staff appraisers or by independent fee appraisers, who usually prepare a narrative appraisal report. The power to exercise the right of eminent domain through a condemnation action is exercised by many different public bodies, among them the federal, state, county, and city government; school districts; public utilities; and flood control districts.

A narrative appraisal report is usually necessary for the public representatives—a real estate agent, right-of-way agent, property agent, or attorney—to be adequately prepared to discuss all the features of the property with the owner. Only then should the property owner be satisfied that the offer to buy his or her property is fair.

The acquisition price should always be fair to both the agency and the seller. Sometimes an agreement cannot be reached, and the property owner acts on his or her right to a court trial, either before a judge alone or before a judge and jury. The agency is the plaintiff in the condemnation action, and the property owner is the defendant. Each side may present its case, calling expert witnesses to testify on value. Under these conditions the need for a more detailed report is apparent. The appraiser must have complete data for proper presentation in court of his or her estimate of value.

Private properties are purchased by a public body for the following uses: freeways, highways, roads, parks, beaches, public boat harbors, and other recreational uses; airports; rapid transit rights-of-way; utility pipelines, such as water, gas, sanitary, and storm sewers; flood control channels; military bases and testing grounds, space and missile launching areas; schools of all grades, including secondary, junior or community colleges, state colleges, and state universities; electric utilities, such as steam generating plants, dams, transmission power lines, and distribution pole lines; urban redevelopment or renewal areas; court and civic center facilities and other government buildings; public libraries; post offices; reservoirs and lakes for water storage; and prisons, rehabilitation centers, mental institutions, and public hospitals.

In exercising their duties, real estate appraisers must consider all factors that act upon value. This is especially important in appraising for eminent domain purposes. Sometimes, a complete narrative report is called for in such cases, however, the new URAR form report with additional photographs and an expanded comments section has become widely accepted by many lenders.

Appraising for Financial Statements

Sometimes an owner will need an updated appraisal of a residence for a financial statement to establish a net worth position for a business venture or to secure additional capital for investment purposes.

Appraising for a Divorce or for Separation Proceedings

Occasionally, appraisers or real estate salespeople are asked to submit an appraisal of a residence for the purpose of a divorce or separation. This situation might occur if the divorce or separation agreement called for one party to receive the residence and the other party to receive other property, either personal or real. Great care should be taken by the appraiser to remain as objective as possible and to avoid becoming an advocate, since there might be some pressure by the party receiving the property to represent its value at a minimum while the party not receiving the property might want it appraised at a maximum value.

Appraising for Real Estate Brokerage

Brokers should realize that listing price must align with market value. They must help sellers price their property so it will not stagnate on the market. If a property is priced too high, potential buyers will pass it by. Brokers are not required to be appraisers, but they should be well informed about the value of property in the area and its pricing on the market. The points indicated in "Appraising for Selling" also apply here.

Appraising for Other Purposes

There are numerous additional reasons for an appraisal, some of which are listed below:

- Review appraising
- Foreclosure
- Partnership dissolution
- Economic studies
- Claims for flood or earthquake damage
- Depreciation in certain income-producing properties
- Appeals to federal tax board for capital gains relief
- Appeals to state tax board for property tax relief

- Feasibility studies
- Bankruptcy
- Wills
- 1041 property exchanges

SUMMARY

Land is a basic commodity vital to our needs, but increasing population means that less land is available per person each day. California continues to lead the nation in population growth. The valuation or appraising of California real estate remains a major economic factor. Appraising has become more technical and is governed by strict and binding rules, creating a continuing need for people trained in real estate appraising. Several types of appraisals are used for varied purposes. For any purpose, however, the appraiser must be objective to be effective. In exercising their duties, real estate appraisers must consider all factors that act upon value.

DISCUSSION QUESTIONS

1. Should real estate appraisal be subjective or objective?

2. Do you consider the tax assessor's appraisal of your single-family residence too high? Why?

3. Generally, the valuations of two qualified, objective appraisers viewing the same single-family residential property and using the same data should be within what percentage of each other?

4. Which type of appraisal usually takes the least time and effort and, when performed by a knowledgeable person, can usually be surprisingly accurate?

5. Give one advantage of the form appraisal report.

6. Why is land not insured against fire damage?

7. At what percent of market value are most California residences assessed?

8. Why is it so important for a real estate broker to be knowledgeable in appraising?

9. What is eminent domain?

10. Do you agree that the government should have the power of eminent domain? Why?

MULTIPLE-CHOICE QUESTIONS

1. An appraisal can best be defined as
   a. An exact science
   b. An educated guess as to value
   c. An estimate of value set on property
   d. An estimate of a listing price

2. The same single-family residence appraised by two *competent, independent, honest appraisers* should generally reflect what maximum percentage difference in value?
   a. 10%
   b. 20%
   c. 0%
   d. 5%

3. The most complete type of appraisal is the
   a. Form report
   b. Narrative
   c. Letter report
   d. Visual comparison

4. Which of the following appraisal purposes would generally require the most complete written appraisal report?
   a. Lending
   b. Insurance
   c. Tax assessment
   d. Selling

5. Which of the following appraisal purposes would generally require the most complete written appraisal report?
   a. Lending
   b. Buying
   c. Inheritance tax
   d. Eminent domain

Chapter 2

NATURE AND CHARACTERISTICS OF PROPERTY AND VALUE

Body of Knowledge Topics

- *Influences on Real Estate Value*

- *Legal Considerations in Real Estate*

- *Types of Value*

The foundations of our law of real property lie in old English common law. Indeed, there has been little change in the method of transfer since medieval times. Interests in property include the right to use, to encumber, to dispose, and to possess to the exclusion of others. Property may be either real or personal; it is sometimes difficult to distinguish between the two.

WHAT IS PROPERTY?

According to *Webster's Dictionary, property* is "the exclusive right to possess, enjoy and dispose of a thing; ownership." More simply, property is anything capable of being owned. It presupposes two basic conditions: an object or thing capable of being owned and an owner.

WHAT IS REAL PROPERTY?

The California Civil Code divides property into two classes: real or immovable property, and personal or movable property.

Real property, according to the California Code of Civil Procedure, Section 1973.5, is "synonymous with *real estate*" (*Dabney* v. *Edwards*, Vol. 5, Calif. 2nd Report, p. 1, 1935). Therefore, real property and real estate in California are land and that which is incidental or appurtenant to land and immovable by law (Civil Code, Sec. 658). Although in some states, the term *real estate* refers to the land and fixtures attached and the term *real property* refers to the rights inherent in the ownership of land—for example, the right to sell, lease, convey, or grant as a gift—in California (and hence in this text), the terms are used interchangeably.

Real property, or real estate, includes, in addition to the surface of the land, the subsurface all the way to the center of the earth and the air above the surface stretching into the sky. Visually, we can think of real property as an inverted, extended pyramid, with its apex at the center of the earth and its base somewhere in infinity. Figure 2–1 shows that owning real estate includes owning not only the ground but also the subsurface minerals, underground deposits, and other material. In addition, the ownership of real estate extends into the air above the surface of the ground. Unrestricted ownership of the air space has been modified through the years, and today, air rights are subject to commercial and military flights.

The most complete ownership of real property is known as *fee simple absolute.* Most appraisals for market value purposes are made on the basis of complete ownership, commonly known as *fee ownership.* Once this value has been estimated, the values of different portions of the property can be estimated.

WHAT IS PERSONAL PROPERTY?

Personal property, as defined by the Civil Code, is every kind of property that is not real property. Generally, it consists of the movable items not securely attached to the real property. The California courts have used five tests to determine whether a given piece of personal property is a fixture.

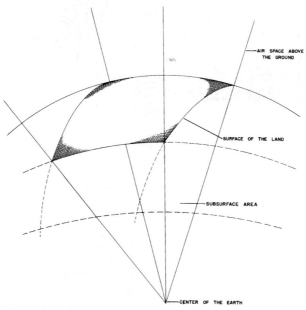

FIGURE 2–1 Extent of land ownership.

1. The intention of the person incorporating the personal property into the land. This test is usually considered the most important.

2. The method by which the property is so incorporated into the land. The degree of permanence of the annexation is significant. Thus, for example, even in the absence of statutory definition, when the attachment is by cement and plaster, the goods so attached are likely to be classified as fixtures.

3. The adaptability of the personal property so attached for ordinary use in connection with the land. If well adapted, it is probably a fixture.

4. The existence of an agreement between the parties involved as to the nature of the property affixed to the land. If the parties have displayed sufficient foresight and properly anticipated the problem, there need be no problem.

5. The relationship between the person who adds or affixes the article and the person with whom a dispute arises as to its character. This would typically involve seller and buyer of the land, or landlord and tenant.

WHAT IS VALUE?

Types of Value

Webster's Dictionary defines *value* as the "monetary worth of a thing; marketplace price." However, in actual use, the term *value* is relative. Although it is regularly used in the concept of the power of one commodity or service to command another commodity in exchange, it is seldom used without another identifying word. Some common types of value are:

1. Insurance value

2. Assessed value

3. Inheritance tax value

4. Market value

5. Rental value

6. Lease value

7. Appraised value

8. Economic value

9. Fair value

10. Depreciated value

11. Cash value

12. Face value

13. Salvage value

14. Interim value

15. Nuisance value

16. Mortgage loan value

17. Book value

18. Tax value

19. Listing value

20. Replacement value

21. Sale value

22. Capitalized value

23. Potential value

24. Exchange value

25. Security value

26. Easement value

27. Contract value

28. Sentimental value

29. Extrinsic value

30. Intrinsic value

31. Corner value

32. Front foot value

33. Square foot value

34. Advertising value

35. Spite value

36. Full cash value

37. Annuity value

38. Junk value

39. Scrap value

40. Antique value

41. Aesthetic value

42. Military value

43. Going concern value

It is easy to see the problem of using the term *value* without a qualifying companion word. In this discussion, however, we address ourselves primarily to the use of the term *value* as it relates to the more specific identification *market value,* and to some other value terms and definitions common to appraisers.

WHAT IS MARKET VALUE?

The Uniform Standards of Professional Appraisal Practice (USPAP) defines market value as:

> The *most probable price* which a property should bring in a competitive and open market under all conditions requisite to a fair sale, the buyer and seller, each acting prudently, knowledgeably and assuming the price is not affected by undue stimulus. Implicit in this definition is the consummation of a sale as of a specified date and the passing of title from seller to buyer under conditions whereby: (1) buyer and seller are typically motivated; (2) both parties are well informed or well advised, and each acting in what he considers his own best interest; (3) a reasonable time is allowed for exposure in the open market; (4) payment is made in terms of cash in U.S. dollars or in terms of financial arrangements comparable thereto; and (5) the price represents the normal consideration for the property sold unaffected by special or creative financing or sales concessions* granted by anyone associated with the sale.

This definition of market value is required by USPAP to be incorporated into appraisal reports, and is a standard part of any form report. This is the only definition that is acceptable for appraisal performed under USPAP guidelines.

Formerly, *market value* was defined as "the price arrived at in the open market by a fully informed buyer and seller, neither being under undue pressure." Practically, although both buyer and seller should ideally be fully informed, this is usually not the case. Also, many market sales, especially of residential property, involve either a seller or a buyer who is under undue pressure to sell or buy.

The concept of an "arms-length transaction" is the principal of a "fair sale," "not affected by undue stimulus." There are four conditions requisite to such a transaction:

1. Neither the buyer or the seller is acting under duress.

2. The property has been offered for sale in an open market for a

*Adjustments to the comparables must be made for special or creative financing or sales concessions. No adjustments are necessary for those costs which are normally paid by sellers as a result of tradition or law in a market area; these costs are readily identifiable since the seller pays these costs in virtually all sales transactions. Special or creative financing adjustments can be made to the comparable property by comparisons to financing terms offered by a third party institutional lender that is not already involved in the property or transaction. Any adjustment should not be calculated on a mechanical dollar for dollar cost of the financing or concession but the dollar amount of any adjustment should approximate the market's reaction to the financing or concessions based on the appraiser's judgment.

reasonable period of time, allowing that some properties are expected to take longer to sell than others.

3. Buyer and seller are aware of the aspects of the property, including any adverse conditions or potential changes.

4. No extraordinary circumstances, such as financing concessions, are involved.

In the usual selling situation, the seller of a single-family residence is much more informed than the buyer about the property for sale. The seller, certainly more aware of drawbacks of the property, will seldom point these out to the buyer. In fact, the average buyer of a single-family residence probably spends a total of less than one hour on the premises before deciding to buy. This is especially true if the home is occupied, since the prospective buyer hesitates to disturb the occupants with an intensive investigation of the premises. In such a short time, it is impossible to discover many problems that may exist, such as poor drainage, a leaky roof, or even noisy or hazardous neighborhood traffic conditions.

Often the seller is forced to sell within a limited period of time or during periods of a poor market because of a job transfer to another city or for some other valid reason.

Because of such inconsistencies, the "conditions requisite to a fair sale" are often variable and difficult to define, resulting in a definition of market value that serves as a guideline and goal, as opposed to an "absolute." In reality, rarely will all conditions be equally met, and buyers set actual values of property when they purchase them.

OTHER COMMON VALUE TERMS AND DEFINITIONS

Price is the amount the property actually sells for—the *sales price*. This amount may differ from the market value due to a number of factors, such as seller concessions for a quick sale or an interfamily sale that is not an arm's-length transaction.

Cost is the amount actually paid for the property and improvements. The price a property may command when resold may not be the same as the cost to purchase the property and construct the improvements.

Investment value is defined in terms of the cash flow requirements and expectations of an investor. The income remaining after all operating expenses have been paid on a property is the cash flow, or revenue stream of a property. The value of this revenue to an investor will depend upon the investor's goals and cash flow considerations.

Assessment value is the property value determined for *ad valorem* taxation by state and local tax agencies.

Insurable value is the amount for which a property may be insured. This amount is generally a percentage of the market value at the time a policy is written or a calculation of future replacement cost, depending upon the type of policy, and the insurer.

Value in use is the value based on a specific use of a property, such as a manufacturing plant used to produce automobiles.

Going concern value is the intangible value, beyond the value of the real estate owned or occupied by a firm, of its on-going business. This value takes into account "goodwill" and longevity.

FORCES AFFECTING THE VALUE OF REAL PROPERTY

Influences on Real Estate Value

The value of all real property is constantly influenced by physical, economic, political, and social forces that motivate human behavior.

Physical Forces   Some of the physical forces that affect real property value are:

1. Size and shape of property

2. Accessibility

3. Drainage

4. Availability of water

5. Underground mineral deposits

6. Soil composition and fertility

7. Climate

8. Whether property is located in a flood zone

9. Whether property is located on an earthquake fault zone

10. Location

11. View

12. Privacy

13. Proximity to schools, shopping, and recreation areas

Economic Forces   Some economic forces affecting real property value are:

1. Expansion or diminution of basic industry production

2. Expansion or diminution of federal military contracts

3. Expansion or diminution of local government activity

4. Discovery of new, or depletion of existing, natural resources

5. Availability or absence of mortgage money and other monies for extension of credit (improvement bonds, etc.)

6. Local private employment expansion or layoffs

7. Expansion or contraction of state and private university activity

8. Opening or closing of military bases

Political Forces   Some political forces that affect real property value are:

1. Federal guarantees in financing (FHA and GI guaranteed loans)

2. Local zoning policies

3. Local building code policies

4. Federal housing and rent subsidies

5. Expansion of federal, state, county, or city highway and public works programs (interstate and state improvements, dams, water projects, flood control projects, etc.)

6. Environmental Protection Agency policies

7. Environmental impact studies

8. Endangered species designations

9. Disabilities acts

10. Police and fire protection

11. Local taxation and assessments

12. Local regulations on business and industry

13. Effect of Workman's Compensation laws

Social Forces   Some of the social forces that affect real property value are:

1. Pride of ownership

2. Attitudes of people

3. Population shifts

4. Changes in size of families

Anyone concerned with the appraisal of real property must be constantly aware of these forces and their part in value determination.

BASIC POWERS OF GOVERNMENT AGAINST PRIVATE REAL ESTATE

Legal Considerations in Appraisal

Although fee ownership, the ownership of land and everything attached to it, lying under it, and extending over it, implies unrestricted ownership, there are actually five necessary powers of government that have some claim on all private real estate in the United States.

1. Local Real Estate Taxation   Most private real property in California is subject to real estate taxation. Exempt properties include those of certain religious, charitable, educational, and nonprofit organizations. Real property taxes are assessed by the local taxing body to provide revenues for city and county governments; school districts; welfare, flood control, and sanitary districts; road bonds; junior college districts; and many other local government and education functions.

As discussed in Chapter 1, local real estate taxes take a relatively smaller bite out of the California homeowner's pocket since the passage of Proposition 13 in June 1978. However, local property taxes, which presently amount to 1 to 1.25 percent of the selling price of a home (or 1 to 1.5 percent of the market value) with annual increments limited to 2 percent per year, are still a concern to most buyers, and real estate licensees and appraisers should be aware of local real estate tax implications on properties with which they are involved.

2. Power of Eminent Domain   Many public and quasi-public agencies have the power of eminent domain. They must show a need for the property and pay market value when they take it. This necessary power is exercised to purchase land for freeways, roads, schools, parks, airports, power lines, reservoirs, military bases, and the like. The power of eminent domain is also called the power of *condemnation,* a term not to be confused with condemnation of unsafe or unsanitary property. The latter type of condemnation is a police power.

The major difference between condemnation under the power of eminent domain and condemnation under police power is that, in the former the public or condemnor must *pay fair market value* for the property that is to be acquired for public use. There is no payment involved in condemnation under police power.

3. Police Power   Police power, according to the 1994–1995 *State of California Real Estate Reference Book,* is "the power in the state to enact laws within constitutional limits to promote the order, safety, health, morals and general welfare of the commonwealth." It includes enacting and enforcing building codes, building setback lines, zoning, installing traffic signals and controls, implementing sanitary and storm drainage requirements, and many other necessary controls.

In condemnation under police power, the public body, or condemnor, generally allows a reasonable time for the private property owner to correct any deficiencies of a property. Also, enforcement of local police powers as they affect private property may not be capricious, arbitrary, or with prejudice. All deficient properties must be treated the same. As stated in the California Department of Real Estate *Reference Book:* "The legislature may not impose onerous, unreasonable or unnecessary burdens upon persons, property or business. Where a law operates upon all persons and property similarly situated, it is not obnoxious to the constitutional provisions guaranteeing equal protection of the law to all persons and classes of persons, or guaranteeing persons' freedom of contract, or guaranteeing that no person shall be deprived of life, liberty or *property* without due process of law" (emphasis added).[1]

4. Escheat　　If a person who owns property in California dies without leaving a will and without heirs, title to the property reverts to the state. This is called *title by escheat.*

5. Air Space　　At one time, landowners' rights extended into the skies above their land. Today, however, with virtually unrestricted air travel, no owner can practically claim the entire air space above a piece of land. The extent of ownership of air space is a moot point. Court decisions have suggested that *ownership* means the reasonable enjoyment of air space above one's land. In the Air Commerce Act of 1926 and the Civil Aeronautics Act of 1938, Congress declared that the United States government has complete sovereignty in the air space over land in this country. As stated in the case of *United States* v. *Causby,* 328 U.S. 256: "It is ancient doctrine that common law ownership of the land, extended to the periphery of the universe—*cujus est solum ejus est usque ad coelum.* But that doctrine has no place in the modern world."

Although some people do not consider control of air space by the federal government one of the basic restrictions on private property, we feel that it is—especially because our original concept of land ownership included the space from the center of the earth into the air above. To illustrate further, suppose the federal government were, for reasons of national interest or well being, to prohibit private individuals from taking oil, minerals, hydrocarbons, or water from a depth of more than 2,000 feet below the surface. Would this not be an additional basic government restriction (although again possibly a necessary one) on the private ownership of land? The only difference between this and restrictions on air space is that, unlike underground deposits, air space above a certain height presently has no market value. We can only speculate on the future value of air space. And who knows how vital to national interests the retention of control of our underground resources might prove to be?

---

[1]California Department of Real Estate *Reference Book,* 1994–1995, p. 3, para. 2.

OTHER POSSIBLE RESTRICTIONS AGAINST PRIVATE REAL PROPERTY

In addition to the basic governmental restrictions on privately owned real estate, private restrictions imposed by previous owners can limit the full enjoyment of real estate by a present or future owner. The appraiser should be aware that *covenants and restrictions* can affect the valuation of a property, since they may impose restrictions such as minimum lot size or minimum house size. These *tract restrictions* are usually on file in the local county recorder's office. Generally, their existence can be determined by a title search; they are usually mentioned in a preliminary title report.

In most cases, when there is a conflict between a *public* (governmental) restriction on the construction or development of a home or lot and a *private* deed restriction on such construction or development, the one that is the most restrictive holds. For example, if the public minimum lot size as determined by police power is stated to be 6,000 square feet, but the private deed restriction states 8,000 square feet, then the one that is most restrictive must be met. In this case, a lot would have to have at least 8,000 square feet in order to place a home on the lot.

SUMMARY

Real estate, or real property, is land and all that is attached thereto. All that is not attached to the land is personal property. Value is the worth of a thing. Market value has been defined by the courts, and more recently, by USPAP, but is difficult, in practice, to apply precisely. Many political, economic, physical, and social forces are acting upon buyers and sellers to motivate their actions. Government of all types has basic powers restricting the complete disposition and use of all private property by owners. These powers are real estate taxes, eminent domain, police power, escheat, and air space. In addition to possible *governmental* restrictions on private property, there are also *private* restrictions imposed by a previous owner. These private deed restrictions are enforceable under the law. Where a conflict occurs between governmental and private restrictions, the most restrictive holds.

DISCUSSION QUESTIONS

1. Define property.

2. Define real property.

3. What term defines the most complete type of real estate ownership?

4. Of the five general tests employed by most courts to determine

whether a piece of personal property is a fixture, which is usually considered the most important?

5. Do you agree that the five government powers over private real estate are necessary? Why?

MULTIPLE-CHOICE QUESTIONS

1. A proper definition of property would be
   a. Land
   b. Automobile
   c. Anything capable of being owned
   d. House

2. Which of the following is not a test to determine whether a given piece of personal property is a fixture?
   a. The intention of the person affixing the personal property to the land
   b. The method of affixation
   c. The use or adaptability of the personal property to the real property
   d. None of the above

3. *Value* can best be defined as
   a. Worth
   b. Price
   c. Money
   d. Fair

4. The market value of a residence is usually closest to
   a. Listing price
   b. Selling price
   c. Replacement cost
   d. Lowest offer

5. The selling price always reflects the market value of a property.
   a. True
   b. False

6. The primary difference between condemnation through exercise of the power of eminent domain and condemnation through the exercise of a police power is
   a. There is no compensation necessary in the exercise of eminent domain.
   b. There is no compensation necessary in the exercise of police power.
   c. One is a power of the public body, and the other is not.
   d. There is no difference.

7. When there is a conflict between a *public* (governmental) restriction on a property and a *private* deed restriction, which one must be adhered to?

    a. The public or governmental restriction
    b. The private deed restriction
    c. The one that is most restrictive
    d. Neither one

8. Of the forces affecting the value of real estate, the size and shape of the property would be
    a. A political force
    b. A social force
    c. An economic force
    d. A physical force

Chapter 3

PRINCIPLES CONTROLLING REAL ESTATE VALUE

Body of Knowledge Topics

- *Economic Principles*
- *Highest and Best-Use Analysis*

Basic economic principles apply to all aspects of the real estate industry. Appraisal is no exception. If we define economics very simply as the material means of satisfying human desires, we realize that the appraisal of real estate is simply interpreting what real property is worth to many potential buyers, each of whom is motivated differently. To understand their motivations we must first understand the basic economic principles controlling value.

PRINCIPLE OF HIGHEST AND BEST USE

USPAP requires that an opinion of highest and best use be incorporated into appraisals for market value, both for the land, as if vacant, and as presently improved, as a measure of property utilization as of a certain date. Before we estimate a property's value, we must determine its most legally profitable and physically permitted use—the highest and best use—that is, the use that will give the maximum net return or benefit.

Consideration of feasible alternatives for land use, without the improvements, provides the basis for land valuation. Evaluating the contribution of improvements to the land provides a complete picture of property value. If the improvements do not represent the highest and best use "as if vacant," an interim use value may be estimated for the improvements.

For example, suppose you are asked to appraise a level, vacant, square parcel of land on a corner of a busy intersection. The parcel is 250 by 250 feet. An old residence that had occupied the lot recently caught fire and burned to the ground. A recent city automobile traffic count indicates that 20,000 cars a day pass by the property.

Your first step would be to determine the reasonable probability of that land being used for some purpose that would result in a higher net return to the land. The parcel could possibly be used for multiple-family residential units, professional offices, or even commercial buildings. In this event, the land alone would probably be worth more in the new use than the land and the old building together were worth as a single-family residence. Until you know which of these uses is most logical (presuming, of course, that the proper zoning could be obtained), you cannot make an intelligent estimate of value.

Note that existing or proposed zoning does not, of itself, create value. It is merely a vehicle whereby highest and best use of a property can be properly realized. Many properties today are zoned for a particular purpose, such as industrial or commercial, but because no demand exists for that particular use, the property value may suffer or the owner may have to wait years for the area to grow or for demand to increase to the point that it becomes economically prudent to develop the property for this use.

There were two criteria that determine highest and best use. These are (1) demand, either existing or imminent, and (2) police power approval (zoning, building site approval, necessary permits, and so forth). There are four tests to explore these criteria for highest and best use. Is the possible use:

1. Physically possible—Is the use physically possible?

2. Legally permitted—Is it likely that the use is or could be legally permitted? If there has been no actual approval, the appraiser can weigh the probability of receiving this approval and apply it to the estimate of value. (In cases where there is a possibility of a zoning change, many properties are sold contingent on the buyer being able to obtain the necessary zoning.)

3. Economically feasible—Is the cost of establishing the use of the property economically sound?

4. Maximally productive—Will the use provide the highest present value?

The highest and best use of a property may change, over time, depending upon zoning changes and other factors. The use providing the maximum return on investment should be determined.

PRINCIPLE OF SUPPLY AND DEMAND

Real property has value only as long as there is a desire for its use. Its value increases as the supply of land decreases, as more and more people compete for the available land. The highest land values are found in the most populated cities, where small parcels of available land bring unbelievable prices.

All private real estate transactions should involve a willing seller and a willing buyer with the ability to buy—best measured in terms of money.

Reduced to its simplest form, then, the principle of supply and demand must include an analysis of population growth, people's ability to pay, and the relative scarcity of available land. For example, within the city limits of San Francisco, where the supply of available land is fixed, the demand for land has become so great in most areas that single-family-home building is precluded, since land can command so much more money for use as a high-rise residential or commercial development. By this means, more people can be accommodated, with the result of a greater monetary return to the land. The result is constantly rising land values as demand grows for the available supply.

If buyers with the ability to pay demand a scarce commodity, its value rises. Even fresh air (the most useful commodity, which used to be most abundant), is becoming more valuable as air pollution threatens urban and suburban areas. Many residential areas, retirement communities, tourist areas, and recreational areas owe much of their value to the supply of fresh, clean air.

PRINCIPLE OF SUBSTITUTION

A buyer will not pay more for a particular real property than the cost of buying a similar property. For example, suppose a person in the market for a new home finds two that are suitable. If the properties are for all practical purposes identical, the lower-priced one will sell first. Or if a buyer finds that it is possible to buy a lot and construct a home with all the attributes of an existing residence for 80 percent of the cost of the existing residence, then the cost of replacement—building a new home—tends to set the top value of the original. (This principle is effective only if there is no unusual delay in the construction of the replacement facility.)

PRINCIPLE OF ANTICIPATION

A real property has value proportionate to the expected use of that property, whether it be a single-family residence or an income-producing commercial property. In the case of an income-producing property, this expected, or anticipated, return can be measured by the amount of money that can be realized over a given period of time. In the case of a single-family residence, the return can be measured by the anticipated enjoyment or amenities.

For example, most high-quality residential properties in exclusive areas sell at prices unrelated to any income-producing capabilities of those properties. Rather, the price reflects the buyer's desire to enjoy whatever future social or physical benefits that property may produce, whether the enjoyment of a quiet, natural setting in an area of large estates, or the social satisfaction of an exclusive address, or even the view of a picturesque coastline.

The principle of anticipation is most obvious and easy to measure in the case of income-producing property. Virtually all multiple residential, industrial, professional, and commercial properties are purchased with the vision of future economic returns. The buyer is interested in past and present production of income only because it suggests *future* earning capabilities of the property.

PRINCIPLE OF CHANGE

Real property is constantly changing, its value influenced by many variables: population shifts, changing economic conditions, increasing government controls, new routes of transportation, new shopping centers, new schools, urban growth and decay, changing social attitudes, changing political ideals, and changing cultural desires. Although change is almost imperceptible to the resident who views an area from day to day, most people have only to go back to the area where they grew up to be struck by the changes that have taken place. Whether these changes reflect a growing, dynamic region or a decaying neighborhood, seldom does a neighborhood remain static for long.

In a dynamic, growing region, professional real estate appraisers, brokers, developers, and investors always take different routes as they move through the area to keep abreast of new developments. In this way, they are constantly informed about what is happening in the real estate industry in that area.

Three Stages in the Life Cycle

All improved real property experiences a three-stage life cycle. The three stages, although not always distinct, can best be described as *development, maturity,* and *old age.* For example, in the life of a single-family residential development, we find the following progression: Development begins with the filing of a subdivision map followed by the laying out and grading of lots, streets, and easements. Next is the installation of off-site improvements including all utilities, sanitary and storm drains, streets, curbs, gutters, sidewalks, and street lighting. Now comes the selling of lots and the construction and sale of homes with the installation of lawns, fencing, and landscaping. Once the neighborhood has developed, there is a period when landscaping continues and the development reaches maturity. Following maturity, the development declines into old age, or its use changes. The time interval for each basic stage varies with each development.

Some developments might take 60 years or more to experience the complete cycle. In fact, some excellent residential areas in the United States are over 100 years old and still have not completed their life cycles, primarily because of continued demand due to an absence of economic obsolescence, as well as good construction, excellent maintenance, and exceptional pride of ownership. Good location and a healthy local economy also contribute to extending the length of the life cycle.

Conversely, developments in some areas of California have gone through the first stages and are well into old age within a period of less than 10 years. Knowing these stages and how to analyze property located in an area of transition is important to anyone in the real estate industry.

PRINCIPLE OF CONFORMITY

A reasonable degree of conformity results in maximum value. A home located in an area of homes of similar size, style, and quality of construction maintains its relative value. (Be careful not to interpret this to mean cookie-cutter or rubber-stamped identicals.)

Homes of varying architectural styles are often located in one neighborhood, especially in an area of exclusive, individually designed homes. However, there is generally conformity in either the economic or the sociological sense in that the homes are of similar price and size or are owned and occupied by people in similar economic circumstances.

For example, the value of a home of 5,000 square feet, of good-quality construction, tastefully landscaped and appointed, will be maintained best when that home is located in an area of similar homes. Generally the larger this area of similar homes, the less vulnerable the home to outside influences that might depress its value.

Conversely, suppose we were to evaluate a substandard home among similar poor-quality, poorly maintained homes in a deprived residential area. The larger this area, the less able most of these properties are to benefit from any outside influences that might enhance their value. Reasonable conformity tends to maintain the status quo, whatever it may be.

Subsidiary Principle of Regression—Overimprovement, or Superadequacy

Occasionally a large, custom-designed, quality-constructed home is found in a neighborhood of homes less than half its size and of inferior construction. A large home of 5,000 square feet, in a neighborhood of similar large, good-quality homes, could be worth $1 million or more. However, in a neighborhood of homes of 1,600 square feet and moderate construction, it might be worth less than $600,000. The unit of higher value loses value when located in an area of lower-value units. This is called *regression*. Overimprovement and superadequacy are alternate terms for the result of regression.

Subsidiary Principle of Progression

The opposite case would be if the 1,600-square-foot home described above were located in an area of large, quality residences. The effect of this turnabout would be value increment to the smaller home. This is known as *progression*.

The effect on value would be different from that discussed in the preceding paragraph. In that case of regression there would be no practical way to salvage the apparent dollar loss brought about by the overimprovement. However, seldom would a 1,600-square-foot home be built on a lot in an area of 5,000-square-foot homes. The cost of the land would not economically justify such a small home. What generally happens is that an older home might be located in a residential area away from urban development in a relatively remote, or farm, setting. Then, as the area is in the path of a newer development, the area may have become much more in demand for any of a number of reasons, such as healthy local economic expansion, open space, semirural setting, natural beauty and amenities, that make newer, larger homes on large lots feasible economically.

The major difference, economically, between regression and progression as discussed in these two examples is that the latter house can be either torn down (if too old) or completely renovated and enlarged to bring it up to the neighborhood standard of 5,000-square-foot homes.

PRINCIPLE OF CONTRIBUTION

Closely related to the principle of conformity, the value of an improvement to a property, whether to vacant land or an existing structure, is worth only what it adds to the property's market value, often less than the improvement's cost to construct. The market value of a swimming pool, for example, may be $10,000, while construction costs may be $20,000. Conversely, adding a second bathroom or an additional bedroom may increase the market value by more than the construction costs. Appraisers must weigh only the actual contribution to value, not the cost of the improvement.

PRINCIPLE OF COMPETITION

Most business ventures need to show a profit. Real estate is no exception. When demand is strong for homes of a certain quality, size, and price, a developer can make a good profit. Other developers may come into the area. With increasing competition, profits decrease, sometimes to the point where profits no longer exist or are so marginal that they are not worthwhile. Moderate profits attract healthy competition. Excessive profits can bring ruinous competition.

PRINCIPLE OF CONSISTENT USE

Land and improvements should be valued on the basis of the same use. Suppose you are asked to appraise a parcel of land a few blocks from the city's central business district. The parcel consists of a lot 80 by 100 feet with a 60-year-old residence. Assume that the highest and best use of the property is to tear down the house and develop a fourplex on the land. You should not value the land as a fourplex site and then add to the land value the value of the house; that would not be consistent. The property can be used for either a single-family residence or a fourplex, but not for both. The proper way to appraise the parcel would be to determine land value and then either subtract the cost of tearing down the house to prepare the lot or, if the house has salvage value, add this nominal value to the lot value. The house might also have interim value as a rental unit until necessary zoning, design, building permits, and financing could be arranged for the fourplex construction.

Another example is a 20-acre cherry orchard that has a highest and best use as a single-family residential subdivision. The best use might represent four times the land's value as an orchard. It would be inconsistent to value the land as a single-family residential subdivision and then add the value of the trees for commercial production. Some orchard trees would add value, incorporated in the development as shade or ornamental trees; however, most orchard trees are removed because their retention would not be worth the added cost of working around them.

PRINCIPLE OF INCREASING AND DECREASING RETURNS

The basic economic principle of increasing and decreasing returns, sometimes referred to as the principle of contribution, reflects that there is a point at which added cost put into a producing unit will no longer produce a worthwhile increase in the net return.

For example, suppose a contractor builds a house to sell competitively on the open market. It is a quality residence of 3,000 square feet in a fine residential community. To realize a profit, the builder may include in the sale of the completed house a front lawn, minor landscaping, and a rear fence. Carpeting, drapes, a patio, and walkways may also be added to increase the salability of the house. However, there will be a point (the point of diminishing returns) after which additional dollars spent for improvement will not yield a worthwhile return when the house is sold. A swimming pool, outdoor brick barbecue and patio, screened lanai, and even carpeting and drapes can be investments that may not show worthwhile return. People's attitudes, desires, and tastes differ so greatly that a builder generally does best by leaving as many personal touches as possible for buyers to install to suit themselves.

Another practical illustration is the addition of extra rooms and a bath. Assume you are asked to appraise an 8-year-old house with such recent additions. You find that the original house was 1,600 square feet in a neighborhood of 1,600-square-foot homes. The added construction contributes an additional 400 square feet, making the house a 2,000-square-foot residence. Although the addition increases the living area substantially, the resulting increase in value does not necessarily make the added investment profitable. Your appraisal should reflect whatever a willing and able buyer would pay for the total property, a value derived from market analysis of the prices new homes or other homes of 2,000 square feet are bringing. Then, after a comparison of all the quality attributes, you can make a final estimate of the value of the home.

In addition to its application to improvements, the principle of increasing and decreasing returns can also be applied to lots that are oversize, either in total square footage or in added width or depth. Are buyers willing to pay the added cost proportionate to the increase in lot size for a lot that might be larger, longer, or wider than the standard lot in the neighborhood?

The principle of increasing and decreasing returns is closely associated with the concept of agents in production.

CONCEPT OF AGENTS IN PRODUCTION

Principles of Balance and Surplus Productivity

The *concept of agents in production,* also known as the theory of surplus productivity and as the principle of balance, is used to determine the value of land based on the primary economic concept controlling all profit-making enterprises that affirms that all production is based on four agents or factors in production. That is, for any production—residential, agricultural, industrial, or commercial—to be profitable, four basic agents must be in proper proportion or balance. They are labor, management, capital, and land. Labor has first claim on returns from production; management, second; capital, third; and the last to be satisfied is land.

Labor includes wages and all payroll except management. In addition, it includes all operating expenses (usually paid monthly), which generally represent a form of labor—maintenance, repairs, electricity, gas, water, rubbish removal, supplies, and the like.

Management includes all charges for coordinating the enterprise. Smaller enterprises are managed by an entrepreneur. In larger enterprises management generally includes salaried management personnel.

Capital covers the costs of constructing the necessary buildings and providing equipment. It includes amortization of loans to pay for capital expenditures. Amortization, of course, includes *return of* money borrowed (principal) and *return on* money borrowed (interest). Capital also includes reserves for future depreciation of capital improvements. Fixed expenses of insurance and taxes also are included. Insurance is generally a protection against capital loss; the major tax assessments are against capital improvements (structure and fixed equipment). Both insurance and taxes are usually payable either annually or semiannually.

Whatever return is left after full satisfaction and payment of the other three agents in production is imputable to the land. This residual, if properly interpreted, can be used as a basis for determining the value of the land. This process occurs in the land-residual method of income approach to value and in the land-residual approach to site valuation, discussed in other chapters.

Although each of the principles discussed here has an individual application in the appraisal of real estate, they are often mutually dependent. Although they appear highly theoretical, they can be directly applied to determine reasonable valuations. The theories must be applied thoughtfully, with regard for the physical, social, economic, and political forces acting constantly on all real property. The appraisal can be only as good as the ability of the appraiser to apply the proper theory at the proper time.

CONCEPT OF OPPORTUNITY COST

Opportunity cost is the realizable dollar amount between various types of investments with differing rates of return. This concept applies when appraising income-producing property, where the appraiser examines alternatives and selects a rate of return for the property, affecting the estimated value.

SUMMARY

The basic principles controlling appraisal of real estate can be applied in varying degrees to all types of real estate. Although some of these principles overlap, the appraiser's basic understanding of each of them will be a good foundation for complete comprehension of the various appraisal concepts discussed in this text.

DISCUSSION QUESTIONS

1. Define the term *highest and best use* and give an example of its application to the appraisal of a parcel of real property.

2. Explain why application of the principle of substitution usually sets the upper limit of value. Give an example.

3. Discuss the variations in the life cycles of several single-family residences in your area. Why do cycles vary?

4. Give an example in your area of ruinous competition bred by excessive profits.

5. Discuss the value of a new, exceptionally high quality single-family residence of 4,000 square feet, in a neighborhood of new, good quality 2,000-square-foot single-family residences. Assume that all are located on half-acre lots.

6. Discuss the value of a modest, 1,500-square-foot single-family residence 30 years old in an area of new, good quality 3,000-

square-foot single-family residences. Assume that all are located on half-acre lots.

7. What principle inhibits inclusion of the value of a 60-year-old residence in the appraisal of a commercial lot whose highest and best use is as a service station site?

8. Name the four basic agents in production. In what order are these agents satisfied?

MULTIPLE-CHOICE QUESTIONS

1. Highest and best use can best be described as that use that will
   a. Be the most expensive to develop
   b. Result in the highest building
   c. Result in the most money
   d. Result in the highest legal return

2. Of the following, the most important variable in determining the value of a parcel of real estate is
   a. Location
   b. Zoning
   c. Credit of the buyer
   d. Credit of the seller

3. As the supply of developable land decreases, and as demand continues to rise, the value of the remaining land will generally
   a. Remain about the same
   b. Tend to rise in value
   c. Tend to fall in value
   d. Demand has no affect on value

4. The principle of substitution can be applied best to
   a. The cost approach
   b. The income approach
   c. The market approach
   d. Any of the approaches, depending on the circumstances

5. The principle of anticipation can be applied to
   a. An apartment building
   b. A single-family residence
   c. A commercial structure
   d. All of the above

6. The principle of regression can be applied when
   a. A small home is built in an area of larger homes
   b. A large home is built in an area of smaller homes
   c. All the homes are identical
   d. All the homes are custom built

7. The principle of progression can be applied when
   a. All the homes are the same
   b. All the homes are custom built

    c. A small home is built in an area of larger homes

    d. A large home is built in an area of smaller homes

8. The principle of increasing and decreasing returns can best be applied when there is
   a. An overimprovement on a parcel of land
   b. An underimprovement on a parcel of land
   c. A poorly designed home
   d. None of the above

9. The principle of consistent use affirms
   a. That all the homes in an area should conform to one another
   b. That land and improvements should be valued on the basis of the same use
   c. That all of the properties should be zoned the same
   d. None of the above

10. Which one of the following is not one of the agents in production?
    a. Land
    b. Labor
    c. Capital
    d. Profits

Chapter 4

ECONOMIC ANALYSIS

Body of Knowledge Topics

- *Real Estate Market and Analysis*
- *Influences on Real Estate Value*

Economics, according to *Webster's Dictionary,* is "the science that investigates the conditions and laws affecting the production, distribution, and consumption of wealth; the material means of satisfying human desires." The second part of the definition is easy to relate to real estate when we realize that people want to own real estate, a material thing, and will spend money to satisfy this desire. The amount of money or economic goods a buyer will pay depends on many factors. To analyze a property properly, an appraiser must be aware of these factors and their effect on a given parcel of real estate. In Chapter 2 we discussed the forces that act constantly on all property to influence values. The effect of these physical, economic, political, and social forces can be measured most logically by briefly studying the international real estate market and the national economy and by making a regional, city, and neighborhood analysis.

INTERNATIONAL REAL ESTATE ACTIVITY

International real estate activity started when explorers from various countries established settlements in foreign lands and later set up colonies that eventually led to claims of ownership by the discoverer nation. Indeed, the United States today consists of some lands that were actually acquired by direct purchase from foreign governments. Most notable are the large land areas included in the Louisiana Purchase from France in 1803 for $15 million and in what was called Seward's Folly, which was purchased from Russia in 1867 for $7.2 million in gold and which eventually became our forty-ninth state, Alaska.

Another relatively good buy, although on a smaller scale, was an island 12.5 miles long by 2 miles wide that was purchased for goods worth $24 from an Indian tribe in 1626 by the Dutch West India Company. Today the lower portion of this island is Lower Manhattan and contains some of the most valuable real estate in the world and comprises a portion of the city known popularly as the Big Apple—New York City.

Much of the rest of the United States was acquired either by conquest or by questionable treaties with the native American Indians.

Since the beginning of the country, foreign individuals, companies, and governments have invested in real estate in the United States. Today this activity continues, as does the investment in real estate in other countries by U.S. corporations and individuals. The rate of investment by foreign governments, corporations, and individuals in real estate in the United States varies depending on many factors. Among them are:

1. Availability of money for investment brought about by international profits, such as those petrol dollars that were accumulated at a prodigious rate in the late 1970s by some oil-exporting countries because of the orchestrated oil crisis of that decade.

2. Availability of money for investment brought about by an imbalance of trade whereby the U.S. consumers purchase many more goods or products from a country than the citizens of that country purchase from the United States. For example, the relative imbalance of trade between Japan and the United States in the mid-1990s produced profits for Japanese firms and individuals, some of which were reinvested in U.S. corporations and real estate.

3. Existing state of political climate in foreign countries. When government leaders, wealthy citizens, and certain others feel threatened by impending political change, they transfer their fortunes out of their countries into a "safe haven" (principally the United States) in the form of bank deposits or the purchase of homes and other real estate. This has been done by citizens of many countries throughout the world over the years.

4. The relative current exchange value between the dollar and other international currencies. When the U.S. dollar loses value relative to a particular national currency, such as the German mark, it is advantageous for those holding German marks to purchase goods, products, or real estate in the United States. When the dollar rises in value, the reverse is true.

5. The availability of relatively low-cost real estate for sale in the United States. For example, in the mid-1980s, large tracts of farmland in many states attracted many foreign investors because U.S. farmland has historically been some of the most productive in the world and because more and more countries seem less able to provide food for their own citizens as world population increases. Other good potential real estate investments, such as multiple residential units in fast-growing urban areas, have also been targeted periodically by foreign investors

from all over the world who realize that U.S. citizens are heading for more and more apartment house living (as are most of the world's urban populations), as the cost of single-family detached housing rises out of the reach of more and more Americans.

6. The availability of relatively low-cost, long-term, fixed-rate financing. Historically, the United States has led the world in this area. In fact, very few countries even have long-term financing available for real estate purchases.

7. The rate of immigration to the United States by those determined to find a new life because of the opportunities that have historically been here for those prepared to work and sacrifice.

8. The amount of illegal, or dirty, money being brought into this country by those profiting from illicit drug trade. The U.S. citizenry continues to be the largest international buyer of drugs from those foreign countries that do little to stem the outflow of drugs from their countries into the United States. Many times, the money is laundered by purchase of real estate.

Adding to the above list of variables are the following:

1. Our laws generally do not restrict foreign individuals or corporations from ownership of real estate in this country. This may change as many foreign countries continue to limit ownership of real estate to only their citizens.

2. The United States has one of the most stable governments in the world, and as the leading world power, ensures the safety of foreign investments.

3. The United States still has a great deal of economic growth potential and an existing healthy, vibrant economy.

4. The U.S. Constitution provides built-in safety features for those residing in or owning property within its borders, whether citizens or not.

The ultimate effect of the ownership of large numbers or large parcels of real estate by foreign investors is difficult to predict. One thing is certain: the more potential buyers for a non-renewable product, such as real estate, the higher the price. Hopefully, the difficult lessons of the savings and loan crisis precipitated by lax federal regulations have brought a new degree of awareness to our government on these issues. One would hope the average American citizen will not ultimately have to suffer with exorbitant prices for homes that will push the American dream of property ownership even further out of reach.

ECONOMIC ANALYSIS

In recent years, there has been a marked increase of foreign buying of all kinds of real estate throughout the United States. The effect on local property values can be dramatic when the normal market is temporarily upset by an extensive outside infusion of funds. Although much of the activity is centered in the agricultural, financial, industrial, and commercial markets, the purchase of various types of residential properties, including single-family as well as multiple-family residences, has also increased markedly.

Generally, foreign buyers are paying top dollar for these properties. In some instances, they have artificially affected market values by paying full asking prices or even bidding the price up higher than the asking price. This competitive bidding sometimes creates a panic situation in which local buyers, afraid of losing out, are also forced to pay excessive prices in a sellers' market created by the additional demand of these outside buyers. This temporary chain reaction of "panic" bidders temporarily distorts selling prices that might not normally qualify as market sales in the truest sense of the term *market value.*

Thus the appraiser must use caution when appraising for market value, remembering that this term presupposes that both buyer and seller are fully aware of relative value and neither is under undue influence to buy or sell. To this end, the appraiser should pay particularly close attention to current sales activity and be as informed as possible as to the reason for any panic buying or selling that might distort market values in an area temporarily.

The student of real estate appraisal must learn to recognize that, when a residential market is being inflated by outside buyers—whether these buyers be from another country, state, or locale, or even speculators who have temporarily driven up prices—it is likely that prices will level off and may even drop as dramatically as they have risen. Whether they do, or the extent to which this happens, depends on many variable and interrelated factors.

NATIONAL ECONOMY

The state of the union is of paramount importance to private property value. Unless the United States is healthy economically, there will be few, if any, economically healthy regions, cities, and neighborhoods. However, economically deprived regions can exist despite a vibrant, healthy national economy.

Of particular importance to real estate activity is the availability of money on a national level at reasonable interest rates. Most real estate ventures, from the construction of homes and apartment houses to commercial shopping centers and industrial parks, rely heavily on the availability of low-cost financing. Since two-thirds of the wealth in the United States consists of real estate, and since the largest single monetary investment that most Americans make is a home, it is easy to see the importance of the availability of large sums of low-cost money.

The Federal Reserve System, established by the Federal Reserve Act of 1913, has a major role in controlling the availability of money. The Federal Reserve System (commonly known as the Fed) is responsible for maintaining a sound credit base to counteract inflation and deflation through a monetary policy that encourages full employment while safeguarding the purchasing power of the dollar. This means basically a high rate of employment and a low rate of inflation. The Fed acts as a banker's bank. Nationally there are 12 Federal Reserve Districts, with each served by a Federal Reserve Bank. *All* nationally chartered commercial banks *must* belong; many state-chartered banks also belong in order to provide depositors with Federal Deposit Insurance Corporation benefits (known as FDIC insurance).

The Fed has numerous functions including issuing currency in the form of Federal Reserve Notes (paper money), supervising and regulating member banks, and assisting in the collection and distribution of income taxes. However, the three activities and controls that have a direct effect on real estate finance are:

1. *Establishing the discount rate* (interest rate) that is charged member banks for borrowing money. The member banks then add to this rate to establish the *prime* rate, which is the rate charged to the various banks' most *creditworthy* customers. When the Fed wants to slow down the economy, it raises the discount rate, which raises the prime rate and slows down borrowing activity. The reverse will speed up borrowing activity.

2. *Establishing reserve requirements,* that is, *increasing* or *decreasing* reserve requirements of member banks. To *slow down* the economy the Fed *increases* the banks' reserve requirement (the amount or percentage of total deposits on deposit with its federal district bank) leaving less money available for loans. To reverse a *slow* or *sluggish* economy, the Fed will *reduce* the reserve requirement, thereby allowing more funds to become available for loans and thus *speeding up* the economy. These reserve requirements vary from 3 to 22 percent of the banks' deposits.

3. *Conducting open market operations.* The Fed is allowed to buy and sell government securities as a further control to balancing the economy. These securities include U.S. Treasury Issues as well as many others, such as securities issued by the Government National Mortgage Association, Ginny Mae, and other federally sponsored housing and farm credit agencies. When the Fed wants to slow down the economy, they *sell* these government securities, thereby attracting investors away from real estate, stocks, and other investments; when they want to speed up the economy they *buy* them, thereby increasing the money supply to investors.

The relationship between interest rates and currency value is determined by management of the value of the nation's currency on the world market, as follows:

All nations want:

- Economic growth

- Cheap imports

- Good prices for their exports

The Federal Reserve Board manipulates interest rates by adjusting its lending rate to banks. This effect ripples down through the economy changing lending rates and interest on deposits.

If rates are raised	*If rates are reduced*
Desirable Effects	
• More investors from abroad buy the nation's bonds and certificates of deposit. • These purchases raise the value of the nation's currency because investors must buy the currency to make investments. • Imports cost less because our country's currency buys more abroad.	• Encourages economic growth; businesses borrow money for expansion. • Encourages exports; our nation's products are cheaper abroad, stimulating export demand. • Encourages refinancing of mortgages and new property purchases.
Undesirable Effects	
• Economic growth slows because it has become more difficult for businesses to borrow for inventory or construction. • Exports slow because our country's products are more expensive to buyers overseas. • Excludes more potential buyers from qualifying to purchase real estate.	• Fewer foreign investors buy the nation's bonds and CDs. They will invest in other nations with higher rates of return. • The value of the nation's currency drops because investors sell the currency to make investments elsewhere. • Imported goods cost more.

There are some important exceptions:

- The government can directly raise the value of our currency by dipping into our reserves of foreign currency and buying back its own currency on world markets.

- In times of crisis, investors rush to buy currencies of stable nations.

A graphic demonstration of these principals at work began in 1977, when an unprecedented series of events in California lead to an inflation rate of 8 percent and an interest rate of 8 percent. This meant that buying residential property was virtually a no-lose scenario, and a buying frenzy ensued, climaxing in 1989, with all-time high property prices. At the same time, federal deregulation of the lending industry, coupled with income tax advantages for real estate development partnerships, and overbuilding of economically distressed cities such as Houston, combined to create the savings and loan crisis, which caused hundreds of banks and thrifts to fail, closing their doors with losses amounting to billions of dollars. Foreclosures on real property peaked in 1987, while property values in highly desirable areas skyrocketed over 40 percent. The effect of the savings and loan crisis on the general economy was devastating and served to drive prices down, radically, in the early 1990s, in some cases as much as 25 to 30 percent. Hardest hit by this were commercial properties, which in some cases were devalued below their purchase and construction costs.

To restimulate the real estate economy in late 1992, the Fed began to reduce the discount rate, resulting in 20-year low interest rates by the summer of 1993. This worked to once again encourage home buyers and created an unprecedented refinancing frenzy but, unfortunately, had little effect on the commercial real estate market.

The appraiser must be aware of the state of the national economy, including the availability of mortgage funds, whether there is recession or inflation, and the short-range economic future. The alert appraiser can make knowledgeable judgments concerning the effects of various national trends that influence real property value.

REGIONAL ANALYSIS

A study of the regional economy is a second step in the economic analysis of a parcel of real property. The value of all real estate in a particular region is maintained, increased, or decreased because of certain factors that have a regional impact.

Increased mobility, made possible by extensive use of the automobile and advanced public transportation systems, has augmented the effect of regional economic activity on local property values. People buy homes 30 to 50 miles from their work. Favorable employment rates, adequate roads, desirable climate, and other factors are important to people interested not only in single-family residential properties but in commercial, industrial, and multiple residential properties as well. A developer of a large shopping center is interested in the regional economy because the success of such a development will depend entirely on the presence of large numbers of people who can buy goods. These people in turn will locate in a desirable area. For example, the addition of 100 new factory jobs in a basic industry has been said to have the following approximate impact on the local economy:

1. 100 additional households

2. 91 additional school children

3. 359 more people

4. $229,000 more in bank deposits

5. 3 new retail establishments

6. 97 additional passenger cars registered

7. 65 additional service-related (nonmanufacturing) jobs

8. $331,000 additional retail sales per year*

The impact of regional employment variations on residential real estate values cannot be overemphasized. Many communities that have relied heavily on a particular industry have suffered when that industry was forced to close. Regional employment changes have been brought on by such classical examples as the Dust Bowl disaster in the 1930s in parts of Oklahoma and Texas; the loss of gold mining in Virginia City, Nevada; the depletion of anthracite coal reserves in the Great Lakes area; the loss of the SST (supersonic transport) contracts in and around Seattle, Washington, in the early 1970s; the loss of tourism in Atlantic City; the conversion throughout the country from a wartime economy in World War II to a peacetime economy; the cuts in federally funded space programs in Texas, Florida, and California in the late 1970s; the loss in jobs in the auto and steel industries because of Japanese and other foreign competition in the early and mid-1990s; the loss in jobs in the lumber industries suffered in the Pacific Northwest (Oregon and Washington) in the early and mid-1980s, and again in the early 1990s; and the layoffs occasioned by the drop in demand for home personal computers in 1990–1991 affecting some high-tech companies.

Some communities have experienced disastrous drops in residential real estate values as a result of these variations. Homes have lost as much as 10 to 20 percent in value in a few months because of these declines in economic activity.

On the other hand, in some areas residential real estate prices have risen 30 to 40 percent in a matter of a few months as a result of mineral discoveries, initiation of large governmental projects, shifts in population due to energy shortages, and many other reasons. Classic among these are the Gold Rush in California in the late 1840s; the oil booms in Texas, Oklahoma, and southern California in the 1920s and 1930s; the TVA (Tennessee Valley Authority) project, Grand Coulee Dam in Washington, and Boulder Dam in Arizona, all in the 1930s and 1940s; the space program in Houston, Texas, and Cape Kennedy, Florida, in the 1960s; and more recently, the dramatic shift of population from the colder areas of the country, such as the Northeast and Midwest, to areas of more mild climate, brought about by the high cost of energy during the oil shortages and the continuing high cost of heating during the late 1970s. These later shifts have had a noticeable effect on the dramatic rise in prices of

*Figures from U.S. Chamber of Commerce, 1994.

residential real estate, particularly in parts of California, where home prices rose from 5 to 10 percent a month in the early months of 1977 in many communities of the San Francisco Bay Area and the Los Angeles Metropolitan Area. These unprecedented price rises of approximately 30 to 40 percent within a period of 4 months (January through May 1977) were caused by a combination of factors in addition to the high energy costs in the eastern part of the United States described above. Some of these factors were:

1. The dramatic influx of industry, mostly high-tech, into the Silicon Valley area of northern California and the similar high-tech expansion that occurred in southern California.

2. Lower-than-normal housing starts occasioned by a 3-year drought prior to 1976, which curtailed water and sewer hookups and created a backlog of anxious buyers.

3. Speculation by opportunistic buyers who saw the chance to turn a handsome profit by purchasing new housing units (homes and condos) and creating a false sellers market by holding them off the market for a few months and then selling them to a horde of panic buyers.

4. A fixed-mortgage borrowing rate that approximated the inflation rate. This allowed speculators, investors, and even those interested in buying their own owner-occupied homes to purchase housing with funds that were virtually "free," since the mortgage could be paid off with "cheaper dollars," and in addition, the IRS allowed mortgage interest to be deducted from income thereby creating a double benefit to those borrowing for the purchase of housing.

This dramatic appreciation was inevitable, with the result that home buyers, whether speculators or owner-occupants, could not lose as home prices skyrocketed to new heights that left California housing the most expensive in the nation. However, recent layoffs, plant closures, corporate relocations, military base closures, decreases in defense-related industries, and corporate down-sizing in the early to mid-1990s have resulted in reduced home prices throughout the state. Commercial real estate prices have dropped, as well.

A good example of a healthy economic base is the medium-sized American county, Santa Clara County, with approximately 2 million people and a total work force of 805,000 described in Table 4–1. The major source of outside revenue is basic industries that attract money from outside the region, for example, automobile and airplane manufacturing, electronic and computer equipment, aerospace development, and even a healthy agricultural economy. These industries are all essential components of the healthy economic base of Santa Clara County.

Another advantage of Santa Clara County is its proximity to many institutions of higher learning. Major universities within one

TABLE 4–1   Wage and salary employment by industry, San Jose MSA (Metropolitan Statistical Area) Santa Clara County, California (in thousands of people employed)

Industry	1994 May	1994 April	1994 Mar.	1993 Mar.
Total, all industries (in thousands)[a]	789.4	786.7	785.5	797.7
Agriculture, forestry, and fisheries	5.4	4.5	3.8	5.3
Nonagricultural total	784.0	782.2	781.7	792.4
Mining	0.2	0.2	0.2	0.2
Construction	26.4	25.9	25.4	25.8
Manufacturing	224.0	224.3	224.9	230.8
Nondurable goods	24.6	24.6	24.5	25.1
Food and kindred products	4.6	4.6	4.5	4.7
Other nondurable goods	20.0	20.0	20.0	20.1
Durable goods	199.4	199.7	200.4	205.7
Electronic group	159.2	159.3	160.0	164.0
Computing, acctg., mach.	43.3	43.4	43.7	47.3
Elect./electronic equip.	77.6	77.5	77.5	76.7
Instruments	38.3	38.4	38.8	40.0
Transportation equipment	18.1	18.3	18.5	20.7
Other durables	22.1	22.1	21.9	21.0
Transportation and public utilities	22.5	22.2	22.5	23.1
Wholesale trade	44.2	44.5	44.6	45.5
Retail trade	109.0	108.4	108.6	110.2
Finance, insur. & real estate	30.8	31.0	31.0	31.0
Services	237.9	236.8	236.1	236.9
Government[b]	89.0	88.9	88.4	89.0

[a]Wage and salary employment is reported by place of work and excludes self-employed, unpaid family workers, domestic, and workers involved in labor-management disputes. Data are benchmarked to March 1994.
[b]Includes all civilian government employees regardless of activity in which they are engaged.

hour's driving time include Stanford University, University of California at Berkeley, University of California at Santa Cruz, University of San Francisco, and Santa Clara University. In addition, San Jose State University and numerous outstanding community colleges such as Foothill, West Valley, De Anza, San Jose City College, Evergreen College, and Gavilan Junior College are available to area residents.

Physically, a pleasant Mediterranean type of climate adds to the desirable living conditions that have brought economic prosperity to the Santa Clara County area from 1946 to the present. Warm summer days and cool nights, along with moderate winter months, add to the general quality of life.

Politically, there are 15 separate jurisdictional seats of government consisting of cities and incorporated areas. They range from the town of Los Altos Hills, which is zoned only for single-family residential one-acre-minimum lot sizes, to the city of San Jose, with all types of land uses and a minimum single-family residential lot size of 5,000 square feet. Some regional problems, such as air and water pollution, transportation, and garbage disposal, are being attacked by regional government. For example, the San Francisco Bay Area, of which Santa Clara County is a part, has a regional government called the Association of Bay Area Governments (ABAG), which comprises most of the jurisdictions in the area and is charged with solving regional problems. As urban areas grow and overlap, area problems can be resolved only by cooperation among the various cities and communities. Also, the Bay Conservation Development Commission (BCDC) controls development in the San Francisco Bay and surrounding areas.

We have seen that economic, political, and physical factors affect property value. In addition, social forces have great influence. Although they are more difficult to isolate and identify, since they result primarily from interrelationships of people and attitudes, the appraiser must still evaluate them.

An effective regional analysis then should include the following considerations:

Physical or Environmental

Climate
Air and water pollution and control
Fresh-water supplies
Waste disposal facilities
Existence and protection of natural scenic beauty
Public transportation facilities
Available open spaces
Available utilities
Natural harbors or waterways
Airports
Noise control
Freeways
Commercial centers
Shopping facilities
Nuclear power facilities
Hazardous waste sites
Electromagnetic fields (EMF)

Economic

Quality and diversification of basic consumer industries
Quality and diversification of defense-oriented industries
Population projections
Quality and quantity of institutions of higher learning
Maintaining strategic military bases

Political

Regional government controls
Cooperation among local government jurisdictions in solving inter-city problems

Social–Public Attitudes Toward

Law and order
Individual responsibilities
Welfare programs
Community improvement programs
Mixtures of cultural, social, and economic groups
Recreation

CITY ANALYSIS

The closer we come geographically to a parcel of real property, the more profound is the effect on its value of the motivational forces acting within this smaller area. Narrowing from regional analysis to city analysis, we reduce the physical size of the area of study. We also reduce the economic ranges, variety of social attitudes, and in some cases, the range of political ideals.

Physical Considerations

Similar forces often act on city and regional property values. For example, an adequate source of fresh water is very important to a city as well as to a region, particularly in California, where some areas did not develop until fresh water was imported by pipes or canals. The Oroville Dam project on the Feather River in northern California has made possible the planning and eventual development of areas hundreds of miles from the source of water. However, in some California communities, fresh water must be rationed or temporary sources provided in late summer and fall, when local wells dry up or because minimal rainfall the previous spring created insufficient storage.

In some areas, water quantity is not the only consideration. Much of metropolitan San Francisco and Oakland is supplied by melted snow carried from the Sierra in eastern California over 100 miles to the bay area. These water systems, constructed in the late 1920s and early 1930s, have provided much of the expanding bay area with snow-melted water of the highest quality.

The demand for high-quality water is especially noticeable in areas near the service boundaries of water suppliers, where homes without high-quality water service lose from $2,500 to $5,000 or more in value; without high-quality soft water, homeowners must install and maintain expensive, bothersome water-conditioning or water-purifying units. In addition, the rates charged by a metropolitan water district are often far below those of small independent water companies, especially where small competing water companies duplicate each other's facilities, preventing the economies of operation realized by the large supplier.

Even though climate is generally a force of regional dimensions, certain areas and communities experience particular climatic conditions. For example, some hilly areas are noted for excessive winds. One community may receive half as much rainfall as another only a few miles away.

Other physical or environmental considerations that affect appraisal include:

Waste disposal facilities

Public transportation facilities

Playgrounds and parks

Utilities

Flood control

Roads, highways, and other public works

Housing of all types

Educational institutions, churches, shopping centers

Medical facilities and cultural centers

Existence of flood-, earthquake-, slide-prone or fire hazardous areas or close proximity to a nuclear power station or other potentially hazardous power-generating facility

Economic Considerations

Job opportunities in any particular city were of prime importance when cities were completely separate communities. However, with the trend toward urban and suburban sprawl, communities tend to overlap one another with the result that many people live in one city or community and work in another. An appraiser need not be concerned with city job opportunities, but rather with regional opportunities.

However, two basic economic considerations should still be noted in city analysis. These are a sufficient tax base to provide needed government services and a sufficient per capita income to support the tax base and to maintain maximum real property values.

Political Considerations

As cities grow and become more crowded, individual property rights become important. Of primary concern to a prospective single-family-residence buyer is the proposed master plan of the city or the planning department's control of zoning. For example, the community of Carmel-by-the-Sea on the California coast is famous not only for its natural scenic beauty but also for its quaint shops, pleasant tree-lined streets, and absence of offensive neon signs. All these advantages are due primarily to strict zoning laws and control. All new construction must pass rigid architectural standards. The result is a community known for its esthetic appeal.

In other cities or communities, the city council may not represent the interests of all the citizens. This is often true in large cities where members of the council reside in one community, yet serve as members-at-large on a council whose decisions affect another community. When this happens, proper city services may not be supported and property values may decline.

Political considerations for appraisal should include:

City master plan

Zoning controls

District representative city council responsive to the needs of the community

Government services

Social Considerations

Of immense importance in maintaining single-family residential real property values are the attitudes of residents toward the following:

Private property

Civic or community pride

Community improvement programs

Law and order

Individual responsibilities

Mixtures of cultural, social, and economic groups

Civic pride is evident almost immediately, even to a stranger, for it shows in many physical ways: in the quality of construction and maintenance of homes and other structures; the existence and use of parks, playgrounds, and cultural centers; the design and care of streets; and the absence or abundance of landscaping throughout the city around homes, private office buildings, government buildings, schools, parks, and streets. Some other social considerations are not so evident to the casual observer, but the experienced appraiser is aware of them and includes them in any analysis.

NEIGHBORHOOD ANALYSIS

The final part of an economic analysis of a single-family residential property must be a study of the properties that surround the subject property and influence its value. A residential property cannot be separated from its neighborhood and the physical, economic, and social makeup of the properties and the residents of those properties that surround it. Neighborhood is more important to residential properties than to many other types of properties. What difference, for example, would neighborhood make to the value of oil- or mineral-bearing real property? It would have little or no influence, as long as proper access and legal authority could be obtained to extract the deposits.

Neighborhood influences single-family residential property more than multiple-family residential property. Many people rent apartments in neighborhoods they would never consider buying in, because they buy a home as a more permanent residence. They may rent a place not entirely to their liking, since it is usually only a temporary residence and does not require a sizable down payment or pose the problem found in selling when they want to move.

What Is a Neighborhood?

Webster's Dictionary defines a neighborhood as "a district or section especially with reference to the condition or type of its inhabitants." Generally, in relating the word to some California single-family residential areas, we can say that a neighborhood is a community whose homes exhibit a certain degree of physical homogeneity and whose occupants exhibit a certain degree of economic homogeneity.

In the past, people gathered in small groups or communities primarily for protection. Usually they had similar economic and social interests and held similar political and religious beliefs. Today the political and religious beliefs of neighbors are often poles apart, but there is still a somewhat homogeneous grouping economically.

It is important to note that the Fair Housing Amendments Act, made effective by Congress in 1989, prohibits discrimination in selling, brokering, or appraising of residential real property on the basis of race, color, religion, sex, handicap, familial status, or national origin. Appraisers must not allow discriminatory factors to be considered in evaluating a neighborhood and must include a disclaimer of discriminatory considerations in each appraisal report.

Changing Neighborhoods

We have already discussed the principle of change. We learned that all improved real property experiences a three-stage life cycle. Single-family residential property is no exception. Neither are the neighborhoods in which the homes are located.

Each neighborhood, or composite of many homes, experiences a complete life cycle. Not only do the improvements or buildings change, usually by physical wear, but the character and attitudes of the inhabitants also change as the neighborhood goes through youth, maturity, and old age. Often as the years pass, people of lower economic levels move into neighborhoods where people of a higher economic status once resided. This is especially common in large urban areas, where succeeding families are often larger and farther down the economic scale than the original families. In some areas, as the neighborhood reaches old age and decay, a new use for the land is generated by an intensified demand for space and the land is zoned for multiple residential units to house more and more people.

Demographic statistics and trend reports are important tools for appraisers, and with the advent of computers, this data is readily available for most of California from on-line information services, such as DataQuick. These reports are based on census tracts, which DataQuick defines as

> small, relatively permanent statistical subdivisions of a county. Census tracts are delineated for all metropolitan areas and other densely populated counties by local census statistical areas committees following United States Census Bureau guidelines. Census tracts usually have between 2,500 and 8,000 persons and are designed to be homogeneous with respect to population characteristics, economic status, and living conditions.

While some professional appraisers may not agree that the census tract designations define neighborhood boundaries, they would certainly agree that these tracts provide a means of correlating demographic data to assist them in neighborhood evaluations.

Four sample reports are provided in Tables 4–2 to 4–5 from opposite ends of the state, showing both demographic and trend figures for different areas. For northern California, both types of reports are presented for the same county, contrasted with reports from two different southern California counties.

The appraiser must be aware of change and how it reflects on value and remember that a neighborhood partially reflects the attitudes of its residents. For example, many modest neighborhoods evidence a great pride of ownership, which maintains maximum property values.

Boundaries of a Neighborhood

What physical boundaries determine a neighborhood? Some single-family residential neighborhoods cover a square mile or more. Others are only a block or two square. Sometimes major traffic corridors—freeways or city streets—determine the boundary of a neighborhood. Other boundaries are natural, such as a stream or creekbed, hills, or a heavily forested area. Often, however, especially in single-family residential developments in California, the boundaries are simply a different quality or style of homes. Boundaries are not limited to physical, social, and economic differences, but may even include a different political jurisdiction or school district. What-

TABLE 4–2   Demographic report—Santa Clara County—census tract 5075.00[a]

Population profile (total population: 5,484)

Age:	0–15	16–21	22–34	35–44	45–54	55–64	65+
Male (%)	9	3	5	7	9	7	6
Female(%)	9	3	6	9	9	6	7

Socioeconomic profile

Tract average household income: $101,883   MSA average income: $57,912

Household income		Education		Profession	
$0–10K	63	No diploma	156	Exec/Admin	867
$10–25K	86	HS Diploma	369	Sales/Tech	943
$25–35K	108	AA Degree	256	Specialty	734
$35–50K	65	BA/BS Degree	1554	Craft/Repair	86
$50–75K	354	Grad Degree	1103	Blue/Other	82
$75–100K	396				
$100K+	896	*Ethnicity*		*Cars owned*	
		Amer-Ind	0	1	187
		Asian	989	2	949
		Black	33	3	477
		Hispanic	73	4	216
		White	4389	None	7
		Other	0		

Housing profile (Total housing units: 2,014)

Housing characteristics				Year	Year movein	Year built
Owner Occ	1836	1 Bedroom	43	1989–90	154	8
Renter Occ	135	2 Bedrooms	152	1985–88	551	77
SFR Det	1893	3 Bedrooms	600	1980–84	217	13
SFR Att	42	4 Bedrooms	885	1970–79	544	244
MF 2–4	32	5+ Bedrooms	328	1960–69	369	875
MF 5+	47			1950–59	136	729
Mobilehome	0			Before 1949	136	68

Mortgage costs		Gross rent		Costs as % of income (1989)	
$0–799	241	$0–499	0	0–20%	522
$800–1249	140	$500–749	10	21–24%	133
$1250–1999	217	$750–999	23	25–29%	114
$2000+	691	$1000+	89	30–34%	106
Avg	$1,626	Avg	$1,141	35+	414

[a]The information was obtained directly from the Economic and Statistics Administration of the Bureau of the Census.
© 1994 DATAQUICK INFORMATION NETWORK
ADDRESS: 9171 TOWNE CENTER DR
           SAN DIEGO CA 92122

TABLE 4–3   Trend report—Santa Clara County—census tract 5075.00—Single-family residences[a]

			Single-family residences			
Quarter	Median price[b]	Trend line[c]	Sales activity[d]	Sales ratio[e]	Number resale loans[f]	Number rf/eq loans[g]
1989						
Jan–Mar	$572,500	100.0	20	1.0%	20	41
Apr–Jun	$639,000	111.6	29	1.5%	27	52
Jul–Sep	$643,750	112.4	22	1.1%	21	70
Oct–Dec	$605,000	105.6	19	1.0%	18	63
1990						
Jan–Mar	$567,500	99.1	7	0.3%	5	61
Apr–Jun	$617,000	107.7	15	0.7%	14	77
Jul–Sep	$645,000	112.6	21	1.1%	19	63
Oct–Dec	$539,000	94.1	9	0.4%	9	53
1991						
Jan–Mar	$550,000	96.0	7	0.3%	7	46
Apr–Jun	$553,000	96.6	30	1.5%	28	93
Jul–Sep	$591,000	103.2	23	1.2%	21	48
Oct–Dec	$575,000	100.4	16	0.8%	15	116
1992						
Jan–Mar	$543,500	94.9	23	1.2%	23	130
Apr–Jun	$590,000	103.0	33	1.7%	32	123
Jul–Sep	$620,000	108.2	26	1.3%	22	143
Oct–Dec	$515,000	89.9	27	1.4%	27	131
1993						
Jan–Mar	$522,500	91.2	20	1.0%	18	142
Apr–Jun	$549,500	95.9	20	1.0%	19	206
Jul–Sep	$533,000	93.1	22	1.1%	21	219
Oct–Dec	$535,000	93.4	21	1.1%	19	235
1994						
Jan–Mar	$568,500	99.3	18	.9%	17	140
Apr–Jun						
Jul–Sep						
Oct–Dec						

[a]The accuracy of the above information is deemed reliable but is not guaranteed.
[b]Median sale price.
[c]Percent of price change from the base qtr. (1st qtr. with med. price).
[d]Number of sales.
[e]Percent of number of full-value sales to number of properties.
[f]Number of resale loans.
[g]Number of refi/equity loans.
© 1994 DATAQUICK INFORMATION NETWORK
ADDRESS: 9171 TOWNE CENTER DR
        SAN DIEGO CA 92122

ever the boundaries, they are usually capable of definition by an experienced appraiser.

Physical Considerations

Sociologists, psychologists, economists, city planners, and others are becoming increasingly aware of the relationship between people and

TABLE 4–4   Demographic report—San Diego County—census tract 0085.09[a]

Population profile (total population: 6,917)

Age:	0–15	16–21	22–34	35–44	45–54	55–64	65+
Male (%)	10	5	13	3	6	6	3
Female (%)	12	4	12	5	5	5	4

Socioeconomic profile

Tract average household income: $42,020   MSA average income: $40,374

Household income		Education		Profession	
$0–10K	541	No diploma	623	Exec/Admin	500
$10–25K	360	HS Diploma	2103	Sales/Tech	1675
$25–35K	781	AA Degree	335	Specialty	778
$35–50K	789	BA/BS Degree	879	Craft/Repair	199
$50–75K	655	Grad Degree	517	Blue/Other	710
$75–100K	200				
$100K+	35	*Ethnicity*		*Cars owned*	
		Amer-Ind	33	1	265
		Asian	463	2	621
		Black	367	3	354
		Hispanic	661	4	74
		White	5342	None	5
		Other	5		

Housing profile (Total housing units: 2,172)

Housing characteristics				Year	Year movein	Year built
Owner Occ	1484	1 Bedroom	659	1989–90	877	3
Renter Occ	1468	2 Bedrooms	799	1985–88	676	78
SFR Det	1490	3 Bedrooms	1662	1980–84	402	469
SFR Att	156	4 Bedrooms	597	1970–79	385	938
MF 2–4	99	5+ Bedrooms	90	1960–69	477	1643
MF 5+	1516			1950–59	45	648
Mobilehome	20			Before 1949	45	36

Mortgage costs		Gross rent		Costs as % of income (1989)	
$0–799	500	$0–499	470	0–20%	709
$800–1249	325	$500–749	371	21–24%	90
$1250–1999	170	$750–999	350	25–29%	168
$2000+	33	$1000+	100	30–34%	80
Avg	$500	Avg	$600	35+	190

[a]The information was obtained directly from the Economic and Statistics Administration of the Bureau of the Census.
© 1994 DATAQUICK INFORMATION NETWORK
ADDRESS: 9171 TOWNE CENTER DR
        SAN DIEGO CA 92122

TABLE 4–5 Trend report—Ventura County—census tract
0003.00—Single-family residences[a]

	Single-family residences					
Quarter	Median price[b]	Trend line[c]	Sales activity[d]	Sales ratio[e]	Number resale loans[f]	Number rf/eq loans[g]
1989						
Jan–Mar	$163,500	100.0	34	1.4%	25	30
Apr–Jun	$170,750	104.4	38	1.6%	27	41
Jul–Sep	$235,000	143.7	45	1.9%	17	44
Oct–Dec	$218,500	133.6	42	1.8%	25	39
1990						
Jan–Mar	$209,000	127.8	36	1.5%	29	29
Apr–Jun	$171,750	105.0	30	1.2%	24	36
Jul–Sep	$202,500	123.8	30	1.2%	24	43
Oct–Dec	$178,750	109.3	28	1.2%	23	26
1991						
Jan–Mar	$205,000	125.3	15	0.6%	10	33
Apr–Jun	$177,000	108.2	27	1.1%	22	33
Jul–Sep	$188,000	114.9	30	1.2%	24	31
Oct–Dec	$189,000	115.5	27	1.1%	21	42
1992						
Jan–Mar	$168,000	102.7	22	0.9%	15	51
Apr–Jun	$160,000	97.8	27	1.1%	18	41
Jul–Sep	$146,000	89.3	18	0.7%	11	46
Oct–Dec	$160,000	97.8	25	1.0%	17	57
1993						
Jan–Mar	$125,000	76.4	21	0.9%	12	32
Apr–Jun	$147,000	89.9	22	0.9%	17	52
Jul–Sep	$155,000	94.8	16	0.6%	15	42
Oct–Dec	$134,250	82.1	28	1.2%	22	63
1994						
Jan–Mar	$131,000	80.1	22	0.9%	15	44
Apr–Jun						
Jul–Sep						
Oct–Dec						

[a]The accuracy of the above information is deemed reliable but is not guaranteed.
[b]Median sale price.
[c]Percent of price change from the base qtr. (1st qtr. with med. price).
[d]Number of sales.
[e]Percent of number of full-value sales to number of properties.
[f]Number of resale loans.
[g]Number of refi/equity loans.
TOTAL PROPERTIES: 2,315
© 1994 DATAQUICK INFORMATION NETWORK
ADDRESS: 9171 TOWNE CENTER DR
          SAN DIEGO CA 92122

their environment. A parcel of real property cannot be separated
from its immediate neighborhood. The appraiser must consider the
quality, size, age, design, utility, and relative value of neighboring
properties. If the homes in the neighborhood are not reasonably homogeneous, what variations are evident, and how can these variations be related to value? Imagine a very good quality 3,000-square-
foot home constructed in an area of moderate 1,500-square-foot
homes. The 3,000-square-foot home will lose value. Conversely, the

1,500-square-foot home constructed in an area of 3,000-square-foot homes will gain in value.

The physical look of a neighborhood is very important to the maintenance of property values. Buyers are the prime determinants of market value. What the potential buyer sees in the neighborhood greatly influences the action that individual will take.

Other important physical considerations are:

Quiet streets of adequate design, width, and maintenance

Pride of ownership exhibited by well-cared-for homes

Adequate, well-planned, and maintained landscaping, both for individual homes and for parkways

Convenience to shopping, schools, churches, playgrounds, and major traffic arteries

Utilities including water, electricity, natural gas, and storm and sanitary sewers

Lot sizes and building setbacks

Use of natural environmental features or amenities

Economic Considerations

The major economic consideration in an analysis of a neighborhood of owner-occupied homes is sufficient household income to maintain each property at its maximum. The first evidence of deterioration in a residential neighborhood is the decreasing maintenance of yards and buildings as the neighborhood progresses from youth to maturity and then to old age. This cycle encompasses different spans of time with different neighborhoods. Some exclusive neighborhoods maintain maximum values for 100 years or more. Other neighborhoods deteriorate into old age in less than 10 years.

Many appraisers estimate the family or household income of a neighborhood by the continuing maintenance of the homes by their owners. An estimate might read as follows: "The neighborhood consists of white-collar semiprofessional, junior executive, and technical types with family incomes ranging from $60,000 to $100,000 per year."

In neighborhoods whose homes are mostly occupied on a rental basis, the primary economic consideration is the amount, quality, and durability of the income or rent for the neighborhood in general. For example, how much rent do homes of similar quality, size, and utility comparable to the subject property command in the neighborhood?

Political Considerations

The two principal political considerations that confront the appraiser in a neighborhood analysis are special assessments and local property taxes. Neighborhoods that lack certain physical facilities, such as water or sewers, may have to pay special assessments for such facilities. Suppose a neighborhood has recently been annexed to an expanding city. The city might require that the neighborhood itself pay for needed water or sewerage facilities. Special assessments, such as a lien on each property in the area, are imposed. The amount of the assessment is usually proportionate to the size and utility of each parcel of property. Suppose that the cost of sewer installation for the average 10,000-square-foot building lot is $5,000. Each such lot is assessed $5,000. If one 20,000-square-foot lot can be split into two building sites, then the sewer assessment will be $10,000 for this lot. If one lot is 15,000 square feet, but the minimum legal lot size is 10,000 square feet, it is probable that such a lot would also be assessed $5,000, since it can be used for only one building site.

The appraiser should also be aware that certain areas carry greater taxes because of their inclusion in a different school, water, or other government service district. Sometimes these tax burdens are not proportionate to increased desirability of the area. The appraiser must measure carefully the effect of extra taxes on market value. For example, some developments have bonds assessed against the properties for payment of infrastructure items such as streets, sewers, utilities, schools (Mello-Roos), etc.

Social Considerations

Of prime importance in a neighborhood analysis are the social forces at work in that neighborhood. However, since social motivations are intermixed with physical, economic, and political motivations, it is difficult to isolate a purely social action. Nevertheless, a neighborhood analysis should consider the following:

Attitudes toward law and order
Attitudes toward people of various cultural, social, and economic backgrounds
Neighborhood pride in property upkeep
Family sizes and age grouping
Homogeneous grouping as to civic interests
Prestige of neighborhood residents

SUMMARY

The appraiser must realize that people's needs, when related to real estate, are best understood through constant study and analysis of their underlying motivations. People are buyers, and buyers principally determine the actions of the market. The appraiser must constantly know what buyers are doing. Although the appraiser will not make a complete economic analysis of a specific parcel of real estate, it is possible to keep abreast of the total economic climate that surrounds the particular property. Appraisers can be effective in regions or areas with which they are familiar. Appraisers usually remain in a particular area, becoming expert in the area economy over a period of years.

DISCUSSION QUESTIONS

1. Discuss how the availability of money on a national scale affects the value of local real estate.

2. In addition to controlling the prime interest rate, how does the federal government directly or indirectly affect local real estate values?

3. What one factor in California has increased the influence of the *regional* economy on *local* real estate values?

4. Discuss what you think is the most important economic influence on the creation and maintenance of local property values.

5. Discuss the diversification (or the lack of it) of industry in your area. What would be the effect on local property values if the major industry in your area were shut down?

6. Explain how institutions of higher learning can contribute to the economic base of a region.

7. Discuss the effect of people's attitudes on the value of single-family residential properties.

8. Do you think a regional government would help your area to maintain single-family residential property values? Why?

9. Discuss what you think is the most important physical force acting on local single-family real estate values.

10. Discuss what you feel is the most important political force acting on local real estate values.

11. What determines the boundaries of a single-family residential neighborhood?

12. How do the boundaries of a single-family neighborhood differ from those of a multiple-family residential neighborhood?

13. What are the three basic stages in the life cycle of single-family residential real estate?

14. List the reasons for the variations in life cycles of different types of single-family residential neighborhoods.

MULTIPLE-CHOICE QUESTIONS

1. Which of the following is not a function of the Federal Reserve Board?
    a. Set discount rate
    b. Set prime rate
    c. Establish reserve requirements
    d. Sell or buy government securities in the open market

2. The Federal Reserve System was established in
    a. 1933
    b. 1953
    c. 1913
    d. 1923

3. To slow down the economy, the Federal Reserve Board would
    a. Lower the discount rate
    b. Lower the reserve requirement
    c. Sell government securities in the open market
    d. Do none of the above

4. To speed up the economy, the Federal Reserve Board would
    a. Lower the discount rate
    b. Lower the reserve requirements
    c. Buy government securities in the open market
    d. Do all of the above

5. Of the actions that can be taken by the Federal Reserve Board to control the economy, the one that affects home sellers and buyers the most is
    a. Lowering or raising the discount rate
    b. Lowering or raising the prime rate
    c. Selling government securities
    d. None of the above

Chapter 5

THE APPRAISAL PROCESS

Body of Knowledge Topic

- *Valuation Process*

The appraisal process begins by defining the valuation problem, identifying the property to be appraised and the type of value to be determined. This process consists of six steps:

1. Definition of the problem: clarifying the assignment
    a. Identify the property to be appraised
    b. Define the purpose and use of the appraisal
    c. Define the interests to be appraised
    d. Define the type of value to be estimated
    e. Determine the date of the value estimate—past, present, or future
    f. Determine any limiting conditions
    g. Determine compliance with license level requirements
    h. Establish fee for appraisal

2. Collection and analysis of data: gathering and interpreting the information
    a. Review national and regional trends for impact on property values
    b. Determine the economic base of the community
    c. Investigate local area and neighborhood composition with regard to:
        (1) Employment opportunities
        (2) Income levels
        (3) Demographic trends
        (4) Access to major traffic corridors and transportation systems
        (5) Convenience to shopping, schools, etc.
    d. Evaluate the site and improvements

3. Perform analysis of highest and best use of property

4. Perform the three approaches to estimating value
    a. Sales comparison: market approach
    b. Cost approach: depreciated replacement cost of land and improvements

   c. Income approach: gross rental multiplier or capitalization methods

5. Reconciliation of the three approaches: correlating the three approaches and making the final estimate of value

6. Communicating the results of the appraisal in a form appropriate to the assignment: producing the appraisal report

USPAP has expanded upon these steps, adding responsibilities to the process, as defined under Standards Rule 1 for performing the appraisal, and under Standards Rule 2 for reporting the appraisal. These additional requirements are briefly summarized below:

The appraiser must:

1. Be aware of, understand, and employ recognized methods and techniques.

2. Not commit a substantial error of omission or commission.

3. Not render appraisal services in a careless or negligent manner, causing the results to be misleading.

4. Include the following specific items, in addition to those defined above:
   a. State the monetary terms of the most probable price.
   b. Consider easements, restrictions, encumbrances, leases, etc.
   c. Determine any pro rata value of fractional interests, if applicable.
   d. Consider any effect of personal property on value, if applicable.
   e. Identify procedures and sources of market information used to perform the appraisal.

5. In reporting the appraisal, it must:
   a. Contain sufficient information as to be understood by the client.
   b. Disclose any extraordinary assumptions or limiting conditions.
   c. State procedures and reasoning that support analysis, opinions, and conclusions.
   d. Explain the exclusion of any of the approaches, if applicable.
   e. State compliance with or departure from the USPAP requirements.
   f. Include a USPAP-approved signed certification statement.

DEFINING THE PROBLEM—CLARIFYING THE ASSIGNMENT

The appraisal process must begin with a concise statement of the questions to be answered in the proper completion of the assignment. Generally, an appraisal is requested by one party from another party. To avoid misunderstandings about the property to be appraised, or the scope of the appraisal, or the license level required for performance of an appraisal, the total assignment must be made clear to all involved. This is best done by dividing the first step into eight manageable components:

1. Identify the property to be appraised.

2. Define the purpose and use of the appraisal.

3. Define the interests to be appraised.

4. Define the type of value to be estimated.

5. Determine the date of the value estimate—past, present, or future.

6. Determine any limiting conditions.

7. Determine compliance with license level requirements.

8. Determine fee for appraisal.

Identification of the Property

The precise location of the property must be determined first. Most single-family residences are identified by a street address, usually adequate to direct even a stranger to a particular property. Many listings and sales contracts include a street address for identification, for example, "all that property known as 13590 Howen Drive, Saratoga, California, being a parcel of land 85 feet wide by 145 feet deep, improved with a one-story, single-family residence and detached garage." Such information is usually sufficient to identify a house for listing purposes. However, to describe a property legally for deed purposes, a more precise description is needed, particularly when the property consists of a large parcel with no street number or address. The three basic methods for writing legal descriptions used in California are government survey, metes and bounds, and lot and block (recorded tract).

Government Survey   After California became a state in 1850, public land not included as pueblos or Mexican or Spanish grants came under the jurisdiction of government surveys under the rectangular system of surveys adopted by Congress on May 20, 1875. This rectangular survey system divided the land into townships 6 miles square. Each township consisted of 36 sections, each 1 mile square. Each standard section contained 640 acres. Townships were delineated by parallel east-west and north-south lines at 6-mile intervals, called range lines. A baseline served as the starting point for the east-west lines, and a principal meridian for the north-south lines. Because of its shape, California requires three principal starting points: the Humboldt Base Line and Meridian in the north, the Mount Diablo

Base Line and Meridian in the central area, and the San Bernardino Base Line and Meridian in the south (see Figure 5–1).

As you can see from Figure 5–2, each township is 6 miles square and consists of 36 sections. Each section contains 640 acres and is generally 1 mile square. From the basic 36 sections, townships are

MAP SHOWING TOWNSHIP AND RANGE SURVEY SYSTEM IN CALIFORNIA

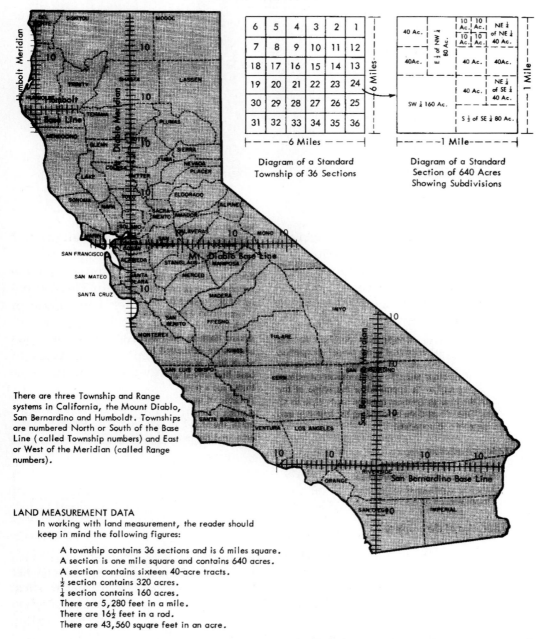

Diagram of a Standard
Township of 36 Sections

Diagram of a Standard
Section of 640 Acres
Showing Subdivisions

There are three Township and Range systems in California, the Mount Diablo, San Bernardino and Humboldt. Townships are numbered North or South of the Base Line (called Township numbers) and East or West of the Meridian (called Range numbers).

LAND MEASUREMENT DATA

In working with land measurement, the reader should keep in mind the following figures:

A township contains 36 sections and is 6 miles square.
A section is one mile square and contains 640 acres.
A section contains sixteen 40-acre tracts.
$\frac{1}{2}$ section contains 320 acres.
$\frac{1}{4}$ section contains 160 acres.
There are 5,280 feet in a mile.
There are $16\frac{1}{2}$ feet in a rod.
There are 43,560 square feet in an acre.

FIGURE 5–1   California government survey lines. (From Homer C. Davey, H. Glenn Mercer, and Albert Sharum, *Real Estate Principles in California,* 3rd ed., 1976, p. 8. Reprinted by permission of Prentice-Hall, Inc., Englewood Cliffs, New Jersey.)

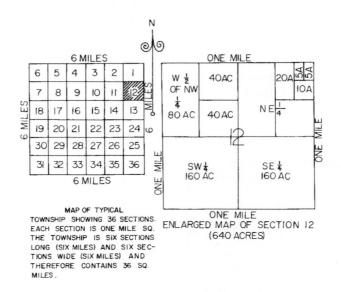

COMMON UNITS OF LAND MEASURE

FIGURE 5–2   Township breakdown.

laid out so that the precise location of a property can be determined by referring to a section or portion of a particular township.

Figure 5–2 shows several identifiable parcels of land. One is the West one half of the Northwest Quarter, of Section 12 of Township 3 North, Range 2 West, of the Mt. Diablo Base and Meridian. (This can be abbreviated as the W. 1/2 of the N. W. 1/4 of Sec. 12 T. 3N., R 2 W M. D. B. & M.) Another is the S. W. 1/4 of Sec. 12, and so on. This method is seldom used today in California, except for large tracts of land that are not definable by reference to either a lot and block or metes and bounds.

Metes and Bounds   According to *Webster's Dictionary, mete* means "measure" and *bound* means "the limiting line." Therefore, *metes and bounds* means "to measure the boundaries."

A metes and bounds description for the parcel illustrated in Figure 5–3 would be "that parcel of land lying in the City of Saratoga, County of Santa Clara," more particularly described as follows:

> Beginning at a point at the intersection of the easterly line of Howen Drive with the southeasterly line of lot 17 as said Drive and lot are shown on that certain map entitled, "Tract No. 1932 Saratoga Village," which Map was filed for record in the office of the Recorder of the County of Santa Clara, State of California, on August 29, 19—, in Book 85 maps, page 1. Thence along said easterly line North 89 dg 24′ East 145.06 feet to the easterly line of said lot 17; thence along said easterly line North 6 dg 11′10″ West 85.40 feet to the northerly line of said lot 17; thence along said northerly line south 89 dg 24′ West 136.75 feet to the easterly line of Howen Drive being also the westerly line of lot 17 previously mentioned; thence along said easterly line of Howen Drive South 0 dg 36′ East 85.00 feet to the point of beginning.

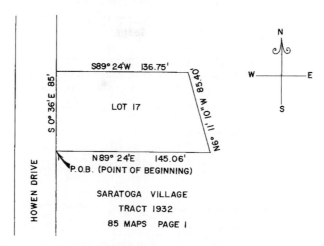

FIGURE 5-3 Metes and bounds description.

The metes and bounds description is obviously cumbersome. Many times this type of description can be interpreted only by a civil engineer, a surveyor, or someone else acquainted with this method of descriptive writing. Often the reference points are objects, such as trees, buildings, or river banks, that are not always permanent and that may be moved or altered so that the description becomes difficult to interpret precisely. Therefore, the metes and bounds description should be used only when a lot and block description is not available, or when the parcel of land is large and irregularly shaped.

Lot and Block (Recorded Tract)   In California, the lot and block system is the most widely used system of writing legal descriptions. Under this system, a tract map (or subdivision map) is filed in the county recorder's office. The map, based on a survey, usually indicates the public streets, easements, and lot lines (see Figure 5–4). It includes statements offering the streets for dedication to the public body, and a statement by the county engineer accepting the roads for public purposes and maintenance. Here is a typical legal description of this type:

> All of lot 17 as shown on the map of Tract #1932 known as Saratoga Village, filed August 29, 19— in Book 85 of maps, page 1, in the County Recorder's office of Santa Clara County, California.

When fewer than five parcels are to be recorded at one time, the map is referred to as a record of survey. Whenever five or more parcels are subdivided from a single parcel, the Subdivision Map Act requires the filing of a subdivision map.

Assessor's Parcel Number   Another method of identification is the assessor's parcel number. Each assessor's office in California maintains a complete record of every parcel of land located in its county, in

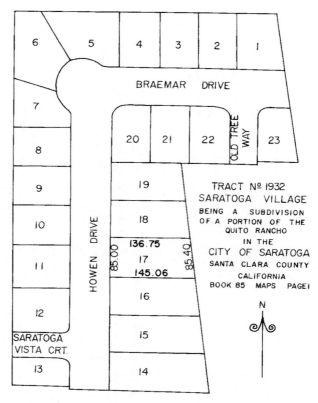

FIGURE 5–4   Example of lot and block (recorded tract).

order to assess property taxes against each property. Each parcel is assigned an identification number that designates only that particular parcel in that county. A master map index of the whole county divides the area into subsections of several square miles each. Each subsection refers to a particular book page that shows an even smaller area of approximately one square mile. Individual parcels are identified by number. Assessor's parcel number 391-09-250 identifies Book 391, page 9, and parcel 250 on that particular page. At the back of each book are listed the names of the persons or firms to whom the tax bill for each parcel is mailed.

The assessor's parcel number is rarely used as a legal description. Its practical use, other than for taxing purposes, is to furnish a ready reference to a person interested in the size, shape, and ownership of a particular property. This is especially helpful when the land is vacant or unoccupied and no other practical means is available for locating the owner of a particular parcel or determining its size and shape.

Purpose and Use of the Appraisal

The next logical step is to determine the purpose of the appraisal. Usually the purpose is to estimate market value. However, it may vary from an estimate of value by a bank for lending purposes to an estimate of value for inheritance tax purposes. An appraisal could conceivably be made to estimate any type of value. After market value is estimated, related value, such as insurance value, can often be determined. Or a bank or lending institution will appraise the market value of a property and decide to lend 70 or 80 percent of the market value. The lender is thus assured adequate security if the borrower defaults and the property must be sold to satisfy the loan.

To gather the proper information and to prepare a report that will be useful to the client, the appraiser needs a clear definition of the purpose of that report. This makes it possible to both avoid needless work and save the client money. For example, an appraisal of a particular property for inheritance tax purposes requires much less time and effort than an appraisal of the same property for condemnation purposes. The inheritance tax appraisal could be acceptable as a letter report, which could be written in about a day. The condemnation appraisal would require a fully detailed narrative report, which might take a week or more to complete.

Interest or Ownership to Be Appraised

An appraisal report is usually made on the basis of total ownership, commonly called *fee*—an abbreviation for the legal term *fee simple absolute*, meaning the most complete ownership. Sometimes, however, an appraisal is performed on a partial interest in a property, for example, an appraisal of a leasehold estate. This simply means appraising the value of a lease on a property rather than of the whole property. An appraisal may also be made on a one-half interest in a property. The appraiser must know from the start what interest or ownership is to be appraised.

Type of Value to Be Appraised

Market value is the most common type of value sought by various clients. Other types of value must be clearly defined by the client so that the appraiser may address the appropriate issues affecting the particular type of value to be estimated.

Date of the Value Estimate—Past, Present, or Future

Because real estate is subject to constant changes, it is important to know the date of valuation desired by the client. An investor might want an estimate of value as of a date 2 years ago or to estimate the future value of the property a year from now. Generally for residential property, value estimates are dated as of the date of physical inspection by the appraiser. The date of completing and signing the report may be several days or weeks later. The date of valuation must be determined so that the appraiser can plan the report and know what information to gather.

Limiting Conditions

The information in an appraisal is based partly on facts uncovered by the appraiser during investigation, partly on representations made by others, and partly on information that is on record. USPAP Standards Rule 2 includes provisions that any written or oral appraisal report must "clearly and accurately disclose any extraordinary assumptions or limiting condition that directly affects the appraisal and indicate its impact on value."

For Fannie Mae and Freddie Mac appraisals, a standard set of limiting conditions has been authorized as an integral part of the appraisal form set. This *Certificate and Statement of Limiting Conditions* can be incorporated into other appraisals, and additional assumptions and conditions may be included, for example:

1. No survey has been made.

2. The legal description is assumed to be correct.

3. No judgments are made as to any matter legal in nature.

4. Information received from others is assumed to be correct; however, no guarantee is made as to its accuracy.

5. The property is appraised as if free and clear of all encumbrances. No title search has been made by the appraiser.

License Level Requirements

With the advent of FIRREA and USPAP, state licensing has generated strict and binding regulations governing the value and complexity of appraisals that an appraiser can perform, based upon the appraiser's current license level. In California, the license levels are as follow:

License-Trainee: Appraisal of properties that the supervising appraiser is permitted to appraise.

License: Appraisal of 1- to 4-unit residential income property up to a transaction value of $1 million if noncomplex, or up to $250,000 if complex in nature. Appraisal of nonresidential property up to a transaction value of $250,000. This includes the appraisal of vacant land where the highest and best use is for 1- to 4-unit residential purposes.

Certified Residential: Appraisal of 1- to 4-unit residential property without regard to transaction value or complexity. Appraisal of nonresidential; property up to a transaction value of $250,000. This includes vacant land, as above.

Certified General: Appraisal of all real estate without regard to transaction value or complexity.

For more information on licensing in California, see Chapter 21.

Determination of Fee

After appraiser and client have agreed on the property and the interest to be appraised, the purpose and date of the appraisal, and the limiting conditions, the appraiser can determine the fee for the required services. It is up to the appraiser to estimate intelligently the time and effort necessary to perform the appraisal.

USPAP ethics provisions expressly forbid accepting an appraisal assignment on the basis of arriving at a particular or specified value. Fees cannot be determined based on value.

COLLECTION AND ANALYSES OF DATA— GATHERING AND INTERPRETING INFORMATION

National and Regional Trends

The appraiser is now prepared to work on the actual appraisal assignment. The first step is to review national and regional trends for their impact on property values. National issues may include real estate financing conditions, as indicated by current interest rates, and regional considerations may include a study demographics for population movements and employment trends.

Economic Base

In considering the geographical area that bears on the value of the subject to be appraised, economic conditions in the city and the neighborhood must also be considered. The economic base of a community is the level and diversity of income-producing business into the area. Property values may be adversely affected by the lack of a strong economic base where the residents do not have adequate services such as roads and police protection; or the values may be higher where a mix of businesses and residential properties provide a tax base that supports such services, making the area more desirable.

Local Area and Neighborhood

The mix of businesses and residential properties, as well as the type of residential subdivisions can affect the value of properties. Access to schools, shopping, and recreational amenities, as well as proximity to traffic corridors, highways, and public transportation, all combine to further influence property values. While census tracts may define neighborhood boundaries for government statistical purposes, subdivision housing tracts more often define boundaries for "comparable" property purposes, because the style, quality, and amenities of homes may vary from tract to tract. In evaluating local and neighborhood influences, the location of the subject property remains the key component.

Evaluate Site and Improvements

Consideration of the site and improvements should weigh the value of the individual parcel as well as its potential when combined with other parcels. The process of acquiring adjacent lots is called *assemblage*, resulting in a larger, more valuable piece of property, referred to as *plottage*.

HIGHEST AND BEST-USE ANALYSIS

Once a study has defined the political, economic, social, and physical makeup of these areas, the highest and best use of the subject property can be determined, and the appraiser can direct his or her efforts productively.

After determining what use will bring the highest net return to the property over a given number of years, the appraiser can begin to gather information regarding sales of comparable properties and cost and income data. (For a more complete discussion of area analysis, see Chapter 4.)

PERFORMING THE THREE APPROACHES

The three basic approaches to the valuation of real estate are the *cost approach*, the *sales comparison*, or *market data approach*, and the *income approach*. Each serves a particular purpose. Depending on the type of property, the data available, and the analysis of that data, each generally reflects a slightly different valuation, and a combination of two or all three of these approaches is used in the reconciliation of the final estimate of value.

The Cost Approach

The cost approach, also called the *replacement cost* approach, *summation* approach, or *physical* approach, appraises the property from the viewpoint of a builder or contractor. The expenses of building a structure at today's costs are computed, the estimated accumulated depreciation is subtracted from the cost of the structure, and then an estimate of the land value is added to that subtotal. The result is a figure indicating the value of the property based on the cost approach.

The five basic steps of the cost approach are:

1. Estimate the expense of building the structure at today's cost.

2. Estimate the total amount of accrued depreciation from all causes—physical, functional, and economic.

3. Subtract the accrued depreciation from the cost of building the structure.

4. Estimate the land value (as though the land were vacant).

5. Add the cost new, less depreciation, to the estimate of land to determine the total valuation of the property.

The Sales Comparison, or Market Data Approach

The sales comparison approach, also called the market data approach or sales analysis approach, appraises property from the viewpoint of a potential buyer-user. This approach is typically weighted most in reconciling the three approaches for single-family residential property. For example, in the case of a single-family residence, the market data approach would compare selling prices of similar or comparable properties.

Recent sales in the same or a comparable area, and of size and quality similar to the subject property, are compiled and analyzed as to utility, size, quality, location, and time. Given sufficient sales data and proper analysis of those data, the market data approach will result in the most accurate indication of market value of the three basic approaches. It is sometimes difficult to find enough recent comparable sales, however, and the analysis of the data must be correct.

The market data approach is generally the most reliable because it does not require estimation of many variables. The cost approach requires the accurate measurement of square footage of the structure, estimation of unit construction costs, accrued depreciation, and land valuation. The income approach requires estimation of gross income, vacancy rate, expenses, interest rate, and recapture rate or remaining economic life.

Since the market data approach requires fewer variables that depend on individual judgment, it involves less chance of error. Most of the variables in the cost and income approaches are actually eliminated from computation in the market approach, since the many buyers of the comparable properties have, by buying the comparable properties, reduced these differences to those of monetary variation. Land size, shape, and utility; improvement size; quality; and effective age are all measured in terms of dollar variations by the difference in sales prices of the various properties. This is especially true in the case of single-family residential appraising.

The market approach, then, consists of two basic steps:

1. Gather information on comparable sales.

2. Analyze and compare these sales with the subject property.

The Income Approach

The income approach, also called the economic or capitalization approach, appraises property from the viewpoint of an investor. It determines how much someone will pay for a property in order to receive the income that the property is capable of producing. Although the capitalization formula of the income approach is normally not used in appraising single-family residences, it has valid application in the appraisal of multiple-family residential properties, such as duplexes, fourplexes, and apartment houses, and often when the single family residence is a rental property. For single-family residential properties, a gross rent multiplier formula is often used.

The income approach analyzes the estimated gross annual income to be derived from the property. An estimate of the anticipated vacancy is deducted. The result is an effective gross income. From effective gross income, a compilation of all the allowable expenses is deducted; the result is called net income. Net income is then capitalized by a process that translates the net income stream into a present value for the property. This process requires the selection of an interest rate for the land and building and a recapture rate for the building. The resulting rate is called the capitalization rate.

The five basic steps of the income approach are:

1. Estimate gross annual income.

2. Estimate a vacancy rate, which is subtracted from the gross annual income to get the effective gross annual income.

3. Estimate the anticipated expenses and subtract them from the effective gross annual income to get annual net income.

4. Select an interest rate for land and building and a recapture rate for building.

5. Translate the net income stream to an estimate of value by employing the interest rates and recapture rate to determine a final value estimate by means of capitalization.

Income property expertise and judgment are required to estimate the projected income, vacancy factor, and expenses and to select a proper interest rate and recapture rate. The interest rate and the recapture rate are added together to determine the capitalization rate.

The gross rent multiplier formula requires knowledge of local property rental rates and produces an estimated value based on a factor generated from the average of the comparable properties sale prices.

RECONCILIATION OF THE THREE APPROACHES AND THE FINAL ESTIMATE OF VALUE

The appraiser has now studied the property from the viewpoints of a builder (cost approach), a potential buyer-user (market data approach), and an investor (income approach). The property has been viewed from all possible directions. The appraiser should now determine which approach is most applicable to the determination of a final estimate of value. If the three approaches have been properly applied, the appraiser has a definitive range of possible values. A proper weighting of the different approaches will lead to one logical conclusion.

Judgment is most important at this stage of the appraisal process. The final estimate is based on the type and condition of the property, the actions of the market, and the availability of data.

Especially in single-family residential appraising, the cost approach will usually set the upper limit of reasonable value and the income approach will usually set the lower limit of reasonable value. The market approach generally falls between them. However, these are generalizations and can vary with other factors affecting the property. The appraiser must weigh all of the factors considered in the three approaches and decide which approach should be given the most weight.

COMMUNICATING THE RESULTS OF THE APPRAISAL

The final step is the actual communicating of the appraisal. This may be oral or written, depending upon the scope of the assignment. Generally, it will be written, and most likely will be prepared using computerized forms. It should be objective, informative, concise, logical, and contain all of the required documentation and certifications necessary for compliance with USPAP regulations. If proper consideration and effort have been given to all of the factors, the report should be worthwhile to all concerned.

Most residential appraisals are reported on computerized forms authorized by Fannie Mae and Freddie Mac, including single-family residences on the URAR, condominiums, 2- to 4-family small income properties (duplexes, triplexes, and fourplexes). Computerization of form generation has facilitated industry standardization of reports and increased appraiser productivity. There are a wide variety of software packages from which to choose suitable programs. Refer to Chapter 16 for a more complete review of this final step.

SUMMARY

The appraisal process is composed of precise steps an appraiser must take to complete the appraisal function properly. Appraisers must work within the limits of their respective license levels, as defined by each state in which they are licensed. Although appraisers generally do not write legal descriptions, they should be skilled to some degree in following a written description to identify the property to be appraised. The interest or ownership to be appraised must be identified, as must the purpose and date of the appraisal. The appraiser and client must agree on the fee to be paid for the appraisal. The client is to be apprised, in writing, of the limiting conditions that apply to the appraisal. Upon performing the cost approach, the market approach, and (in cases of income-producing property) the income approach, the appraiser reconciles the applicable approaches and determines a final estimate of value. When these are complete, the report should be prepared in an objective, competent, informative, concise, logical, and aesthetically pleasing manner.

DISCUSSION QUESTIONS

1. Of the several methods of writing a legal description, which method is used most in California? Why do you think this particular method is most widely used?

2. Of the three approaches to the appraisal process, which involves more estimates and is therefore open to more criticism as to its exactness?

3. Why does California have three baselines from which government survey descriptions are made?

4. Why is a specific date of appraisal important?

5. Why should the fee be discussed before completion of the appraisal?

6. Name a drawback—other than lengthiness—of the use of a metes and bounds description.

MULTIPLE-CHOICE QUESTIONS

1. Which of the following should be the first task of the appraiser?
   a. Performing the three approaches
   b. Correlating the three approaches
   c. Clarifying the assignment
   d. Gathering and analyzing the data

2. At what stage should the fee for the appraiser be understood?
   a. At the very beginning
   b. In the middle of the appraisal
   c. At the end
   d. When the bill is submitted

3. The tract map, or lot and block, method of describing a parcel of real estate
   a. Is the most commonly used method because it is recorded in the County Recorder's office
   b. Is the most commonly used method because of its simplicity and accuracy
   c. Is not the most commonly used method

4. In the government survey system of description writing, one-fourth of a section contains
   a. 460 acres

    b. 40 acres
    c. 160 acres
    d. None of the above

5. A township consists of
    a. 6 sections
    b. 36 sections
    c. 1 section
    d. 48 sections

6. The most complete ownership of a parcel of real estate is called
    a. Grant deed
    b. Underlying fee
    c. Fee simple absolute
    d. Fee simple qualified

7. A statement of limiting conditions is necessary in an appraisal because
    a. It notifies the client of items subject to which the appraisal is made
    b. It protects the appraiser against conditions of which he or she has no control
    c. It limits the liability of the appraiser against claims not of an appraisal nature
    d. All of the above

8. Of the three approaches to valuing a parcel of real estate, which one values the land separately from the improvements?
    a. Income approach
    b. Market approach
    c. Comparable approach
    d. Cost approach

9. Generally, the most reliable approach in the appraisal of single-family residential property is the
    a. Market approach
    b. Cost approach
    c. Income approach
    d. Summation approach

10. Another name for income approach is
    a. Investment approach
    b. Capitalization approach
    c. Capital gains approach
    d. None of the above

Chapter 6

CONSIDERATIONS IN
SITE ANALYSIS

Body of Knowledge Topic

• *Property Description*

Every parcel of land and its location are unique. No two sites, no matter how similar, can be identical. In the case of improved properties, analysis and valuation of the site must sometimes be made separately from analysis of the improvements, for several reasons:

Local tax assessment
Claim on federal income tax return for depreciation allowances on improvements
Cost approach and certain income approaches of appraisal
Insurance
Eminent domain
When the existing improvements do not represent the highest and best use of the land

Whatever the reason for separate valuation, the appraiser must keep in mind the factors that make one parcel of land more desirable than another. These physical factors may all be combined into the word *utility*. Utility, of course, takes many forms, but for our purposes, it relates to *desirability*. In this discussion, we limit ourselves to land whose highest and best use is residential. We do not discuss land that could be used for commercial, industrial, or other purposes.

A common saying among real estate professionals is that the three most important aspects of any property are location, location, and location. Although other physical attributes also contribute to value, location is certainly the most important factor. Land cannot be moved. Only one parcel of land in any area has the best location. From this one parcel or area, the value of every other parcel or area is measured. Since a parcel of land occupies only one fixed spot on earth, we say that land translates to location. Following this premise to its logical conclusion, we find that location translates to use, since land in a certain location has a specific use now and in the future. If demand is great enough and zoning and building permits are available, use translates to value, which translates to return. Return can be measured in terms of money. Reversing this simple progression, we find that to be worth money, a parcel of land must have a return. To have a return, it must have value to someone. Value requires a use. The use of any parcel of real estate is a direct function of its location. Therefore, we can say that location is money.

The utility of land depends not only on its location but also on the type, size, and shape of the lot and other factors. To discuss residential land analysis and valuation in its proper perspective, we must study the following features:

1. Type (e.g., corner lot, cul-de-sac)

2. Size

3. Shape

4. Slope

5. Drainage

6. Soil composition

7. Existence of natural growth (trees)

8. Exposure to sun and weather

9. View, setting, natural environmental features

10. Accessibility

11. Availability of utilities

12. Off-site improvements (special assessments, accessibility, roads and sidewalks)

13. Deed restrictions, easements, rights-of-way

14. Availability of public transportation

15. Proximity to earthquake zones and faults

16. Proximity to nuclear facilities or hazardous waste sites

17. Proximity to electric and electromagnetic fields (EMF)

Other features to be considered are included in a neighborhood analysis. General accessibility; whether the property is in a flood-prone, earthquake-hazardous, fire-hazardous, or slide-prone area; quiet, well-landscaped streets; convenience of shopping, schools, and churches; and social prestige of neighborhood residents are certainly important. However, they relate to the entire neighborhood. The physical features listed earlier relate differently to each specific parcel of land. Since parcels in one neighborhood vary in size, shape, slope, and so on, we must consider these final variables and their definite influence on utility and, hence, value.

TYPE OF LOT

This section discusses the different types of residential lots, such as corner and cul-de-sac, and how these different types are valued in the eyes of buyers. Our discussion focuses on a hypothetical subdivision where the minimum lot size is 6,000 square feet. (If the minimum lot size in a subdivision is 43,560 square feet or one acre, some of the following comments might not be applicable.) For example, a corner lot in a subdivision of lots of at least 6,000 square feet would necessarily be larger than 6,000 square feet in order to accommodate the front-yard setbacks required for a house placed on the corner. Because a corner lot actually has two front yards, the lot must be wider than normal to accommodate the two front-yard setbacks. In such a subdivision, the corner lot would probably be 8,000 square feet or more as opposed to an interior lot that could be only 6,000 square feet and still conform to the front-yard setback required for improvements. However, in a subdivision of one-acre-minimum lots, all the lots would be approximately one acre whether they were corner, interior, or cul-de-sac lots, and all would have sufficient room for setbacks.

Corner Lot

In some single- and multiple-family residential areas, a corner lot (lot A, Figure 6–1) is more desirable than other types of lots. The developer of a subdivision may charge more for a corner lot both because

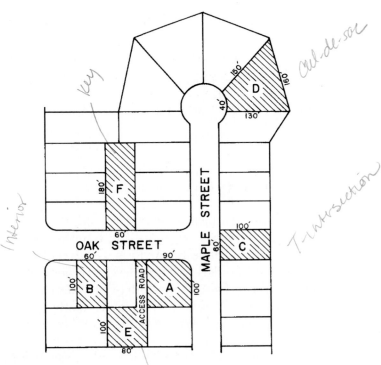

FIGURE 6–1   Lot types.

of this and because it usually costs more in terms of off-site improvements, such as streets, sidewalks, and utilities. This is because the corner lot has two sides that require off-site developments.

However, a corner lot may not command a higher price. What is an advantage to one prospective buyer may well be a disadvantage to another, and vice versa. For example, a large backyard may be desirable to some buyers whereas others might wish a smaller backyard.

Possible advantages of a corner lot:

1. Generally larger than interior lots.

2. Affords more privacy, since only two sides of the lot have abutting neighbors.

3. House looks larger because it is seen from two sides; can be more a showplace.

4. Better access to rear yard for trailer or boat storage or for heavy equipment used to excavate a swimming pool.

5. More street parking (particularly if there is no fire hydrant).

6. In some areas where alleys provide access to rear garages of interior lots, corner lot permits access to garage direct from street. This is safer at night and also more accessible in snowy areas where snow removal equipment usually does not clear alleys.

7. A street light is usually located on the corner. (Some people consider this a disadvantage.)

Possible disadvantages of a corner lot:

1. Larger front yard requires more maintenance to an area that family uses very little, including removal of snow from sidewalk in snowy areas.

2. Smaller backyard area.

3. Children and dogs shortcut across front of lot.

4. Close to intersection and possible objectionable noise and headlights.

5. Fire hydrant often located on corner lot.

6. Street light can be objectionable after family has gone to bed.

7. At least two sides of house are exposed to street, lessening privacy and requiring additional maintenance of those two sides. (Some owners feel compelled to paint the side or sides exposed to the street more often than the sides not exposed to the street.)

To relate these advantages and disadvantages to real estate value is difficult. The appraiser should know the desires of buyers in that area. For example, one California city enacted an ordinance forbidding overnight parking of boat and house trailers in the front yard or on the street in single-family residential neighborhoods. This ordinance resulted in an almost overnight rise in the value of most single-family residential corner lots. People who could no longer park their trailers in their front yards had either to rent space at a trailer storage yard or to park their trailers in their backyards. The only single-family lots of moderate size that had enough room on one side or the other for trailer access to the backyard were corner lots. In one confirmed case, a buyer purchased a corner lot, paying more than a 20 percent premium to be able to store a house trailer and a boat and trailer. The standard interior lot in the area was worth $100,000. He paid $120,000 for the corner lot and built his home to provide access to both sides of the rear yard. The alternative would have been to rent two trailer spaces at a commercial yard for a monthly minimum of $150 apiece. By buying a corner lot, he saved $3,600 per year in rental and had the convenience of having his boat and trailer in his own yard for weekend trips and minor maintenance. To him, the corner lot, even at a 20 percent premium, was a bargain.

No competent appraiser would immediately attach a 20 percent premium to all corner lots just because of this illustration, however. The appraiser must be aware of the many reasons people have for buying different lots at different prices in various areas.

Interior Lot

Most people prefer interior lots, and most single-family residential lots are interior lots (lot B, Figure 6–1). An interior lot is surrounded by other lots on three sides, generally by no more than five lots.

Possible advantages of an interior lot:

1. Backyard larger than front yard, affording more private play and entertainment area.

2. Small front yard requires less development and maintenance.

3. Farther removed from intersection and offensive traffic noises.

4. More private access can be had via an alley way.

Possible disadvantages of an interior lot:

1. Three (or more) abutting neighbors, as opposed to only two for corner lot.

2. In subdivisions of small lots, once residence is constructed, it is difficult to gain access to backyard for storage of family recreational vehicles or boats or for excavating for a swimming pool.

3. In snow areas where alleys serve interior lots, snow removal can be a problem. Interior lot value is usually the benchmark from which other lots are valued, primarily because most lots are in-

terior lots. Interior lot prices can be estimated by using the market approach.

T-Intersection Lot

The T-intersection lot (lot C, Figure 6–1) is basically an interior lot. However, it suffers from its location at the end of a T intersection.
Possible advantages of a T-intersection lot:

1. Spacious feeling afforded by view from front of house, looking *down* a street rather than at homes *across* a street.

2. View of hills or other scenic view, if any, is less obstructed by other homes.

Possible disadvantages of a T-intersection lot:

1. Automobile headlights may shine into house at night.

2. Possibility that errant vehicle may run into house. Especially vulnerable when lot is below grade of street.

In a well-planned subdivision, the house is positioned so that people in the living area are not bothered by the headlights of approaching automobiles. In such a case, if any improvement is directly in the path of an errant automobile, it would be a garage.

Cul-de-sac Lot

Many families with young children prefer cul-de-sac lots (lot D, Figure 6–1) because they offer more seclusion and safety than other lots. In a subdivision of moderately sized lots, a cul-de-sac lot generally has a greater number of square feet than other types of lots because of its shape.
Possible advantages of a cul-de-sac lot:

1. Minimum front yard requires minimum maintenance.

2. Maximum rear yard provides greater private living area for swimming pool, patio, vegetable garden, dog run, children's play area, and so on.

3. Absence of through traffic ensures privacy and greater safety of small children playing in street.

4. Depending on precise lot shape and size, house can be designed and positioned to take advantage of sun and still conform to building setback requirements.

5. Generally among first lots to sell in new subdivisions of moderately sized lots, all other things being equal. In older subdivisions of moderately sized lots, residences located on cul-de-sac lots seem to sell more easily.

Possible disadvantages of a cul-de-sac lot:

1. Minimum street parking area in front of residence.

2. Minimum front-yard privacy, since front yards are relatively narrow and angle toward one another.

3. The cul-de-sac may become overrun with children since it is generally a good place to play. (This can be an advantage, depending upon one's outlook.)

Flag Lot

The flag lot (lot E, Figure 6–1) is so named because of its similarity in shape to a flag on a staff. The "staff" portion generally includes the access road to the lot itself. A flag lot is usually behind, above, or below a lot that fronts on a public or even a private street or road. The flag lot can be worth more than other lots in the area if it enjoys a better view; for example, a flag lot may be on a higher elevation than another lot, or it may enjoy better access to a lake, stream, or ocean frontage if it is located below another lot. Generally, however, the flag lot has less value because of the costs of extending a private road and utilities to serve the lot. The appraiser must be aware of the pros and cons of such a lot in terms of market value, depending on location and other physical aspects. For example, in the heavy snow areas of California, a flag lot might require additional snow clearing for winter access, a factor that would decrease its value.

Possible advantages of a flag lot:

1. Can be more secluded.

2. Better access to ocean, lake, or stream if lot is located on any of these.

3. Better view if lot is above surrounding lots.

Possible disadvantages of a flag lot:

1. Generally requires a private road needing private maintenance.

2. Public utilities must be extended to the site at cost of lot owner.

3. Construction on such a lot might be difficult to finance, depending on access.

4. Less view and privacy if lot is below surrounding lots. Might also present drainage problems.

Key Lot

The term *key lot* is somewhat misleading. The sides of a key lot (lot F, Figure 6–1) touch a number of other lots, usually more than six others. Many key lots were not originally incorporated into the plans of a development, for some reason. In the case of a single-family residential development, the key lot may already have been improved with a residence when the area was subdivided; in the case of a commercial or industrial development, the key lot may have an older structure that is still economically functional and can be incorporated into the new plans. It is usually an exceptionally deep lot, or it may have some other odd shape. In a residential area, a key lot is generally less desirable because it has so many abutting properties. However, such a lot might be more desirable and valuable to a developer who wanted to assemble a group of residential lots under one ownership for the purpose of rezoning for a higher and better use, such as for commercial purposes. The key lot would be the first lot the developer would try to control, since it touched all the other lots; in this way it could be a "key" for a development that would include the surrounding lots.

The appraiser should realize that, in different areas and at different times, buyers will seek certain lots for a variety of reasons; these reasons can change. The appraiser must keep abreast of the changing desires of prospective buyers.

SIZE

Utility is a function of size as well as of location. In some areas a 3,000-square-foot lot is large enough to qualify as a single-family residential building site. In other areas, the minimum lot size is one acre or more.

A multiple-family residential site must have a certain number of square feet for the first unit and for each additional unit. Square-foot requirements generally include off-street parking needs; for example, in many areas each living unit requires parking space for a car and a half. Land value can usually be related to the price buyers pay per living unit. A site large enough to accommodate 20 units might be worth $50,000 per unit, or $1 million for the land. In the same area, another multiple site capable of accommodating a 40-unit apartment house would probably be worth $2 million. The values of multiple residential sites are usually proportionate to their size. As size increases measurably, value increases—assuming, of course, that the shape of the parcel is not unusual.

On the other hand, increases in the size of single-family residential sites do not necessarily create proportionate increases in value. For example, a single-family residential site of 6,000 square feet in a neighborhood of 6,000-square-foot lots might be worth $20 per square foot, or $120,000. However, it does not necessarily follow that a 10,000-square-foot lot in the same area would also be worth $20 per square foot, or $200,000. The appraiser must carefully determine through market analysis what buyers are paying for lots larger than the standard for the area. In the case above, the 10,000-square-foot lot would probably be worth not more than $140,000 to $150,000.

SHAPE

In the consideration of value per square foot, the most valuable lots are usually those nearest in shape to a square. Suppose two lots are under consideration, each of which is 10,000 square feet. One lot is a square, 100 by 100 feet. The other is a rectangle, 50 by 200 feet. Obviously, the square lot is more adaptable by almost any kind of development, multiple or single-family, than the rectangular lot that is four times as deep as it is wide. The appraiser must use good judgment in considering the utility of the parcel as affected by its shape.

SLOPE

As more and more of the level land in California is developed, builders and developers are forced to choose hillsides for all types of residential projects. This is especially true in larger cities near the coast, such as Los Angeles, San Diego, San Francisco, Oakland, and San Jose. Modern building methods and materials have greatly increased the number of potential building sites. In the future, all but the most precipitous slopes will likely be developed.

The appraiser should note however that, as more and more hillside areas are developed, the danger of slides brought about by a combination of cuts made for roads and building sites increases. California hills, in some areas, are not noted for extremely solid base material and can be subject to slides brought about by occasionally heavy rainy seasons. Also, California has a somewhat unique combination of either heavily timbered or heavily brushed hills and mountains that can become extremely dry and fire hazardous during the fire critical months of July, August, and September. Either of these conditions should be considered by the appraiser, and adjustments should be made to properly reflect any *buyer or lender* concern.

As the slope of a lot increases, building costs also increase. It is more expensive to install streets and utilities and to carve out building sites in a hilly area. The appraiser can best determine the effect on lot value of varying degrees of slope by referring to recent sales prices of similarly sloped lots. In some areas, depending on terrain and degree of slope, there is even a marked difference in value between an *uphill* lot and a *downhill* lot. The skilled appraiser is aware of these differences and knows the reasons for them.

The percentage or steepness of slope of a residential lot is very important in determining value:

Level to nearly level	0–3% slope
Gently sloping	3–10%
Moderately sloping or rolling	10–15%
Hilly	15–30%
Steep	30–45%
Very steep	Over 45%

The steeper the slope, the more pronounced are some problems. Some hill lots do not precisely fit major classifications because of the virtually unlimited variances in the physical aspects of a particular lot; however, many can be identified as *uphill, downhill, sidehill, top-of-hill,* or *bottom-of-hill.*

Uphill Lot

An uphill lot is uphill from the road of access—the road following the contours of the slope, that is, horizontal to the slope. Since the road traverses the slope horizontally, uphill lots can be found on slopes ranging from gently sloping (3–10 percent) to very steep (over 45 percent) (see Figure 6–2).

Possible advantages of an uphill lot:

1. Residence appears larger and more impressive from the road because more of residence is visible.

2. Safe feeling of being above the road; little chance of an errant vehicle endangering occupants of residence.

3. Easier to drain water from front steps and driveway; water will run downhill to catch basin in street.

4. Less road dust settles on house since residence is above road.

Possible disadvantages of an uphill lot:

1. Additional cost to prepare site for residence (all extra cut material from excavation must be hauled away).

2. Additional cost during construction (all concrete, wood, etc., must be hauled up to site).

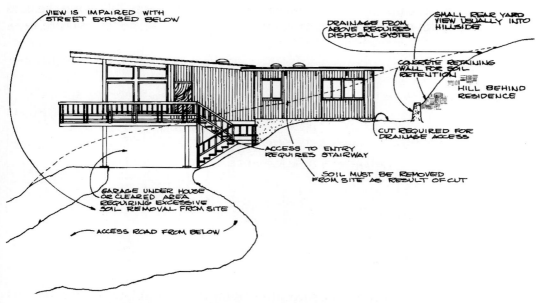

FIGURE 6–2   Residence situated on an uphill lot.

3. Generally more flood drainage problems, especially if there is a large hill behind the residential site. Surface runoff seeking lower level might go under or even through a house constructed on such a lot if the house is not equipped with adequate drainage facilities.

4. Generally expensive terracing or extensive retaining walls required to provide sufficient backyard area for residence.

5. Groceries and other supplies must be carried up to house; especially burdensome if slope is steep. (If possible, architect should design residence with garage in rear, level with entrance of house for easy access.)

6. Some privacy is lost because view side of site overlooks road; possible traffic noise.

7. If electricity for neighborhood is carried on telephone poles in street, view might be impaired. (In newer, high-quality developments utilities are underground.)

8. Difficult to build swimming pool in backyard.

9. Difficult to have sufficient drainage for septic tank installation and leaching lines downhill from facilities in residence yet within private property line.

10. In areas of heavy snowfall, the problems of snow removal may be intensified.

11. In areas of heavy moisture and low temperatures, a steep driveway may become hazardous due to icing.

Downhill Lot

A downhill lot is downhill from the road of access following the contours of the slope, that is, horizontal to the slope (see Figure 6–3).

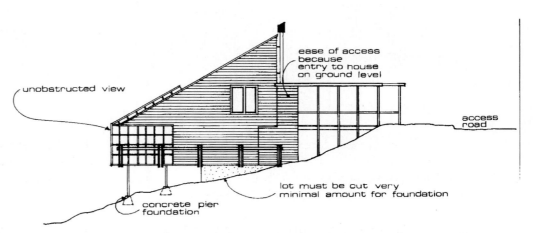

FIGURE 6–3   Residence situated on a downhill lot.

Downhill lots can be found on slopes ranging from gently sloping (3–10 percent) up to very steep (over 45 percent).

Possible advantages of a downhill lot:

1. Savings in cost to prepare site for residence—excess material from excavation can be pushed down slope.

2. Savings during construction of residence—all concrete, wood, and other materials can be lowered to site.

3. Savings in drainage cost. In a properly engineered development, road above downhill site should have facilities for catching storm runoff from surrounding higher elevations in storm sewer catch basin.

4. Concrete pier footings and porches can be used to maximize living areas without resorting to expensive retaining walls.

5. All groceries and other supplies for house can be carried down to house.

6. More privacy; view side is generally away from access road.

7. Ability to control view (e.g., control of trees that might block view) since major portion of lot is generally below residence and within control of lot owner.

8. If septic tank system is required, there is more area for drainage and leaching lines downhill from house.

Possible disadvantages of a downhill lot:

1. Residence not as impressive from road as one on uphill lot; actually looks smaller than it is.

2. Unsafe feeling of being below road traffic; chance that errant vehicle may endanger occupants of residence.

3. If lot is served by sewers, pumping may be needed up to sewers in road above.

4. In certain climates, if site is served by a steep driveway down to the residence, snow removal may be difficult, and icing of the driveway may create hazardous conditions.

Sidehill Lot

A sidehill lot is a lot at the side of a street or access road that is vertical or perpendicular to (straight up) the slope (see Figure 6–4). Sidehill lots usually can be developed only on a slope of less than 15 percent.

Possible advantages of a sidehill lot:

1. Construction costs of a residence on such a lot are kept to a minimum, depending on steepness of access street or road. Because

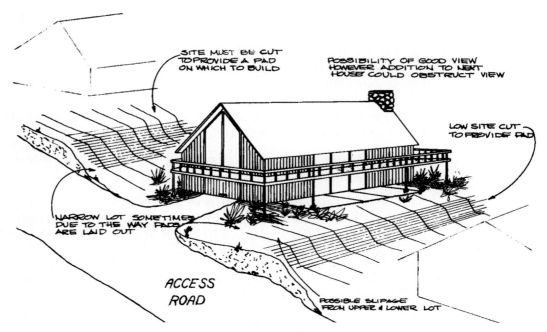

FIGURE 6–4 Residence situated on a sidehill lot.

road is usually vertical or perpendicular to slope, terrain usually varies from gently sloping (3 to 10 percent) to moderately sloping or rolling (10 to 15 percent). Access is therefore easy, excavation costs are moderate, and retaining walls and other costs of construction on a hill are kept at a minimum.

2. Lots enjoy basically the same view as other surrounding sidehill lots.

3. Drainage of storm waters can be engineered so that runoff from each lot goes directly into street drainage facilities.

Possible disadvantages of a sidehill lot:

1. To maximize number of lots fronting on road, lots are sometimes laid out so that narrow side of lot fronts on road. This limits view control over the lot downhill from a particular lot; trees or improvements such as a two-story residence can block view, since such obstacles will be close to property line.

2. Sliding or slipping occurring in any lot uphill or downhill from a particular sidehill lot tends to have a negative effect on that lot.

Top-of-Hill Lot

A top-of-hill lot is at the apex (summit) of a hill. The hill can vary from gently sloping (3 to 10 percent) to very steep (over 45 percent) (see Figure 6–5).

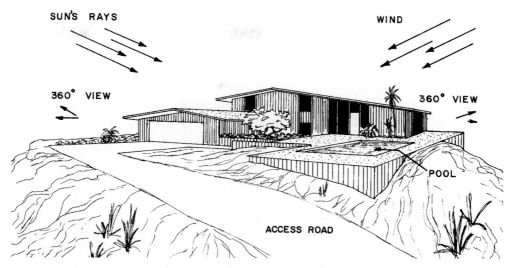

FIGURE 6–5 Residence situated on a top-of-hill lot. Can be designed and oriented to take advantage of view (can face any view), wind (to protect against cold or to capture a cooling breeze), sun (to maximize backyard and pool use), or access road.

Possible advantages of a top-of-hill lot:

1. Full 360-degree view.

2. House can be designed and oriented to take advantage of view, weather (wind), sun, and access road.

3. Lot drains well.

Possible disadvantages of a top-of-hill lot:

1. Usually most expensive lot in a development.

2. If elevation is too high, consideration must be given to water source. Lot may be situated higher than local facilities can supply, and water must be privately found, pumped, and stored.

3. Costs of preparing lot for residence are high; for example, cost of private access road is borne only by top-of-hill lot.

4. Underground utilities cost more.

5. If access is provided mainly by public road, a cul-de-sac must be provided to permit cars, trucks, and fire engines to turn around.

6. A public cul-de-sac attracts sightseers and others who can create a nuisance.

7. If lot is above in elevation or beyond in distance the normal range of city or community utilities, cost of providing utilities may be prohibitive.

8. If a relatively steep driveway or road is required to provide ac-
    cess, there may be problems of snow removal and icy conditions
    in certain climates.

Most disadvantages of such a lot can be cured by spending
enough money. Therefore, the most expensive site in a community is
normally the one having the character of a top-of-hill lot, provided
that all community utilities are available at the site.

Bottom-of-Hill Lot

A bottom-of-hill lot is at the base of a hill.
   Possible advantages of a bottom-of-hill lot:

1. Usually the least expensive type of hill lot.

   Possible disadvantages of a bottom-of-hill lot:

1. Traffic going uphill can be noisy and bothersome.

2. Drainage from lots above can cause problems during rainy or
    snowy periods.

3. View restricted to looking up at hill above.

4. In areas of heavy snows or icy roads, a home situated on such a
    lot can be in a hazardous position due to unsafe road condi-
    tions.

DRAINAGE

The least understood physical aspect of site analysis and valuation is
probably the adequacy or inadequacy of drainage facilities. Many
residential lot purchasers are extremely disappointed when they discover the need for spending additional money to provide adequate
drainage facilities. In some cases, a qualified appraiser can estimate
the cost of providing these facilities. Often, however, the opinion of
an engineer or other drainage expert is needed. The reasonable cost
of providing adequate drainage is often discounted from the value of
a site that compares in all ways except drainage to other sites in the
area.
   The appraiser should be especially wary of possible drainage
problems when a lot is located at or near the bottom of a hill; near a
shallow water course; near a creek or water course's outfall into a
lake, a bay, or the ocean; on a steep slope; at the bottom of a dead-
end street; on the lower side of a street; in an area that lies below the
high flood stage of a river; or in an area where unusually heavy rains
cause flooding.

SOIL COMPOSITION

The average appraiser cannot be an expert in all fields. Most soil composition analysis should be done by someone trained and equipped for the job. Professional soil engineers perform analysis on all types of land for a variety of uses. In addition, city and county agencies often employ soil analysts who determine, for example, the percolation ability (ability to absorb water) of soil in order to set minimum lot sizes in areas where sanitary sewers are not available, necessitating the installation of septic tanks with leaching lines. (Refer to the discussion of septic tanks later in this chapter.)

Soil composition is of paramount importance in determining not only the percolation ability of soil but also the ability of the base material to support intended structures. Our discussion, of course, refers to residential land. Other soil tests are conducted to determine the productive capabilities of the soil for agricultural uses or extractive industries, such as gravel mining or strip mining.

Most level land in California poses no significant soil composition problems for residential development. For this reason, unless the base material is entirely unsatisfactory for percolation or support, the appraiser normally need not be concerned with soil composition of level or near-level land provided adequate drainage is available.

TREES

Mature shade, fruit, or ornamental trees may add value to a lot depending on their type and placement on the lot, their age and condition, and the attitudes of buyers. For example, a 200-year-old, 6-foot-diameter California live oak in excellent condition, situated on an exclusive one-acre residential lot and oriented so as to shade the backyard, could add 10 percent or more to the lot value. However, simply because one such tree adds 10 percent, the appraiser cannot add 20 percent if the lot contains two such trees or 30 percent if it contains three! In addition, all trees do not necessarily add such value. For example, a mature 110-foot-high eucalyptus might add no value to an exclusive one-acre lot. As a matter of fact, such a tree could actually detract from value; many people consider eucalyptus messy, unattractive, and dangerous (they can blow over in a storm since they are so tall and are relatively shallow-rooted). Redwood trees, found mostly in northern California, can be an asset; however, since they become so large, they fit best on large residential sites. Other mature, native shade and ornamental trees should be considered as each affects a particular lot and the motivations of buyers.

Fruit trees can add to or detract from residential lot value depending on their age, condition, and type. When a number of mature fruit trees of the same type, such as cherry, apricot, peach, or plum, are located on a lot, it is usually because they were once part of a commercial orchard. Such trees, often nearing the end of their economic life, are sometimes retained in a subdivision to facilitate selling the lots. Although some buyers might consider such fruit trees an asset, others may not want to bother pruning, spraying, thinning, cultivating, and irrigating them. The appraiser must determine what buyers are seeking by comparing the prices of comparable lots with similar trees.

So far, we have not discussed lots improved with a residence and containing ornamental or shade trees or a family orchard. In such cases, the existence of the trees can be included in the value of the whole property. The appraiser should try to estimate objectively what value increment attaches to the whole property because of the existence of the trees; this is best done by comparing the prices of similar properties having similar trees. If no such sales are available, then an estimate must be made.

Placement of trees can add to or detract from a lot's value. In Figure 6–6, the trees are situated to provide energy-saving shade in the summer months. Proper placement of such trees can reduce inside residence temperatures by 20 degrees and, when placed along sidewalks, can reduce the surface temperature of the sidewalks by 60 degrees. But if a home has a swimming pool where the sun can be used for additional heating of the water (through a black-bottom pool and a solar heating system), poorly positioned shade trees would detract from the home's value.

The attitudes of buyers toward trees are influenced by quality of residence, locale, and ability to pay. For example, some feel that all mature trees should be valued on the basis of the cost to replace them. In the case of a mature oak, sycamore, silver maple, or even European white birch, the cost of planting a mature specimen on a

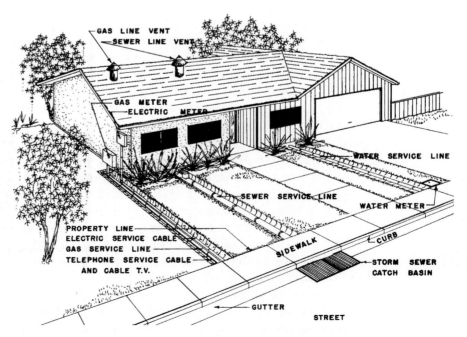

FIGURE 6–6   Facilities in a developed residential lot.

lot would be prohibitive and not at all reflective of the value increment of the existing trees to the property.

EXPOSURE TO SUN AND WEATHER

Many people prefer a particular weather and sun exposure for
their home. Some want a backyard with a northerly exposure (or
southerly, easterly, or westerly). In much of California, a backyard
with a southerly exposure to the sun is most popular. Californians
like to enjoy outdoor living as much of the year as they can. If the
backyard faces south, they can enjoy the sun on the patio or the
porch throughout the fall, winter, and spring months as well as
during the summer. Winds in most parts of California generally
blow from the northwest. Therefore, if the backyard faces south,
the house or apartment itself acts as a shield and adds to the outdoor living enjoyment. Residences with south-facing backyards
suffer less sun damage to the paint on the front of the structure.
Since the front is usually more extensively decorated and more
carefully maintained than the back, less maintenance means less
expense.

The appraiser should learn the desires of buyers, as many sec-
ond- or third-time home buyers insist on a particular exposure.

VIEW

Given a choice, most people would prefer a site with a view toward
the ocean, a lake, a bay, the mountains, or a valley. As good-quality
residential sites become more scarce and urban areas grow more
crowded, the need for space becomes more acute. Most people find
that a feeling of space in the environment is comforting. Especially in
areas of exceptional scenic beauty, such as the Lake Tahoe region,
residential view sites sometimes sell for twice the price of sites without a view. Even in suburban areas, it is not unusual for view sites to
bring 50 percent more than nonview sites, all other features being
equal.

The precise location of the site determines whether it will have
a view. Of course, it is also important that the house be designed and
constructed to take full advantage of natural environmental features.
In most subdivisions where a variety of sites are available, the view
sites, even though priced the highest, are the first to sell. A rule of
thumb is that the minimum premium for a view site is 10 to 20 percent. The same principle is true of multiple residential sites. Buildings erected on sites with views command considerably higher rents.
Good examples of such higher rents can be found in any urban area
where view sites are available. Nob Hill in San Francisco is an excellent example.

ACCESS

A residential site must have access by some means, either a public or private road. A private road provides privacy, the main reason for its installation; however, maintenance and repairs must be provided by the owners of the properties served by the road. Although a public road provides less privacy, maintenance costs are borne by the public body—city, county, or special district. Some property owners prefer to depend on their own initiative to keep access roads properly maintained, since the public body is not always responsive to road maintenance needs. On the other hand, in the case of private roads that serve more than one owner, disagreements among the private parties may cause road maintenance to suffer.

Security provided by public and private roads can vary greatly depending on their location, the patrolling activity of the local police or sheriff, and fencing and gates erected (for private access roads).

The appraiser should recognize that road engineering, including width, grade, drainage facilities, materials, and construction, can determine whether access to a site is adequate or inadequate. Value allowances should be made, for example, in the case of a road that may be virtually impassable during the winter because of rain, ice, or snow or in the case of a road too narrow for fire equipment. In the latter case, a construction loan may be difficult to obtain since fire insurance to cover the loan may be nonexistent or exorbitant in cost. Local fire districts usually require a minimum paving of 20 feet wide, properly designed and engineered, if they are to provide fire protection to a residential site.

AVAILABILITY OF UTILITIES

Utilities include water, electricity, natural gas, sewers, telephone, and sometimes cable television. Most quality residential areas in California now require underground installation of all utilities, primarily for aesthetic and safety reasons. This adds to the cost of the site; however, the market value of the site will usually increase to offset the cost.

The following list explains the diagram of utilities in a developed residential lot (Figure 6–6).

Water: Meter generally at the property line.
Electricity: Meter generally at the front of the residence.
Telephone: No meter at the site.
Natural gas: Meter generally at the front of the residence.
Sewer: Generally no meter. Vent and clean-out generally on street side of residence; hookup of residence to sewer main generally indicated by letter S on curb or in driveway.
Cable television: Generally no meter, flat monthly rate.
Sidewalk: Generally concrete, placed at property line, located within

public road right-of-way; property owner obligated to maintain and keep clear.

Curb: Generally concrete; can be squared or rolled. Generally within public road right-of-way.

Gutter: Concrete; sometimes cast as one piece with curb.

Storm sewer catch basin: Accommodates water runoff from private property and the street.

Street: Generally paved macadam or asphaltic concrete over crushed-rock base over engineered soil. Local county or city generally obligated to maintain and keep clear in the case of a dedicated public road properly accepted for maintenance by local city or county. Maintenance of private roads is obligation of owner of property served by such roads.

In a well-planned and properly coordinated development, all facilities should be installed so as to minimize their cost. As many services as is safe and possible should be installed in a single trench. The cost of these facilities is included in the asking price of the lot or residence.

Water

A residential site must have an ample supply of fresh water. If the lot is supplied with water by a local or mutual water district or public or private water company, the appraiser should determine the quality of the water, its source, and whether the water company or district has sufficient storage facilities to provide a continuing supply of fresh water for the foreseeable future. If the future supply of water is doubtful, for whatever reason—be it polluted water, low water table, or an ineffective or inefficient public mutual or private water system—the appraiser must give this question prime consideration when appraising the residential site.

In remote areas where lots rely on individual wells for fresh water, the appraiser might gain some insight from the counsel of a well-drilling or water expert. Usually, however, if no adequate system is operating yet, the *foretelling* of water sources and supplies in much of California is a risky venture not to be undertaken by the appraiser or real estate professional.

In hilly areas throughout much of the state, even if existing private wells supply ample water for existing residences, there is little guarantee that sufficient supplies are available for additional users or that enough water will be available during dry years. In northern California, the problem is usually less acute; there, greater rainfall results in more underground water supplies, and fewer people mean less development and demand for water.

Where an abundant supply of good fresh water is available now and for the foreseeable future, a lot can realize maximum value, depending on other features.

Electricity

Electricity is usually available even in the most remote sections of California. Private and public electrical utilities have supplied the state with an electrical system second to none. With hydroelectric dams and power plants, steam-generating plants, nuclear power plants, and even some geothermal power plants, the supply of power—most provided by private companies—seems assured for the present. However, the cost of electrical power is continually rising because of increasing production costs. Also, additional power sources may become a problem in the future.

Hydroelectric sources have for the most part been tapped; this places the main burden of future electrical power expansion on increased steam generation, which presently provides the major portion of electrical power in the state, and on nuclear power (fission). (The use of geothermal power is in its infancy, and its economic use may be questionable.) The continuing expansion of steam generation requires increasing use of oil or natural gas, fossil fuel sources that may become prohibitively expensive because of depletion of existing supplies and difficulty of obtaining what remains. Construction of additional nuclear (fission) reactors may be slowed by disagreement over their safety and over means of disposal of waste materials. A new power source, nuclear fusion—a relatively safe and clean power source—is only in its infancy, perhaps several decades away from practical use. Solar energy, an inexhaustible, clean, safe, relatively inexpensive power source, will probably become more practical as the available supply of fossil fuel decreases.

Natural Gas

Most urban areas of California are presently supplied with efficient, low-cost natural gas, most of which is brought into the state from Texas and Canada by private utility companies. (This situation may change, however, as the energy crisis becomes more acute.) For heating a home, natural gas is generally more economical than bottled gas or even electricity. Many homes in outlying suburban areas are not served by natural gas because of the cost of pipeline installation. Many of these homes rely on manufactured bottled or tanked gas that is much more expensive than natural gas. For the present, lots supplied with natural gas realize maximum value.

Sanitary Sewers

Sanitary sewer hookup (not to be confused with storm sewers) provides the lot with the means of disposing of waste material away from the site. Kitchen, laundry room, and bathroom facilities are directly connected to the sanitary sewer main located in the street (see Figure 6–6). The cost of sanitary sewer facilities, including hookup, sewer main, pumping station, sewerage treatment plant, and all other attending facilities for sewerage disposal, is usually borne by the local sanitary district and paid for by property taxes and a special hookup charge at the time the residence is tied into the system. The developer charges the cost of installation of mains and other facilities to each lot, and the price of the lot reflects these charges.

Outlying properties have often been serviced for years by individual septic tank systems, either relatively sophisticated septic tank systems (see Figure 6–7) or, in more rural areas, cesspools. As the city services of a nearby metropolitan area expand to these suburban or rural areas, the residents agree to annex to the sanitary district to have the convenience and safety of sanitary sewer hookups. An assessment district is formed to extend the sanitary sewer main and other facilities to the remote areas. Each lot is assessed a certain charge (usually based on the number of legal building sites per specific property), and the property assumes this indebtedness until it is paid.

Septic Tank System

If a lot is not served by a sanitary sewer system, it must have facilities for waste and sewerage disposal on the site. This necessitates the installation of a septic tank system.

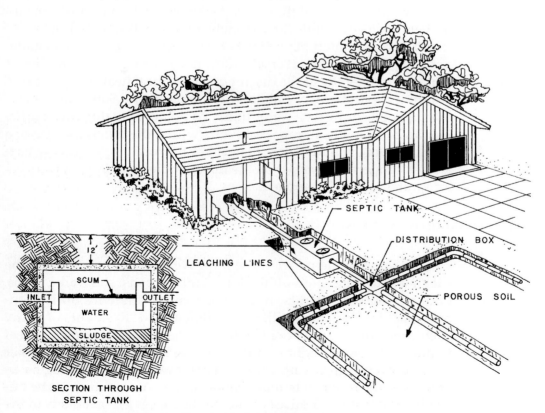

FIGURE 6–7 Septic tank installation.

The disposal of waste material at the residential site poses several problems. First, will the local public body allow such a system? Under a police power the local health department, building department, or in some cases, department of public works sets up health and safety requirements to be met by each lot before it will issue building site approval. The requirements generally include the following:

1. That there be a sufficient supply of fresh water at the site

2. That the site pass a percolation test

3. That the installation of a septic tank system not endanger other water sources or supplies in the area

We discussed the first requirement, sufficient supply of fresh water, earlier in this chapter. The percolation test determines the porosity of the soil for drainage purposes. Several 8-inch-diameter holes about a foot deep are drilled in the land and filled with a measured amount of water. Depending on the type of soil (e.g., sandy loam, rocky, or adobe), its compaction, and other characteristics, the water will drain at varying rates. The rate of drainage is measured and the lot either approved or disapproved for a building site. In the case of a slow drain, a larger lot size might be required to accommodate more extensive *leaching lines* to maximize drainage. If the water does not drain at all within a proper time period, building site approval is denied, and the lot cannot be used as a residential site.

The determination of whether a particular septic tank installation may endanger or adversely affect neighboring water supplies or systems is generally at the discretion of the local health department, building department, or public works department. Sometimes, however, a public or private water utility company operating in a particular area or having storage reservoirs within the *watershed* area of a particular lot or subdivision, may either buy out the potentially hazardous properties or insist on the installation of sanitary sewers before water service is supplied.

OFF-SITE IMPROVEMENTS

Off-site improvements are those improvements not directly on the site that add to the site's utility, for example, roads, sidewalks, curbs, gutters, and street lights. In exclusive areas, the only off-site improvement, other than utilities, is often a road. Residents of many such areas do not want sidewalks, curbs, gutters, or even street lights, since these might detract from the rural atmosphere. Other areas, however, may suffer from lack of these facilities. Imagine an area recently annexed to an expanding city. A condition of the annexation is that a special assessment must be levied on all lots in the annexed area to provide sidewalks, street lighting, curbs, and gutters. In this case, the amount of the special assessment would have to be considered as a value differential.

DEED RESTRICTIONS, EASEMENTS, AND RIGHTS-OF-WAY

Some sites, especially single-family residential sites, are encumbered with tract or deed restrictions that can affect their value. These restrictions, usually imposed by a previous owner, may set minimum house square footage, restrict the keeping of farm animals, and so on. Such restrictions might have a minimal effect on value; however, they should be considered.

An easement is one person's acquired right to use the land belonging to another person. Easements may have a restrictive effect on site value. Imagine, for example, a single-family residential site with a 25-foot-wide underground storm sewer easement running diagonally across its backyard, prohibiting construction of a swimming pool or even a patio. Such a restriction would be difficult to value precisely; however, the value detriment might easily exceed 20 percent of the value of the lot.

A road right-of-way may be imposed along one side of a lot to provide access to a lot in the rear. Suppose a lot 100 feet wide by 200 feet deep has a 20-foot right-of-way along one side. The negative effect of the right-of-way may be a 20 percent or more devaluation of the front site, not only because the right-of-way takes 20 percent of the land from the site but also because of the added nuisance and inconvenience of automobiles and people using the road. A more detailed discussion of valuing easements can be found in Chapter 19.

AVAILABILITY OF PUBLIC TRANSPORTATION

In some areas, the close proximity of public transportation boosts the value of both multiple- and single-family residential sites. This is especially true in neighborhoods occupied predominantly by older people and by those who do not have private transportation. The close availability of public transportation can add 5 to 10 percent to the value of such residential lots.

PROXIMITY TO EARTHQUAKE FAULT ZONES AND FLOOD HAZARD AREAS

In California, proximity to earthquake zones or faults is of major concern, primarily to insurance companies and lenders, and realtors must disclose this proximity information to potential buyers. The Alquist-Priolo Special Studies Zone Act, passed in 1973, established earthquake zones and produced maps for these areas for the entire state. Close proximity to a fault line or zone may influence market prices in an area, and the appraiser must be careful to consider and document these factors. The paired sales technique for arriving at an adjustment value may be effective in this case, comparing sales located in the same or similar fault zones.

The Federal Emergency Management Agency (FEMA), an arm of the Housing and Urban Development Department, has established flood zones, which, again, are important to insurers and lenders, and these zones must be disclosed to potential buyers, as well. The flood zone map number and zone code, along with the date of the map consulted by the appraiser, are required for Fannie Mae and Freddie Mac appraisal reports.

Many of the area maps used by realtors and appraisers show both earthquake and flood zones, but these zones are subject to change, as land and conditions change. These maps are updated from time to time, so that appraisers should have access to current zone data.

PROXIMITY TO NUCLEAR FACILITIES OR HAZARDOUS WASTE SITES

The impact of close proximity to nuclear power plants or hazardous waste disposal sites is generally obvious by the lack of sales in the area, coupled with extremely depressed sales of those properties that do sell. The government is grappling with how to clean up the waste sites, and how to minimize risk to the surrounding areas. Many of the nuclear power plants have been built in areas where a sales history can be evaluated, assisting in the determination of current value. However, the long-term effects on land and people have yet to be determined.

PROXIMITY TO ELECTRIC AND ELECTROMAGNETIC FIELDS (EMF)

Recent public awareness of electric and EMF emissions has created a volatile political environment in which contradictory scientific evidence abounds. Without definitive answers, it is difficult to assess the true impact of proximity to power towers and other EMF-emitting objects. Buyers, in general, seem wary of the power towers and believe that close proximity to these towers is negative, adversely affecting the price a buyer is willing to pay. Until conclusive scientific evidence is available, this issue will remain a gray area. Generally, however, aesthetic considerations typically reduce the value of properties located near such facilities.

SUMMARY

Before proper valuation can be determined on a lot or site, the appraiser must consider not only the location of the lot in the community but also the specific features of the lot, including type (e.g., corner lot), size, shape, slope, drainage, type of soil, native growth, exposure to sun and wind, view, access, and availability of utilities. These features will vary with every lot, since no two parcels of land are precisely the same. The appraiser must therefore consider these features and relate each lot to existing market demands.

DISCUSSION QUESTIONS

1. Compare the advantages and disadvantages of single-family residential corner lots in your area. Do the advantages outweigh the disadvantages or vice versa?

2. Do you feel that the cul-de-sac single-family residential lot is becoming more popular or less popular? Support your answer. Discuss the cul-de-sac multiple-family residential lot.

3. In your area, do single-family residential lots that are 50 percent larger than the standard lot size sell for at least a 50 percent higher price? Explain your answer. If your answer is no, tell what principle discussed in a previous chapter applies.

4. What do you think a *multiple-family* residential lot 50 percent larger than the standard lot size might sell for in your area? Would it sell for a 50 percent increase in price over standard lot prices? Is your answer different from your answer to question 3? Explain.

5. Do you agree that the residential lot nearest a square shape (within reason) usually has maximum value per square foot? Explain your answer.

6. Compare the values of single-family residential lots in your area, sloped and not sloped. Which generally bring the higher prices?

7. What are the differences in value, in your area, of view lots over nonview lots?

8. In your area, does the lack of availability of public transportation to some neighborhoods affect the value of homes in those neighborhoods?

9. Can you think of any advantages or disadvantages of hill lots, whether uphill, downhill, or any other type, that are not discussed in the chapter?

MULTIPLE-CHOICE QUESTIONS

1. In which of the following cases would it not be necessary to value the site separately from the improvements?
   a. Local tax assessment
   b. Fire insurance
   c. For selling purposes
   d. Cost approach

2. In which of the following cases would it be necessary to value the site separately from the improvements?
   a. Market approach
   b. For listing purposes
   c. For buying purposes
   d. When the existing improvements do not represent the highest and best use of the land

3. Which of the following variables is generally the most important in determining the value of a parcel of real estate?
   a. Size
   b. Shape
   c. Slope
   d. Location

4. Which of the following types of suburban lots generally occupies the most area?
   a. Corner lot
   b. Cul-de-sac lot
   c. Flag lot
   d. Interior lot

5. Which of the following improved lots generally has wider access to the backyard?
   a. Corner
   b. Cul-de-sac
   c. Interior
   d. None of the above; all have the same width of access to the backyard.

6. Which of the following types of lots generally allows more safety and privacy from street traffic?
   a. Corner lot
   b. Cul-de-sac lot
   c. T-lot
   d. None of the above; they all provide the same safety, quiet, and privacy.

7. Which of the following generally is the most common type of *lot*?
   a. Corner
   b. Interior
   c. Cul-de-sac
   d. Flag

8. Generally speaking, which of the following types of lots will be the most expensive to prepare for site development?
   a. Uphill lot
   b. Downhill lot
   c. Sidehill lot
   d. All of the above; all generally cost the same.

9. Generally speaking, of the following, the least expensive type of residential lot would be the
   a. Top-of-hill lot
   b. Bottom-of-hill lot
   c. Uphill lot
   d. Downhill lot

10. In which of the following areas should an appraiser feel least qualified to render an opinion?
    a. View
    b. Floor plan
    c. Drainage
    d. Lot size

11. In hill areas, the appraiser should be more inclined to seek outside professional opinion on
    a. Soil composition
    b. Drainage
    c. Geological hazards
    d. All of the above

12. In considering exposure to the sun in valuing a single-family home site, the appraiser generally gives the most value to a backyard facing
    a. North
    b. East
    c. West
    d. South

13. The most widely available utility service for single-family homes is
    a. Natural gas
    b. Electric
    c. Propane
    d. Sanitary sewers

14. One primary difference between a sanitary sewer hookup and a septic tank system is
    a. Necessity for a percolation test
    b. Necessity for a survey
    c. Necessity for a title report
    d. None of the above; there is no difference between them.

15. Which of the following is an on-site improvement as opposed to an off-site improvement?
    a. Sidewalk
    b. Sewers
    c. Streets
    d. Residence foundation

Chapter 7

FUNDAMENTALS OF SITE VALUATION

Body of Knowledge Topic

• *Site Value*

There are six basic methods of valuing land. They can be applied to any type of land including commercial, industrial, professional, and residential. Our discussion will be limited to the application of these methods to the valuation of residential land. The basic methods are:

Sales comparison, or market data, approach
Allocation approach, or the ratio of total value to site value
Abstractive, or extraction, approach
Land development approach—Subdivision development analysis
Land-residual approach
Ground rent capitalization

THE SALES COMPARISON, OR MARKET DATA, APPROACH

The market approach is the best of the five, as it is the most direct. To be effective, it must meet three conditions: First, there must have been a sufficient number of recent comparable sales, generally from three to five such sales. Second, the sales information must be available to the person making the appraisal. In some cases, and for a variety of reasons, this information is not given out by those knowledgeable of the price and terms of the sale. Third, the analysis of the available comparable sales must be performed by someone knowledgeable in such matters.

The market approach is a model of simplicity. It requires only the gathering of sales data for comparable land that has been recently sold. These sales are then compared to the parcel under discussion. The problem in most areas is the difficulty of finding enough recent sales of vacant lots. Once enough data are found, the second step involves only judgment by a competent individual.

Difficulty of Finding Lot Sales

Most residential property, especially single-family residential property, is sold as a total package including land and improvements. Bare lot sales for single-family residential use are rare; when they occur, it is often in an area measurably different from the area under consideration. Suppose you are appraising a single-family residential lot located in an area of 20-year-old homes. It is highly unlikely that there would be any vacant lots, let alone any recent *sales* of vacant lots. To determine lot value, you must therefore seek recent sales of bare lots that may be quite different from the subdivision in which the subject lot is located. If no other sales information is available, this is exactly what an appraiser must do. If this information is not conclusive, he or she will use one of the other appraisal methods as a check on the land value estimate.

The same problem may arise with *multiple* residential lot sales. In this case, the income, or land-residual, approach can be employed more effectively.

Sources of Data

Sales data on comparable vacant land can be found through owners, buyers, sellers, real estate brokers, land developers, multiple-listing services, computerized on-line information services such as Data Quick or CD-ROM compact disc information subscription services such as Metroscan, sales periodicals, title insurance companies, appraisers, banks, mortgage loan offices, and county recorders' offices.

From all except the county recorder's office, the required information, if available, can sometimes be had for the asking. Data available from the county recorder must usually be interpreted before any useful information can be obtained. The county recorder keeps a record of all land deeds properly presented. This record is usually a microfilm of the actual deed that transfers the property. However, the law does not require that the price of the land be noted in the document. Sometimes *real property* transfer tax stamps are placed on the deed, and the price of the property can be determined from these stamps. These stamps are generally not, however, too reliable an indicator of the sales price of a certain property for some or all of the following reasons:

1. Real property transfer tax stamps sometimes are not placed on the deed.

2. Real property transfer tax stamp requirements vary in different communities, depending on the amount of tax collected by the local governmental body.

3. Real property transfer tax stamps generally are paid only on new money trading hands and would not indicate an assumption of an existing loan.

4. Sometimes buyer or seller will place more stamps than are required to indicate a higher price was paid for the property than actually was paid.

5. Real property transfer tax stamps do not show terms of the sale; that is, down payment, amount of loan, secondary financing, or bonded indebtedness assumed by the buyer.

Although the county recorders' offices maintain a record of all documents submitted for public recordation, they are usually filed or recorded chronologically. People seeking information on a particular property must know the book and page of recording, or if they know the approximate date, they can check the grantor-grantee index, providing they also know the name of either the buyer (grantee) or seller (grantor).

Another governmental body, the assessor's office, also keeps a record of real estate sales transacted within the county. This information is generally requested from each buyer and seller of a property after the transaction has been completed, but it is confidential and is not revealed to those outside the office.

Computerized on-line and CD-ROM compact disc data services are efficient resources for gathering information compiled from country, tax assessor, and title company records. These types of services offer sales histories, prices and dates of sale, document numbers, statistics about the property and improvements, and plat maps, as well as access to flood zone and demographic information. These programs offer computer search capabilities that seek comparable properties within a given geographical area, based on the characteristics of the subject property.

The appraiser can usually gather whatever recent sales information exists by contacting one or more of the other sources we have listed. Real estate brokers are usually helpful and knowledgeable, especially if the property in question lies within the area in which the broker is active. Some appraisers are also real estate salespeople and brokers and may have access to this information.

Criteria of Data

Obviously, a comparable sale must meet certain tests of comparability. These are:

1. Similar location

2. Similar utility

3. Similarity in time to date of appraisal

4. A voluntary market sale

5. An actual market sale

Since no two locations are precisely alike, the appraiser must look for sales of land as similar as possible in locational factors to the parcel being appraised, and preferably as close to the subject parcel as possible.

Similar utility means that all the parcels must be nearly alike in size, shape, highest and best use, zoning, soil composition, drainage facilities, accessibility, and amenities.

Similarity in time means that all sales should have occurred within a reasonable period of the date of the appraisal. Usually, any sale within 2 years of appraisal can be adjusted with a time factor to bring it up to date. Accuracy depends on sales activity; that is, if enough comparable sales have occurred within the 6 months before the date of the appraisal, then the time problem is less, since less adjustment is needed.

A voluntary sale is one in which the seller of the land was not forced in any way to make the sale. Courts will not consider sales to public agencies having the power of eminent domain as comparable sales. Examples of other forced sales are a trustee's sale in the case of a foreclosure, a tax sale, or any other sale instituted against the wishes of the owner.

An actual market sale is real; that is, it actually occurred in the market. Sometimes sales are fabricated between members of the same family, business partners, or others who wish for some reason to misrepresent a sale. For example, land speculators may purchase land lying in the path of a proposed freeway and indicate through tax stamps on a deed a higher price than they actually paid. In this way, they hope to obtain a higher price for the land when it is purchased by the public agency for the freeway.

Listing of Data

Once the necessary sales information has been obtained, the appraiser should list the important aspects of the sale. A typical comparable sales sheet on a parcel of land might include the following elements:

Location
Name of grantor (seller)
Name of grantee (buyer)
Date of sale
Size of parcel
Amount of sale
Amount of real property transfer tax stamps
Assessed value
Encumbrances (existing liens, special assessments)
Remarks and analysis of sale

Analysis of Data

The appraiser now sorts this information so a meaningful analysis can be performed. The criteria for comparable sales must be met for a proper analysis. Perhaps the easiest way to analyze the relevant data is to prepare a chart that will make it easier to compare the features of the comparison lot sales with those of the subject site.

A chart that included all the possible variables would be too cumbersome. A few major headings will afford a reasonable comparison. Charts vary depending on the features to be rated, the area, and the type of site. For example, if the subject property is a view site, then a separate measurement comparing sale sites and subject property as to view is justified. A reprinted or computerized report form may be used to facilitate this process.

Let us prepare a chart with adjustments for time, utility (size, shape, slope), location (such as nearness to schools), and view (see Table 7–1). By applying adjustment factors to each sale for each of the major rating features, we can compare the various sales and indicate a value for the subject site.

The adjustment factors used in all cases are those required to make the sale site equal to the subject. For example, in sale 1 (Table 7–1), a site without a view, the adjustment factor 1.20 has been used since the subject does not have a good view. Conversely, sale 4 enjoys a location superior to that of the subject. In this case, the factor 0.90 is used, which means that the subject enjoys a location 90 percent as good as that of sale 4.

Another method of adjusting comparables uses actual dollar amounts assigned to the various features. This method uses paired data set analysis to determine the effect on value of a single individual factor, such as an extra bedroom or bathroom in a particular neighborhood. By taking the difference between sales prices of similar homes where the only difference in price can be attributed to a single feature, an approximate dollar value can be derived for that

TABLE 7–1   Land sales summary and adjustment[a]

Sale no.	Time of sale	Sales price	Utility (size, shape, etc.)	Location	Time	View	Indicated value of subject
1	1 year ago	$46,000	5,000	Equal	1,000	10,000	$62,000
2	1 month ago	$54,500	3,500	5,000	Equal	Equal	$63,000
3	2 years ago	$42,000	5,000	10,000	5,000	10,000	$60,500
4	6 months ago	$63,500	−2,500	−5,000	−2,000	2,000	$62,000
5	Presently listed for sale (asking price)	$76,500	−5,500	−10,000	Equal	Equal	$61,000

[a]This table could also be shown in dollar adjustments.

feature. Then a sufficient number of sales must be used in order to establish a relative value for a feature.

Adjustment factors are subject to criticism, of course, since they depend on the judgment of the appraiser. However, if the appraiser can remain objective in all the analyses, the factors should reflect a composite factor that approximates the value differential.

Sale 5 is really a listing, not an accomplished sale. It is considered in the chart only to set the upper limit of value of the subject.

Generally an averaging of the comparable sales is to be avoided as the only means of estimating market value, since such an arithmetic average tends to be distorted by extreme highs or lows. However, if the high and low fall within 10 percent of one another, such an arithmetic average can be used as a check, with the final estimate still left to the judgment of the appraiser.

Use of Listings to Sell

Sometimes too few recent sales are available to make a valid market comparison. There may be several listings of lots or land for sale, however. The asking prices for these lots can usually be considered as setting the upper limit of value for that particular type of property. Most real estate asking prices are set a little higher than market value. The appraiser can therefore get an idea of approximate upper limit of value by checking listing prices.

Use of Offers to Buy

Just as the listing to sell, or asking price, generally sets the upper limit of value, valid offers to buy generally set the lower limit of value. It is difficult to document such offers because they are usually not in writing. Prospective sellers may casually refer to a verbal offer made for their property in order to influence a value judgment. They may or may not have had such an offer. If it is not in writing as a valid written offer, it may be difficult to substantiate. Unless it can be substantiated, it should not be included in an appraisal.

THE ALLOCATION APPROACH—THE RATIO OF TOTAL VALUE TO SITE VALUE

The allocation approach assigns a certain percentage of the total value of a property to the land. For example, in a single-family residential area, comparable sales of improved properties may average about $200,000. In many single-family residential areas, the ratio of the total value to the value of the land approximates 4 to 1. If this entire property sells for $200,000, then the land or site is worth one-quarter of $200,000, or about $50,000. This ratio varies slightly depending on the neighborhood; most appraisers and brokers know what it is in their particular area. In some states, where the demand for available land

and the ability to pay for that land are not as great as they are in others, property-to-land ratios will be 6 to 1 or higher. The site value of a $200,000 single-family property might be $32,000 or less. In many single-family residential areas in California, however, a ratio of 3 to 1 is not at all unusual. For example, a $200,000 property might have one-third, or $66,000 or more of its total value imputed to land. As a community prospers and as overall real estate values continue to rise, the ratio of land value to total value will rise; that is, it is not unusual in some desirable urban areas to find land accounting for 50 percent of the total value of a single-family residential property.

In the case of *multiple*-family residential properties, the ratio varies depending on whether the site is purchased individually or as acreage for a development of apartment houses. The values are usually related to individual units. In other words, a site for a 10-unit apartment might be worth $20,000 per unit, or $200,000. If the cost of constructing the building is $80,000 per unit, or $800,000, the total value then would be $1 million, or a ratio of 5 to 1 ($1 million to $200,000).

A variation of the allocation approach is to use the assessor's office estimate of the land value. This amount is usually stated separately from the improvements and can be used if the land has been recently reassessed.

The allocation approach can be used if there is insufficient information for the market approach. The appraiser should not rely on this approach entirely but can use it as a check on another method.

THE ABSTRACTIVE, OR EXTRACTION, APPROACH

The abstractive approach is performed by abstracting (taking away) the depreciated replacement cost new of all improvements from the total value or sales price of a property to determine the value of the land. For example, suppose you are seeking the market value of a single-family residential lot, whether vacant or improved—let's call it the *subject* property. Assume there are no *vacant lot* sales available and that several single-family homes have sold in the vicinity of the subject single-family residential property. By estimating the replacement cost new, less depreciation, of the improvements on these comparable residential properties that have recently sold and subtracting each of these depreciated costs from the various selling prices, you should arrive at a very close estimate of the values of the residential lots. These values can then be used as comparable lot values to aid in solving your lot appraisal problem. See sample in narrative appraisal report in Appendix II.

THE LAND DEVELOPMENT APPROACH (lrg parcels)

The land development approach is best applied to the appraisal of large parcels of vacant land. Suppose you are asked to appraise a 25-acre parcel with a highest and best use as a single-family residential

THE LAND-RESIDUAL APPROACH

development of 20 exclusive sites of one acre each. (Five acres will be devoted to streets.) The analysis of this proposed subdivision would include several steps. First, determine what probable market exists for one-acre sites in that area; in other words, learn what price can be realized for each lot. Suppose you determine that such residential sites would sell for an average of $500,000 per developed acre site. Your computations to determine what a developer could pay for the 25 acres of raw land are shown in Table 7–2.

The developer could pay $5 million for the 25-acre parcel, or $200,000 per raw acre, and still make the development worthwhile. This approach justifies the appraiser assigning a value of $200,000 per acre to the 25-acre parcel.

Engineers, developers, bankers, lenders, and others familiar with costs of development can often help the appraiser estimate the value of larger tracts of land by the development approach.

THE LAND-RESIDUAL APPROACH (individual lots)

The land-residual approach has also been called the *concept of agents in production*. It is somewhat similar to the land development approach; however, it is best employed in estimating value of individual sites. Although this approach can be employed effectively in the valuation of a commercial site, such as a service station site, a site for a restaurant, or another commercial or industrial possibility, we discuss here its application to apartment site valuation.

Suppose you are assigned the job of valuing an apartment house site in an area where there have been no comparable sales of

TABLE 7–2   Computation for the land development approach

a.	Projected sales of all lots: 20 lots @ $500,000			$10,000,000
b.	Direct costs of construction to prepare lots for sale:		
	(1) Cost for roads	$1,000,000	
	(2) Cost for underground utilities including electricity, water, gas, and sewers (both sanitary and storm sewers)	1,000,000	
	(3) Cost for grading and leveling all the sites (20 × $500)	100,000	
	(4) Cost of engineering and surveying soil tests, environmental impact studies, and geological hazard reports	100,000	
	(5) Cost of marketing lots	320,000	
	(6) Profit to developer	800,000	$3,320,000
c.	Indirect costs:		
	(1) Cost of financing	600,000	
	(2) Taxes during construction and before sale	300,000	
	(3) Administrative, legal, accounting, appraisal, title fees, and other professional services	780,000	$1,680,000	$ 5,000,000
	What developer could pay for raw land			$ 5,000,000

any kind. Your client wishes to know what can economically be paid for such a site. Before you can estimate the valuation, you need the following information either from your knowledge and research or the knowledge of your client, the entrepreneur:

1. Available zoning and necessary permits, number of units proposed to be constructed, anticipated yearly income from rents for the given economic life of the structure, and anticipated vacancy rate

2. Total anticipated annual labor, operating, and maintenance expense

3. Total management expense

4. Total costs for amortizing (paying in full) whatever capital expenditures are required to build the structure and develop the land; fixed expenses and reserves for future depreciation

5. Expected percent of return sought by the entrepreneur on his or her investment in the land

Once these questions have been answered, you can estimate the value of the land by the land-residual approach. This approach, also called the *theory of surplus productivity,* uses the method of capitalizing whatever money is surplus to the land after all necessary costs of producing this income have been paid.

To simplify this approach, let us relate the income stream to be derived from this investment to a stream of water and a series of barrels that must be filled before any residual will be imputable to the land (see Figure 7–1).

Assume an anticipated annual effective gross income of $480,000. (*Effective gross* means that a vacancy factor has been allowed from gross income.) From the effective gross income, assume wages, labor, operating, and maintenance expenses of $200,000 per year; coordination and management of $50,000 per year; and annual cost of borrowing money to build the apartment house, including return *of* capital (principal) and return *on* capital (interest), reserves for future depreciation, and fixed expenses at $150,000 per year. With this information, we may proceed with our illustration.

The residual of $80,000, which is imputable to the land, can be capitalized at the going rate, say 10 percent, to determine the value of the land. *Capitalizing* means converting a projected income stream to a present-day value by employing a capitalization rate.

$$\$80,000/0.10 = \$800,000$$

Using this approach, we estimate the value of the land in this case at $800,000.

The term *going rate* refers to whatever rate of return is generally expected for this type of investment, either by the specific investor

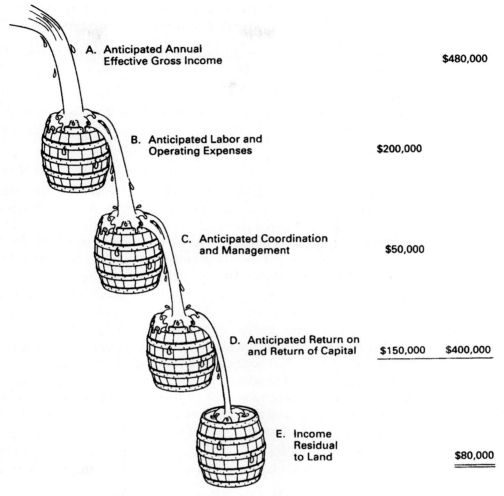

A. Anticipated Annual Effective Gross Income		$480,000
B. Anticipated Labor and Operating Expenses	$200,000	
C. Anticipated Coordination and Management	$50,000	
D. Anticipated Return on and Return of Capital	$150,000	$400,000
E. Income Residual to Land		$80,000

FIGURE 7–1   Land-residual approach.

(entrepreneur) or other investors in similar types of properties. This is more fully explained in Chapter 14.

PLOTTAGE, OR ASSEMBLAGE

The act of combining two or more parcels into an economically more worthwhile single parcel is discussed in Chapter 19, "Special Purpose Appraising."

GROUND RENT CAPITALIZATION

This method of determining land value may be used when the property owner retains title to the land, while leasing the right to develop and use it. The *ground lease* provisions and the amount to be paid—the *ground rent*—are determined by the location and type of development intended. The lease term is set by California statute, as follows:

1. Property located in a city or town, or land leased for oil, gas, or other hydrocarbon products, the maximum term is 99 years.

2. Agricultural land or land used for horticultural purposes, the maximum term is 51 years.

3. For property owned by a minor, or a person deemed by the court to be incompetent, the maximum term is set by a court.

SUMMARY

In the valuation of multiple- or single-family residential sites, appraisers must keep in mind the buyers' desires. Appraisers must be objective; their personal preferences must be entirely eliminated from their comparisons of sites. They must remember that single-family residential site purchases are made according to people's individual preferences. Multiple-family residential sites, on the other hand, are usually purchased with a view to the potential income that can be derived from the construction of living units, whether in the form of cash flow, a tax shelter, or investment for appreciation.

Whatever the reasons for market activity in any type of residential land, competent appraisers will be familiar with them and make sound judgments accordingly.

In valuing a site, appraisers must use a method applicable to the problem to be solved and the data available. The judgment of the appraiser is still the final determinant in a value estimate.

DISCUSSION QUESTIONS

1. Which method of site valuation is generally the best?

2. What is the major drawback, in most areas, of the market approach to site valuation?

3. List the five criteria of comparability that a lot must meet to be considered a comparable lot sale. Discuss each.

4. Explain the practical use of considering comparable listings to sell and offers to buy in the valuation of a residential lot.

5. What basic limitation can you see in the practical use of the land residual approach in the valuation of a single-family residential lot?

MULTIPLE-CHOICE QUESTIONS

1. Which of the following is not a basic method of land valuation?
   a. The market approach
   b. The land development approach

   c. The capitalization approach

   d. The land-residual approach

2. Which of the following is usually the best approach in land valuation?

   a. The market approach

   b. The capitalization approach

   c. The land development approach

   d. The abstractive approach

3. The most important variable of the market approach to land valuation is

   a. Sufficient number of recent sales

   b. Proper tax records

   c. Proper tax assessment

   d. Land and improvements assessed on the same basis

4. The allocation approach to land valuation can also be called

   a. The market approach

   b. The comparative approach

   c. The abstractive approach

   d. Ratio of total value to site value

5. Which of the following land valuation approaches considers the depreciated value of the improvements?

   a. The comparative approach

   b. The abstractive approach

   c. The land development approach

   d. None of the above

6. In appraising a bare 40-acre parcel of land, ripe for residential development, which of the following approaches should be used?

   a. Abstractive approach

   b. Allocation approach

   c. Land development approach

   d. Capitalization approach

7. In appraising a vacant lot with highest and best use of a 100-unit apartment building, which of the following land valuation approaches is best to use?

   a. The allocative approach

   b. The land-residual approach

   c. The abstractive approach

   d. Ratio of total value to site value

8. The concept of agents in production is most closely associated with which of the following land valuation approaches?

   a. Land development approach

   b. Land-residual approach

   c. Abstractive approach

   d. Allocation approach

9. The theory of surplus productivity is most closely associated with which of the following land valuation approaches?
   a. Land development approach
   b. Land-residual approach
   c. Allocation approach
   d. Abstractive approach

10. In the land-residual approach to land valuation, which agent in production is usually satisfied (or paid) first?
    a. Land
    b. Labor
    c. Capital
    d. Management

Chapter 8

CONSTRUCTION METHODS AND MATERIALS

Body of Knowledge Topic

- *Property Description—Basic Construction and Design*

The overall desirability of a house depends partly on its shape, the quality of its construction, and the materials and equipment used to build it. The appraiser must keep abreast of developments in the construction industry to be able to properly judge the effect on value of the use of various shapes, building materials, and construction methods.

The residential construction industry is one of the most competitive in the nation. In an attempt to cut costs yet not necessarily sacrifice quality, many builders are using economical construction methods, such as precut lumber, panelized walls, and unit construction. The unit method produces modular units for expandable homes that economically accommodate growing families. Besides cutting original construction costs, the family avoids the financing expenses, property taxes, and maintenance costs they would otherwise pay for a residence that might at first be too large for their needs.

Unit modules are assembled at a factory from two interlocking modules of 12 by 20 feet each, for example, or 480 square feet per unit. They are completely preplumbed and prewired, with factory-installed heating and ductwork. The floors are finished with carpeting, hardwood, or whatever other surface the buyer desires. A family might begin with two such 480-square-foot units, or a total of 960 square feet. As the physical needs and the financial resources of the family expand, additional modular units can be added to the core unit. The result is that the family can earlier afford a home of their own.

The modular concept adapts readily to multiple residential construction. Larger modules built of reinforced concrete are constructed at the factory. These modules can be stacked one upon another like building blocks, each an individual apartment with complete plumbing, electricity, heating, and ducting installed at the factory.

Although cost-cutting devices, such as precut lumber, panelized walls, and unit construction, are presently used in California to some degree, most existing residences were built conventionally, framed and finished at the site rather than at the factory. Indeed, builders' attempts to institute cost-cutting methods have been thwarted in many areas by outmoded building codes and consumer reluctance to purchase homes built using such innovations. However, increasingly prohibitive construction costs may cause changes in the building codes and influence consumers' attitudes so that they will accept these economically sound cost-cutting methods.

Whatever methods and materials are being used, a proper estimate of value can be made only by those who keep constantly informed of consumer desires. In all three valuation approaches, the appraiser should be concerned with the quality of construction and the materials used in the residence, along with the shape of the floor plan. These factors are especially important in the cost approach and the market approach. Knowledge of residential construction methods and materials is a must for a completely competent appraiser.

Construction economies do not necessarily mean inferior construction; in fact, such economies may have been instituted in a certain area where residences sell at a premium. This may be because of other factors, such as neighborhood desirability or excellent planning of a particular development. Conversely, some residential structures may have excessively overbuilt support members or more elaborate equipment than is needed, for example, a 60-gallon water heater in a one-bedroom apartment. For maximum marketability of residential property, all these components must be in balance and must contribute to the whole in proportion to their individual cost. It would be economically unsound for a developer to put expensive slate roofs on homes of modest construction in a suburban tract development.

CLIMATE AND AVAILABLE MATERIALS

Since prehistoric times, climate and available materials have been major influences on the types of homes people have built. From being simply a shelter from the elements, housing has evolved into a more permanent, useful, aesthetically pleasing structure.

However, climate and the availability of materials still influence construction methods, even in California. A mountain cabin in the Sierra has a steep-pitched roof to ward off annual snowfalls that may exceed 200 inches and heavy insulation to protect against temperatures that drop below zero. An adobe brick home in the California desert region, where summer daytime temperatures soar past 130 degrees in the shade and nighttime temperatures may drop below freezing, has walls 2 feet thick. Contrasting with these extremes are the stucco and wood homes in San Francisco, where moderate temperatures usually range from 40 to 75 °F throughout the year.

Most types of building materials can be found in California. Redwood, native to this state, is found in few other places in the world. Douglas fir, pine, cedar, spruce, and other timber trees grow in the forests of northern California. Almost every type of masonry brick and block is manufactured in the state, including adobe brick, wire-cut brick, red and white brick, and concrete building blocks. In addition, many types of natural river and mountain rock are available for construction purposes. Many large cement manufacturers operate throughout the state. Because of the wide assortment of available materials and the excellent low-cost means of transportation, virtually every type of material can be found in California residential construction.

ANALYSIS OF THE STRUCTURE

We shall study general shape or floor plan and construction methods and materials in the order in which they are used in construction: foundation, framing, roofing, exterior walls, floors, interior walls and ceilings, cabinets, doors, and windows. Figure 8–1 shows the construction details of a house.

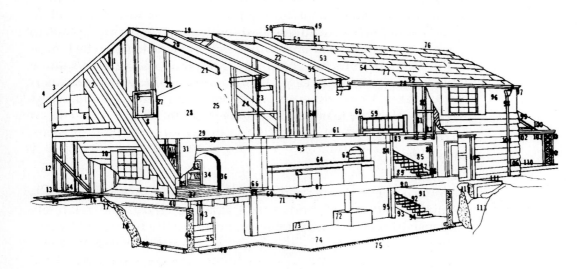

KEY TO CONSTRUCTION DETAILS

1. Window Head Frame
2. Wall Sheathing, Diagonal
3. Verge Board
4. Gutter
5. Window Jamb Trimmer
6. Wall Building Paper
7. Window Sill Frame
8. Cripple Stud
9. Wall Siding
10. Window Shutters
11. Corner Bracing 45
12. Corner Studs, Double
13. Sole Plate
14. Box Sill
15. Basement Areaway
16. Basement Sash
17. Grade Line
18. Gravel Fill
19. Ridge Board
20. Collar Beam
21. Roof Rafters
22. Interior Partition Plates
23. Interior Studs
24. Cross Bracing
25. Plaster Base, Lath

26. Gable Studs
27. Interior Window Trim
28. Plaster Walls
29. Cross Bridging
30. Second Floor Joists
31. Arch Framing
32. Insulation, Batts
33. Dining Nook
34. Interior Door Trim
35. Plaster Base, Rock Lath
36. Finish Floor
37. Floor Lining Felt
38. Sub-Flooring, Diagonally
39. Sill Plate
40. Termite Shield
41. Girder
42. Plate Anchor Bolt
43. Post
44. Foundation Wall
45. Frame Partition
46. Tarred Felt Joint Cover
47. Drain Tile
48. Footing
49. Flue Liner Tops
50. Chimney Cap

51. Brick Chimney
52. Flashing & Counter Flashing
53. Spaced 1" x 4" Sheathing (Wood Shingles)
54. Tight Roof Sheathing (All Other Coverings)
55. Ceiling Joists
56. Exterior Wall Plates
57. Lookouts
58. Furring Strips
59. Stair Rail & Balusters
60. Stair Landing Newel
61. Finish Floor Over Felt Over Sub-flooring on Wood Joists
62. Book Shelves
63. Picture Mould
64. Mantel and Trim
65. Damper Control
66. Base Top Mould
67. Ash Dump
68. Baseboards
69. Shoe Mould
70. Hearth

71. Plaster Ceiling
72. Boiler or Furnace
73. Cleanout Door
74. Basement Concrete Floor
75. Cinder Fill
76. Roof Cover (Shingles)
77. Roofing Felts
78. Soffit or Cornice
79. Facia of Cornice
80. Vert Board & Batten Siding
81. Fire Stops
82. Ribbon Plate
83. Stair Wall Partition
84. Stair Rail or Easing
85. Starting Newel
86. Cased Opening Trim
87. Main Stair Treads & Risers
88. Wall Stair Stringer
89. Face Stringer & Moulds
90. Starting Riser & Tread
91. First Floor Joists
92. Basement Stair Rail & Post
93. Basement Stair Horses

94. Basement Stair Treads & Risers
95. Basement Post
96. Facia Board
97. Cornice Bed Mould
98. Leader Head or Conductor Head
99. Belt Course
100. Porch Rafter
101. Porch Ceiling Joists
102. Porch Ceiling Soffit
103. Porch Roof Beam
104. Porch Beam Facia
105. Entrance Door Trim
106. Leader, Downspout or Conductor
107. Porch Trellis
108. Porch Column
109. Porch Column Base
110. Concrete Porch Floor
111. Concrete Stoop
112. Entrance Door Sill
113. Stoop Foundation

FIGURE 8–1 Construction details of a house.

Floor Plan or Shape of Structure

The appraiser should consider whether the overall floor plan of the structure is in the shape of a box or some other shape that would be a factor in its cost or marketability (value in exchange). Figure 8–2 shows four basic floor plans of single-family residences. Note that the box shape (A), although the same square footage (1,600 square feet) as the more complex H shape (D), has only 4 corners as compared to 12 corners for the H. Note also that as the shapes progress from a simplified box, even though the square footage remains the same, the lineal feet of perimeter, the square feet of wall area, and the number of corners all increase, adding considerably more cost to identical square footage. These cost increases will be realized in the added cost of the increased foundation, interior and exterior walls, insulation, number of windows and doors, weather-stripping, wiring, plumbing, heating ducts, and roofing. The H shape requires an intricate combination gable and hipped roof, its additional valleys and ridges requiring additional flashing, gutters, and downspouts to facilitate rain runoff. Not only will the cost of construction be higher for the H shape, but the cost of heating and cooling will also be higher because of the increased wall area exposed to outside temperature changes. Depending upon the availability and cost of energy, this could affect the marketability of the residence.

Foundations

The foundation material used most often in California is concrete, a mixture of sand, gravel, and cement. It is strong, durable, relatively inexpensive, available, adaptable, and can usually be poured by ma-

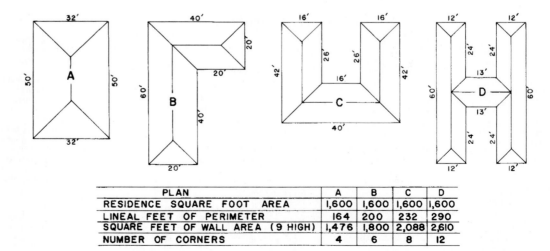

PLAN	A	B	C	D
RESIDENCE SQUARE FOOT AREA	1,600	1,600	1,600	1,600
LINEAL FEET OF PERIMETER	164	200	232	290
SQUARE FEET OF WALL AREA (9 HIGH)	1,476	1,800	2,088	2,610
NUMBER OF CORNERS	4	6	8	12

FIGURE 8–2 Residential floor plans with identical square footage. The drawings also indicate the different roof contours required to accommodate the four floor plans.

chines instead of by hand, saving a great deal of time. Steel is sometimes used for reinforcement. Building blocks are occasionally used instead of concrete, especially in remote and rugged areas to which cement trucks do not have access because of terrain or distance from a cement plant. Both concrete and building blocks, also called cement blocks, can be made water resistant. In some areas, native rock is used as the major foundation material; however, native rock requires much more work and skill to install than concrete and is therefore more expensive.

The concrete foundation usually takes the form of the exterior load-bearing walls. Precast concrete piers are sometimes used with supporting girders of lumber or lightweight steel for interior load-bearing walls.

Steel framing is required by code in some areas for any multiple residential structure exceeding a certain height. However, in most of California, wood—Douglas fir—is still the most popular, versatile material for residential framing. The frame consists of a bottom horizontal member, called a sill, to which are nailed vertical members called studs. A variety of bracings, called joists, fire stops, and headers, and numerous other members whose names serve little purpose to an appraiser, complete the frame. For the most part, the frame is not readily visible once the structure is complete, except in the garage, where the skeletal framing and roof support members are often visible. The average appraiser, however, makes no specific allowance for framing in comparing one residence with another.

The importance of framing and other construction components to the appraiser is as a part of the overall quality of construction. Various qualities of construction are more fully discussed and visually portrayed later in this chapter. For general information for the appraisal student, Figures 8–3 and 8–4 show construction details of a low-cost (minimum quality) California ranch house and of a very good quality California ranch. Figure 8–5 shows construction details of a good-quality masonry house. The figures show major construction differences even in components not normally visible to the eye. Although new construction requires wall and ceiling insulation, older, low-cost homes did not generally include such insulation.

Roofing

The material used to construct the roof is usually very visible in residential buildings, especially single-family units. There is more variety of materials for roof construction than for any other component of a residence (see Figure 8–6). The following is a partial list of the roofing materials in common use in California, in order of increasing expense:

Corrugated metal
Tin
Rolled tarpaper

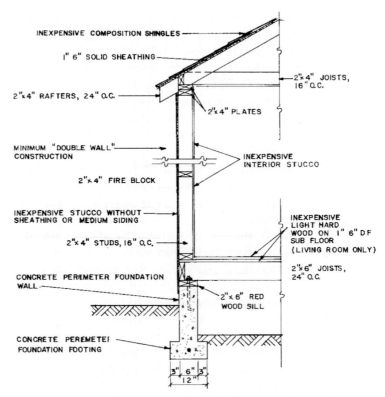

FIGURE 8–3 Construction details of a low-quality California ranch style wood frame house.

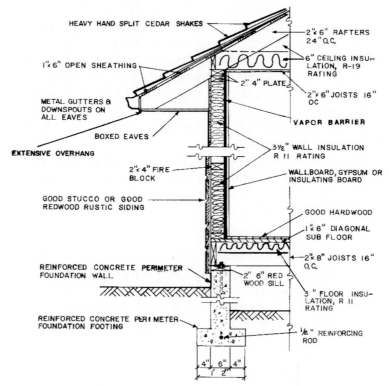

FIGURE 8–4 Construction details of a very-good-quality California style wood frame ranch house.

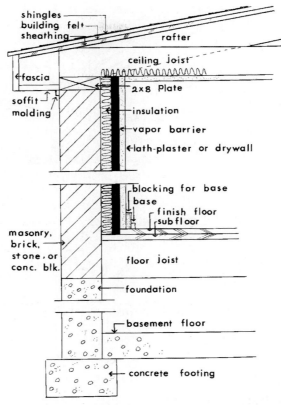

FIGURE 8–5 Construction details of a good-quality masonry house.

Tar and gravel ("built-up" roof)
Composition
Composition shingle
Asphalt shingle
Aluminum (sheet)
Cedar shingle
Hand-split cedar shake
   Light
   Medium
   Heavy
   Hollywood (extra heavy shake doubled)
Hand-split redwood shake
Fiberglass shingles
Tile (flat)
Mission tile (curved)
Concrete tile or shake
Aluminum rustic shingle (simulated hand-split shake)
Clay flat tiles

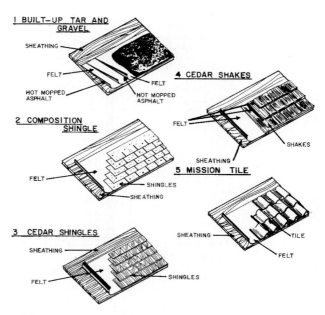

FIGURE 8–6   Most common roof coverings.

Metal tiles
Perlite shakes
Manufactured slate
Slate
Anodized aluminum
Copper

Other roofing materials can be found, but those listed here are the ones most commonly used. The most popular style is the gable roof, illustrated in Chapter 9, Figure 9–37.

Each material has a unique advantage, depending on the desires of the builder and the buyer as to appeal, cost, and durability. Although the materials used most in single-family residential construction are the composition shingle and the cedar shingle, the hand-split cedar shake roof has more appeal, gives better insulation, and is more durable than the cedar shingle roof. The thicker the shake, the greater the advantage. A cedar shingle roof might last 30 years, a heavy shake roof 40 or more.

The lifetime of a cedar roof, whether shingle or shake (in fact of any wood roof), is dependent on such variables as care (whether it is continually treated), exposure to continual dampness, quality of installation, and whether people walk on the roof.

The wood or cedar roof generally has one big disadvantage, and that is its propensity to burn. Many homes burn because the wood roof is so susceptible to flying embers that land on the roof. Unless the roof is treated continually with a fire-retardant mixture, it becomes a fire hazard, especially in those fire hazardous areas in California that experience extreme hot and dry weather conditions over a prolonged period of weeks and where there is a dense amount of dry vegetation including grass, undergrowth, and trees that might provide fuel for a devastating fire. This type of fire occurs periodically in the southern, central, and northern California foothills and mountains, destroying tens of thousands of acres and many homes in the process. In fact, fire insurance rates will continually rise as more and more homes are being built away from the urban areas and in these more remote areas that generally have drastically insufficient fire protection systems in the way of storage tanks and water systems with fire hydrants. Although swimming pools, local reservoirs, and other water sources can be used to fight fires, it seems probable that more and more building codes will require tile or other masonry-type roofs that are not merely fire retardant but fireproof. This would measurably reduce the danger of fire.

The devastating fires in the Oakland hills in 1991, and subsequent fires in the Los Angeles area, have motivated many county and city governments to require Class A-rated roof materials to reduce fire danger.

The metal roof is used widely in heavy snow areas where summers are not unbearably hot. The slickness of metal when properly sloped prevents layers of heavy snow from accumulating on the roof. More conventional roofs might collect 10 or more feet of snow, necessitating constant, laborious snow removal or exceptional beams and framing to support the added weight. Mission tile, used mostly in warm areas, has a double advantage: long life and excellent insulation qualities because of the layer of air inside the curved portion of the tile. Slate, anodized aluminum, and copper are practically indestructible by the elements. Roofs of these materials will last almost indefinitely.

Some roofs are constructed with gutters and downspouts to carry rainwater and melting snow into surface and underground drainage facilities. Gutters are usually of galvanized iron, aluminum, copper, or other sheet metal and are generally painted. Wood is sometimes used, but it is much less serviceable since it is subject to warping and splitting. Some quality residences lack gutters and downspouts; however, these items are usually omitted to save money.

There are methods of prolonging the life of existing roofing material. Silicone, used in the past as a rubberized bathtub caulk, an aquarium sealant, and an automotive sealant, is noted for its ability to provide long-life seal under even the most adverse conditions. After it cures, silicone expands and contracts with changes in atmospheric conditions and allows for structural changes and shifts in buildings. In the case of a low-pitched roof, a liquid silicone coating can be rolled on over exterior-grade plywood to provide a low-maintenance roof covering with a life expectancy of 30 years. New coverings will no doubt be introduced to add life and low maintenance to existing roofing materials.

The following list shows the life expectancy of various roofing materials, rated by class:

Class	Roof type	Life span (yr)	Approx. cost 1900 SF Hm (per SF)	Appearance	Advantages/Drawbacks
A	Built-up	10–15	$3,500–$5,000 ($110–$150)	Tar & gravel flat, low slope	Class A required 9 layers fiberglass roofing felt.
A	Cedar shake press.-treated	12–20	(Newly approved as Class A—No data)	Treating darkens color.	Requires 2 layers wood sheathing sandwiching 1/2 in. gypsum board.
A	Clay tiles	Lifetime	$6,500–$9,000 ($200–$275)	Classic red Spanish roof	Durable but fragile—requires strong framing, solid sheathing.
A	Concrete tiles	Lifetime	$5,500–$7,000 ($170–$220)	Many forms, colors, textures	Good value over time, but fragile—need strong framing.
A	Fiberglass shingles	20–30	$3,000–$4,000 ($90–$130)	Mineral-faced shingles	Easy to apply and economical. Cost depends on weight.
A	Metal tiles	Lifetime	$6,500–$7,500 ($200–$240)	Variety of shapes	Requires 1/2 ft gypsum board felt. Cost varying with style.
A	Perlite shake	Lifetime	$7,000–$8,000 ($220–$250)	Similar to cedar shake	High initial cost, but looks like wood shake and lasts.
B	Built-up	10–15	Same as class A	Tar & gravel	Mineral cap sheets may replace 400 lb of gravel or slag.
B	Cedar shake press.-treated	12–20	$6,500–$8,000 ($200–$250)	Same as Class A	Underlayment may be metal foil—life cycle cost high.
B	Metal tiles	Lifetime	Slightly lower than Class A	Same as Class A	May apply directly over sheathing on new homes.
C	Asphalt shingles	15–25	$3,000–$4,000 ($90–$125)	Variable colors	Inexpensive and easy to apply.
C	Built-up	10–15	Slightly lower than Class A & B	Tar & gravel	Only 3 layers for Class C.
C	Cedar shake press.-treated	Same	$5,500–$7,000 ($180–$210)	Same as Class A & B	Standard installation with no special underlayment.
D	Built-up	Same	Slightly lower than Class C	Same as Class B	Asphalt or paper-based felts can be flammable.
D	Cedar shake	12–20	Approx $4,500 (Approx. $135)	Lighter color	Low-life expectancy and may be flammable.

Exterior Walls

Stucco is the most common exterior wall material used in California. It is the most versatile and one of the least expensive. Stucco is applied after diagonal wood sheathing or plywood has been covered with building paper and chicken wire. The chicken wire supports the stucco, which is applied with a trowel in a wet, muddy consistency. Once dry, this material can be sealed with a waterproofing compound and painted. Another popular exterior covering is wood. Often a rustic (wood) finish is applied to the front of a stucco residence to add to the appeal of the structure, or the whole exterior siding may be good-quality Douglas fir. Wood surfaces require slightly more maintenance than stucco surfaces, especially in areas where the chemical action of heavily salty air deteriorates painted surfaces. However, untreated redwood is more impervious to termites and adverse weather conditions. Many untreated redwood-exterior homes are still in good condition after more than 80 years of exposure to the weather; the years seem to add charm to the surface of redwood siding.

Other materials used for exterior walls are building board (composition board), concrete building blocks, brick, adobe brick, stone, Arizona flagstone, weatherproofed construction plywood, corrugated sheets, tarpaper, wood shingles, and some materials more commonly used for roofing. Painted aluminum siding has found some acceptance. Although it is relatively maintenance free, a blow can dent it. Some manufacturers produce painted aluminum siding that remarkably resembles painted, rough-sawn lumber.

Masonry siding, such as brick, is usually used as a veneer. The brick does not actually give support but acts only as a pleasing exterior siding. Very few residences in California are constructed entirely of brick, mainly because of cost. Also, the mild weather in California does not justify the insulation qualities of a completely brick house. Although many people believe that brick tends to crack in areas of frequent earthquakes, many entirely brick California residences, both single- and multiple-family, are still in good condition after more than 50 years.

Another type of exterior siding used primarily for multiple residential construction is precast, reinforced, lightweight concrete siding with built-in electrical circuits and conduit pipes. In a multiple residence of any size, this siding material effects noticeable economies.

Single-family residential construction is slow to change from conventional construction methods; however, continually increasing labor and material costs may force builders to adopt, and consumers to accept, the more practical construction methods used by builders of multiple residential units and industrial and commercial buildings.

In addition to bringing increased unit and modular construction, the future may bring revolutionary materials, such as injection-molded polyvinyl chloride bricks that snap together like a child's plastic building blocks. With the increasing use of nonwood products, other exterior building materials—all mineral laminated shingles, urethane plastics, fiberglass, vinyl, and other long-lasting, no-maintenance materials—may become the preferred exterior residential siding materials. Most of these materials can be made to look surprisingly like wood, yet are immune to most of the things that harm wood siding, such as warping, peeling, cracking, and even burning.

Figures 8–7 through 8–12 illustrate typical California construction qualities. One of California's indigenous architectural styles, the

FIGURE 8–7   California ranch, low-cost (minimum quality) construction. This is usually a small (800–1,000 square feet, 2 bedroom, 1 bath) residence with a boxlike shell, single carport, and gabled tar and gravel roof. Exterior walls are usually stucco or low-grade building plywood, with little or no exterior rustic treatment. There is usually no fireplace. Heating is generally by electric wall panels. Interior and exterior finishes are plain and inexpensive.

California ranch, is so popular that we present six versions and grades of construction quality: low-cost (minimum), fair (just below average), average, good, very good, and excellent. Many variations of this informal, livable style are found throughout California.

Figures 8–13, 8–14, and 8–15 illustrate the contemporary architectural style most common in California. The three examples show only homes of fair, good, and excellent construction, although the contemporary style is built in as many construction qualities as the California ranch. The difference in construction grade is visible primarily in the size, equipment, and quality of materials used in each home.

Figures 8–16 and 8–17 illustrate mountain cabins of minimum and good construction, showing how the size and construction quality of cabins used primarily for vacations or weekends differ from those of year-round residences. Some cabins, of course, match or exceed the construction standards of year-round residences; generally, however, mountain cabins are more moderately constructed and smaller than their urban equivalents.

FIGURE 8–8   California ranch, fair (just below average) construction. Built in many areas throughout the state, it is usually between 1,000 and 1,300 square feet (3 bedrooms, 1 or 2 baths), with a 1- or 2-car attached garage, unit fireplace, tar and gravel or composition shingle gabled roof, and exterior walls of stucco or building plywood. Heating may be by electric wall panels or forced air. Interior and exterior are slightly more refined than in the low-cost California ranch.

Floors

Most residential floors have a diagonal subflooring—2 inches of tongue and groove or heavy plywood over supporting beams—covered by any of a variety of materials: oak hardwood, ceramic tile, carpeting, or even vinyl. Oak was a popular covering for many years; however, because it demands constant maintenance and usually must be carpeted to eliminate cold and the risk of unsure footing, its popularity has declined. In its place, more and more people choose high-quality commercial fiber, wall-to-wall carpeting, laid directly on the subfloor. Carpeting is serviceable, warm, safe, and easy to maintain.

For kitchens, baths, and service rooms, vinyl, asphalt, and rubber tile are popular floorings. Some homes still have linoleum floors, but vinyl is more resilient and maintenance free. However, even in these rooms, serviceable new blends of wall-to-wall carpeting are being used. Carpeting varies widely in quality and cost. Foam-backed indoor-outdoor carpet, laid wall-to-wall, is easy to maintain and surprisingly durable in utility rooms, laundry rooms, bathrooms, and even kitchens.

FIGURE 8–9   California ranch, average construction. Very popular, it is usually between 1,300 and 1,800 square feet (3 or 4 bedrooms, family room, 2 or $2\frac{1}{2}$ baths, custom fireplace, 2-car attached garage). The roof is usually gabled or hipped of composition or cedar shingle or light cedar shake; exterior walls are stucco with rustic treatment, sometimes augmented with brick or stone on the front of the house. Interior and exterior finishes are more refined than those of the fair-quality ranch construction, with a better grade of materials and appointments.

Another common floor base, or subfloor, is concrete slab. It is usually less expensive than hardwood, since a resilient tile, parquet wood floor, or even a rubber pad covered with wall-to-wall carpeting can serve as the entire floor covering. In homes with radiant heating, a concrete slab floor holds the copper tubing best. The slab, 5 to 8 inches thick, is generally poured on a gravel base. Any tubing or conduits are laid before the slab is poured. Reinforcing steel often is also laid under the slab to inhibit cracking. Some people complain of tired legs and feet after walking or standing for any length of time on a floor with a concrete slab base. To eliminate such complaints, builders have installed raised hardwood floors directly on the slab base, an approach that creates good insulation. Another modification of the slab floor is slab sections precast with spaces for conduit and tubing. Butting the pre-stressed, reinforced sections to one another provides a continuous conduit for the installation of many facilities within the subfloor.

An appraiser can determine whether a residence has a concrete slab subfloor by noticing whether there are air vents around the ex-

FIGURE 8–10   California ranch, good construction. Popular in suburban areas, it is usually between 1,800 and 2,400 square feet (3 or 4 bedrooms, dining room, family room, $2\frac{1}{2}$ to 3 baths). The roof is gabled or hipped, and of medium or heavy hand-split cedar shake. Exterior siding is of stucco, wood, or masonry with extensive rustic treatment. There may be 1 or 2 fireplaces. Interior and exterior finishes are noticeably more refined than those found in average-quality ranch construction, with better materials and appointments. The minimum lot size for such a house is usually one-quarter acre (10,000+ square feet) to one-half acre (20,000+ square feet).

terior base of the house. Also the front door stoop of a residence with a slab subfloor is not elevated 4 to 6 inches, as it is in a residence with conventional hardwood flooring.

Interior Walls

The interior wall material most often used in California residential construction is drywall, also called sheetrock, plaster board, or gypsum board. Lath and plaster used to be the most common material; however, sheetrock is less costly to install. It is nailed to the studs in sheets, the butted sides are taped, and a textured material is either sprayed or troweled on to give the effect of plaster. A $\frac{5}{8}$-inch sheetrock layer has the same fire protection qualities as a plastered wall.

Other interior wall coverings are plywood, simulated wood paneling, hardwood paneling, and tile. Exterior support materials

FIGURE 8–11 California ranch, very good construction. Can be identified by its 2 or 3 custom fireplaces, heavy hand-split cedar shake or tile gabled or hipped roof, extensive brick and wood exterior walls, and 2- or 3-car attached garage. It is usually between 2,400 and 4,000 square feet (4 or 5 bedrooms, 4 baths, dining room, den, pantry, family room, double front doors, tile or rock entryway). Exterior and interior finishes show high refinement and quality in materials and appointments. Such houses are usually custom built for individual lot owners on one-half to one-acre lots.

are sometimes carried through to the interior, in wall-bearing masonry, such as brick, adobe brick, or concrete block. Durable, aesthetically pleasing nonwood interior materials, such as urethane plastics, plastic foam, plastic laminate, aggregate-covered plywood, and vinyl-faced hard-board, are increasingly accepted. Specialized liquid finishes can add years of service to many existing interior wall surfaces. For example, wood surfaces can be coated with latex paints, enamels, stains, lacquers, sealer preservatives, or polyurethane varnish. Metal vents, pipes, and hand railings can be maintained by applying pigmented aluminum paint, heat-proof epoxy enamel, latex, or even a moisture-proof primer and enamel. Masonry interior surfaces can be maintained with coatings such as silicone, epoxy, enamel, and latex.

Most interior residential walls are painted or papered with a variety of paper types. Painting is originally less expensive; however, good-quality washable wallpaper, properly installed, will be more serviceable and require redecoration less often.

Ceilings

The ceilings in most residences are covered with the same material as the walls. Other materials besides the aforementioned ones are sometimes used. Heavy beams create a special architectural effect, the

FIGURE 8-12 California ranch, excellent construction. Can be readily identified by its 3 or more fireplaces, heavy hand-split cedar shake gabled or hipped roof, extensive brick and wood rustic exterior walls on all sides, and 3-car attached garage. Usually more than 4,000 square feet with solid milled double front doors, tile or rock entryway, living room, dining room, family room, den, wet bar, utility or laundry room, pantry, at least 5 baths, 5 or more bedrooms, extensive closet and cabinet space, built-in bookcases, sliding glass doors from master bedroom to private patio, and other custom features. Usually situated on lots of at least one acre and up to 5 acres or more, such houses are almost always custom designed and built, equipped with complete climate control including heavy-duty air conditioning, dehumidifier, electronic air filtering, etc. Interior and exterior finishes show the highest refinement and quality of materials and appointments.

FIGURE 8–13 Contemporary, fair construction. Usually distinguished by a flat or sloping roof of tar and gravel and by straight, uncluttered lines. The house illustrated here is between 1,000 and 1,300 square feet (2 or 3 bedrooms, 1 or 2 baths, carport). Exterior walls are generally wood or stucco with wood rustic or brick veneer on the front.

beamed ceiling. Exposed 4- by 8-inch wooden beams, 3 to 4 feet apart, support the roof with either a gable or a horizontal effect. Other ceiling materials include acoustical tile, acoustical sprayed-on material with the appearance of rough stucco, heavy plywood, and even two-by-fours laid edgewise abutting one another for a special effect.

Insulation

As fossil fuel energy sources dwindle and become more expensive, more homeowners, builders, and buyers will insulate homes to conserve energy. Heating costs can be reduced by 50 percent in a completely insulated house that has double-paned windows and sliding glass doors. Insulation is generally rated by its resistance to heat flow, called its R value. The higher the rating of a material, the better its resistance or insulating quality. According to the National Association of Homebuilders, a thickness of 4 inches of blanketed fiberglass or rock wool, classified as R-11, is equal to 9 inches of lumber or 4 feet of brick in its ability to resist heat transfer. Generally, ceilings should be insulated to a rating of R-19, floors and walls to R-11. The Federal Housing Authority and the Veterans Administration require 6 inches of insulation in the ceilings and 3.5 inches in the walls of all newly constructed homes on which they guarantee loans. All new construction is required to have insulation.

FIGURE 8–14   Contemporary, good construction. Distinguished by a gently sloping roof with exposed interior beams; generally designed for privacy and outdoor living in atrium-style patio, with few windows facing the street. This is a popular, utilitarian design for maximum family living at a relatively modest square-foot cost. Usually of slab floor construction with radiant heating and exterior walls of stucco or wood siding. Generally between 1,300 and 1,800 square feet (3 or 4 bedrooms, family room, 2 or $2\frac{1}{2}$ baths).

FIGURE 8–15   Contemporary, excellent construction. Generally over 3,500 square feet, an individually designed structure embodying the basics of contemporary architecture. The structure is solidly built with brick or other masonry material exterior walls and built-in privacy (few street windows; sky bubbles or sky windows are used instead).

FIGURE 8–16   Mountain cabin, low-quality construction. Of rough wood exterior and galvanized corrugated steel roofing, this basic shelter is insufficient protection from the cold weather of the Sierra. It is usually found at elevations less than 3,000 feet and is used primarily as a summer vacation cabin. Such cabins are usually less than 500 square feet. Most present building codes would prohibit this type of construction.

It is less expensive to insulate walls, ceilings, and floors during construction of a house than to install insulation after its completion. Insulation materials include fiberglass, mineral or rock-wool balls laid between the rafters, blown or poured wool (like cotton balls), cellulose, poured vermiculite (like lightweight pea gravel), celotex, insulating board, and styrofoam.

If a residence has a pitched roof and a crawl space, the appraiser need only crawl in the attic and under the house to learn whether ceiling and floor are insulated. However, it is difficult to inspect for ceiling and wall insulation in flat-roofed homes. To check for perimeter wall insulation, place a thermometer on the wall inside the house. With room temperature at 68°F and outside temperature about 50°F, a well-insulated wall should register about 65°F. If it is much lower, the wall is probably not insulated.

The market value of an average, or better, constructed residence usually increases by the cost of insulation at the time of its construction. Almost all residences of good, very good, and excellent construction were completely insulated when they were constructed.

FIGURE 8–17 Mountain cabin, good construction. Built mostly of fir, pine, or redwood with a roof of hand-split cedar shake, this type of cabin usually has an expanse of glass for viewing purposes and is found throughout California in summer and winter recreational areas. It is usually larger than 1,000 square feet. A popular roof style for this type of cabin is the A-frame.

Vapor Barrier

A vapor barrier is a means of preventing the moisture contained in the air within a house (which, in cool climates, is significantly greater than the moisture contained in the outside air) from seeping through the interior wall and condensing on the insulating material, thus destroying its thermal qualities. It also prevents condensation of moisture of the inner surface of exterior siding, eliminating the probability of paint peeling or dry rot. (See Figure 8–4.)

Nearly all insulation manufactured in batt or roll form (always used in open-wall or open-attic-ceiling installations) includes a vapor barrier either of asphalt-impregnated paper, foil, or some other impervious material. The barrier or membrane must be installed on the warm or inside surface of the wall, that is, toward the inside of the house.

When insulation is blown or poured into a closed or finished wall, an effective vapor barrier may be created by coating the interior wall with two coats of aluminum paint and a good grade of latex, oil, or acrylic paint.

When the normal difference between indoor and outdoor temperatures approaches 30°F, a vapor barrier becomes highly desirable. As this difference increases, the barrier becomes an absolute necessity if the thermal qualities of the insulation are to be preserved. For California, cold climates, such as those found in the Sierra, some insulation is made in envelope form, that is, it is completely wrapped in a waterproof material to prevent moisture penetration from any source or direction.

Although the appraiser cannot normally tell whether a vapor barrier has been installed or applied, it is usually found on better-quality construction, and this discussion is included for informational purposes.

Cabinets, Doors, and Windows

Most cabinets are made of solid hardwood (rare because of its high cost); hardwood veneer such as maple, birch, or black walnut; or softwood such as pine or fir stained to resemble one of the hardwoods. Some cabinets are made of building board (composition board) or even sheet metal—most often used in bathrooms. Although some cabinets are milled or paneled, most are flush. Wood moldings are occasionally glued to a flush cabinet to create a paneled effect.

Doors can be made of anything from solid hardwood, milled or paneled, to hollow hardwood veneer, painted, stained, or varnished to bring out the natural grain and color. Many closets have sliding doors, which take up less room than hinged doors. Folding and pocket doors are also used, especially where a separation is sometimes desired—between a family room and a kitchen, for example.

Windows, although visible from the outside, help sell a residence because of their placement from within. Their size, style, and utility either add to or detract from the residence as a whole.

Many types of windows are common in California today: casement, pivot, or swing-out type; sliding type (move horizontally); and double-hung (with two movable sashes raised or lowered vertically); these and other types are shown in Figure 9–39. The double-hung window is the most elaborate, requiring weights and pulleys. Usually made of wood, it is subject to warping and sticking. The sliding type, generally the least expensive, is usually made of aluminum. The casement, pivot, or swing-out type seldom sticks, but when open it may be dangerous to someone walking beside the house.

Window glass varies from high-quality double-pane insulated glass and reflective glass to inexpensive, poor-quality glass. The quality can usually be judged from the clearness of the view through the window. A house should have enough windows to give each room ample light and ventilation. One mark of a high-quality residence is the number of windows with high-quality frames and glass. Steel is sometimes used for window frames and casements; however, steel made some time ago tends to rust and must be scraped and repainted periodically. Some newer steel alloys are practically mainte-nance free. Most metal window frames are made of aluminum.

A combination window and door with the attributes of both is the sliding glass door, extremely popular in California because of ex-tensive outdoor living. Most are framed in aluminum. Sliding glass doors are usually installed in the family room or living room just off the patio. In larger homes, one or more bedrooms may have direct patio access through sliding glass doors. Many people put decals or other ornamentation on the glass to warn others, especially children, when the door is closed; many serious accidents have occurred when people who thought the door was open have walked into the glass.

EQUIPMENT IN THE BUILDING

The quality of the facilities provided in a residence has an increasing influence on its attractiveness. Our advanced knowledge of environ-mental control is increasingly reflected in the equipment offered in California residences. In California, the state with the largest popula-tion and one of the highest per capita incomes, buyers make increas-ing demands for comfort and convenience.

Most equipment is installed during initial construction of the residence; however, older residences, multiple as well as single fam-ily, are being modernized according to the desires of owners and renters. Each year, more homes are constructed with more built-ins as standard equipment.

The appraiser must be aware of equipment and know how it adds to the utility and desirability of a residence. Since many items do not last the lifetime of the residence, the appraiser should know which items need to be replaced during its economic life. Then he or she can compute a realistic depreciation figure.

Electrical System

The most important basic equipment of any residence is the power source—the electrical system. Most homes and apartments have many appliances and other electrical conveniences.

Most modern residences have a 220-volt system feeding into the home, controlled by a master switch either inside or outside. A cir-cuit breaker automatically disengages the power, should an overload occur. The circuit breaker is then manually engaged to return power to the residence. Older houses have a fuse box system. When an overload occurs, a fuse blows and it must be replaced. In older houses, the 110-volt system may have to be modified or replaced if an electric clothes dryer is installed.

Completing the electrical system are wires, conduits, connec-tions, outlets, and switches. The appraiser can best evaluate the elec-trical system by noting the quality of lighting fixtures and the num-ber of porch and closet lights, outlets, and switches. Most quality residences have three or more outlets in almost every room. Hall and garage lights should have two-way switches to facilitate entrance or exit after dark. Long halls should have more than one light. Many new residences have silent mercury switches. The switch box (circuit breaker) should be inside the house, for convenience. The master switch is usually outside the house, generally at the point of service from the distribution line. Most newly constructed homes include GFCIs (ground fault circuit interrupters) in the kitchen and bathrooms to protect against possible electrocution in high-risk areas.

The electrical system usually lasts the economic life of the residence with only periodic updating or replacement of a fixture, switch, or outlet.

Water

The water in most residences has come from a distant source. The city or the utility company pumps water to the house and meters it at the property line. We shall not discuss water systems, such as private wells with pumps, that are included with a property. The appraiser confronted with this situation should consult an expert in the field about the quantity, quality, and adequacy of the water source and system.

As many areas of California build up industrially with high-tech industries that sometimes discharge toxic wastes into the ground, the underground water supplies become more threatened. This is especially true in those areas that rely principally on wells to provide domestic water on a day-to-day basis. The appraiser should consider the sources and quality of the local water supply and be certain to consider comparable sales that share basically the same water supply.

The appraiser should also consider the adequacy of water supplies and facilities to provide a maximum of fire-fighting protection, especially in those areas of high fire hazard discussed previously in the roof section of this chapter.

A primary concern of the appraiser should be not only the quality and quantity of the water but also the adequacy of the water pressure. Is it sufficient for the residence? Is there enough pressure, for example, to operate the lawn sprinkler system? If the pressure is too great, is there a pressure-reducing valve at the main faucet? Ideal residential water pressures range from 20 to 60 pounds per square inch. The appraiser should know the area water sources, whether the service is gravity fed or electrically pumped, and the adequacy of local reservoirs and stand-by supplies.

In many parts of California, the water source is either local well water or water transported from many miles away. Water from these sources is usually high in mineral content—hard water. Hard water is generally less desirable for residential use than soft water, which is low in mineral content. Hard water requires more soap and conditioners to clean clothes, hair, or dishes properly. Minerals may accumulate in water pipes. Because of these problems, many people insist on having a water softener to reduce the hardness of the water.

A softener may be a simple tank installation, commercially serviced and replaced with a recharged tank every 2 to 4 weeks, or it may be an elaborate, almost completely automatic unit that needs only periodic refilling of the rock-salt tank. In some areas of California, notably portions of the San Francisco–Oakland area, melted-snow soft water from the Sierra is provided in ample amounts by local utility companies. However, in areas having only hard water, a water softener is a desirable feature. The availability of natural soft water may mean an increase in value of $10,000 or more for a single-family residence. A mechanical water softener in the home probably adds no more in value than the cost of installation of the unit. The cost of a commercially serviced unit is usually nominal, since many companies provide for a small charge the plumbing modifications required to bypass the garden water system and hook up the softener, in order to attract future service business from the homeowner. The cost of a completely automatic unit, including the cost of standard installation, would probably be under $1,000.

Hot water usually comes from tanks heated by electricity, bottled or compressed gas, or natural gas. Natural gas is used most often in California. Hot water heater capacity usually varies between 30 to 60 gallons; some larger residences with three or more baths have larger water heaters.

Except for some pipe deterioration and clogging, many water systems will last the economic life of the residence. Water heaters, however, must normally be replaced four or five times during the economic life of the residence.

Plumbing

As residences increase in size and utility, they require more plumbing facilities. The average buyer or appraiser does not analyze the actual piping and the conduits in the walls and under the house, but does notice the quality of such plumbing fixtures as toilets, sinks, tubs, and showers. Are the toilets the silent flush type? Is there a wet bar, or additional sink with water facility, in the family room? Is there a double sink or even a triple sink in the kitchen? The third small sink is actually the garbage disposal unit so that both sinks and the disposal can be used at once during kitchen cleanup. Is there a double laundry tub in the laundry area? Are the faucets and spouts of good quality? Do the shower heads adjust for various water concentrations? In short, is the hardware of good quality? All these features add desirability and therefore value to the residence.

Pipes may have to be replaced if they are rusted, clogged, or corroded beyond use. It is often difficult for the appraiser to discover pipe deterioration unless there is outside evidence of leaks, such as water stains on walls or floors. Clogging by hardened mineral deposits will sometimes render a system inefficient in older homes. This is evidenced by lack of water flow when more than one faucet is turned on at the same time. If the pressure is found to be sufficient (this can be checked at the meter point by the local water department), then new pipes will have to be installed to restore the flow volume.

Heating

Many forms of heating are available to most California residences. Some homes are heated by gas floor or wall furnaces or electric wall panels. The most popular system, where available, is central heating by natural gas with an electric blower and duct system to carry the heated air to various rooms of the house. Most residences so equipped have an automatic thermostatic control unit that can be set to maintain a fairly constant desired temperature. The heat registers are located on the floor in the baseboard, or in or near the ceiling. The exhaust or return register is usually in the ceiling. Most people prefer floor or baseboard registers. Since heat rises, the heat is more useful the lower the source. See Figure 8–18 for illustrations of gas heating systems.

There are many types of forced-air systems and furnaces, either natural gas fired or oil fired. These can include conventional updraft, general return; conventional updraft, individually ducted returns; downdraft; perimeter heating; ducted return; and others. If the valuing of a residence depends on great sophistication in analyzing the type of forced-air heating system, the appraiser should consult a person schooled in this area. Generally, the appraiser's knowledge of the major types of heating systems, such as forced air, perimeter baseboard, solar, or radiant, is sufficient for appraisal purposes.

Innovative modifications of existing forced-air systems are meeting consumer acceptance because of a desire to combat general air pollution. In addition, many people are allergic to dust and pollen. Because of this, buyers desire greater control over the climate in their homes. In higher quality residences, the trend is toward complete climate control. Air-cleaner units can be installed on many existing forced-air heating and cooling systems. These electronic units remove more than 90 percent of all airborne particles, even minute dust particles. Compact units that accomplish heating, cooling, dehumidification, and electronic air filtering are used increasingly in excellent quality residences.

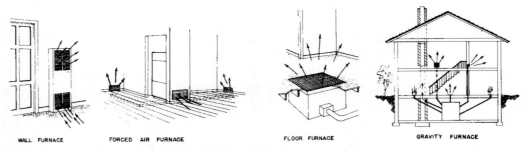

WALL FURNACE   FORCED AIR FURNACE   FLOOR FURNACE   GRAVITY FURNACE

FIGURE 8–18   The major types of residential gas heating systems.

Heat Pump

An efficient alternative to furnaces is the *heat pump*, which supplies two to three times as much heat as the electrical energy required for its operation. To put it another way, the heat pump is about *three* to *four* times more *efficient* than gas or oil furnaces—and the same heat pump will also provide air-conditioning.

A heat pump is basically an air conditioner with a reversing valve that switches the flow of refrigerant so that it can provide heat as well as cooling. It uses electrical energy to move heat from a colder to a warmer location. This moving of heat by electrical energy is more efficient than converting electrical energy into heat, which is what other electrical heating systems do. The heat pump's comparative efficiency, the changing energy picture, and constantly improving technology and hardware are reasons for its growing popularity in most areas of the United States.

Electric heat is usually achieved through an electric baseboard. Although electric heat might be cleaner than a forced-air system, it is usually considerably more expensive to operate and is generally used only when natural gas or oil is not available.

In some sections of the country, oil is the main fuel for heating homes. An oil storage tank, generally in the basement, is refueled periodically by truck. The recent international politics of oil-producing nations will probably have a continued negative effect on the reliability of oil as a dependable, economical fuel for home heating.

Bottled or compressed gas, such as butane or propane, is used in remote areas where natural gas or oil is not available.

Radiant heat, which gives the feeling of standing near a lighted fireplace or an old pot-bellied stove, comes from heated pipes or coils, usually in the floor or subfloor but sometimes in the walls or the ceiling. If the heat comes from pipes below the floor, it is usually provided by recirculating hot water, heated by gas or electricity. Hot air is sometimes circulated through the pipes instead of water. The copper tubing is usually installed in a concrete-slab floor base. Sometimes galvanized (steel alloy) or steel piping is used; however, copper is most desirable because it does not break easily even if the concrete slab shifts or cracks. In areas of shifting base material, a crack or break in a line necessitates expensive repairs. Copper has the ability to bend and is therefore easy to install. It is an excellent conductor of heat, and it resists corrosion. Many people will have no other type of heat, claiming that radiant heat is clean, comfortable, and efficient.

Some older multiple- and single-family residences have fin-type cast-iron radiators that provide radiant heat by means of hot water circulating through the radiator. The water comes from a central heating system, either on the site or at a city- or privately owned facility several blocks away. Some older central business district commercial offices are also heated this way. This is also known as steam heat.

Fireplaces, although not a primary part of residential heating systems, are popular nevertheless. Most buyers want an attractive, maintenance-free fireplace, built with a good draft, located conveniently. Brick is usually the best material, although stone, rock, building block, and steel are sometimes used. Many quality residences have gas-fired simulated-log fireplaces with the aesthetic appeal of a cheerful fire and the maintenance-free aspect of natural gas. Unit fireplaces of simulated brick are becoming common in average-quality residences.

The appraiser should know what types of heating systems are the most desirable in a particular area and why.

Use of Solar Energy

As fossil fuel sources (coal, oil, and natural gas) become more scarce, and therefore more expensive, more and more homeowners, builders, and developers will consider installing some sort of solar energy system to augment existing energy systems. As the technology, production, and marketing of residential solar energy systems become more advanced, more sophisticated systems should become available at more competitive prices. Costs for a complete system now run between 5 and 10 percent of the cost of the structure. Although the direct use of solar energy is as old as the human race, its use in the modern home is more or less in its infancy; very few maximum systems are in use today, most of these in areas where there is sufficient sunlight for operation during most of the year. However, many homes now use solar energy to help defray the rising cost of heating the swimming pool or heating water for household use. In addition, rooms are space heated with solar heating panels, plastic tubing, or any of a great many other ways to use this unlimited, relatively pollution-free, inexpensive power source available at the site. Figure 8–19 is a simplified version of one type of installation that might be employed to heat and cool a home. The air is brought in at ground level during the sunlight hours, heated through flat plate solar collector panels on the roof, and transmitted through the house on chilly days. The rooftop solar panels, if made of cadmium sulfide or copper sulfide, would be much less expensive than the solar cells that provided much of the power for the U.S. space program. Excess warm air can be stored in the rock chamber as long as 5 or 6 days for use on cloudy days.

In much of the United States, the air cools considerably at night even if the days are warm. During hot weather, cool air can be brought to the rock chamber during night and early morning hours and pumped through the house during the heat of the day. Chemical salts could be used instead of rocks in the basement chamber. The salts would melt during the day, storing heat for evening use. In summer, the system would work in reverse: the cool incoming night air would freeze a mixture of salts, which would cool the warm air coming in during the day for cool air distribution throughout the

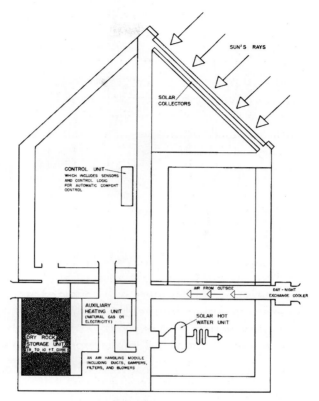

FIGURE 8–19   A residential solar energy system that provides heating and cooling of space and heating of water.

house. Of course, this system would function best if the home were insulated in the walls, floor, and ceiling, with weather-stripping on all doors and double-paned glass used in windows and sliding glass doors.

Figure 8–20 is a simplified diagram of solar heating of water in a swimming pool; the method is in scattered use today, but it is sure to become more common because of the relative ease of incorporating such a unit into the existing pool heating system. Figure 8–21 shows a residential floor plan that would make good use of solar energy.

Although appraisers need not be expert in solar energy systems, they should keep abreast of trends and learn how different systems can add to, or detract from, value. This judgment is best supported by comparable sales information of homes with similar systems. If no such comparable sales are available, then the appraiser must judge what value increment a particular solar energy system adds to, or subtracts from, a particular residence in a specific location. The advice of a solar engineering expert might be worthwhile in some cases. In general, an efficiently functioning unit should add value relative to the cost of its installation.

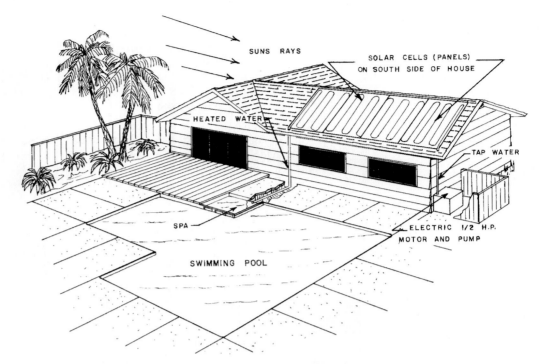

FIGURE 8–20   Solar heating a swimming pool.

Air-conditioning

Air-conditioning units can be simplified, inexpensive window units that might cool one room of a residence up to expensive, elaborate central units capable of completely cooling a fine large residence. The cost, and generally the resultant added value, can range from $150 to many thousands of dollars.

In many parts of the country, because of relatively oppressive, muggy summer weather, a built-in, or central, air-conditioning unit is a must in homes of good, very good, or excellent quality construction.

The appraiser generally includes the depreciated cost of the air-conditioning unit as the value increment to the residence.

Wind Energy

Another form of natural, inexpensive, nonpolluting energy that is being reconsidered in certain areas is wind energy. The windmill helped develop much of the farmland of the midwestern and western United States. Simple, efficient, modern windmills are now being manufactured and installed in some areas where sufficient winds prevail to supply a small portion of home energy needs. These units are usually functional only if the wind has an average velocity of 6 to

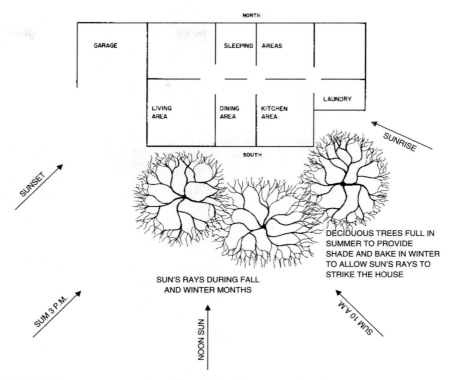

FIGURE 8–21   Functional floor plan for use of solar energy.

10 miles per hour. They are often no more visible or objectionable than a television aerial.

Wind energy is changed to electrical energy by means of a generator that powers electrical appliances. Excess electrical power is converted to chemical power by storage in batteries in the basement or below the house; it is reconverted to electrical power during windless days and nights, when the electrical appliances are run by the power stored in the batteries. The cost of installing a wind energy system is reasonable, usually about 1 percent of the cost of the structure. If proper comparables are unavailable, the appraiser must make a value judgment of the value increment such a unit adds to a residence.

Insulation

The energy efficiency of homes is generally directly related to the type and quality of insulation methods used in construction. Title 24 of the federal building codes established minimum insulation requirements and established a rating system. Using this system, local building commissions set insulation standards for their areas based primarily on weather conditions and the type and purpose of the structure. Different types of insulating materials have varying degrees of resistance to heat flow. An R value, or rating, is given to each type of material, and when building plans are drawn, energy effi-

FIGURE 8–22   Energy-efficient home. This diagram indicates those areas discussed below that help to ensure that a home is as close as possible to being completely energy efficient. The more energy efficient it is, the more comfortable and economical the home will be. Generally, these items will add value beyond their cost.

1. Six inches (R30) or more of attic insulation
2. Insulation between floors: a minimum of $3\frac{1}{2}$ inches (R19)
3. Storm windows and doors: also thermal-pane or double-pane windows
4. Caulking and weather stripping around windows and doors
5. Minimum $3\frac{1}{2}$ inches (R11) insulation in side walls
6. Insulated basement walls
7. Adequate attic ventilation with a blower to blow out hot air in attic, thus allowing house to remain cooler
8. Light-colored roof to reflect the sun in warmer climates
9. Trees shading the home from the sun during the summer but losing leaves during winter to admit winter sun for solar energy collectors on the roof
10. Properly maintained and adjusted heating and cooling equipment
11. Cupola with fan to keep garage cool during summer
12. Solar collector panels for heating and cooling; should be placed on south side of roof
13. Skylights
14. In addition, the home should have pilotless natural gas appliances and equipment and should also have a heat pump, watersaving flush toilets and showers, fluorescent lighting wherever acceptable, and a positive damper fireplace proportionate to the cost of installing a built-in air-conditioning, vacuum cleaning, or even burglar alarm system.

ciency calculations are made to ensure that the proposed structure meets or exceeds the local R ratings for ceilings, walls, floors, etc. For example, the minimum R values in Saratoga, located in the annually temperate climate zone of the South San Francisco Bay Area, are different than in an area with radical season temperature changes, such as Truckee, located in the Sierra mountain range near Lake Tahoe:

Local	Ceiling	Walls	Floor
Saratoga	R19	R13	R13
Truckee	R30	R19	R19

Use of double-pane windows is another Title 24 requirement. Homes constructed since Title 24 regulations took effect will generally have higher energy efficiency rating than those built previously.

Energy-Efficient Home

Figure 8–22 illustrates a home that has been built or updated to be energy efficient. As energy becomes more expensive (and it appears it will), energy-efficient homes will realize maximum value. The appraiser should be aware of these basic energy-saving features of residences. The value increment of a particular home or residence equipped to be partially or fully energy efficient can only be made on an individual basis; the appraiser must consider such factors as local cost of gas, oil, or electricity; extremes in local weather; construction quality; size and shape of the structure; and the availability of other similar residences in the marketplace.

Appliances

More and more homes are being constructed with built-in appliances, such as stoves, ovens, dishwashers, and garbage disposals. Many multiple residences even have built-in refrigerators and clothes washers and dryers.

Although older residences may have no built-ins, the appliances in them are sometimes sold with the residence. However, the appraiser should not really allow the value of any but a *built-in* appliance to be included in an appraisal of a single-family residence. Unattached stoves and refrigerators are usually included as *personal* property in the appraisal of residential properties.

Appliances normally have a service life less than the economic life of the residence. Few of those discussed here have a service life greater than 20 years. In the cost approach, the appraiser allows for depreciation of such built-in appliances. He or she must consider the quality and make of the appliances. For example, is the oven self-

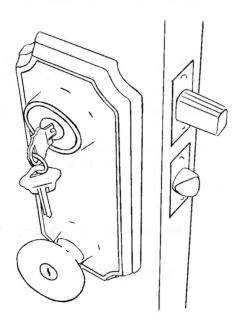

FIGURE 8–23   Dead-bolt lock provides security from outside entry and safe exit from inside in case of fire, with both locks activated simultaneously by the door handle from inside. Outside knob spins free when door is locked; it can't be twisted off.

cleaning? Is the refrigerator frost-free; does it have an automatic ice-maker? Are the washer and dryer operative? Washers and dryers usually have the shortest lives. If built-in appliances are worn out or outmoded, they add little or no value to the residence.

Hardware

The quality of hardware, including faucets, door hinges and handles, locks, and shower and tub fixtures, is a good indicator of construction quality. Most good-quality homes will have locks and door handles of solid brass and other quality fixtures throughout the house. The experienced appraiser can often judge quality by the brands of such hardware. For example, in a good-quality residence, a dead-bolt lock (see Figure 8–23) will be found on front doors. This type of lock provides security from outside and safe exit from inside in case of fire, with both locks activated by the door handle from inside. Other security precautions in side and rear doors would be hardened steel rollpins to prevent cutting through the bolt and tapered brass cylinder collars that rotate from the outside when the door is locked from the inside to prevent the handle from being wrenched off.

Specialty Equipment

Specialty equipment, such as built-in air-conditioning, intercommu-nications, burglar alarm, and vacuum cleaning systems, can be found in quality residences. The vacuum cleaning system is especially use-ful and efficient in two-story homes, where it avoids the necessity of carrying heavy cleaning equipment up and down stairs or of having two separate hand vacuum cleaners.

The value of specialty items depends heavily on the value of the whole residence. It is doubtful, for example, that a small, modest res-idence in an area of similar houses would show a market value in-crease proportionate to the cost of installing a built-in air-condition-ing, vacuum cleaning, or even burglar alarm system.

Smoke Detector Units

Responsible studies have indicated that most deaths due to fire in homes are actually caused by smoke inhalation, and therefore most states now require the installation of smoke detector units for all res-idential construction. Inexpensive, self-contained smoke-sensitive detectors can be installed in a house. One popular type is the individ-ual unit that can be affixed to the ceiling in the hall near the bed-rooms and in several other parts of the house to alert the residents to a fire. These battery-powered units, small enough to be held in a per-son's hand, buzz loudly when smoke reaches a certain density. If the residents are smokers, or if excessive smoke results from cooking, they can adjust the unit to a less sensitive position. Periodic adjust-ment is necessary because the battery loses power over a period of time. The units can be installed by the resident with nothing more than a screwdriver. Another type of smoke detector, powered by the residential electrical system, is simply plugged into a socket. The dis-advantage of this type is that if the electrical power is off in the house, the unit will not work.

The value increment to a residence equipped with one or sev-eral smoke detectors should offset their cost.

Interior Sprinkler Systems

For new residential construction, many communities in high fire danger areas now require ceiling sprinklers in every room. This adds approximately $3 per square foot to the construction cost.

YARD EQUIPMENT AND MATERIALS

To permit unrestricted access to the main structure during construc-tion, yard improvements are usually installed after the residence has been completed. It is occasionally difficult to install a major yard improvement, such as a swimming pool, after the house, landscaping, and fencing are completed; however, many homeowners install pools years after construction of the residence. Major yard improvements for multiple residential units are usually installed during construction. The important consideration in valuing a yard is its *present* utility and desirability, not *when* it was installed.

Swimming Pool

One of the more popular major yard improvements in many parts of the country is the swimming pool. Most single-family residential pools are less than 40 feet long by 20 feet wide and cost less than $25,000, but size, shape, and style variations are almost limitless. Each year, swimming pools and equipment become more elaborate. Many are equipped with automatic cleaning devices as well as a filter system, lights, heater (electric, gas, or solar), slide, skimmer, spa, and diving board for total family enjoyment. The operating costs of pools vary with the amount of professional service necessary. Costs include increased taxes, insurance, cleaning, and maintenance. Heating even a moderate-sized pool three-fourths of the year more than doubles operation costs over those of an unheated pool. In the case of a multiple residential unit, the swimming pool cost is usually offset by increased rents.

To estimate the value increment for a swimming pool, the appraiser must study the market to learn what value swimming pools have added in comparable sales. The addition of a $35,000 swimming pool will not necessarily add $35,000 to the value of the whole property. In the case of an average $150,000 house, a $35,000 pool might add only $10,000 to $15,000 value to the whole property. Yet the same addition to a $400,000 home might add the full cost of $35,000 to the total value of the residence.

Patios and Walks

Most residential yard areas have a patio and walkways for added outdoor enjoyment. Most of these improvements are made of concrete, either exposed aggregate or smooth finished. Some patios and walks are brick, Arizona flagstone, redwood, adobe brick, building block, or some other material. The cost generally determines the value increment to the residence. Brick, either used or wire-cut red, has certain advantages over concrete. Brick can be installed by one person, whereas concrete demands several people for proper installation. Brick gives less glare and is more porous, so that wet spots dry quickly. Many people feel that brick is more attractive. Concrete patios and walks are popular for the same reasons concrete foundations are popular. Concrete can be installed quickly; it is adaptable to different contours; it is serviceable and relatively inexpensive. Many people add lampblack or another darkening agent to the concrete to cut down the glare of white concrete. Generally, the cost of installing patios and walks is offset by a proportionate increase in value. Cost per square foot of the patio or walkway is the unit used in computing value by the cost approach.

Custom outdoor barbecue pits vary greatly in size, shape, style, and utility, although most are made of brick. Like some other yard improvements, they usually add value proportionate to their cost. An exception would be an extremely elaborate barbecue pit in an area of modest homes where outdoor living is restricted much of the time by inclement weather.

Lawns, Shrubs, and Trees

For every type, size, and quality of residence, there is a standard of adequate landscaping. Extensive landscaping does not always add value proportionate to its cost. A large lawn can be a drawback, since it requires extensive maintenance.

What is the value increment to a property of a large ornamental shade tree? Many people believe that a 300-year-old, 6-foot-thick live oak in excellent condition, growing in a perfect spot, is worth what it would cost to replace the tree. Actually, the cost of installation of a tree of that age and size would be prohibitive. The cost of digging, wrapping the roots, transporting, and planting a giant weighing more than 40 tons would greatly exceed the expected value increment. In exclusive areas the existence of such a tree might add 10 percent to the value of the lot; that is, a $400,000 lot with such a tree might sell for $440,000. However, trees of all types—fruit, ornamental, and shade—contribute only to the value of the whole property and are seldom appraised separately. (One exception is in part takes of property by condemning agencies, covered in Chapter 19.) Proper landscaping helps sell a residence. However, the actual valuation of the plantings can be judged only in comparison to residences with similar landscaping. See the discussion on trees in Chapter 6.

Outdoor Sprinkler Systems and Lighting

As Americans have more leisure time, they want more and more to eliminate the drudgery of garden maintenance. Since hand watering is time wasted to most people, built-in sprinkler systems are becoming more popular. Many are made of plastic pipe with fixed or pop-up heads. Some are of galvanized metal or other metal pipe. Some sprinkler systems have rain bird, or revolving, sprinkler heads.

Outdoor lighting is generally an extension of the home's interior lighting. Both sprinkler systems and outdoor lighting generally add value proportionate to their cost. Both may require periodical maintenance and even replacement during the economic life of the residence.

Fencing and Retaining Walls

Residents of some sections of the country demand privacy in their outdoor living. In these cases, backyards are completely fenced. Most residential fences are made of redwood, from basketweave, the least expensive, to hand-split redwood grape stake fencing, the most expensive of wood fences.

Much more costly fences are made of the materials used in retaining walls: brick, rock, adobe brick, building block, and even concrete. Another favorite retaining wall material is creosoted 10-inch by 10-inch railroad ties. For full advantage, the material should be suited to the residence. The depreciation of such improvements is generally not separated from that of the whole property, although wood fencing might occasionally need periodic maintenance. In other sections of the country few yards are fenced. Here the people sometimes rely on well-placed shrubs and trees to provide desired privacy.

Specialty Outdoor Equipment

Unusual outdoor improvements are occasionally included in a residential property, for example, a tool shed, playhouse, thermostatically controlled greenhouse, or even a bomb shelter installed more than 25 years ago in the early 1960s. The valuation of an expensive greenhouse or bomb shelter installation might be difficult even for an experienced appraiser, since comparable sales are not often available. Generally, such installations add some value to a residence, although the increment is not in proportion to their cost. A $15,000 bomb shelter in the backyard of a $200,000 single-family residence would probably not bring a commensurate increase in the sales price; it is unlikely that many people would want such a structure. However, a prospective buyer might want to convert such a structure into a workshop, photographic darkroom, or other hobby shop, and would be willing to pay $5,000 more for that residence than for one without a bomb shelter. The appraiser must be practical when valuing a property with such improvements. Similar sales should be considered; if they are not available, the appraiser should make a reasonable estimate of possible use and resultant value.

Another specialty item is an electric garage door opener. Openers usually have dual control units activated both by direct wire from inside the garage and by remote control from an electronic unit installed inside the car. When approaching the garage, the operator activates the remote control unit inside the car to raise the garage door.

Electric garage door openers are relatively inexpensive and usually add value approximating their cost.

FACTORS IN ANALYSIS OF HIGH-QUALITY RESIDENCES

The following list, which can be expanded, is a handy reference for the appraiser for factors to consider in the analysis of a high-quality residence. For sales appeal, some builders may include one or more of the quality features in the construction of moderate or even modest homes. However, if many of the features are in evidence, the residence is probably expensively constructed.

1. Gable or hip roof with slate, tile, or heavy shake roofing material

2. Gutters and downspouts

3. Extensive overhang—more than 5 feet

4. Boxed eaves

5. Two or more fireplaces, each gas-jet fired, with tempered glass screens

6. Many upper vents

7. Good-quality wood or brick exterior walls

8. Wood or aluminum sashes

9. Many lower vents

10. Many windows—at least two in every room except bathrooms

11. Double front doors

12. Solid milled doors throughout residence

13. Six or more outside entrances

14. Eight or more outside hose bibs

15. Three-car detached garage with individually operated electric doors

16. Covered porches with extensive overhang

17. Underground utilities

18. Many corners with extensive doors and windows

19. Extensive walkways of brick or exposed aggregate

20. One or more patios of ample size, made of brick, exposed aggregate, or redwood

21. Completely insulated walls and ceiling; weather stripping on all outside doors

22. Extensive outdoor lighting

23. Built-in adjustable television aerial in the attic, or hookup to an underground TV cable

24. Separate tool house and garden working center

25. Electric doorbell with varied chimes

26. Marble or tile entry

27. Wide entryway

28. Entry closet with double doors

29. Built-in intercommunication system

30. Wide window ledges

31. Extensive built-in bookshelves, cabinets, seats, and storage space throughout the house

32. Several pocket and folding louvered doors for room separation

33. Silent mercury switches throughout

34. Chandelier with dimmer switch (rheostat)

35. Separate dining room with built-in shelves

36. Large rooms

37. At least three bathrooms

38. Beamed ceilings with insulation

39. Sunken tub with outside window or sliding door viewing private garden to let in sunlight and air during pleasant weather

40. Private patio off master bedroom bath

41. Built-in seat in shower

42. High-quality hardware in kitchen and bathrooms; colored bathroom fixtures

43. Separate bath off utility room, with private access to yard

44. Skylights

45. Outside security lights

46. Outside electrical outlets

47. Extensive use of wallpaper

48. High-quality covered flooring in kitchen and utility room

49. Built-in heat lamps and infrared lamps in bathrooms

50. Silent flush toilets

51. Large walk-in closets with built-in drawers and shelves in every bedroom

52. Two to three electrical outlets in every wall

53. Built-in vacuum system

54. Wet bar in den or family room

55. Breakfast bar in kitchen

56. Telephone and television jacks in each major area throughout the residence

57. Double sinks in kitchen; utility room with screen door

58. Ceramic tile drain in kitchen

59. Built-in breadboard

60. Built-in sliding desk or fold-out kitchen desk

61. Magnetic latches on all cabinets

62. All-hardwood cabinets

63. Built-in roller-type drawers

64. Ample heating and air-conditioning vents for proper receiving and exhaust (at least one outgoing exhaust vent in every major portion of the house and at least one incoming vent in every room)

65. Recirculating hot water system

66. Automatic water softener system connected to all interior plumbing

67. At least two 50- to 60-gallon water heaters, glass lined

68. Built-in pantry with shelves

69. Built-in outdoor barbecue

70. Built-in desk in family room

71. Variations in ceiling heights

72. Circular staircase in two-story residence

73. Electric drapery pulls

74. Floor-to-ceiling, wall-to-wall draperies (or custom wood shutters)

75. Many built-in lighting fixtures

76. Built-in stereo

77. Screened and covered patio

78. Brick or stone wall or grape stake fencing

79. Built-in burglar alarm

80. Rotary antenna on the roof if no cable television

81. Solar energy unit, either for heating swimming pool or more sophisticated system for heating and cooling home, professionally designed and installed

82. Double-paned glass in all windows and sliding glass doors

83. Reflective glass in all windows and sliding glass doors for privacy and increased insulation

84. Smoke detector units throughout the house

85. Garbage compactor in kitchen area

86. Built-in electric blender and shredder in kitchen

87. Heavy-duty built-in air conditioner unit with dehumidifier and electronic air filtering; two or more units for very large homes

88. Heat pump

89. Microwave oven

90. Marble or granite counter tops

FACTORS IN ANALYSIS OF FAIR-QUALITY RESIDENCES

In analyzing low-cost construction methods, materials, and omissions, the appraiser must realize that because of the intensely competitive nature of the residential building industry, some builders may employ cost-cutting methods, materials, and omissions that may adversely affect value, unlike economically sound cost-cutting methods that have little effect on value.

The following list presents the most common cost-cutting methods, materials, and omissions in the construction of residences of fair quality.

1. Flat roof, tar and gravel

2. Composition shingles if gable-type roof

3. No insulation in walls or ceilings

4. No gutters or downspouts

5. No overhang

6. Square or rectangle shape (boxlike); only four corners

7. No fireplaces

8. Minimum venting, upper and lower

9. Completely stucco exterior

10. Minimum number of windows

11. Single hollow front door

12. Hollow doors throughout interior

13. Two or fewer outside entrances

14. Two or fewer outside hose bibs

15. No garage

16. No porch

17. Aboveground utility facilities

18. No outdoor patio, walkways, or barbecue

19. No outdoor lighting

20. No built-in television antenna or telephone jacks

21. No out-buildings, such as tool shed

22. Redwood basketweave fencing

23. Crank-type manual doorbell

24. No entry hall

25. Narrow hallways

26. No window ledges

27. No built-in bookshelves or extra storage space

28. Small closets, not walk-in

29. No separate dining room

30. Living room and kitchen not separate

31. Only one bathroom

32. No glass doors on tub or shower

33. Only one window in each room

34. Small rooms

35. Small shower

36. Minimum-quality hardware and fixtures in kitchen and baths

37. Noncoved linoleum in kitchen and baths

38. Only one electrical outlet per room

39. Single sink in kitchen

40. Composition board cupboards

41. Only 30-gallon hot water heater, not glass-lined

42. No pantry

43. All ceiling heights the same

SUMMARY

Although residential appraisers do not have to be experts in construction methods, materials, and equipment, they must be better informed than the average person to make an intelligent, practical analysis of residential property. They should be aware of good-quality construction, materials, and equipment, and of readily visible cost-cutting features.

The lists above enumerate the factors to be considered in the determination of the overall quality of a residence. The first list contains positive factors to consider in appraising a high-quality residence. The second contains negative (cost-cutting) factors to consider in analyzing a fair-quality residence. Most residences, of course, fall between these extremes.

The appraiser should not rely heavily on any one factor or even on several factors, as an indicator of the quality of construction. For example, a flat roof is usually less expensive than a gable roof. However, many quality residences of a particular architectural design have flat roofs. Another misleading feature is concrete slab subflooring. Again, although concrete slab is usually a cost-cutting feature, all homes with concrete slab subflooring are not necessarily of modest construction. A high-quality residence with radiant heating may have a concrete slab subfloor. However, if many of the items on one or the other of the two lists are in evidence, the appraiser can be fairly sure of his or her assessment of the quality of the residence.

The factors are most logically applied to single-family residences; however, the appraiser can sensibly use portions of each list for multiple residential analysis as well.

The appraiser's estimate of value depends on his or her knowledge, investigation, and judgment of the construction methods, materials, and equipment used in residential construction. New construction methods, materials, and equipment are constantly being developed, and the appraiser must keep abreast of them. Only then can he or she make an intelligent, practical value estimate.

DISCUSSION QUESTIONS

1. Why is such a wide variety of construction materials used in single-family residences?

2. Why does a hand-split cedar shake roof give more insulation than a cedar shingle roof?

3. Why does concrete serve so well for foundation construction?

4. Why does a tile roof give more insulation than a corrugated metal roof?

5. What material is used for exterior wall covering in most single-family residences in your area?

6. Why is wood such a popular exterior covering?

7. How does a circuit breaker function in the electrical system of a single-family residence?

8. What quality is the domestic water distributed in your area? Is a water softener often found in single-family residences in your area?

9. Discuss the types of heating systems in general use in single- and multiple-family residences in your area. Which are most popular? Why?

10. Discuss the effect on value of the inclusion of built-in air conditioners in single-family residences in your area.

11. Do you think swimming pools add *value* to single-family residences in your area, proportionate to their *cost?*

MULTIPLE-CHOICE QUESTIONS

1. Assuming four different shapes of a 1,600-square-foot house, which would be the most expensive to build, assuming the same materials and quality of construction?
    a. A rectangle
    b. An L shape
    c. An H shape
    d. A U shape

2. Assuming four different shapes of a 1,600-square-foot house, which would be the least expensive to build, assuming the same materials and quality of construction?
    a. A U shape
    b. An L shape
    c. An H shape
    d. A rectangle

3. Assuming four different shapes of a 1,600-square-foot house, which would be the most expensive to heat in the winter and to cool in the summer, assuming the same building materials and quality of construction?
    a. A rectangle
    b. An H shape
    c. A U shape
    d. An L shape

4. Which of the following roof coverings is generally most expensive?
    a. Wood shingle
    b. Tar and gravel
    c. Composition shingle
    d. Mission tile

5. A noticeable difference between a low-cost, or minimum-quality, residence and an average-quality residence would be
    a. Lack of a built-in kitchen
    b. Lack of a fireplace
    c. Lack of forced-air heating
    d. All of the above

6. Generally the most recognizable feature of a new low-cost (minimum-quality) house would be
    a. Small size, under 1,000 square feet
    b. Small windows
    c. Stucco exterior
    d. Composition shingle roof

7. A low-cost (minimum-quality) residence will seldom have
    a. A bathroom
    b. A kitchen
    c. Gutters and downspouts
    d. A gable roof

8. Which of the following building materials affords the most insulation per inch of material?
    a. Brick
    b. Stucco
    c. Wood
    d. Slump stone

9. Diagonal subflooring is used in most home construction. The purpose is
    a. To increase the cost
    b. To improve the looks
    c. To improve the quality
    d. None of the above

10. As a floor covering, carpeting has increased in popularity over the years. The reason is
    a. Provides warmth
    b. Easy to maintain
    c. More choice of colors
    d. All of the above

11. One easy way of determining whether a house has a slab floor is to
    a. Check the title report
    b. Check the grant deed
    c. Check for air vents around the exterior base of the house
    d. Go to the planning department and look up the records

12. Generally on all new-home construction, ceiling insulation must have a minimum R value of
    a. 9
    b. 19
    c. 11
    d. 49

13. In home construction, a vapor barrier is primarily used to
    a. Combat accumulation of moisture
    b. Add cost to construction
    c. Insulate the ceiling
    d. Reduce heating bills

14. One good indication of excellent construction is
    a. One custom fireplace
    b. A built-in, all-electric kitchen
    c. Solid hardwood doors throughout the house
    d. Sliding glass doors off the family room

15. Which of the following improvements to an older home will generally result in a proportionate increase in the value of the home?
    a. Adding insulation
    b. Putting in a swimming pool
    c. Putting in hardwood floors
    d. Remodeling the living room

16. Which of the following types of windows is the most expensive to install in a house?
    a. Double-hung
    b. Casement
    c. Fixed-glass
    d. Horizontal sliding

17. Most window frames (sash) are made of
    a. Steel
    b. Wood
    c. Aluminum
    d. Bronze

18. Which of the following heating systems is the most expensive to install?
    a. Wall furnace
    b. Forced-air furnace
    c. Floor furnace
    d. Perimeter baseboard

19. One drawback of radiant heating would be
    a. Expensive to operate
    b. Long lag time
    c. Uneven heat distribution
    d. Causes drafts

20. Which of the following heating methods is generally the most efficient and least expensive to operate?
    a. Open fireplace
    b. Butane
    c. Propane
    d. Natural gas

21. Which of the following improvements to a home would best add proportionate value relative to its cost?
    a. Adding a solar energy water heating unit
    b. Adding central air-conditioning
    c. Adding a wind energy unit
    d. Replacing all doors with solid hardwood doors

22. Which of the following would best add energy efficiency to a home?
    a. Adding 6 inches of insulation in the ceiling
    b. Insulating a water heater
    c. Venting the fireplace
    d. Putting in a vapor barrier

23. Which of the following exterior wall coverings requires the least maintenance?
    a. Brick
    b. Stucco
    c. Wood
    d. Building plywood

24. Which of the following kitchen appliances is seldom included in a built-in kitchen in most new-home construction?
    a. Stove
    b. Oven
    c. Dishwasher
    d. Refrigerator

25. Which of the following improvements to a 25-year-old average-size, average-quality home would generally be the least cost-effective?
    a. Adding an extra half-bath
    b. Installing a swimming pool
    c. Remodeling and updating the kitchen
    d. Installing new carpeting

Chapter 9

ARCHITECTURAL STYLES
AND UTILITY

Primarily because of the wide range of weather and natural environmental conditions in California, single-family residences in the state represent almost every architectural style found in the nation, from mountain chalets in the Sierra to beach homes at Newport Beach, from magnificent Hollywood mansions to fine old San Francisco Victorian homes. Old-world charm with new-world convenience are typical of traditional styles, such as English half-timbered (Elizabethan), Pennsylvania Dutch, Norman French, Dutch colonial, French provincial, Spanish, Italian, Moorish, and Oriental. American styles such as Cape Anne colonial, pueblo or adobe, New England colonial, Southern colonial, Georgian colonial, and Cape Cod can be found in many areas. In addition, California has two styles of its own: the Monterey, developed by early Spanish settlers, and the California ranch. The California ranch and its modifications are the basic style found in the largest numbers throughout the state. California also boasts contemporary homes and a wide variety of individual designs by some of the world's foremost architects.

CONSUMER ACCEPTANCE OF STYLES

Since individual tastes in architecture vary, it is difficult to value a particular style except relative to its acceptability on the market. When a particular style becomes popular, overbuilding sometimes inhibits consumer acceptance. For example, the international modern (Figure 9–20), popular in the late 1930s, characterized by a flat roof, stucco exterior, some rounded corners, and occasional round windows, experienced such a decline in popularity that five decades later it has still not had the slightest resurgence. Other period types are revitalized from time to time but may experience short periods of consumer rejection.

The appraiser need not usually be concerned with interpreting the style whims of the buying public, except in cases of extreme design variations. For example, some designs are styled expressly to meet the owners' particular desires and their and the architect's interpretation of the best use of a particular site. In the Frank Lloyd Wright one-design home on the coast near Carmel, the owner wanted no square (90-degree) corners in any part of the house. The result was an octagonally designed floor plan, a one-bedroom home with native rock walls and an anodized aluminum roof. The home is very attractive, designed especially for its site on the rocks at the edge of the ocean. To value such a home, however, is difficult because of its unusual features, its extremely attractive site, and an unusual design by a world-renowned architect who is no longer living.

Other, less exceptional one-design homes can be found in most communities. Most appraisals of such residences are conservative, since there are no sales homes of similar design with which to compare.

Figures 9–1 through 9–5 show variations of the ever-popular California ranch style: single story, split level, two story, combination California ranch–Cape Cod and a contemporary.

The next group of figures (Figures 9–6 through 9–19) shows some basic residential styles that have been popular for over 100 years, both in this country and in their countries of origin. These

FIGURE 9–1   California ranch, single story. This extremely popular style is found in almost every part of California, especially in suburban areas. It is characterized by a slightly sloping gabled (double pitch) roof with a relatively wide overhang and a rambling style generally designed for indoor-outdoor living. Depending on the construction quality, it usually has a composition, wood shingle, or shake roof, and exterior walls of stucco, wood rustic, masonry, or adobe brick. Size ranges from 800 to 4,000 square feet or more; construction quality ranges from low cost to excellent. The house shown is of good quality.

FIGURE 9–2   California ranch, split level. A type well suited to sloping terrain, usually above 1,600 square feet in area and from fair to excellent construction quality. The house shown is of average quality.

styles are usually associated with larger residences, but some are used in modest-sized residences.

Figure 9–20 shows an international style popular in the 1930's.

Figures 9–21 through 9–26 show architectural styles that originated in the United States. Some of them have survived from when the United States was a British colony; they are identified with the word *colonial*. All are still popular and are found throughout California.

Figures 9–27 through 9–36 are examples of individual contemporary architectural styles. They illustrate the range of basic shell structures and roof styles.

Figures 9–37 through 9–39 show a wide range of roof types and window styles that may be used. Variations are almost limitless, depending on the setting and the imagination of architect and owner.

AESTHETIC APPEAL OF MATERIALS

Although few buyers would agree completely on what makes an attractive architectural style, most would agree the mixture of too many styles in one house is unattractive. Exterior design should balance building textures and materials. Most styles have withstood the years, and some the centuries, because of a proper balance of horizontal and vertical lines, building materials, and roof lines that blend into something functionally useful as well as attractive.

(a)

(b)

FIGURE 9–3   California ranch, two-story: (a) original style; (b) contemporary version. A type that provides maximum living area at the most reasonable cost. It may also provide maximum living area on a minimum-sized lot. Construction quality ranges from fair to excellent; the residence shown is of good quality.

To economize, builders occasionally substitute one material for another, generally cheapening the total effect. Or they may add gingerbread—for example, artificially extended roof lines to convey the impression of a larger house or other artificial additions meant to convey something other than what actually exists. These additions are often installed at the expense or omission of a more important item; these omissions may not be readily apparent upon casual observation.

FIGURE 9–4   California ranch–Cape Cod combination. This residence is large (3,000+ square feet) and exhibits some Cape Cod influence in its shutters, curved support members on the covered porch, and combination wood and native stone exterior. Roof is usually of cedar shingle or hand-split cedar shake. This residence is of very good quality construction.

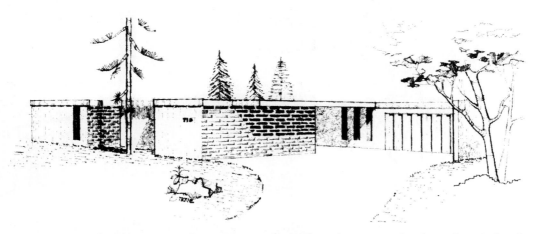

FIGURE 9–5   Contemporary. This basic style has been built throughout California. It is characterized by a flat or slightly sloping roof; concrete slab floor; stucco, masonry, or wood exterior; and extensive window areas facing an interior court (atrium). It is usually one story. Size ranges from 800 or less to 4,000 square feet or more; quality ranges from low cost to excellent. The residence shown is of excellent quality.

FIGURE 9–6 Traditional French provincial. A large (generally more than 4,000 square feet), formal estate type with recessed upper windows, two or more high chimneys, steep hipped roof of slate or wood shingle, and exterior walls generally of masonry, plaster, or stucco. Situated on formal grounds.

FIGURE 9–7 Conventional French provincial. Two-story with steep hipped roof. Of medium size for this style (2,500 to 3,500 square feet), formal, generally with dormer windows, slate or shingle roof, and exterior walls of masonry, plaster, or stucco. Extremely popular in many parts of California.

FIGURE 9–8 Contemporary French provincial. Combination hipped and mansard roof. Of small size for this style (2,000 to 2,500 square feet); formal; generally with slate, wood shingle, or shake roof and exterior walls of masonry, plaster, or stucco. Usually one story.

FIGURE 9–9 Normandy French. A round tower is the distinguishing feature of this formal French style, usually situated on a fairly large site. The tower usually serves as the main stairway. The standard steep-pitched hipped roof of most French styles is also a distinguishing feature of this style.

FIGURE 9–10   Country French. The charm of the French country-side is captured in this fine example of a homey country estate featuring the oversized brick chimney; sloping, steep hipped roof of slate shake or wood single; and an exterior of brick or native stone.

FIGURE 9–11   Dutch colonial. The distinguishing feature of this style is the gambrel roof, commonly associated with the red barns in the midwestern and eastern United States. The roof is usually of cedar shingles; exterior material is wood, masonry, or a combination of the two. Window shutters are generally painted white or green in contrast to the exterior wall color. When two-storied, it usually has dormer windows on the second story.

FIGURE 9–12 Victorian. This picturesque, multigabled, ornate style with wood exterior and wood shingle roof, can still be found in California, primarily in fine residential areas of bygone days. Built just before the turn of the century, examples of this style that have been restored to their former elegance can be found in some California cities and towns. The extensive, time-consuming artistry required in the construction of this architectural style precludes present-day repetition because of prohibitive labor costs. The Winchester Mystery House in San Jose is probably the most extensive example of this architectural style.

ROOF STYLES

One of the most distinguishing architectural features of a single-family residence is its roof style. An appraiser should be familiar with the various types, since many homes are identified by their roof type—for example, hipped roof or mansard roof. Figure 9–37 shows 21 roof types and styles.

The least expensive roof to install is a flat roof, although this type adds little, practically, to the overall livability of a home. A flat roof makes cold- or hot-weather insulation difficult. During the winter, heating costs are considerably higher than for houses with other roof styles, eating up the savings realized in lower construction costs for a flat roof. In the summer months, especially in the Central Valley and the southern California desert area—Palm Springs, Indio, and so on—the flat-roofed house, unless air-conditioned, is virtually impossible to keep cool.

FIGURE 9–13 English Tudor. This formal style with its medieval, castlelike look features an extremely steep-pitched roof of slate and a cathedral-like entrance. Exterior walls are of carved granite, building-stone masonry, or plaster, and are often ivy-covered. Many older colleges and universities have adopted this architectural style.

FIGURE 9–14 English half-timber (Elizabethan). This popular, appealing style has survived since the reign of Queen Elizabeth I. It features a steep roof of slate or wood shingles (in England, thatched roofs are not uncommon) and exterior walls of plaster, masonry, or stone and roughhewn half-timbers, previously used as support members but now primarily decorative.

FIGURE 9–15   English cottage. Often constructed of native stone, this style is of English heritage, a close relative to the English half-timber. Extremely picturesque, it is sometimes called a Hansel and Gretel cottage. The distinguishing feature is its heavy gabled roof of wood or composition shingles with rolled edges. Exterior walls are sometimes of plaster or stucco. In early England the roof was thatched.

Many architects specify a gabled roof with split cedar shake, not only for insulation and durability but also for aesthetic reasons. The heavy, coarse look of such a roof adds appeal and emphasizes contrasting materials, such as adobe, stucco, or even brick.

Some roofs serve a dual purpose: They also accommodate skylights or sky windows, solar heat collectors, and other practical additions to the residence. One such addition is the cupola, which can be installed to help keep the residence cooler in hot weather (see Figure 9–38).

WINDOW STYLES

Another distinguishing architectural feature of a single-family residence is the type and style of its windows. See Figure 9–39 for the more popular window types.

FIGURE 9–16 Traditional Italian. A large, formal style with rounded heads over exterior openings and a hipped mission-tile roof. Note the sheltered front porch and the enclosed upstairs balcony. The exterior walls are usually of masonry, plaster, or stucco. This type is usually found on large, formal grounds.

FIGURE 9–17 Spanish. This popular style, found especially in the warmer parts of the state, is designed primarily for casual and comfortable living with its enclosed patio and construction of adobe brick or stucco. Its mission-tile roof acts as cooling insulation from the summer heat. The exterior walls are usually white or cream-colored with brown or red shutters and woodwork that blends with the red of the tile roof.

FIGURE 9–18 Conventional Mediterranean. This style is similar to the traditional Italian, but on a much smaller scale. It is characterized by a mission-tile roof with rounded ornamentation above the first-floor windows. It can be one or two stories and usually has a covered porch. Exterior walls are normally of plaster or stucco.

FIGURE 9–19 Contemporary Mediterranean. This variation on the conventional style is being used in many suburban and metropolitan areas in California. There are many variations of this recent adaptation. The distinguishing features are a stucco exterior, generally with a tile roof.

FIGURE 9–20 International modern. This style was popular in the late 1930s. It is characterized by a flat, uncluttered roof line and corner windows, sometimes of glass and occasionally round. The roof is generally of tar and gravel and the exterior walls of plaster or stucco. Very few examples of this style were built in California after 1940.

FIGURE 9–21 New England colonial. This classic style is extremely popular in many parts of the state. It is characterized by a gabled, wood shingle roof. Its boxlike exterior surface is of painted wood, usually white, laid horizontally, and it has contrasting dark shutters and occasionally a bay window.

FIGURE 9–22   Contemporary colonial. This modification of the New England colonial continues to be extremely popular in California. It may be single or two story. It is characterized by a steep-pitched, gabled, wood shingle roof with dormer windows. The exterior side and rear walls may be of wood and the front of wood, native stone, or red brick. The back portion of the roof on the residence shown here is a combination of the gable and shed types.

MULTIPLE-FAMILY RESIDENTIAL STYLES

The same basic architectural styles apply to both single- and multiple-family residences. For most single-family residential styles, there is a multiple-family residential counterpart. However, the appraiser should be aware that the importance of styling in multiple-family residences is not equal to the importance of style in a single-family residence. People will rent an apartment regardless of objectionable styling if it offers advantages, such as accessibility, and extra services, such as a swimming pool and spa.

FUNCTIONAL UTILITY IN SINGLE-FAMILY AND MULTIPLE-FAMILY RESIDENCES

The architectural needs of a residence are not met until a useful floor plan is designed to make the living unit as desirable as possible. Architects are often confronted with the choice of sacrificing style for functional utility, or vice versa. Each component is important, and

FIGURE 9–23   Traditional colonial. The exterior of this style has remained virtually unchanged since revolutionary days. It is generally characterized by a boxlike exterior, a gabled roof of wood shingle or slate, redbrick wall construction, a balanced number of windows with green or white shutters, a chimney at each end, and an ornate entry with a solid milled wood door.

only with the proper blend of style and utility does the residence reach its maximum desirability. Two residences may be practically identical from the outside, may have the same square footage inside, and may even have been built by the same builder; however, one may be much more desirable than the other because its interior has been planned for functional utility.

Room Layout

Most people prefer a home organized to move people from the front to the back of the residence. The entryway is usually an alcove or hallway in the front where guests can be greeted and their coats put in an entryway closet. The living room generally connects directly with the entryway. There are various alternatives for the rest of the room layout. Sometimes the kitchen and family room area are off to one side, the bedrooms and baths to the other. Or the living area—living room, dining room, kitchen, family room, and an extra bath—may be separated from the rest of the residence.

Basic common sense in room and access arrangements provides

FIGURE 9–24 Southern colonial. The distinguishing feature of this ever-popular style is the tall columns supporting the two-story covered porch. This style, almost always two stories, is built very large (over 3,500 square feet). The roof is usually slate or wood shingle with exterior walls of wood laid horizontally and painted white. There are numerous windows and contrasting dark shutters.

maximum livability. It is generally undesirable, for example, to direct any foot traffic through one room to get to another. Most California building codes prohibit bathrooms directly off a kitchen or dining room. If such an arrangement is allowed, no fewer than two doors should separate the two rooms. A bedroom directly off a dining room or kitchen is also undesirable.

The appraiser must be aware of popular room layouts and floor plans and know why they are popular. Common sense is helpful.

Figures 9–40 and 9–41 show poor and good floor plans. (The plans are only for comparison of major features, and are not intended to show house details.) The residences shown are of average construction and of identical shape and square footage. They have the same size garage on the same size lot. The good floor plan embodies many of the factors we have discussed, such as an entryway with a good traffic flow. The poor floor plan incorporates the following undesirable features:

1. Entry directly into the living room makes it difficult for guests to avoid other household traffic.

2. There is no inside (covered) access from the garage to the house for use in bad weather.

FIGURE 9–25 California Monterey. This is one of the two original California architectural styles (the other is the California ranch), found throughout the state. The style was formerly constructed of solid adobe brick with either a mission-tile or a wood shingle (cedar) roof. However, exterior walls now can be of masonry, wood, or even stucco. A distinguishing feature of the style is the front veranda or balcony, usually covered, that extends the full width of the house.

FIGURE 9–26 Cape Cod. A homey style of East Coast heritage, it features second-story dormer windows and leaded bay windows. The gabled roof is of wood shingle or slate; exterior walls are of wood and native stone. Another distinguishing feature is the weather vane, which formerly warned Cape Cod fishermen of approaching storms but now serves primarily for decoration.

FIGURE 9–27   Contemporary architectural design or Pacific island hut roof.

FIGURE 9–28   Modified gambrel roof.

FIGURE 9–29 Geodesic dome.

FIGURE 9–30 Modern mansard, single story.

FIGURE 9–31   Contemporary mountain chalet.

FIGURE 9–32   Classic A-frame mountain cabin.

FIGURE 9–33 Log cabin—manufactured, or "kit" home. This type of home is generally of high-quality logs that provide excellent natural insulation and, when properly assembled, are extremely solid, with a long life expectancy.

FIGURE 9–34 Contemporary shed roof.

FIGURE 9–35   Pyramid.

3.   The kitchen is too far from the garage; carrying groceries into the kitchen will be inconvenient.

4.   There is no doorway between the kitchen and the family room.

5.   The view from the living room is of either the driveway or the utility yard, neither of which is desirable.

6.   Corner bedrooms do not have two windows to aid in cross ventilation.

7.   Family room is next to master bedroom.

FIGURE 9–36   Modern mansard, two story.

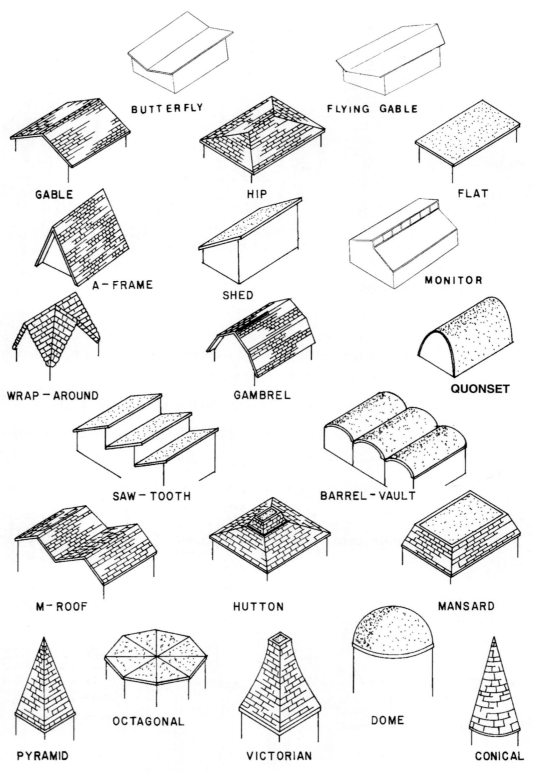

FIGURE 9–37   Roof styles.

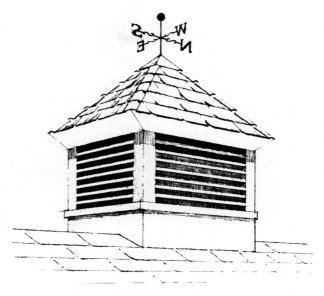

FIGURE 9–38   The cupola not only is an attractive addition to a residence but also can be designed to be functional, allowing hot air from the house to escape or to be blown out by a fan on hot days.

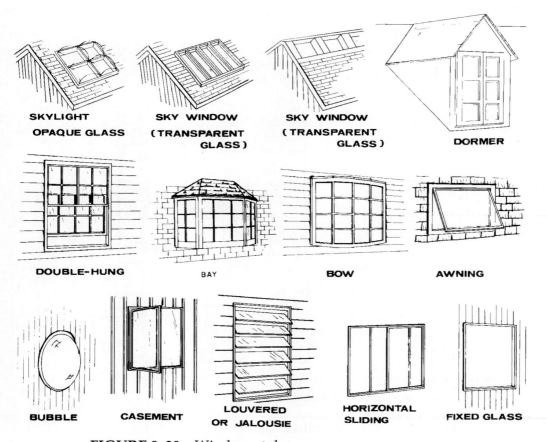

FIGURE 9–39   Window styles.

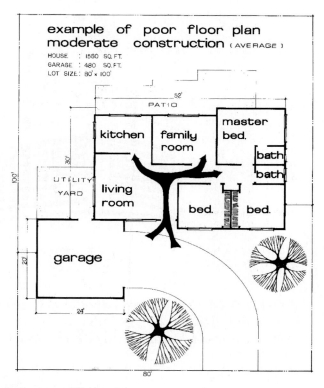

FIGURE 9–40 Poor floor plan.

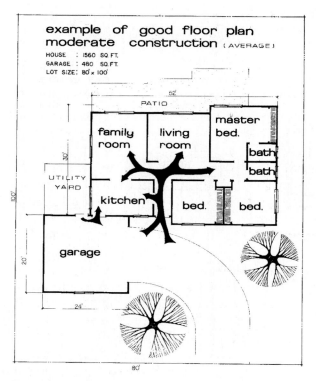

FIGURE 9–41 Good floor plan.

Room Sizes

Most residential buyers or renters want a medium-sized living room, a kitchen large enough to hold all equipment but small enough for convenience, a dining area large enough to accommodate the family and a few guests, a master bedroom larger than the others, an adequate family room or den, and bathrooms large enough to provide comfort and utility. They also want ample hallway width and closet and cupboard space to serve the needs of the family. The relative size of the rooms, of course, depends on the size and quality of the whole unit.

Automobile and Storage Utility

With more than one car for every two people, California is in need of parking space. Many California homes have facilities for parking at least two cars under a roof, sometimes three or more. The garage and storage area is usually attached to the house on the street side. The architectural style of the garage generally follows the style of the house. Sometimes a carport (roof only) substitutes for an enclosed garage.

The appraiser should be sure to consider the on-site parking facilities of a residence. Sometimes a full-sized car cannot fit into the existing garage of an older home. Most modern garages are large enough for two cars with some room left for a laundry area, storage, cupboards, or a workbench.

Garage Conversions

In some single-family residences, the garage has been converted into a family room or another bedroom or for some other use. The appraiser must judge whether the conversion is aesthetically pleasing and functionally sound and whether it serves an added purpose that will increase the appeal of the residence. Sometimes the appraiser must balance the benefits of the added room against the disadvantage of not having a garage. This can be important to the potential buyer; also, lenders and loan insurers may not approve a loan if there is no garage. This could adversely affect the marketability of the residence.

Many garage conversions result in additional living space that lacks the heating and electrical facilities of the remainder of the house. This factor is important not only in the market approach, requiring a judgment by the appraiser but also in the cost approach. For example, if a 400-square-foot garage has been converted to a family room by finishing the interior walls and laying a floor covering such as vinyl tile over the concrete pad, but no extensions of the forced-air heating system and the electrical system have been completed, then the garage conversion would not be computed in the cost approach at the same cost per square foot as the other living areas of the house. For example, if building cost for average construction is $60 per square foot, then such a garage conversion would be computed at a cost between the square-foot cost of a simple garage—say $20 per square foot, and the square-foot cost of a house—say $60 per square foot. In such a case, $40 per square foot might represent a realistic cost to replace the converted garage.

Additions to, and Remodeling of, Existing Residences

Additions, whether vertical or horizontal, and remodeling can affect the value of a residence positively or negatively, depending on a number of factors:

1. Does the addition or remodeling increase the utility of the residence to potential buyers?

2. Does the addition or remodeling architecturally fit the existing structure and the neighborhood?

3. Are the other residences of sufficient size and utility, whether originally constructed or added to, so that the house does not suffer by *regression*?

4. Does the addition or remodeling conform to local building codes? Was a building permit obtained and were all other legal zoning requirements satisfied before construction?

5. Does the addition or remodeling conform to all private legal deed restrictions (CC & Rs—conditions, covenants, and restrictions)? For example, does any addition or remodeling have to be approved by an architectural committee composed of adjoining property owners? Was such approval received?

Yard Utility

Yard utility is extremely important in California because of the predominantly moderate weather throughout most of the state during spring, summer, and fall.

The minimum size of most yards—front, side, and rear—is usually set by local zoning ordinance. The functional utility of the yard should relate to the residence. In addition to aesthetic appeal, the yard should have room for facilities for outdoor living. Depending on the size of the lot and the style of the house, walks, patios, fences, planting, and a utility area should be considered.

Additional Multiple Residential Utility Factors

The appraiser should realize that many of the desires of buyers are the same for single- and multiple-family residential units. However, some basic considerations of functional utility are unique to multiple-family residences, since most of these are built for rental. Some of these additional considerations are:

1. Economic use of space in exterior and interior planning

2. Easy exterior and interior maintenance, including landscaping

3. Availability of off-street parking

4. Inexpensive utility services

UNDESIRABLE STYLE AND FUNCTIONAL UTILITY FACTORS

When considering architectural style and utility, the appraiser should be aware of obvious undesirable features. Some of the following negative factors apply only to single-family residences, but most apply to multiple-family residences as well.

1. Unappealing mixture of exterior architectural styles

2. Misplaced architectural style that does not fit the site or is incompatible with other styles in the neighborhood

3. Improper situation of residence on the site

4. No central hallway or entryway

5. No hall closet or linen closet

6. Minimum-sized bedroom closets

7. Inadequate closet or cupboard space for bathroom and kitchen storage

8. No separate pantry

9. No separate laundry room

10. Fewer than three entrances to the residence (an entrance to the kitchen through the garage counts as an entrance)

11. Windows too few or too small to provide adequate cross ventilation and light to all rooms

12. No dining area separate from the kitchen

13. No den or family room

14. Inadequate or excessive room size

TWO-STORY VERSUS SINGLE-STORY RESIDENCES

Although most single-family residences in California are single story, many traditional styles have two stories. The appeal to buyers of two-story homes is not only the style; there are other advantages also:

1. *Lower basic construction costs per square foot of living area.* One foundation and one roof, both expensive components of a home, can serve twice as much floor area.

2. *Lower cost of electrical, plumbing, heating, and air-conditioning systems.* These facilities can serve two rooms with minor extensions. For example, two electrical outlets set vertically to serve two rooms will be less than 10 feet apart (the height of a room) as opposed to 15 feet or more apart (the length or width of a room), which they would be in a one-story residence.

3. *Conservation of fuel both for heating in winter and for cooling in summer.* The extra story acts as additional insulation. Because heat rises, the second floor is warmed from the first floor during the winter; conversely, the first floor is cooler in the summer because of the additional insulation above it.

4. *Less land required for more living area.* This is especially important in California, where the ratio of land value to total value is greater than in most other states. In many areas of the United States, the ratio is 1 to 6 or 8; however, in urban and suburban areas of California, the ratio of land value to total value many times is greater than 1 to 3.

5. *Upper floor generally has more view and gives more feeling of space.* This is especially true in a neighborhood where most homes have only one story.

6. *In flood areas, people and goods can be moved to upper floor in case of flooding.*

7. *Upper floor does not require guest-perfect maintenance.*

Two-story homes have some disadvantages, too:

1. *Some people have difficulty negotiating stairs.* The labor of interior cleaning and maintenance is increased.

2. *Less privacy.* Since each room borders another either above or below it, there may be less privacy in a two-story residence.

3. *Exterior maintenance is more troublesome.* Some work must be done from a ladder.

4. *More potential damage in the event of an earthquake.*

5. *More danger in case of a fire.*

6. *Heat escapes up stairway during cold weather in the event there is no stairway hatch.*

The advantages and disadvantages of single-story homes are the converse of those listed above.

Split Level

A style very popular in California is the split-level home, embodying features of both the single-story and the two-story home. Its primary advantage is its adaptability to a moderately sloping lot. Because it is half one story and half two stories, the advantages and disadvantages of both apply selectively to the two components of this style.

SUMMARY

The appraiser should study architectural style and functional utility to determine their effect on the salability of the residence. It is important to know which styles are currently popular, because in each area certain architectural styles and utility are favored over others. The appraiser must consider style and utility as objectively as possible.

DISCUSSION QUESTIONS

1. Discuss the advantages and disadvantages of flat-roof construction in single-family residences.

2. Discuss the advantages and disadvantages of gable roofs in single-family residences.

3. Do you feel that architectural style is as important to multiple-family residences as it is to single-family residences? Explain your answer.

4. Explain why it is usually less expensive, per square foot, to build a two-story house than to build a single-story house.

5. Discuss advantages, other than reduced cost per square foot, to be realized in the construction of a two-story house as opposed to a single-story house.

6. Discuss four considerations in appraising a residence that has had an addition to, or remodeling of, the original structure.

7. What is one possible disadvantage, as far as market value is concerned, of a home with a garage that has been converted into a family room or some other type of room?

MULTIPLE-CHOICE QUESTIONS

1. A mansard roof is generally associated with which of the following architectural styles?
   a. Southern colonial
   b. Ranch
   c. Contemporary French provincial
   d. Dutch colonial

2. A gambrel roof is generally associated with which of the following architectural styles?
   a. Victorian
   b. Normandy French
   c. Cape Cod
   d. Dutch colonial

3. Another name for the English half-timber architectural style is
   a. Elizabethan
   b. English cottage
   c. English Tudor
   d. Traditional English

4. Enclosed patio, adobe, brick, or stucco walls, and mission tile roof can best be associated with which of the following popular architectural styles?
   a. International modern
   b. Spanish
   c. New England colonial
   d. Country French

5. A multigable, ornate style, with wood exterior and wood shingle roof, best describes which of the following architectural styles?
   a. Contemporary
   b. International modern
   c. Traditional Italian
   d. Victorian

6. Which of the following is not an original American architectural style?
   a. Ranch
   b. Monterey
   c. Victorian
   d. Southern colonial

7. A second-story balcony or veranda extending the full width of the house best describes which of the following architectural styles?
   a. Traditional colonial
   b. Cape Cod
   c. Monterey
   d. International modern

8. Which of the following window styles is generally the most expensive to install?
   a. Bay window
   b. Fixed-glass
   c. Casement
   d. Horizontal sliding

9. Which of the following window styles can present a hazard to someone outside walking close to the house?

a. Double-hung
b. Horizontal sliding
c. Dormer
d. Casement

10. Which of the following window styles is generally found only in two-story homes?
    a. Casement
    b. Bay
    c. Horizontal sliding
    d. Dormer

11. Which of the following would be the most obvious difference between a bad floor plan and a good floor plan?
    a. Front entry directly into the living room as opposed to an entryway
    b. Kitchen in the back of the house
    c. Living room next to the family room
    d. No rear porch

12. Which of the following would generally not be considered living area of the home in computing square footage?
    a. Garage conversion
    b. Living room
    c. Kitchen
    d. Bathroom

13. Which of the following is an advantage of a two-story home over a single-story home?
    a. Stairs
    b. Lower construction cost per square foot
    c. Easier to paint and maintain exterior
    d. Less danger in case of fire

14. Which of the following is a disadvantage of the single-story home as opposed to a two-story home?
    a. More land required for same square footage of house
    b. More danger in case of fire
    c. Harder to paint the exterior
    d. Lower construction cost per square foot

15. For an addition to a home to be cost-effective, which of the following conditions is most important?
    a. The addition must not cause the house to suffer regression.
    b. The addition must be architecturally attractive.
    c. The addition must not be noticeable.
    d. The addition must not cause the house to suffer progression.

Chapter 10

COST APPROACH: ESTIMATING COSTS

Body of Knowledge Topic

- *Cost Approach—Reproduction versus Replacement Cost*

The cost, or summation, approach figures the cost new of the improvements, less accrued depreciation, plus land value. This process is logically reduced to five basic steps:

1. Estimate the value of the land as if it were vacant and available for development to its highest and best use.

2. Estimate the present cost to replace or reproduce the existing improvements.

3. Estimate accrued depreciation, or loss in value, to the improvements from all causes.

4. Deduct accrued depreciation from cost of new improvements to get depreciated improvement cost.

5. Add depreciated improvement cost to land value to arrive at value indicated by cost approach.

Cost of improvements new	−	Depreciation on improvements	+	Site value	=	Property value

Cost estimates are commonly divided into two categories: direct costs and indirect costs. Direct costs are the labor and materials directly associated with construction of the improvements, including contractor's overhead and profit as well as building and professional services, such as surveying, design, and engineering. Indirect costs are expenditures of time or money not directly related to the physical construction but necessary and usual in the development of the property. Indirect costs include financing fees, interest and taxes during construction, administrative expense, and fees for the professional services of lawyers, accountants, and appraisers. It is often difficult to label costs as clearly direct or indirect. However, all cost items must be included in the cost estimate, regardless of their category.

REPRODUCTION COST AND REPLACEMENT COST

There are two distinct and often dissimilar types of building cost estimates: reproduction cost and replacement cost. Reproduction cost is the present cost estimate of constructing an exact replica of the improvements under consideration. Replacement cost is the present cost estimate of replacing improvements with some of similar type, utility, and amenities.

Making a reproduction cost estimate of an older house may entail obtaining cost data for materials, construction methods, or building components no longer used. Items such as lath and plaster interior walls may far exceed in cost the methods presently used.

In practice, a combination of replacement cost and reproduction cost is normally used. We estimate cost on the basis of known current costs of structures as similar as practical to the subject, while attempting to eliminate obsolete items that would otherwise have to be deducted from the cost new as depreciation. In appraisal parlance, any type of cost estimate not strictly reproduction cost is called replacement cost.

A replacement cost estimate is usually recommended because it allows latitude in choosing materials and labor, it is simpler to calculate, it eliminates some obsolescence, and more data are available. The appraiser decides to use either replacement or reproduction cost after considering the age, type, and design of the building as well as the intended use of the appraisal. An appraisal for insurance purposes or for an eminent domain action would probably require consideration of the actual cost to reproduce the improvements.

METHODS OF ESTIMATING COSTS

The four most common methods used today for estimating replacement or reproduction cost of improvements are:

1. The comparative, or square-foot, method

2. The unit-in-place method

3. The quantity survey method

4. The index method

A variation or adaptation of any method is acceptable if it reflects current practices in the construction industry. The type of property and/or the use of the appraisal often dictate the general method to be used in making a cost estimate. The appraiser's experience and knowledge of construction may also eliminate some of the available methods. An appraiser may use two or three different methods to arrive at a final cost estimate. Be aware of your limitations when you make cost estimates; if the building is unusual and the appraisal assignment warrants it, retain a building contractor to make a cost estimate on a fee basis.

Remember that cost estimates *are* estimates. Bids received for construction of a residence, based on identical specifications, may vary in price from 5 to 10 percent.

Comparative, or Square-Foot, Method

The comparative, or square-foot, method directly compares a building of known cost with the subject building. Construction costs are reduced to an average cost per square foot of floor area (a cubic-foot unit is used in some areas outside California). The comparative method, based on a square-foot cost, is the method most often used by appraisers to estimate cost new. It is also often used by contractors and cost estimators.

The building used as the cost basis must be similar to the building for which the cost is to be estimated. To meet the test of similarity, the building should be intended for the same type of occupancy, be approximately equal in size, be similarly constructed, and be approximately the same quality of construction.

The base cost per square foot is calculated by dividing the total known cost by the square footage of the building. The cost must reflect current building prices. Building size is computed from exterior dimensions: To compute the square footage of a building, multiply the width by the length. If the building is not rectangular, draw a plat of the building, with measurements. Divide the plat into sections, from which you can calculate the area. If some of the walls do not form right angles, calculate the area by forming triangles or by some other reasonable process. Appraisers often round off measurements to the nearest half foot for ease in calculations. A tolerance of 20 or 30 square feet is acceptable in a calculation of the size of a typical residence. Two appraisers calculating the size of the same house seldom arrive at an identical figure.

When you calculate the size of a house, compute areas of different construction or use separately. The first and second floor, garage, open porch, enclosed porch, unfinished room, basement, and so on should be segregated. Figure 10–1 shows a building plat and area calculation for a typical residence.

The real estate appraiser must keep up with construction industry costs. Because locating and analyzing new construction costs is so time-consuming, many companies provide current building cost data as a service. New construction is continually analyzed and average cost figures made available to subscribers. Most cost service companies provide average costs for base buildings, designated by type and quality of construction. Costs are periodically updated, often monthly, by a current cost multiplier. Since most cost service compa-

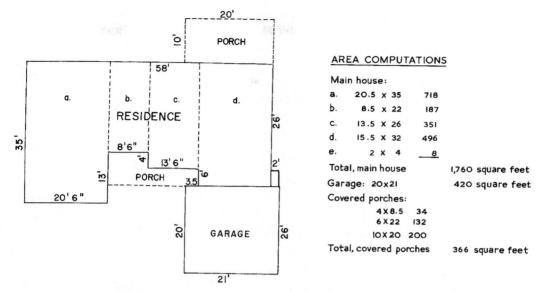

FIGURE 10–1   Measurement of living area, porches, and garage of single-story home.

nies are national, local cost multipliers must be used to adjust for area differences.

When you develop a comparative cost estimate, determine exactly what items have been included in the base cost. The cost of a house constructed under contract usually includes the builder's overhead and profit. Design plans may have been drawn by the contractor and their price included in the price of the house; an architect's fee of 7 to 10 percent of the improvement costs may be payable by the owner under a separate contract. If data are obtained from the builder of a larger tract of homes, costs will probably include indirect cost items, such as legal services, loan and appraisal fees, interest, and property taxes.

If you develop cost data from a recently constructed home, find out what was included in the price. A 2,000-square-foot house built at a contract price of $120,000 cost $60 per square foot. However, the unit price might include the garage, porches, driveway paving, and other site improvements. As long as the subject house contains the same appurtenant improvements as the base house, you can apply the average cost per square foot directly. If the size of the garage, porches, or site improvements of the subject house differs substantially from that of the base house, you must segregate building costs or make appropriate adjustments.

Cost figures obtained from building cost service companies are usually computed separately for buildings differing in type or occupancy. The actual living areas of the house, garage, storage area, porch, driveway, patio, and so on are each calculated separately. You must know what is included in the cost data you have and apply them to the subject improvements accordingly.

Adjustments and refinements are often necessary before you can make a comparison. Adjustments are usually made by the unit-in-place method. The net adjustments to be added to or subtracted from the base cost may be converted to cost per square foot of the subject building and combined with the base square footage cost, or they may be added to or subtracted from the extended base cost of the subject building.

To adjust for quality differences in a particular building component, you add or subtract the cost of the component in the base house from the cost of the component in the subject. For example, if the subject house has a heavy shake roof and the base house a wood shingle roof, you estimate by the unit-in-place method the cost of a heavy shake roof and a wood shingle roof. Suppose the heavy shake roof costs $6,000 and the wood shingle roof only $5,000 (both estimates based on the size of the subject improvement). Add the $1,000 difference as a lump sum to the cost of the subject house, which you computed from the base per-square-foot cost. Table 10–1 shows the computation of the cost of a residence by the square-foot method, with typical adjustments.

The net adjustments could be converted to a square-foot unit and combined with the base unit cost to indicate an adjusted cost per square foot for the subject house. The primary advantage of the comparative method is its simplicity and direct application. If an appraiser is overly meticulous with adjustments and refinements, he or she loses the advantage of the method without making the final cost estimate any more accurate.

Unit-in-Place Method

The unit-in-place method has many variations, with different names. Basically, this method prices building units, including both material and labor, as installed components of the building. It is actually a simplification of the quantity survey method. Costs have been analyzed, either by quantity survey or by comparison with actual costs, and translated to a logical component, or unit, cost. Cost units are normally segregated by building trade and/or stage of construction.

Some unit-in-place costs, such as floor and ceiling framing, are priced by square foot of floor area. Outside dimensions are used to

TABLE 10–1   Adjusted cost estimate

Base cost of subject house: 1760 sq. ft. @	$60	$105,600
Refinements		
Add for second fireplace	$2,000	
Add for self-cleaning ovens	500	
Subtract for 1/2 bath	1,500	
Net addition	1,000	
Estimated cost of house		$106,600

compute the size of a structure for a cost analysis. Electrical costs may be based on the number of outlets and capacity of service, plumbing on the number and type of fixtures, and painting on the total surface area. The method used to calculate cost per unit varies depending on the source of the data. Any method is acceptable as long as it logically relates the unit costs to the building being appraised and includes all items.

The data sources for the unit-in-place method of estimating costs should be examined carefully to determine what is actually included in the unit cost. Most cost estimates include material, labor, contractor's overhead and profit, and incidental expenses.

Several unit costs are usually listed for each building component depending on the type and quality of the building, and the components of the unit cost must be rated accordingly. It may also be necessary to make an adjustment for size of the structure. Cost data sources are often based on an average-sized structure. If the building being appraised is much larger than the model used for cost data, a downward adjustment for some of the unit costs may be necessary.

The unit items should be presented in the cost estimate in a logical, concise form. Often the items are listed according to the approximate order of construction. Necessary data include the item or component, number of units or other measurement, price per unit, and total cost for the component. Table 10–2 gives a typical unit-in-place cost estimate for a single-family residence.

The unit-in-place method is normally used by contractors and cost estimators. Building trade subcontractors use the method to calculate cost estimates quickly when they are engaged in that particular type of construction. Cost estimates received from subcontractors are *hard costs.* When preparing an estimate, the general contractor usually allows 10 to 15 percent of the subtotal for overhead expense and anticipated profit.

Appraisers should use this method only if they are aware of their limitations. Only if they understand basic construction practice can they be sure to include all building components and to recognize differences in material and workmanship quality. The unit-in-place method of cost estimating is useful in other real estate appraisal techniques. Unit costs are used in the market approach to make adjustments for improved sale properties, in the cost approach to estimate accrued depreciation, and in the income approach to establish reserve accounts. For example, suppose that in making a market analysis you find a house comparable to the one under appraisal. The only major difference between the two is that one has two fireplaces and the other only one. By simply adding the unit cost of the extra fireplace, you can include the probable value difference between the two structures.

Quantity Survey Method

The quantity survey method requires that all materials and labor that will be expended in the construction of a particular building be

TABLE 10–2 Unit-in-place cost estimate

Building permit		$ 1,200
Site preparation		1,000
Construction utilities		500
Foundation		
210 lineal ft. @ $20.00	$4,200	
22 piers @ $30.00	660	
Total		4,860
Lumber		
1,760 sq. ft. @ $6.00		10,560
Framing (labor)		
1,760 sq. ft. @ $4.50		7,920
Plumbing		
9 fixtures @# $500.00	4,500	
Sewer hookup	2,000	
Gas service	1,500	
Total		8,000
Electrical		
72 outlets @ $25.00	1,800	
Range and dryer service	500	
Fixtures (allowance)	750	
Service box	800	
Total		3,850
Sheet metal		
Furnace	900	
10 heating outlets @ $140.00	1,400	
240 lineal ft. gutter @ $3.00	720	
6 downspouts @ $50.00	300	
Flashing	200	
Total		3,520
Stucco siding		
210 sq. yards @ $18.00		3,780
Sheetrock		
6,200 sq. ft. @ $0.60		3,720
Cabinets		
40 lineal ft. @ $80.00		3,200
Painting		
8,100 sq. ft. @ $0.30	2,430	
Cabinets and doors	600	
Total		3,030
Kitchen appliances		1,200
Fireplace		1,800
Roof covering		
20 squares @ $150.00		3,000
Floor covering		
140 sq. yards carpet @ $18.00	2,520	
50 sq. yards linoleum @ $14.00	700	
Total		3,220
Finished lumber		
1,760 sq. ft. @ $0.60		1,056
Finish carpentry		
1,760 sq. ft. @ $1.20		2,112
Bath accessories		200
Rough hardware (nails, etc.)		500
Finish hardware		500
Door (prehung)		
9 @ $150.00		1,350
Windows		
14 @ $80.00	1,120	
Sliding glass door	400	
Total		1,520

TABLE 10–2   Unit-in-place cost estimate (continued)

Ceramic tile		
Entry	600	
Shower enclosure	450	
Tub enclosure	300	
Kitchen counter	1,000	
Total		2,350
Insulation (walls and ceiling)		1,400
Final grading		400
Clean-up		500
Contingencies		1,000
Subtotal		77,248
Contractor's overhead and profit (15%)		11,587
Total direct cost		$88,835

priced. Complete improvement specifications and drawings are necessary for this method. The number and type of labor hours are estimated and priced according to the wage rates for each particular function. Material and labor costs are combined to indicate the hard cost of the building. The estimated overhead expense and the anticipated contractor's profit, usually a percentage of costs, are added to the hard cost estimate.

The quantity survey method is not often used by appraisers; it is reserved for building experts. Actually, few contractors or cost estimators are qualified to make a complete, accurate quantity survey cost estimate. Building construction includes many crafts. Materials and labor methods and their costs are constantly changing. It would be difficult for any single contractor to be familiar enough with all facets of construction to prepare a current cost breakdown, item by item, of materials and labor.

A building contractor or general contractor usually negotiates with the owner for complete supervision and responsibility for constructing a building. The general contractor will hire licensed subcontractors for various components of the building. Some builders subcontract construction of the entire building. Larger contractors usually have a carpentry crew, subcontracting for other craft work, such as plumbing, electrical work, and masonry.

A general contractor may prepare a quantity survey cost estimate for the work within his or her field and request similar estimates from the other craft contractors. A quantity survey breakdown of the electrical system alone for a single-family residence might include 130 different items. Obviously, the quantity survey method of cost estimating requires an expert in all construction fields and is time-consuming to prepare. A cost estimate on a single-family residence by the quantity survey method could easily require one or two days' work.

Because of the time factor, few contractors use the quantity survey or any other such detailed method in estimating building costs. Building craft contractors may be justified in spending the time for a detailed cost estimate when they are submitting a bid on construction of large numbers of identical houses or when a house is unique in design and construction and does not lend itself to other methods of cost estimating.

Index Method

The index method merely adjusts the subject improvements from their original cost to current cost. The original construction cost is increased or decreased by the percentage of change indicated by a construction cost index. A number of replacement cost multipliers are available. The cost index is often broken down by type of construction, including adjustments for regional differences.

To compute the cost factor from the comparative cost index, the present-year index (or that of any other year for which the cost is desired) is divided by the index for the year of construction. This factor is multiplied by the known cost to indicate present reproduction cost. For example, a house constructed in 1985 cost $90,000. Current reproduction cost is desired. Therefore,

$$\frac{\text{Present index (19??)}}{\text{Former index (1988)}} \quad \times \quad \text{Original cost} \quad = \quad \text{Present cost}$$

or

$$\frac{402.2}{327.2} = 1.23 \text{ (factor)} \times \$90,000 \text{ (1985 cost)}$$
$$= \$110,700 \text{ (present cost)}$$

When you use the index method, you should substantiate the original cost and determine what it includes. Make sure that building components have not been changed or added since the original construction.

The index method is not often used by appraisers. When it is, it should be used in conjunction with one of the other cost estimating methods. The index method applies best to newer buildings and to unique and unusual improvements.

SOURCES OF COST DATA

An appraisal office must maintain a cost data file. Collection and classification of cost data are a continuing process. Building costs constantly change, usually upward, and require continual updating. Cost data are factual information, not someone's opinion or estimate. The three sources of cost data most often used by appraisers are recent local construction, building contractors, and published building cost data. All three sources are based on actual construction; the difference is how the appraiser obtains the information.

Comparable Buildings Constructed

Analyzing comparable buildings recently constructed is the most
time-consuming of the sources. However, an inspection of a building
of known cost gives the appraiser a reliable basis for comparison
with the subject improvements. It is also reassuring to be able to inspect a building firsthand rather than trust someone's description of
a "typical" building.

Buildings under construction or recently completed can usually
be found locally. The most useful information can be obtained from
the general contractor. Not only the total contract price but also a
cost breakdown into house, garage, yard improvements, and so on
should be obtained if possible. The contractor can often provide a
breakdown by subcontracts. The appraiser should measure the improvements rather than rely on the contractor for building size figures. It may be possible to inspect a copy of the building plans, from
which measurements can be taken. The plans give the name of the
architect or designer, who can be contacted if the appraiser needs
more information.

Costs of recently completed buildings can be obtained for the
comparative (square-foot) method and the unit-in-place method. The
cost data should be classified by type and quality of building. Special
construction problems should be noted; for example, building on
filled land might require increased foundation construction. When
talking with the contractor, the appraiser should determine whether
the contractor would contract at the same price to reconstruct the improvements. The original cost estimate may have been found to be
too low, building costs may have increased enough during the construction period to dictate a higher cost.

Because it takes so long to obtain current cost data from actual
buildings, appraisers seldom rely on this method of cost comparison,
especially as their sole source of building cost data. The time spent
for an extensive analysis of actual building costs may be warranted
in two instances: (1) if the appraiser is valuing many similar properties by the cost approach or (2) in an eminent domain case, where it
is important to substantiate the appraisal witness's estimate of the reproduction cost of the subject improvements.

Building Contractors

An experienced building contractor can provide a wealth of information; however, the data you get this way are usually only as good as
the price you pay for them. A builder's estimate of the current construction cost of an arbitrary building is as accurate as an appraiser's
valuation of a good residential lot. Discussing building costs without
reference to a particular building or specifications will produce, at
best, a ballpark figure seldom suitable for the basis of an appraisal.

Some appraisal assignments warrant engaging the services of a
building contractor or cost estimator. Like any other professional

consultants, they should be paid for their services. The scope of the contractor's service varies with the appraiser's knowledge and the intended use of the appraisal. If the appraiser is to testify in court about the valuation of a property, and the replacement cost of the improvements is a major consideration, a cost estimate by a competent contractor may be well justified. Such an estimate should be prepared with the same care and accuracy as if the contractor were submitting a bid, and the contractor should be paid accordingly for the services provided.

Published Building Cost Data

Numerous building cost services provide cost data to their subscribers. Some of the more prominent publications are *Marshall Valuation Service, National Construction Estimator, Dow Building Cost Calculator,* and *Boeckn Appraisal Manual.*

Building cost services provide a base cost handbook with descriptions, pictures, and average cost figures for various types of structures. The *Marshall Valuation Service* lists 40 types of buildings. Buildings are further classified by type and quality of construction. Building costs are based on national averages, and multipliers are provided to compensate for local differences.

Building cost services list cost data from one or more of the four methods we have discussed. The cost method used may be called by a different name depending on the particular service, but it usually falls into one of the four standard categories or is a hybrid of two methods. The *Marshall Valuation Service* reports building cost data by three methods: (1) calculator method (comparative, or square-foot, method), (2) segregated method (composite of unit-in-place and square-foot methods), and (3) index method. The *National Construction Estimator* classifies all construction items alphabetically, with materials and labor separated. Data from this cost manual can be used as a basis for the quantity survey method or for computing unit-in-place costs.

When using any building cost service, pay careful attention to the explanations and instructions provided. You will be told the correct method of applying the cost data. (Again, it is important to know what items are included in the data.) Appropriate adjustments and refinements of building costs will also be described.

Let us outline the process of estimating the replacement cost of a residence by the comparative, or square-foot, method based on a building cost service publication.

1. Find the base cost per square foot from a table, based on residence type and construction quality.

2. Make refinements for differences in building components (usually as a lump sum, by the unit-in-place method).

3. Adjust for differences between the base structure and the subject structure, for example, number of stories, height per story, and ratio of exterior perimeter to floor area. (Adjustments are usually made with factors available from prepared tables.)

4. Apply adjustment factors to bring cost data up to date and to compensate for local cost deviation from national averages.

Construction costs reported by most services are based on a continual investigation and analysis of new construction. Updated cost sheets or current multipliers are usually sent monthly or quarterly. In a period of rising labor and materials costs, it is difficult to keep abreast of construction costs by any source other than a building cost service. Most appraisers use all three sources of cost data but rely largely on published building cost material because of the detail, variety, and newness of available information.

SITE OR YARD IMPROVEMENTS

Most appraisals include improvements, other than buildings, that are part of the real property. Such improvements, called site or yard improvements, include patios, driveways, walkways, fences, retaining walls, sprinkler systems, landscaping, and so forth. The replacement cost of most site improvements is estimated on a per-unit basis. Concrete or asphalt paving is usually estimated by the cost per square foot; fencing, by the cost per lineal foot; water sprinkler or outdoor lighting systems, by the cost per sprinkler head or lighting fixture. Cost data for these items can be obtained and computed in a manner similar to that used for building improvements.

Landscaping is one of the most difficult improvements to measure and value, because cost and value are mixed. The cost of lawns can be computed per square foot, but large trees and shrubs must be considered on the basis of the value they add to the total property. Some large trees are irreplaceable, or the cost of replacing them is greater than the actual value they add to the property. The placement and appearance of landscaping is very important. A large oak tree may be worth $10,000 to a site, but it is very unlikely that 10 oak trees on the same site would be worth $10,000 each.

Like any other type of improvement, landscaping must be considered in relation to the rest of the property. An extensively planted yard with specimen trees and shrubs may be economically justified with an $800,000 home, but it would be a great overimprovement with an $80,000 home.

Landscaping is usually valued for its contribution to the value of the total property, as judged by the appraiser. If site improvements are a relatively minor portion of the property value, a lump-sum estimate based on contributed value is often used.

INDIRECT COSTS

An estimate of construction cost must include all expenditures in time and money. Direct costs are those relating directly to the physical development of the structure: materials, labor, engineering, and design. Indirect costs are not directly related to the physical construction but are originated and necessitated by such construction. Items usually classified as indirect costs are interest, taxes, and insurance during construction; accounting, legal, and appraisal fees; administrative and management expenses; leasing or rental fees; and loss in rental until normal occupancy is established.

Although indirect costs cannot be estimated as accurately as direct costs, the appraiser should attempt to estimate reasonable anticipated expenses in a construction project.

There is a general relationship between indirect cost and direct cost; however, indirect cost varies greatly depending on the length of construction, financial conditions, and competency of the general contractor and subcontractors.

Insurance

Liability and fire insurance policies should cover the property during the construction period. On large projects, the insurance policy may be written so that premiums are charged according to the progress of the construction. Most insurance policies are written for a period of 36 months, beginning when construction commences. A 10 percent discount is usually given on a policy that includes the construction of the improvements. In effect, this gives free insurance for 3.6 months, which often covers the entire period of construction.

Taxes

Real estate taxes are assessed as of the first day in March, with the tax beginning the first of July. Taxes are assessed separately on land and improvements. Only those improvements in existence as of the first day in March are taxed during the following fiscal year (July 1 to June 30). Suppose construction of a house begins on the first of January. By the first day in March, the house is framed. The county assessor places a value on the partially completed improvements as of the first day in March. On the first of July, taxes on the partially completed improvements begin. Of course, taxes on the land continue regardless of the improvements. Often a supplemental tax bill will be sent after the improvements are completed.

Interest

Interest during construction includes both interest paid on borrowed money and interest on the equity of the owner. If the owner is paying cash for the construction, the interest return on the value of the lot and on the money expended are estimated. Interest is usually estimated on the average construction cost of the improvements. If the construction cost is estimated at $90,000, interest is computed on the basis of the average construction payments (one-half of the total, or $45,000) for the total construction period. Assume the following: improvement cost, $90,000; lot value, $50,000; construction period, 6 months; interest rate, 12 percent. Interest, as an indirect cost, would be computed as follows:

Land:	$50,000 at 12% for 6 months	$3,000
Improvements:	$45,000 at 12% for 6 months	$2,700
Total interest		$5,700

A construction loan is often obtained to finance the construction of improvements. In that case, indirect costs should include an allowance for loan fees, usually between 1 and 3 percent of the loan principal, and the cost of a policy of title insurance, necessary to obtain the loan.

Administration and Management

A large project may necessitate an office staff to coordinate and oversee the project. The estimated cost of this administrative expense should include an appropriate proration of employee's salaries, office rent and utilities, vehicles, and other normal office expenses. In a large development, administrative expense can be substantial.

When estimating the cost of a single-family residence or small apartment house, we tend to overlook the cost of management or administration. However, purchasing the site, approving the plans, arranging the financing, and overseeing the entire project are important and often time-consuming. The monetary value of entrepreneurship must be included as an indirect cost.

Loss in Rental

In the case of rental property, the lack of a return on investment until normal occupancy is achieved is also an indirect cost. This lag in earnings until the property has reached normal occupancy is often classified as a development cost. If it is estimated that 4 months will elapse after completion of an apartment house before normal occupancy and a fair return on the investment are established, the average loss in rental—in this case the normal rent schedule for 2 months—should be included as an indirect cost. The same principle holds for a new single-family residence offered for sale. The owner is entitled to a return on the investment for a reasonable holding period until the home is sold.

Whatever the details, the main consideration is not the classification of the building and development costs but the inclusion of all reasonable and usual costs in the building cost estimate.

DISCUSSION QUESTIONS

1. What are the five basic steps in the cost approach?

2. Distinguish between direct and indirect costs in building construction.

3. Give some examples of indirect costs as used in the cost approach.

4. Distinguish between replacement cost and reproduction cost as used in the cost approach.

5. In what two types of appraisals might it be preferable to use reproduction cost over replacement cost?

6. What are the four methods commonly used for estimating replacement or reproduction cost of improvements? Which method is most often used by appraisers?

7. When is the index method of estimating improvement cost most applicable?

8. Why is the quantity survey method of estimating building costs seldom used by appraisers?

9. What are the three sources of the cost data used by appraisers?

MULTIPLE-CHOICE QUESTIONS

1. In the cost approach, which of the following is considered an indirect cost?
   a. Labor
   b. Contractor's overhead and profit
   c. Financing fees
   d. Materials

2. What is the difference between replacement cost new and reproduction cost new?
   a. Reproduction cost new is an exact replica; replacement cost new is not.
   b. Replacement cost new is an exact replica; reproduction cost new is not.
   c. Reproduction cost new is the cost to reproduce the same utility.
   d. There is no difference.

3. Which of the following is considered a direct cost in the cost approach?
   a. Surveying
   b. Interest and taxes during construction
   c. Appraisal services
   d. Lawyers' fees

4. Which method of estimating costs of a residence is most used by appraisers?
   a. The unit-in-place method
   b. The index method
   c. The comparative or square-foot method
   d. The quantity survey method

5. Which method of estimating costs requires the most time and detail?
   a. The index method
   b. The quantity survey method
   c. The comparative or square-foot method
   d. The unit-in-place method

6. To determine the square footage of a house for appraisal purposes the dimensions are taken
   a. Interior of the house
   b. Exterior of the house
   c. Neither a nor b
   d. Both a and b

7. A tolerance of how many square feet is generally acceptable in the measurement of the square footage of a typical house?
   a. 100 to 200 square feet
   b. 50 to 100 square feet
   c. 5 to 10 square feet
   d. 20 to 30 square feet

8. Which of the following is normally computed as part of the living area of a home?
   a. Bathroom
   b. Converted garage
   c. Covered porch
   d. Screened porch or lanai

9. In the cost approach, which of the following improvements is valued based on its contribution to the overall value of the residence and not on its cost of replacement?
   a. Garage
   b. Swimming pool
   c. Fencing
   d. All of the above

10. In the cost approach, which of the following improvements would be included in the lot or site value?
    a. Utilities in the street
    b. Sewer hookup
    c. Water hookup
    d. Foundation

Chapter 11

COST APPROACH: ACCRUED DEPRECIATION ANALYSIS

Body of Knowledge Topics

- *Accrued Depreciation*

- *Methods of Estimating Depreciation*

To complete the cost approach, the appraiser deducts accrued depreciation from the estimated improvement cost new to find the present value of the improvements. Accrued depreciation, in appraisal terminology, is the difference between the reproduction cost of the improvements and the value of the improvements, measured at the same date. With this definition we have backed into the theory of depreciation. Obviously, the appraiser who knew the present value of the improvements would not need to be concerned with reproduction cost and depreciation. A careful examination of the definition of accrued depreciation will make depreciation theory and measurement easier to understand.

1. Accrued depreciation is a lump sum. It has occurred in the past and continues to the date of measurement.

2. Accrued depreciation is the difference between cost new and present value.

3. The amount of accrued depreciation can be estimated only as of a particular date.

4. To measure all items of depreciation, the appraiser must theoretically use the reproduction cost of the improvements rather than the replacement cost. If the replacement cost or a modified reproduction cost is used, the appraiser may automatically eliminate some of the depreciation.

Appraisers have categorized the elements of depreciation and have developed methods of measurement. The three basic categories of accrued depreciation are:

1. Physical deterioration

2. Functional obsolescence—intrinsic or internal

3. Economic obsolescence—external

Physical deterioration and functional obsolescence can be either curable or incurable. Economic obsolescence is almost always incurable. As in most other appraisal theorems, there is not always a clear distinction between the classes of depreciation. As long as all depreciation is considered, the classification used is not critical.

PHYSICAL DETERIORATION

Physical deterioration is the actual wearing out of a building through age and use. All buildings deteriorate physically, commencing at their construction. Deterioration can be curable or incurable. Curable physical depreciation involves items or components of the building that are normally replaced during the life of the structure, such as roof, painting, furnace, water heater, kitchen appliances, and floor covering. For instance, a roof that is 10 years old and that has an expected life of 25 years would be 40 percent depreciated. If the present cost of replacing the roof is $6,000, the accrued depreciation for this building component would be $2,400. Curable items of depreciation that require immediate repair to prevent further damage or to make the property salable, such as replacing broken window glass or repairing a broken step, are classified as deferred maintenance and are measured by the present cost to cure.

Incurable physical depreciation is deterioration to the bone structure of the building, that is, all components of the building not normally replaced during the life of the structure. Any element of the structure not classified as curable would be treated as incurable. In measuring physical depreciation, the appraiser must consider *all* components of the structure; classification as curable or incurable depreciation is not so critical.

FUNCTIONAL OBSOLESCENCE

Functional obsolescence is depreciation caused by the design of the structure itself; in other words, the building does not function as well as the currently acceptable replacement. Functional obsolescence is usually the result of a poor floor plan, outdated architectural styling, excessive construction, inadequate building components, outmoded equipment, or abnormal building features. Functional obsolescence can occur because of a gradual change in the typical buyer's wants and needs or because of faulty judgment at the time of construction.

Wants and needs are constantly evolving. A three-bedroom house with one bath may have been considered totally adequate 50 years ago. Now a three-bedroom house is usually considered deficient unless it has two and one half bathrooms. In another 10 years, a two-and-one-half-bathroom house may be considered inadequate.

As tastes change, buildings depreciate faster than they are physically wearing out. Building components may not be adequate to meet present needs. A 30-amp electrical service was adequate 60 years ago, when a radio was the major electrical appliance. A 100-amp electrical service, adequate today, may be totally inadequate 40 years from now.

Excesses in construction usually cause immediate functional obsolescence. An inordinately adequate foundation may be reassuring, but the market rarely reflects its additional cost in the price buyers are willing to pay. All building components must bear the proper relationship to each other. It does little good to have one component outlast the total useful life of the structure.

Functional obsolescence may be curable or incurable. The repair of a curable functional deficiency is economically justified. Practically any functional deficiency may be cured if enough money is spent. However, to be economically justifiable, the value created by curing the deficiency must equal or exceed the cost of curing it. Replacements or improvements to eliminate or reduce functional deficiencies may involve minor items, such as replacement of outdated plumbing and electrical fixtures, or they may involve major remodeling and room additions: adding a second bathroom or modernizing a kitchen. Examples of incurable functional obsolescence are overadequate construction in foundation or framing, excessive ceiling or wall heights, wasted space because of oversized rooms, and poor room arrangement. A functional deficiency that is curable in one instance may be incurable in another.

Note: Overbuilding or excessive construction can be included as functional obsolescence incurable or economic (external) obsolescence, which is also incurable. Whatever way this item of incurable obsolescence is treated, and appraisers differ as to treatment for an infinite variety of reasons, the important point is to be certain that it *is* treated as an incurable obsolescence item whether functional or economic. It is not really important to which category it is assigned as long as it is included in the appraisal.

ECONOMIC OBSOLESCENCE—EXTERNAL OBSOLESCENCE

Economic obsolescence is caused by factors external to the property being appraised. Such depreciation usually affects many properties in the area and is beyond the control of an individual property owner. Examples of economic obsolescence are the proximity of an improvement to a freeway or railroad, infiltration of inharmonious land uses, changes in legislation or zoning, and changes in the character of population in the neighborhood. The important distinction between functional and economic obsolescence is that functional obsolescence is caused by factors within the structure itself, while economic obsolescence is caused by factors outside the individual property and affects both land and improvements.

Practically speaking some items such as proximity to freeways or inharmonious land uses are difficult to specifically assign to either economic obsolescence or to the land value, however, the important thing is to include such depreciation in the appraisal.

MEASUREMENT OF ACCRUED DEPRECIATION

Methods of measuring depreciation are by no means standardized. The five basic methods of estimating accrued depreciation have numerous hybrids and variations. In addition, new depreciation theory is constantly developing. The five methods of measuring depreciation discussed in this chapter are:

1. Age-life method

2. Observed condition method

3. Cost-to-cure method

4. Capitalization-of-rental-loss method

5. Sales data method

Different methods may be used to measure various elements of depreciation of one particular improvement. Certain methods are designed primarily to measure one class of depreciation, whereas others may be used to measure the total depreciation of a building. Remember that measuring depreciation is an estimate, just like estimating the cost new of the improvements; the most important aspect of measuring depreciation, as in most appraisal techniques, is the exercise of sound judgment in attempting to reflect actual market conditions.

A word of caution: Depreciate an item once and only once. Do not compound depreciation, and do not depreciate items not included in the original cost estimate. Depreciation may be measured either as a percentage of cost new or in dollars. All items of depreciation should include a proration of indirect costs as well as direct costs.

Age-Life Method

The age-life method uses the relationship between the age of the improvement and the estimated total life of the improvement. Total life is divided into age to indicate the percentage of accrued depreciation. There are many variations of the age-life method. Before explaining and demonstrating this method, we must understand the terms used.

Chronological age (also called physical, or actual, age) is the number of years that have elapsed since the structure was built. *Effective age* is the age the building appears to be, based on its present condition. Effective age depends on modernization, replacement of building components, and degree of general maintenance. *Physical life* is the number of years that the structure as a whole will stand. *Economic life* is the estimated number of years of anticipated usefulness of the improvements. Factors other than the physical aspect of the improvements must be considered. Economic life is usually shorter than the physical life of an improvement because of functional and economic conditions. It can be estimated on the basis of comparison with buildings of similar class and quality that have reached, or are reaching, the end of their economic lives.

Suppose we are appraising a 30-year-old residence. We estimate its total physical life to be 100 years. Dividing the age by the estimated total life indicates 30 percent depreciation. The apparent defect in this method is that no consideration has been given to the physical condition of the residence at the date of appraisal. We compensate for this by estimating the effective age of the residence. A 30-year-old residence that has been modernized and well maintained may have an effective age of 20 years. Accrued depreciation based on a 20-year effective age would be computed at 20 percent, rather than the 30 percent based on chronological age. Or the residence may have been poorly maintained and reflect an effective age of 40 years, thus 40 percent accrued depreciation.

Since we are measuring actual age against physical life, we are computing only physical depreciation. If an estimate of economic life is used instead of physical life, the computed depreciation will include normal functional and economic obsolescence as well as physical deterioration. The usefulness of a building seldom terminates because of physical deterioration alone. All factors of depreciation are constantly at work, usually increasing with the age of the building. Economic life is also easier to measure, because an abundance of examples are available for study. For a residence estimated to have an effective age of 20 years and an economic life of 80 years, the straight-line age-life method would indicate an accrued depreciation of 25 percent. Functional and economic obsolescence of a nature not found in most buildings of similar age would have to be estimated by another method and added to the age-life figure.

Many building components are normally replaced during the life of the structure. Therefore, these components depreciate faster than the bone structure of the building. These shorter-lived items—such as roof covering, floor covering, paint, plumbing and lighting fixtures, water heater, furnace—can be depreciated at a different rate from the bone structure. An estimate of the total economic life is based on an average of the total structure. Therefore, if the shorter-lived items are depreciated separately, the total economic life of the bone structure should be increased. The shorter-lived components should be depreciated as a group. Depreciation of individual components is part of the observed condition method.

Observed Condition Method

The observed condition method is used to estimate accrued depreciation caused by physical deterioration and some functional deficiencies. Basically, this method compares the subject structure in its condition as of the date of the appraisal with a hypothetical new structure of similar design. A percent or dollar figure expresses the adjudged difference in value between the subject building and the new structure; the difference is usually determined by valuing the individual building components.

Physical and functional deficiencies are estimated separately. The physical deterioration of each building item is compared to the new item. The item breakdown may be similar to the unit-in-place method of reproduction cost estimate, or it may be a consideration of individual units of mechanical equipment, fixtures, and other building components. Table 11–1 gives an example of the physical deterioration of a 20-year-old residence estimated by the observed condition method.

Physical depreciation, estimated by the observed condition method, is $16,605, approximately 28 percent of cost new. If the reproduction cost estimate included direct cost only, an additional allowance for the depreciation of indirect costs would have to be added.

The observed condition method does focus the appraiser's attention on the actual physical condition of individual building items.

TABLE 11–1 Physical deterioration estimated by observed condition method

Item	Reproduction cost	Observed deterioration (percent)	Deterioration in dollars
Site preparation	$1,000	0	$0
Foundation	4,000	5	200
Floor structure	5,000	10	500
Wall framing	8,000	10	800
Exterior wall cover	3,500	20	700
Interior wall cover	3,500	30	1,050
Cabinets and wardrobes	3,000	25	750
Kitchen appliances	1,200	40	480
Floor covering	2,500	60	1,500
Doors and windows	2,500	30	750
Plumbing	7,000	40	2,800
Heating and sheet metal	3,000	60	1,800
Electrical	3,500	40	1,400
Roof structure	4,000	10	400
Roof cover	2,500	70	1,750
Painting	3,000	50	1,500
Masonry	1,500	15	225
Total	$58,700		$16,605

If the unit-in-place method has been used in the original estimate of reproduction cost new, the observed condition method may have some practical applicability. However, this method can be very time-consuming, and it is largely a matter of judgment. In addition to the time and experience it requires from the appraiser, it has several other disadvantages.

Building components are made of items that often accrue depreciation at different rates. For instance, the electrical system in a house has three major parts: service, lines, and fixtures. They depreciate at different rates. Therefore, the accrued depreciation estimate for the electrical system is actually based on an average condition of many subcomponents.

Only a few of the building components are actually available for inspection. Wiring, plumbing lines, and framing are usually not exposed.

It is often argued that no building component, regardless of its physical life, can have a longer economic life than the improvements as a whole. A foundation, for example, may have a physical life of 200 years, but a shorter effective life because of limitations by other building components.

The observed condition method can be used for measuring functional obsolescence due primarily to excess construction. Depreciation caused by an overadequate foundation can be measured by deducting the cost of a typical adequate foundation from the reproduction cost of the subject foundation. The result would probably reflect the actual functional obsolescence. Make sure that depreciation for excess construction is not deducted unless the reproduction cost of the excess item is included in the estimated cost new of the structure.

Cost-to-Cure Method

The cost-to-cure method can be used to measure curable physical deterioration and curable functional obsolescence. Curable physical deterioration usually means a deferred maintenance condition and can be measured directly as the dollar cost to replace or repair the particular deferred maintenance items. Physical cost-to-cure expenditures are usually for minor repairs, such as spot painting or replacing window glass. If you include larger repair jobs, such as replacement of roof or floor covering, in the curable physical deterioration category and estimate them by the cost-to-cure method, be sure not to include depreciation for the same items a second time by some other method.

Curable functional obsolescence is usually due to an outmoded item or the omission of an item. Plumbing fixtures may be too outmoded to be acceptable in the market as of the date of appraisal. The cost-to-cure would be similar to that for curable physical deterioration, that is, the dollar expenditure to replace the item.

Estimating functional deficiencies due to omission by the cost-to-cure method is more difficult. Suppose there is no second bathroom in a four-bedroom house. If the deficiency is to be classified as curable functional obsolescence, the addition of a second bathroom must be economically feasible. Since a second bath was not included in the original cost estimate of the improvements, the total cost of constructing a bathroom cannot be deducted from the cost new as a depreciation item. The addition of a bathroom, heating system, or electrical service to an existing house usually costs more than if the same item had been installed with the construction of the house. The amount of curable functional obsolescence is the difference between the cost of *adding* the item at the date of appraisal and the cost of *installing* the item as part of the house construction as of the date of appraisal. In our example, functional obsolescence measured by the cost-to-cure of adding a second bath is calculated as follows:

Estimated cost of adding bathroom to the existing house:	$6,500
Estimated cost of bathroom included as part of house construction:	−4,500
Functional obsolescence:	$2,000

Capitalization of Rental Loss

The capitalization of rental loss can be calculated to measure incurable functional and economic obsolescence. Assume that an incurable deficiency exists in a three-bedroom house because of the necessity of going through a bedroom to enter the only bathroom. Because of the poor floor plan, the house will rent for $10 per month less than a similar three-bedroom, one-bath house with a good floor plan. The future loss of $10 per month over the remaining economic life of the house can be capitalized to reflect the existing depreciation because of this deficiency. Capitalization merely converts the periodic rent loss into a present value (negative in this case). What is measured is the difference in value between the subject house and a similar house without the deficient floor plan.

The monthly rental loss can be capitalized in several ways. The usual method is to multiply the estimated rental loss by a gross rent multiplier. The gross rent multiplier is based on the relationship of sales price to rent. We discuss it more fully in Chapter 14.

Economic obsolescence is caused by factors outside the subject property. Similar to incurable functional obsolescence, it can be measured by capitalizing the rent loss. The obsolescence reflected by the capitalized rent loss affects the total property, both land and improvements.

For example, suppose your investigation shows that houses located adjacent to a freeway rent for $50 per month less than similar houses away from the freeway. Multiply this rental loss by a gross rent multiplier to determine the capitalized value, which reflects the depreciation in value due to the proximity of the freeway. However, when you appraise the site, the value of which will be added to the depreciated improvement value, remember that the adverse effect of

TABLE 11–2   Functional obsolescence

Rental loss per month due to floor plan	$ 20
Estimated gross rent multiplier	110
Functional obsolescence $20 × 110	$2,200

the freeway on the land should be reflected in your estimate of the value of the site.

If you find that lots next to the freeway sell for $2,000 less than lots away from the freeway, you know that the $2,000 reflects the economic obsolescence attributable to the land. If the capitalized value of the rental loss is greater than $2,000, the difference is attributable to the improvements. If the effect of the freeway on the land value cannot be measured by land sales, some other method of allocating the economic obsolescence between land and improvements must be used. Tables 11–2 and 11–3 contain examples of estimated incurable functional and economic obsolescence, measured by the rental loss.

Sales Data Method

An analysis of comparable sales can be used to measure either total depreciation to a property or a particular element of depreciation. When using the sales data method (or the abstractive method) for estimating overall accrued depreciation, the appraiser attempts to analyze the amount of depreciation reflected by purchasers in the market. The theory is to abstract, or segregate, the depreciation to the improvements from the sale price of the property. Sales of a number of properties similar to the subject are analyzed in the following manner:

1.   Estimate the reproduction cost of improvements for each of the sale properties.

2.   Estimate the land value of each sale property based on sales of vacant land.

3.   Deduct the estimated land value from the sale price to determine the indicated sale price for improvements only.

TABLE 11–3   Economic obsolescence

Rental loss per month due to freeway	$ 50
Estimated gross rent multiplier	110
Total economic obsolescence $50 × 110	$5,500
Economic obsolescence to land	$2,000
Economic obsolescence to improvements	$3,500

4. Deduct the indicated sale price of improvements from the esti-
    mated reproduction cost of improvements for each sale prop-
    erty. The result is the indicated accrued depreciation expressed
    in total dollars for each sale property.

5. Divide the amount of depreciation by the estimated reproduc-
    tion cost to determine the percentage of depreciation to the sale
    improvements.

Table 11–4 contains an example of accrued depreciation estimated by
the sales data method.
    Depreciation to each of the sale properties is abstracted in this
manner. The percentages of depreciation are correlated to determine
an indicated percentage of accrued depreciation applicable to the
subject improvements. If the percentage of depreciation to the sale
properties is not considered equal to the subject improvements, adjustments have to be made by some other method. Obviously, such
an analysis of several sale properties is time-consuming, and the accuracy of the results is doubtful.
    Depreciation tables, supposedly based on an analysis of market
transactions, have been prepared by several building cost service
companies. Depreciation is abstracted as we have described, classified according to construction and use, and plotted. From statistical
curves, tables are prepared. Most tables are based on the relationship
between effective age and typical life expectancy. The tables are designed to measure all types of "normal" accrued depreciation. "Abnormal" items of depreciation are estimated by some other method
and added to the depreciation indicated on the table.
    Most published tables indicate that relatively little depreciation
occurs during the first few years, but that the yearly rate progres-
sively increases during the middle and latter years of the structure's
economic life. This progressive rate of depreciation increase is probably closer to actual market conditions than is the straight-line age-life
method. Older buildings usually suffer proportionately greater functional and economic obsolescence than new ones.
    Published depreciation tables are a convenient source of ready
data for analyzing accrued depreciation by the sales data, or abstractive, method. However, there are major disadvantages in relying on

TABLE 11–4 Accrued depreciation estimated by the sales
                data method

Estimated reproduction cost of sale improvements		$90,000
Sale price of property	$130,000	
Less estimated land value and site improvements	− 60,000	
Indicated sale price of improvements		
Indicated accrued depreciation		70,000
		$20,000

$20,000 / $90,000 = 22%

these tables: (1) The sales data used are usually nationwide and may not accurately reflect depreciation in a particular area. (2) There are no specific sales data on which to substantiate the percentage of depreciation used. (3) Depreciation tables usually measure normal depreciation, but the term *normal* may vary with the individual and the region. (4) For every 10 sets of depreciation tables published, there will be 10 different schedules of depreciation. This is understandable, but disconcerting when you are asked to defend the table you use over another table.

An analysis of sales can give the greatest substantiation to some items of functional and economic obsolescence. The difference in the sale prices of similar properties, with and without an abnormal deficiency, is a direct measure of depreciation for that deficiency. Sales of houses both adjacent to and away from a freeway or railroad supply realistic means of measurement. Likewise, comparisons are made of sales with and without a poor floor plan or other functional deficiency. Economic obsolescence measured by the market sales method reflects depreciation to the total property and may have to be broken down into land and improvements.

There are disadvantages in using the market sales method to measure items of functional or economic obsolescence: (1) The particular deficiency of the subject property must be common enough to be found in sale properties. (2) Sales used must be similar in all other respects in addition to the deficiency being measured.

The advantage of using the market sales method of measuring depreciation is that the measurement is direct and reflects the actual response of buyers and sellers in the market. It is often difficult for the appraiser to remain objective and to avoid using their preferences to judge items of obsolescence. In appraising a house adjacent to a freeway, an appraiser's logical subjective judgment may be that obsolescence exists because of the noise, fumes, inharmonious use, and loss of privacy caused by the freeway. However, if his investigation shows that similar houses, both adjacent to and away from the freeway, sell at the same price, he can charge no depreciation to the freeway.

LIMITATIONS OF THE COST APPROACH

1. Requires an accurate estimate of the value of the site. This may be very difficult if there are no vacant lot sales available.

2. Requires accurate estimates of all replacement cost new figures of all improvements.

3. Requires accurate estimates of all forms of depreciation.

4. Is generally used most effectively in conjunction with one of the other approaches.

5. Loses validity when applied to properties with old improvements.

6. Loses validity when applied to significantly overimproved properties.

7. Difficult to apply to condos or planned unit development units commonly called town homes.

8. Requires estimate of effective age.

9. Best applied with a special-purpose property, such as a church or public building, where it is not possible to use the income or the market approaches.

SUMMARY

Valuation by the cost approach entails estimating the cost new of improvements, subtracting accrued depreciation, and adding the value of the land. The improvement cost estimate can be based on either the reproduction or the replacement cost of the improvements. Reproduction cost refers to duplicating an exact replica; replacement cost refers to the duplication of the structure's utility and amenities.

Of the several methods of estimating building costs, the one most often used by appraisers is the comparative, or square-foot, method. Building costs per square foot, obtained from recent construction and published cost data, are adjusted and applied to the subject improvements.

In estimating cost new, the appraiser must include all costs—both direct and indirect. Direct cost is the actual cost of construction including the builder's overhead and profit, engineering costs, and architect's fees. Indirect costs are expenditures in time and money and loss in income associated with the development but not directly a part of the construction.

Depreciation is the difference between the reproduction cost new of the improvements and their present value, measured at the same date. Depreciation can take the form of physical deterioration, functional obsolescence, or economic obsolescence. Of the many methods of estimating depreciation, the most common is the age-life method based on the ratio of effective age to economic life. It is important when using this method not to compound depreciation or to depreciate items not included in the original cost estimate.

The older the building, the more difficult it is to estimate reproduction cost and depreciation accurately. The cost approach is most reliable when the improvements being appraised are relatively new and represent the highest and best use of the site.

A summary of cost approach conclusions should be included in the appraisal report. A detailed explanation and justification of cost and depreciation estimates should also be included in the report and referred to in the summary sheet. The summary sheet in Figure 11–1 is only an example. Any clear, concise method of outlining cost approach conclusions is acceptable.

FIGURE 11–1 Sample summary sheet.

Reproduction cost of improvements			
Residence			
1,760 sq. ft. @ $50.00		$88,000	
Covered porches			
366 sq. ft. @ $10.00 =		3,660	
Garage			
420 sq. ft. @ $20.00 =		8,400	
Concrete driveway			
600 sq. ft. @ $3.00		1,800	
Fencing			
200 lineal ft. @ $6.00		1,200	
Indirect costs		5,000	
Total cost of improvements		$108,060	
Depreciation			
Physical deterioration			
Curable		5,000	
Incurable		8,000	
Functional obsolescence			
Curable—addition of			
bathroom	2,000		
Incurable—poor floor			
plan	2,200		
Economic obsolescence			
Proximity to freeway	3,500		
Total depreciation		20,700	
Depreciated cost of			
improvements		87,360	
Land value		40,000	
Landscaping		5,000	
Property value indicated by			
cost approach			132,360
Rounded			$132,000

DISCUSSION QUESTIONS

1. Explain the term *accrued depreciation* as it is used in appraisal practice.

2. Name and describe the three basic classifications of accrued depreciation.

3. What are the five basic methods of estimating accrued depreciation?

4. Explain effective age of a building in contrast to chronological age of a building.

5. What is the meaning of the term *economic life* as it is used in appraising? How does economic life differ from future physical life?

6. Under what conditions is the application of the cost approach most reliable in the appraisal of real estate?

7. What is the most common method used by appraisers to estimate depreciation?

8. Distinguish between curable and incurable physical deterioration.

9. How are comparable sales analyzed to indicate accrued depreciation?

MULTIPLE-CHOICE QUESTIONS

1. In the cost approach, accrued depreciation is closely associated with
   a. Physical deterioration
   b. Functional obsolescence
   c. Economic obsolescence
   d. All of the above

2. Which of the following types of accrued depreciation is an item of physical deterioration?
   a. Only one bath in a three-bedroom home
   b. House in need of paint
   c. Kitchen appliances in need of replacement
   d. Both b and c

3. Which of the following types of accrued depreciation is an item of functional obsolescence?
   a. One-car garage
   b. One fireplace
   c. One bathtub
   d. An alternating current electrical system

4. Which of the following types of depreciation is always, for all practical purposes, incurable?
   a. Economic obsolescence
   b. Functional obsolescence
   c. Physical deterioration
   d. None of the above; all types of depreciation are, practically speaking, curable

5. Chronological age of a structure is
   a. The age indicated by the condition of the structure
   b. The actual age of the structure
   c. The effective age of the structure
   d. All of the above

6. A loss in value due to the existence of a freeway in back of a residence would be considered which of the following types of depreciation?
   a. Functional obsolescence
   b. Physical deterioration
   c. Economic obsolescence
   d. All of the above

7. The capitalization of rental loss is used to measure which of the following types of depreciation?
   a. Incurable functional and economic obsolescence
   b. Curable functional and economic obsolescence
   c. Curable physical deterioration
   d. None of the above

8. Which of the following is a limitation of the cost approach?
   a. Need to find a sufficient number of comparable sales
   b. Loses validity when applied to significantly overimproved properties
   c. Need comparable rental information
   d. Need proper capitalization rate

9. In which of the following ways does the cost approach differ from the market approach?
   a. Need separate estimate of land and improvements
   b. Need updated cost-to-replace figures
   c. Neither a nor b
   d. Both a and b

10. Depreciation in a residence is which of the following?
    a. The difference between the replacement cost new of the improvements and their present value, measured at the same date
    b. The loss in value from any cause
    c. The difference in value between the improvements and the land
    d. Both a and b

Chapter 12

SALES COMPARISON, OR MARKET DATA, APPROACH

Body of Knowledge Topic

- *Sales Comparison Approach*

The sales comparison, or market data, approach, sometimes called the comparative approach, directly compares the subject property with sales of similar properties. The basic principle underlying the market data approach is *substitution:* A buyer should not pay more for a property than the cost of a substitute property of equal utility and desirability. (The market data method of valuation should not be confused with the cost and income approaches, in which the basic data also come from the market.)

The market data approach is well suited to the appraisal of residential properties, especially single-family residences. The reliability of any method of valuation depends largely on the availability of data necessary for its application. Because people today are so mobile, data on home sales are usually readily available. The average ownership period for a single-family residence is approximately 5 to 7 years. It is apparent that, in any given neighborhood, there probably have been a number of recent sales.

The market data approach has four basic steps: (1) collection of sales data, (2) processing of sales data, (3) analysis of sales data, and (4) comparison of sales data with the subject property to arrive at a value estimate. The application of the market data approach is essentially the same in the valuation of all types of property, although the units of comparison between the sale properties and the subject may vary.

The real estate appraiser investigates both property transactions that have taken place in the open market and properties presently offered for sale. From analyzing these data, the appraiser deduces the probable selling price for the property being appraised—an estimate of value indicated by the market data approach.

COLLECTION OF SALES DATA

Before sales data can be collected, four questions must be resolved:

What are the characteristics of the subject property?
What area should be searched for sales?
What time period should be investigated for sales?
What source should be used to find sales?

The experienced appraiser does not consciously consider each of these questions but immediately initiates a plan for gathering sales data.

Characteristics of the Subject Property

Before a search can be conducted, the characteristics and features of the subject must be defined. This information can be found in multiple listings, if the property has been listed for sale, in county records, from previous appraisals done for tax or mortgage loan purposes, and from on-line and CD-ROM subscription services offering sales histories and property profiles. Companies such as DataQuick (see Figure 12–1) provide data that is a composite of these resources, offering such pertinent information as lot size, square footage of improvements, number of bedrooms and bathrooms, and previous sales transaction data. Often, the name of the subdivision or development is included, along with the assessors parcel and census tract numbers.

Area of Search

The area to be searched for sales obviously depends on the type of development surrounding the subject property and on sales activity. The immediate neighborhood or subdivision will usually yield adequate sales data for the appraisal of a tract home. In the case of an unusual residence or an apartment house, it may be necessary to extend the search area. If sales are not available in the immediate neighborhood, the appraiser attempts to find other areas that may yield sales of properties similar to the subject. Normally, investigations are confined to the neighborhood of the subject property, the search area widening only if a preliminary analysis does not furnish adequate sales data.

Time Period for Sales

The time period for comparable sales depends on the sales activity in the area of the subject property. Sales close to the valuation date for

```
                    Property Profile - Santa Clara

                    Dataquick new house account
      Prepared For:                          Acnt Rep:
      Attention   :                          C/S  Rep:

**************************************************************************
*                                                                        *
*      APN   : 403-57-053                                                 *
*      Owner1: CALIFORNIA FEDERAL BANK          Phone :                   *
*      Owner2:                                  OwnShp:                    *
*      Site  : 2341 GRIMSBY CT                  Pg-Grd: 65-D4             *
*            : SAN JOSE CA              95130   Census: 5066.04           *
*      Mail  : 5700 WILSHIRE BLVD               Zoning: R1               *
*            : LOS ANGELES CA           90036   FloodP: 060349 0035      *
*      Legal Desc    : TR 3791 LOT 236                                    *
*                                                                        *
*                     ------------------------                           *
*                     Property Characteristics                          *
*                     ------------------------                           *
*                                                                        *
*      Use   : SINGLE FAM RES                                             *
*                                                                        *
*      YrBlt : 1965       SqFeet: 1,181         Firepl:                   *
*      BedBth: 3/2.0      Addtns:               Ht/Cl :                   *
*      #Rooms: 5          Basmnt:               Dishwh:                   *
*      #Dinng:            GarSf : 494           Elevtr:                   *
*      #Famrm:             Offic:               Pool  :                   *
*      #Utlrm:            LeasSf:               Sauna :                   *
*      #Units: 1          LotSz : 5,227         Tennis:                   *
*      RecRm : 1          Dimens: 58x94         Sprnkl:                   *
*      #Story: 1                                WallHt:                   *
*                                                                        *
*                     ----------------------                             *
*                     Sale/Loan Information                             *
*                     ----------------------                             *
*                                                                        *
*      Last Trans W/O $:                                                  *
*      SaleDt: 03/29/94    Doc#  : 12423223     Buyer : CALIFORNIA FEDER  *
*      SaleAm: $223,777 T  $/SqFt:              Seller: DOE, JOHN         *
*      1st Td:             LoanTy:              Lender:                   *
*       +Addl:             PrevDt: 12/17/93     Title : FIDELITY          *
*                          PrevAm:                                        *
*                                                                        *
*                     --------------------------                         *
*                     Assessment/Tax Information                        *
*                     --------------------------                         *
*                                                                        *
*        Assd  : $248,700        Tax   : $3,032.02                        *
*        Land  : $86,822         Status: CUR                             *
*        Improv: $161,878        TRA   :                                 *
*           perc: 65%            Exempt:                                 *
*                                TaxYr : 93-94                           *
*                                                                        *
**************************************************************************
            *** THE ACCURACY OF THIS INFORMATION IS   ***
            *** DEEMED RELIABLE BUT IS NOT GUARANTEED ***
            Copyright (c)1994 Dataquick Information Network
```

FIGURE 12–1   Sample sales history—DataQuick.

the subject property are most desirable, especially when the market is rapidly changing.

Sales within 6 months of the valuation date for the subject property are usually acceptable. In a stable market, or if there are few sales of property similar to the subject, a period of 1 or 2 years may be necessary. Older sales, considered too old for direct comparison with the subject property, are often useful for establishing a trend in sale prices of a particular type of property.

The valuation date for the subject property is usually the date of the current appraisal. If the property is being valued as of some prior date, sales both before and after the valuation date should be used.

Sources of Sales Data

Each appraiser develops sources for sales data. Most use more than one source. The intended use of the appraisal and the type of property being appraised often influence the selection of the sales data source. We list the most common sources for sales data.

County Recorder's Office   Counties maintain a file of all documents recorded in the county offices, including all deeds transferring ownership of real estate. Indexing methods vary. The index system in some county recorders' offices provides a quick and simple method of searching an area for sales; in other counties, the filing system may be to complicated for practical use.

Title Insurance Companies   Title insurance companies, like county recorders' offices, maintain files of all recorded county documents. Real estate transfer deeds are usually filed according to the physical location of the sale properties. This filing system facilitates the appraiser's job of obtaining sales within a specified area. Some title companies gather sales data as a service to their customers. They usually charge an hourly fee.

Real Estate Board Multiple-Listing Service   Most local real estate boards provide a cooperative listing service to their members. New listing sheets are distributed daily or weekly to subscribers. Sales of listed properties are reported at regular intervals. A summary of sales and expirations of listings, grouped by geographical area and property type, is published periodically. Many multiple-listing services have this information available to members' offices via computer terminals (see Figure 12–2).

Published Services   Several private companies in California publish a weekly, monthly, or quarterly list of all recorded property transfers within each county. The information available from these publications is very brief—usually location of the property by assessor's parcel number or street address, date of sale, buyer's and seller's names, recorded document number, price indicated by revenue stamps, and concurrent deed of trust. Examples are, California Market Data Cooperative (CMDC) and Real Estate Data Inc. (REDI).

Computerized Services   There are a host of on-line and CD-ROM information services available to appraisers on a subscription basis. This data includes sales history data, as depicted in Figure 12–1, plus many additional types of data such as flood zone, demographic, population trend, and most importantly, comparable property data. The capability of these computerized data systems to perform program-

```
SOLD DATE:18-Mar-94   $192,500     DOM: 282   TRMS:CV CBFF01
Ad: 14128 HANSEL                 Ar:09 9TD    # 31156
Subd:TDNR10            Lt:436 Blk/U:10  Apn#45-530-11    N
Zn:R-1    Lt Sz:70,180            Acr:         Soil Class:
View:           Sq Ft:  1740 ME   Arch:M  Str:2  Topo:DOWNSLO
Bdrm: 3         F/P:F             Adl Rm:                PT:RS
Bath:2.50       WdStv:            Heat:PRO             Furn:N
Lft:N Den:      Flrs:H,TL,CV      Roof:CO           Fndtn:PRCO
Fr:Y  Dr:N      Deck:YES          Swr Pmp:
YrBlt:93        Gar:1             Ease:
Extras:                   HO $  510 A   H Opt:N  Other:
Wtr Co:TDPUD         Init Fee:         H/O Amen:BE,PI,PL,TN,GF,SP
Incl Feat:CA,RO,MW,DS,DW          Excl Feat:RF,FN
       LOANS    TYPE     RATE    PMT   TERM  LENDER
   1st
   2nd
  Bonds
Opt Fin:            Trade:       Type List:ER  Mtg Bal:
             Spec Discl:
Purchase Term:C.T.N.L.

Remarks:Custom designed and built by top builder on
a beautiful sunny lot with lots of trees,
nice view and level driveway, lovely family
room with fireplace 3 bed 2.5 bath.
Own:Candler              Ph:            Fee:3%
Ten:                     Ph:            Rent Hist:
Agt:Ed Candler           Ph:587-4802       T.D.S.
Rlt:First Realty         Ph:916-582-8022
H Shw:GO        Alarm:N Sec Acc:N  Sign:Y   $197,500
```

FIGURE 12–2 Multiple listing—closed sale transaction.

mable searches, based on the configuration of the subject property—square footage, number of bedrooms, number of bathrooms, lot size, etc.—makes these services efficient and powerful resources. In addition, this information is constantly updated, and is sent monthly, in the case of CD-ROM, or is available almost immediately with the on-line services. (See Figures 12–3 and 12–4.)

Real Estate Brokers   Most real estate offices can provide data on property sales handled by their office. "For Sale" signs in an area indicate which offices are active. Since real estate offices like to advertise their success, "Sold" signs often remain on a property for some time after the sale has been consummated.

Real Estate Appraisers   Most real estate appraisers maintain a file of the sales data collected for prior appraisals. A sales sheet with all pertinent data is prepared for each sale property. The sales sheets are indexed, usually by location, for easy access. Appraisers use their own files and may also solicit comparable sales data from other appraisers. Appraisers normally reciprocate in the exchange of sales data.

Number of Sales

The number of comparable sales used to value a property by the market data approach depends on the comparability of the sales to the subject property and the intended use of the appraisal. Three or four sales similar to the subject in essential aspects are usually suffi-

```
[[[[[[[[[[[[[[[[[[[[[[[[[[[[[[[[[[[[[[[[[[]]]]]]]]]]]]]]]]]]]]]]]]]]]]]]]]]]]]]]]]
[[                1994 COPYRIGHT BY DATAQUICK INFORMATION SYSTEMS              ]]
[[                 DETERMINATION OF FLOOD ZONE RATING                         ]]
[[             INFORMATION DEEMED RELIABLE BUT IS NOT GUARANTEED              ]]
[[[[[[[[[[[[[[[[[[[[[[[[[[[[[[[[[[[[[[[[[[]]]]]]]]]]]]]]]]]]]]]]]]]]]]]]]]]]]]]]]]
Property Street Address  : 13590 HOWEN DR
City, State, & Zip Code  : SARATOGA CA 95070
County                   : SANTA CLARA
Assessor's Parcel Number : 393-38-006
------------------------------------------------------------------------------
Community Number : 060351          Flood Zone        : B
Map Panel        : 0002 - B        Flood Elevation   : N/A
Map Date         : 01/17/79        Community FIRM Date : 01/07/79
------------------------------------------------------------------------------
Flood Zone Description:
Area of moderate or minimal hazard from the principal source of flood in
the area.  Flood insurance is available in participating communities but
is not required by Federal regulations.
Special Flood Hazard Area :  NC         Participation : REGULAR / ELIGIBLE
==============================================================================
```

Disable Printer, Press <Return> to continue...

FIGURE 12–3 Flood zone determination—Western Flood, a DataQuick series (on-line or CD-ROM).

cient. If sales of overall comparability to the subject property are not found, a larger number of sales must be used.

If the appraisal is being made for a taking in eminent domain, the appraiser's report must be prepared in anticipation of court testimony and will probably include 8 to 10 sales. In appraising for loan purposes where the loan will be limited to 70 or 80 percent of property value, 3 sales of reasonably similar properties should be adequate.

The appraiser may have to investigate 20 or 30 recorded transactions to find 3 or 4 comparable sales. After analyzing recorded documents, the appraiser does a visual inspection to determine whether the improvements are similar to those on the subject property.

PROCESSING SALES DATA

Processing sales data involves extracting and organizing pertinent sales information for convenient analysis. The preliminary processing depends largely on the source from which sales were gathered.

If the sales data come from recorded documents furnished by the county recorder's office, a title insurance company, or a publication service, the information will be in the form of a copy of the recorded deed or an extraction of data from the deed. Information available from a deed is limited to the names of buyer and seller, date of deed, date of recording, legal description, transfer tax, and recording number. A deed gives no information about improvements on the sale parcel, if any.

If the appraiser's data come from the multiple-listing service, the appraiser's own files, real estate brokers, or other appraisers, basic information on improvements is available. The street address

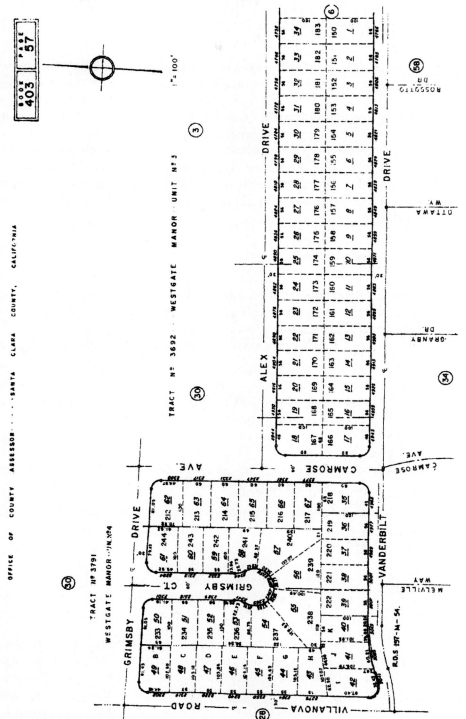

FIGURE 12-4 Plat map—DataQuick (CD-ROM, only).

of the sale property is also known, whereas on the recorded deed the only location given is the legal description.

Plotting of Sales

When sales data are extracted from the various sources, the appraiser must plot each of the sale parcels on a map to locate the properties in the field. Such a map is referred to as the sales map. When sale parcels are located within a recorded subdivision, the tract map of the area is normally used for plotting the sales. When sale properties extend over a large geographical area, a smaller-scale map is used or several maps may be joined. The sales map not only locates sales but also enables the appraiser to view (1) the sale parcels in relation to the subject property and (2) other characteristics of the neighborhood.

Comparable Sale Form

After plotting the sales on a map, the appraiser prepares a lender-approved form as a worksheet to extract and organize the pertinent data from the various sources. The standard residential appraisal form is the URAR, revised in June of 1993. It includes the following data:

Seller
Buyer
Date of sale
Location
Lot size
Description of improvements
Confirmation (person with whom confirmed and date)
Recording index
Transfer tax
Sale price
Terms of sale
Remarks

The data obtained from the sources can be recorded in the appraiser's office prior to the property inspection. The remaining data are filled in by the appraiser during or after the inspection of the property. The appraiser may obtain a copy of the plat map, either from a CD-ROM subscription service such as DataQuick, from a microfiche service, or from a title company or the county recorder's office.

The worksheet is numbered to correspond with the prepared sales map. The appraiser takes the worksheets into the field when inspecting the sale properties. If sales data are obtained from multiple-listing sheets, they can be transferred to the appraiser's worksheets or the listing sheet may be used in place of the worksheet.

Inspection of Sale Properties

The appraiser *must* inspect the sale properties. This inspection may be only a brief observation of the property, or it may be as thorough as the inspection of the subject property itself. A thorough inspection of the sale properties allows the appraiser to make a more precise comparison between the sale and subject properties. An appraiser seldom inspects the interior of sale houses, because it is often difficult to gain entry to an occupied residence and a thorough inspection is time-consuming.

If the sale data are obtained from a multiple-listing service or similar source, most of the pertinent information will be available from the listing sheet. Then an inspection for the condition and attractiveness of the property is all that is necessary.

Confirmation of Sales Data

All comparable sales used in an appraisal should be confirmed with one of the principals in the transaction, the real estate broker or salesperson who handled the sale, or someone familiar with the terms and conditions of the sale. Sales may be confirmed either in person or by telephone. More information can usually be obtained by interviewing in person than by telephone, but personal interviews may be impractical.

The data solicited in an interview with the buyer, seller, or real estate broker depend on the type of property and the information already available. In addition to the sale price, confirmation data usually include the following, pertinent at the time of the sale:

1. Terms of sale

2. Any extenuating circumstances in the sale (imminent foreclosure)

3. Description of improvements (number of rooms, baths, etc.)

4. Occupancy status

5. Rental, if not owner-occupied

6. Condition of property at the date of sale

7. Personal property included in the sale

8. Assessments or encumbrances against the property at the date of sale

The sale price can often be deduced from the transfer tax stamp affixed to the deed (see Chapter 7). Find the sale price by dividing the amount of tax by 11 and moving the decimal four places to the right. The tax will not indicate the correct sale price if an existing loan has been assumed by the buyer. Also, additional stamps may have been purchased and placed on the deed, or the stamps may have been affixed to the deed after recordation.

Sales data from multiple-listing services include sale prices as reported by the real estate broker handling the sale. This confirmation and the other data provided on the listing sheet are usually adequate for making an appraisal.

ANALYSIS OF SALES DATA

After processing, the sales data must be arranged systematically to make analysis convenient for the appraiser. An appraiser must learn to discriminate in the selection of sales data, discarding information not relevant to the appraisal of the subject property.

Analysis involves separating comparable sales into parts that can be more readily examined. The appraiser can make meaningful comparisons between the desirability and utility of the sale property and the subject property.

Units of Comparison

In the appraisal of single-family residences, total properties are compared after making adjustments for differences between the sale and subject properties. A common denominator is established.

Design, size, and utility of apartment houses usually differ too greatly to allow a direct comparison between total properties; however, several units of comparison have been developed for analysis of such sales. The most common units are:

1. Per square feet of living area

2. Per living unit

3. Per room

4. Gross rent multiplier

Appraisers often use three or four units of comparison when analyzing sales of apartment houses.

In appraising commercial and industrial properties, the appraiser normally uses square feet of building area and gross rent multiplier as units of comparison.

COMPARISON BETWEEN SALES AND SUBJECT PROPERTY

The most difficult—and important—aspect of the market data approach is the adjustment for differences between the comparable sales and the subject property. No property is identical to the subject property. The appraiser attempts to find sales or property as similar as possible to the subject property and adjusts for differences. To be considered comparable, the sale property must be similar to the subject property in location, utility, and date of sale, and the transaction must be voluntary and open.

The sale price of the comparable property is always adjusted upward or downward to reflect the differences between the sale property and the subject property. The major categories of adjustment for all comparable sales are time, location, and physical characteristics. Adjustments may be made by any of the following three methods:

1. As a percentage of sale price

2. By a dollar amount—the most common and practical method

3. By pluses or minuses

When measuring differences between sale properties and the subject property, the appraiser must avoid personal preferences and attempt to reflect only differences that affect sellers and buyers. Adjustments are not normally made for elements less than $500 in value, since smaller elements are relatively insignificant in relation to the value of the total property and cannot usually be realistically measured by the appraiser.

Time

Adjustment for time reflects the change in value between the date of the comparable sale and the valuation date of the subject property. It is difficult to measure accurately differences in value over a period of time. If enough sales of similar properties are available, a value trend can sometimes be established and measured. Published studies summarize surveys measuring changes in various types of property values. In a rapidly changing market, the more recent sales and listings of property for sale should be given the greatest weight in the market data approach. Normal practice among appraisers is to analyze sales occurring within 6 months of appraisal date and make no time adjustments providing sufficient recent sales are available.

Location

Adjustment for location includes differences in desirability between neighborhoods or between specific locations within a neighborhood. In appraising single-family residences, comparable sales are normally limited to the neighborhood of the subject property. Dissimilarity exists between neighborhoods in public transportation, shopping facilities, schools, parks, natural amenities, socioeconomic status of residents, care and condition of properties, and so on.

The location of sale properties should resemble that of the subject property within the immediate neighborhood. Unless there is a shortage of comparable sales in the area, sale properties adjacent to stores, freeways, or the like should not be used. Sales affected by natural amenities, such as trees, view, or creek, the value of which is difficult to measure, should not be used unless the subject property also includes these amenities. Likewise, if the subject property has any amenities or undesirable characteristics, similar sales should be used for comparison.

Physical Characteristics

Adjustments for physical differences between the sale properties and the subject property are the most difficult kind in single-family residence appraisal. The appraiser must be aware of quality, quantity, and design differences between the sale and subject properties and must be able to express them in terms of market value.

Physical characteristics are generally classed as site (or land) improvements and building improvements. Site and land improvements include lot size, street improvements, utilities, natural amenities, and landscaping, which is usually considered in relation to its effect on the total property.

In adjusting for differences in building improvements, the appraiser must consider age, condition, size, type, and quality of construction. A comparable sale property must have major similarities to the subject property. Adjustments should be necessary only for minor differences. For instance, a two-story house should not be compared to a one-story house; a brick building to a wood frame building; or a two-bedroom, one-bath home to a three-bedroom, two-bath home.

The appraiser adjusts for differences by anticipating market response. How much more will buyers pay for an inside utility room, additional half bath, second fireplace, dishwasher, built-in range and oven? Each significant difference between the sale property and the subject property must be translated into dollars.

The most common method of measuring differences in improvements is by depreciated cost. Suppose the cost of an additional half bath is estimated at $4,000. The half bath is 15 years old, so 20 percent depreciation is deducted from cost new. An adjustment of $3,200 is made for the half bath. Adjustments are often necessary for differences in size between the sale houses and the subject. Since the average depreciated cost of a residence includes the kitchen, bath, fireplace, heating system, and other items that are basic regardless of the size of the house, the adjustment for size should be less than the average square foot depreciated cost. Suppose a sale house has a living area 150 square feet larger than that of the subject house. This extra living area may be included as larger rooms than those of the subject house, or it may include a dining room or family room that the subject residence does not have. If the depreciated cost of the residence is estimated at $40 per square foot, an adjustment of $30 per square foot or $4,500 for the 150-square-foot difference in size may be considered proper. If a second fireplace costing $2,000 to construct is considered 20 percent depreciated, the adjustment would be $1,600.

Of course, depreciated cost in our examples may not reflect the exact difference in value. However, appraisers know that buyers find features such as an additional half bath, larger living area, and a second fireplace desirable and are willing to pay for them. Depreciated cost is merely one method for expressing building differences in terms of money.

The appraiser must carefully analyze overimproved sale properties. The over improvement may be the relationship of the building to its neighborhood, for instance, a $400,000 house in an area of $150,000 homes; or it may be the relationship of an improvement to the total property, such as a $30,000 swimming pool with an $150,000 home. An overimproved, or superadequacy, comparable sale property should not be used for comparison unless the subject property has a similar overimprovement.

Terms of Sale

In real estate appraisal, the subject property is normally valued as free and clear of all liens and encumbrances; that is, existing mortgages, deeds of trust, and assessments against the property are not considered. Most definitions of market value are in terms of money. Therefore, in real estate appraisal the estimated value reflects a cash or equivalent dollar sale price.

What is "equivalent to cash"? Most property sales are financed partially by loans. In appraising, an equivalent-to-cash value generally includes financing that is typical for the property being valued. Typical methods of financing vary with the type, location, and price range of a property and the general economic conditions that affect the availability of investment funds.

The appraiser estimates how the terms of sale or financing affect property values. When analyzing a comparable sale, it may be necessary to adjust for atypical terms of sale. A $100,000 residence priced at a small downpayment whose seller carries a large second deed of trust would generally be considered atypical. If the appraiser feels that the $100,000 sale price does not represent the true market value of the property because of the terms of sale, the sale price must be adjusted or the sale rejected as not comparable to the subject property. In the case of an appraisal for a conventional loan, it is normal to adjust sale price downward if the seller pays for the buyer to obtain a loan, such as in VA or FHA financing, or if the seller pays some of the buyer's closing costs. In these instances, the price of the sale property is usually increased to compensate for the seller's additional costs. The appraiser may deduct from the comparable sale price an amount approximately equal to the fee paid by the seller of the sale property, if a similar fee is not being paid in the sale of the subject property. The appraiser adjusts for terms of sale according to personal judgment and experience with financing and property values.

There are many possible methods of adjustment for cash equivalencies, depending on an almost limitless variety of seller financing plans. Two possible types of sales:

1. Comparing sale prices of similar homes, one with special owner financing and the other with conventional financing. If, after making all necessary adjustments, there is still a difference, then this difference in dollar amount would reflect the difference in value because of special owner financing.

2. Comparing sale prices of buy downs by a developer who is selling homes, condominiums, or townhomes (planned unit development), the same type of comparison might be made using a development in which no buy down is being offered. [*Note to student: A buy down is where a builder or developer, because of a pre-arranged preferred rate with the lender during the initial period of the mortgage, is able to pass an initial lower interest rate on to the buyer—for example, a rate of 8 percent when the market interest rates are 10 percent.*]

The payment of loan points, as the payment of an extra fee by the seller in the case of a VA, FHA, or any other lower-interest loan can be directly adjusted since such payment of points is an actual dollar amount that the seller pays as an incentive for the buyer to buy that house because of a lower interest rate available on a loan. For example, a buyer might obtain a loan at a lower interest rate, say 8.75 percent, when conventional financing is 9 percent. This would then call for a point payment of 2 points (8 points per full percent; therefore 2 points for 0.25 percent or a fourth of a percent). The 2 points would translate to a 2 percent fee on the loan. Therefore a $100,000 loan with a charge of 2 points really means $100,000 × 2% or $2,000. This $2,000 fee is paid up front and is, in reality, a prepayment of future interest that the lender will not receive over the given life of the loan. This $2,000 can then be deducted from the sale price of a comparable property as being a special discount or concession.

Due to the endless possibilities of financing and the many variations in ways appraisers can measure the apparent value differences, it is difficult to be precise in measuring many cash equivalencies. For example, one seller may ask for 10 percent down with a 10 percent interest-only note due in 5 years, another may ask only 5 percent down with a 10 percent interest-only note due in 10 years, and another may ask nothing down with a 10 percent fully amortized note due in 1 year. One may offer 6 months rent free and another a lease for 5 years with an option to buy. One seller may accept another property, or even a car, as part payment; the list goes on. Although some appraisers have a tendency to think that most of these variations in financing arrangements can be measured by use of certain mathematical tables, this is generally not true because the buyer and seller reach their agreement through negotiations that reflect an infinite variety of reasons for which it is difficult to assign a mathematical formula.

Another problem that remains for the appraiser lies in obtaining the correct information. Sometimes sellers and buyers will not want to give out the details regarding a sale. If they give any information, it may be false or misleading for any number of reasons. The only precise way to know the details in some transactions is to be a party to the contract, to have access to the escrow details, or to have the IRS or some other legal power obtain all of the necessary details. Even the escrow information can be deceiving because the seller and buyer may have some prearranged secret return of money to the buyer after close of escrow. This is sometimes done so it will appear that the buyer either paid a higher price for the property or paid more money down to qualify for certain third-party financing. Because of these and many more possibilities, it is really best to discard any so-called comparable sales of unusual, questionable, or deceptive seller financing.

Rating Grid

After adjusting for comparable sales differences, the appraiser prepares a rating grid, or comparison chart, listing the items of difference. [See Figure 16–1 (page 296 and page 297).] The grid enables the appraiser to visualize the differences between the sale properties and the subject property and to make a more meaningful comparison. The rating grid is normally included in the appraisal report.

The rating grid contains as many adjustment factors as the appraiser desires. Adjustments may be expressed in dollars, percentages, or pluses and minuses. Table 12–1 is a typical chart adjusted by dollars.

If adjustment is made by percentages, all adjustments are multiplied together to indicate the adjustment factor. Percentage adjustments are expressed in relation to 100 percent: An adjustment of plus 10 percent would be 110 percent; an adjustment of minus 15 percent would be expressed as 85 percent. Table 12–2 is a rating grid adjusted by percentages.

Dollar adjustments to comparable sale prices are usually preferred to percentages because most adjustment items are estimated in terms of dollars and because small adjustments are difficult to measure by percentages. When all necessary adjustments are minor and relatively equal, a rating grid indicating merely an upward or downward adjustment is often preferred.

TABLE 12–1   Rating grid adjusted by dollars

	Sale 1	Sale 2	Sale 3
Sale price	$139,000	$142,000	$140,000
Adjustments			
Time	+1,000	0	+2,000
Location	+1,000	0	0
Lot size	0	−1,000	−1,000
Condition of improvements	0	−1,000	−1,000
Improvement size	+2,000	0	+1,000
Quality of construction	−1,000	0	
Net adjustment	+3,000	−2,000	+1,000
Adjusted sale price	$142,000	$140,000	$141,000

CORRELATION OF MARKET DATA SALES

The adjusted sale prices of the comparable sales should bracket the value of the subject property. In the appraisal of a relatively new residence within a subdivision of similar houses, the bracket range will not normally exceed 5 percent between the high and low adjusted sale prices. The spread may exceed 5 percent for older or unusual residences.

Do not average the adjusted sale prices to find a final estimate of value by the market data approach. If you have used a large number of comparable sales, you may narrow the indicated price range by eliminating some of the less comparable sale properties. Give the greatest weight to the sales that are most comparable to the subject property.

LIMITATIONS OF THE MARKET DATA APPROACH

1. Requires recent sales of comparable properties.

2. Requires expert analysis of the comparable sales information.

TABLE 12–2   Rating grid adjusted by percentages

	Sale 1	Sale 2	Sale 3
Sale price	$144,000	$154,000	$144,500
Adjustments			
Time	112%		105%
Location	110%		
Lot size		90%	99%
Condition of improvement		95%	98%
Improvement size	90%		102%
Quality of construction	95%		
Net adjustment factor	105%	86%	104%
Adjusted sale price	$151,200	$132,440	$150,280

(This would include, among other considerations, the ability to determine whether the comparable sales reflected the actions of knowledgeable buyers and sellers. Also it would include the ability to analyze various financing arrangements.)

3. Has less validity in appraisal of some income properties.

SUMMARY

The market data approach directly compares the subject property to sales and listings of similar properties. A comparable sale or listing must be similar to the subject in location, time, and utility and must be an open market transaction.

The appraiser collects, processes, and analyzes the sales data and adjusts for time, location, and physical differences between the sale properties and the subject property.

Sales data are available from several sources. The type of property being appraised and the intended use of the appraisal influence the appraiser's choice of a data source. The search for sales data is limited to the neighborhood of the subject property unless the appraiser cannot find enough comparable sales, in which case the search expands to other areas similar to the subject neighborhood. Three or four comparable sales are usually enough for appraising a single-family residence. Sales close to the valuation date of the subject property are most desirable, especially in a rapidly changing market.

The sale price and other pertinent information are confirmed with the real estate broker or one of the principals in the transaction. Then the sale and listing properties are compared with the subject property. Comparable sales must be adjusted for (1) changes in value from the date of sale to the appraisal date, (2) differences in desirability of location, and (3) differences in physical characteristics of the land and improvements. Adjustments are made in dollar amounts, by percentages, or by pluses and minuses.

The appraiser prepares a rating grid or chart to help visualize the differences between the sale and subject properties. The grid shows adjustments made to the comparable sales for the differences the appraiser considers significant.

The adjusted sale prices are correlated to arrive at the subject property value indicated by the market data approach.

For a more practical and complete market approach presentation, your attention is directed to the sample Narrative Appraisal Report in the supplement to this text.

DISCUSSION QUESTIONS

1. Outline the basic steps in the application of the market data approach.

2. Discuss the usual adjustments made to comparable sales in the appraisal of a single-family residence.

3. What are the three methods of adjusting sale properties to the subject property?

4. Explain the principle of substitution as it applies to the market data approach.

5. Why is the market data approach usually considered well suited to the appraisal of single-family residences?

6. Discuss the purposes of a comparable sales map.

7. What information should be included on a comparable sales sheet for a single-family residential property?

8. Why are inspection and confirmation of comparable sales important?

9. What data should be obtained through confirmation of a comparable sale?

10. In analyses of comparable apartment house sales, what are the common units of comparison?

11. Explain the purpose of a rating grid in the adjustment of comparable sales.

MULTIPLE-CHOICE QUESTIONS

1. *Comparable approach in appraising* is another name for
    a. The capitalization approach
    b. The market approach
    c. The cost approach
    d. None of the above

2. *Summation approach in appraising* is another name for the
    a. Market approach
    b. Economic approach
    c. Cost approach
    d. Comparison approach

3. Which of the following variables is the most important consideration in the market approach?
    a. Quality of construction
    b. Number of square feet of residence
    c. Number of bedrooms
    d. Location

4. Normally for a form report for loan purposes the minimum number of comparable sales is
    a. Ten
    b. Eight

    c. Three

    d. Five

5. In the market approach, which of the following groups of variables is most important?

    a. Architectural style, number of bedrooms, quality of construction, terms of sale

    b. Time, location, utility, terms of sale

    c. Size of residence, location, architectural style, financing

    d. Location, square footage, number of bedrooms, terms of sale

Chapter 13

INCOME APPROACH: INCOME AND EXPENSE ANALYSIS

Body of Knowledge Topics

- *Estimation of Income and Expenses*

- *Operating Expense Ratio*

Real estate appraisal estimates a present value for the future benefits of real property. The income approach directly measures the present value of property based on its expected future benefits, expressed in dollars. Benefits vary with the type of property. The expected future benefits from ownership of a single-family residence include not only the basic utility of housing but also pride of ownership, stability, prestige, and freedom of use. The intangible benefits of home ownership, called amenities, obviously cannot be readily expressed in dollars. Therefore, the income approach is seldom used in the valuation of single-family residences. In single-family residence appraisal, we substitute for the income approach a method called the gross rent multiplier. (This method is more fully described later in Chapter 14.)

The income approach is applicable to property whose future benefits are measured by the expected net income to the owner. This includes most investment property—apartments, stores, offices, and in some cases, vacant land. The income approach measures the present worth of the net income a property will produce during its remaining economic life. (Economic life is the number of years the property will produce a net income to land and improvements.)

The seven basic steps of the income approach are:

1. Estimate the gross income.

2. Estimate an allowance for vacancy and rent loss.

3. Subtract the allowance for vacancy and rent loss from the gross income estimate to determine the effective gross income.

4. Estimate fixed expenses, operating expenses, and reserves for replacement of short-lived items.

[handwritten margin notes: "gross rent multiplier — SFR" and "income approach applied to investment prop."]

250

5. Deduct estimated expenses and reserves from effective gross income to determine net operating income.

6. Select a capitalization rate applicable to the subject property.

7. Capitalize, or discount, the estimated net income to indicate the present value of the property.

We shall study the income approach in relation to multiple-family residential property. The basic theory of the income approach applies to the valuation of all income-producing properties; however, the techniques vary slightly, depending on the type of property appraised.

GROSS INCOME

The gross income estimate is actually the potential gross income to the property, as of the date of appraisal. Income includes all receipts generated by the property; it is usually classified as either rental income or service income. Rental income for an apartment house is the total of the economic, or fair, rent for each of the apartment units. Service income includes receipts from laundry facilities, vending machines, selling of utility services to tenants, and the like.

Contract rent is the actual, or contracted, rent received from the property. *Economic rent* is the rent the unit would bring in the open market at the date of appraisal. Economic rent should be estimated for all living units, including manager's and janitor's units, even though rent is not actually being collected. If parking or storage space is rented separately from the living unit, such income should also be included. The gross rental estimate assumes that the property is in good, rentable condition and has competent management. The estimated cost of repairing any deferred maintenance is deducted from the value of the property indicated by the income approach.

Rental data come from two sources: the present rent schedule and a survey of rents from similar properties. Although the rent schedule and rental history are an important source of data, they should never be used for a gross income estimate without first being compared with other apartment rentals in the area.

If it is practical, the rental survey should cover only those apartments in the general area that are of similar age and construction. Usually, apartment units with the same number of bedrooms are compared. There are more detailed bases for comparisons, such as rent per room or rent per square foot of living area. However, since most tenants choose apartments to fit their bedroom requirements, this is usually the most practical unit of comparison.

In collecting rental data, obtain enough information for meaningful comparison with the subject units. Determine basic facts such as rent, furnishings, utilities, number of rooms, acceptance of children or pets, vacancies, date or rent schedule, and type of tenants. Apartment house managers are usually cooperative and will provide much information. An inspection of the comparable apartment building will provide additional data on the age and condition of the building, recreation, laundry, storage, and parking facilities.

It may be necessary to make adjustments in comparing the comparable rental units with the subject units. After analyzing the comparable rental data, the appraiser estimates a rental schedule for the subject property. The economic rent schedule may be less than, the same as, or greater than the actual rent schedule. If the economic schedule differs substantially from the existing schedule, that should be well documented and supported. Rent schedules are usually established on a monthly basis; they are converted to annual income for use in the income approach.

If the actual rent schedule is substantially below the estimated economic rent schedule, the appraiser must consider the probability of raising existing rents to their economic levels. In areas governed by rent control, it may be necessary to use the existing rent schedule. The appraiser must be familiar with any municipal regulations that may affect rental property and develop an estimated rent schedule accordingly.

Some personal property, such as stoves, refrigerators, and drapes, is usually included in the rental of an apartment unit. In addition, it is normally included in the sale of the real property and is often treated in the appraisal as real property. However, any personal property included in an appraisal of real property should be clearly identified. In the appraisal of an apartment house that includes all furnishings, estimated value should be categorized as real property or personal property. In this case, the estimated economic rent must be allocated between real and personal property.

In a small apartment house, the only service income normally comes from the laundry facilities. The appraiser should determine whether the machines are to be included in the appraisal or are in the building on a rental basis. In a large apartment complex, utilities may be purchased wholesale by the apartment house and sold to the individual units. In either case the service income estimate can usually be based on past income to the property.

VACANCY AND RENT LOSS

An allowance must be made for vacancy and rent loss. This allowance is deducted from the estimated gross income to determine the effective gross income, that is, the amount of money that should actually be collected. The vacancy and rent loss allowance is not estimated solely on conditions existing at the date of appraisal but reflects the expected vacancy and rent loss over an extended period of time. The appraiser estimates an average loss, knowing that vacancy and rent loss may sometimes exceed this estimate while at other times there may be no loss.

The vacancy and rent loss allowance in apartment properties is normally estimated at between 2 and 10 percent of gross income. The allowance is set by the appraiser based on his or her judgment of the subject property and the surrounding neighborhood. Remember that the estimated allowance is for *future* vacancy and rent loss.

If a property has a history of no vacancies, the rent schedule has probably been too low. Any apartment house should experience some vacancy and rent loss. It is often desirable to have a vacancy period between tenants to facilitate interior painting and maintenance. Remember that the allowance is considered in relation to the prevailing *economic* rent, not the existing *contract* rent.

EXPENSES

All expenditures necessary to produce income are deducted from effective gross income to determine the net income attributable to a property. The term *expenses* is used differently in appraisal from the way it is used in accounting terminology. In appraisal, expenses are *estimated* on an annual basis regardless of the period in which they are incurred or paid. The owner must estimate the dollar value of the time spent to produce income from the property; it is deducted as an expense item. Like the vacancy allowance, expenses must be considered in relation to the future productive life of the property and expressed as a yearly figure at costs prevailing as of the date of appraisal.

The expenses deducted from effective gross income are usually classified as one of the following:

1. Fixed expenses

2. Operating expenses

3. Reserves for replacement

Expense items do not have to be separated into categories. However, be sure to consider all expenses necessary to produce income and to allow for future replacements when you determine estimated net income.

Fixed Expenses

Expenses that are incurred yearly with relatively little change are categorized as fixed expenses. Real estate taxes, license fees, and insurance are the only items normally classified as fixed expenses. Real estate taxes are assessed for the fiscal year, from July 1 to June 30, and are usually paid in two installments. Under Proposition 13, real property is reappraised with the change in ownership. The assessed value usually increases over the previous assessment, and the taxes increase. The definition of market value assumes the sale of the subject property. In estimating taxes, the appraiser must use the anticipated taxes to the potential buyer, not the past taxes to the present owner. The tax rate is set at 1 percent of property value plus any bonds or assessments outstanding. Usually, the total tax rate is 1.1 to 1.25 percent of value. Insurance on a property usually includes fire, liability, and extended coverage. The insurance coverage normal for the type of property being appraised should be used as a cost basis. The appraiser must be careful when extracting insurance charges from the owner's operating statement. Many policies are written and paid for on a 3-year basis and must be prorated for one year. Separate policies may have been written for fire and liability coverage, while the payment indicated may include only one of the policies. If the accuracy of the insurance charges is doubtful, obtain current rates from a local insurance agent.

Operating Expenses

All expenditures to provide services for tenants are classified as operating expenses. Operating expenses usually cover utilities, administration, and maintenance and repairs.

Utilities furnished by the owner vary with the type of property and the terms of the rental agreement. In an apartment house, the owner usually provides water, garbage service, electricity for common area lighting and utility rooms, and gas for central water heaters. In some apartment projects, the owner provides all utilities except telephone. Utilities may be charged to the tenants at a flat monthly rate; however, they are usually included in the rent. Owner and tenant both can save by purchasing each utility service through one meter rather than through separate meters for each apartment. The appraiser should determine what utilities the owner provides the tenants before estimating the economic rent schedule and utility expenses.

If it is practical, the appraiser should itemize separately the estimated cost of the various utilities—water, electricity, gas, garbage service, and so on. The cost of utilities varies with type and age of apartment building, size of apartment units, and type of occupancy. Obviously, expenses for electricity and water are greater in a garden apartment with extensive landscaping and outside lighting than in a high-rise apartment. A two-bedroom apartment occupied by a family may use four times the amount of utilities used by a single-occupancy one-bedroom unit.

Utility expenses can be obtained from the operating statement of the subject property. Analyze the expenses for at least one full year to compensate for seasonal differences in utility costs.

Administration expense is the cost of direct management and services related to the management of property. In a small apartment house, the only administrative expense is usually the wages of a resident manager, who shows and leases apartment units, collects rent, maintains the grounds, and sometimes performs minor building maintenance and repairs. Payment to the resident manager is usually in the form of reduced rent for the living unit, amounting to approximately 5 percent of rent collected. Additional payments are often made for maintenance and repair work. If the property has no resident manager and the owner performs the management functions, an estimated cost for management must still be included as an expense.

In a large apartment complex, administrative expenses may also include supervisory management, leasing fees, office expense, and legal and accounting fees. Many real estate and management companies will completely operate an apartment house, hiring resident managers and other personnel, arranging for repairs and maintenance, leasing units, and keeping the books. The owners receive a monthly statement accounting for rent collection and disbursements of funds. Real estate companies charge approximately 5 percent of collected gross income for their supervisory management, in addition to the normal costs of the resident manager, repairs, and maintenance.

Maintenance expenses include both buildings and grounds. Building maintenance and repairs are closely allied and usually grouped together. The annual cost of maintenance and minor repairs should be estimated. Do not rely on the owner's operating statement when you estimate maintenance and repair expenses. Many major maintenance items, such as painting, may be incurred only once every 3 to 5 years and may or may not be included in the owner's operating statement as an expense item in any one year. If the operating expenses of the property for the past 5 years or so are available, you can estimate average maintenance and repair expenses from the past experience of the property. The actual operating expenses are useful for establishing monthly or yearly maintenance costs for items under service contract, such as swimming pool, gardening, elevator, and air-conditioning.

Estimates for maintenance and repairs are often based on a percentage of gross income or on dollars per square foot of building area. Although guidelines have been established for various types of property, expenditures vary widely with facilities. In a small apartment house the major maintenance expense is usually painting. A large apartment complex may have 5 to 10 major maintenance items. You will make the most accurate expense estimate by considering major maintenance items separately from the allowance included for miscellaneous repairs.

Reserve for Replacements

An annual reserve allowance for replacement of building components and chattels having a life shorter than the future economic life of the property should be estimated and deducted as an operating expense from the gross income. Replacement items may be grouped as (1) components that are an integral part of the building, (2) chattels normally included in the sale and lease of the real property, and (3) furniture.

Building components having a shorter life than that of the total structure include roof covering, floor covering, water heaters, furnace, elevators, and air conditioners. These items may be replaced two or three times during the economic life of the building. Some appraisers argue that replacement of major building items increases the economic life of the building and upgrades the structure, and therefore should be treated as a capital addition rather than an annual expense. This may be true; however, some allowance must be made for replacement of these items during the life of the building, the time period for which the anticipated income was estimated.

The annual allowance for replacement of building components is usually determined by estimating the replacement cost new of each item and dividing it by the anticipated useful life of that item (assuming the item were new). For example, if the replacement cost of a furnace is $2,400 and its estimated useful life is 20 years, an annual reserve of $120 would be made for each furnace. An allowance is made in this manner for each applicable building component. In practice, one lump sum is usually included as a reserve for all short-lived building components. In estimating the useful life of building components, the appraiser should consider the estimated expense for maintenance and repairs, which is also deducted from gross income. Maintenance and repair extend the useful life of building components.

Chattels that are normally included in apartment houses and considered part of the real estate—stoves, refrigerators, carpets, and drapes—usually have shorter lives than the building itself. Therefore, reserve allowances similar to those for short-lived building components must be estimated for their replacement. The amount of reserve for chattel replacement is estimated in the same manner as the reserve for the building components.

Furniture in an apartment house includes household furnishings such as beds, dressers, tables, and chairs. A reserve for replacement of furniture is established only if the gross income estimate included the income attributable to the furniture. The annual reserve for furniture replacement is estimated in the same manner as the reserve for replacement of building components.

BROKER'S NET

People in the real estate field often refer to broker's net when discussing income-producing properties. *Broker's net* is the net income from a property as computed by the real estate broker or salesperson. There is no standardized method for determining broker's net income. It usually differs from the appraiser's estimate of net income in the following ways:

1. The appraiser estimates an economic rent schedule for the property. Broker's net is based on the actual income schedule.

2. Broker's net usually does not allow for vacancy and rent loss.

3. Only the actual recurring expenses are deducted in computing the broker's net; existing taxes are used rather than increased taxes caused by a change in ownership.

4. Broker's net provides only a minimal allowance, if any, for repairs and maintenance and no allowance for replacement of short-lived building components and chattels.

The broker's net is usually higher than the appraiser's estimate of net income. The appraiser tries to base estimates on the anticipated future expenses of the property. The broker's net, on the other hand, reflects an optimistic analysis of the property for use as a sales tool in the brokerage business.

RECONSTRUCTED OPERATING STATEMENT

The summary of income and expenses prepared by the appraiser is called a reconstructed operating statement. It is basically a reconstruction of the operating statement for a property as prepared by the owner. The owner's operating statement is prepared for a one-year period and is used primarily for tax purposes. The appraiser's reconstructed operating statement is intended to reflect a stabilized estimate of income and expenses. Some items normally included in an owner's operating statement, such as interest and principal payments on loans, depreciation (*accounting* depreciation, that is), and so forth, are not included in the operating statement prepared by the appraiser. Conversely, allowances for vacancy and rent loss, reserves for replacements, and management expense (where management is performed by the owner) may be incorporated in the appraiser's operating statement but not in the owner's accounting statement. Although appraisers should not incorporate into their operating statements the actual income and expenditures of the subject property, they must be prepared to support their estimates, which may differ from the actual history of the property.

Many publications outline typical expenses in apartment house operations. Expenses are usually expressed as a percentage of gross income. Since expenses in apartment houses vary so greatly, published averages should be used only as a guide in analyzing the expenses reported for the property being appraised.

Table 13–1 is a reconstructed operating statement for a 16-unit garden apartment. The total expenses for a modern garden apartment are normally between 30 and 40 percent of the gross income from the apartment. As the building ages, expenses usually increase in relation to income.

DISCUSSION QUESTIONS

1. Outline the basic steps of the income approach.
2. Differentiate between contract rent and economic rent.
3. Define the term *effective gross income* as used in the income approach.

TABLE 13–1   Reconstructed operating statement—16-unit garden apartment

Annual gross rental		
16 units @ $500 per month		
($8,000 per month × 12)		$96,000
Service income		
Laundry facilities (rental basis)		800
Annual gross income		$96,800
Vacancy and rent loss (5%)		4,840
Effective gross income		$91,960
Expenses		
Fixed expenses		
Taxes	$11,000	
Insurance	2,000	
License	100	
Total fixed expenses		$13,100
Operating expenses		
Resident manager 5%	4,600	
Other management 2%	1,840	
Water	1,200	
Gas and electricity	2,400	
Garbage service	800	
Pool service	1,200	
Gardening maintenance	1,800	
Building maintenance	3,000	
Total operating expenses		$16,840
Reserves for replacement		
Stoves, refrigerators, carpets, drapes	3,000	
Building components	2,000	
Total reserves for replacement		$ 5,000
Total expenses		$34,940
Net income		$57,020

4. What are the three categories of expenses considered in estimating the net income attributable to a property?

5. What is a reconstructed operating statement? How does it differ from a similar statement prepared by the owner's accountant?

6. What items are usually classified as operating expenses?

7. Why is the income approach not normally used in the valuation of single-family residences?

8. What is the reserve for replacement allowance, as used in appraising? What items does it include?

MULTIPLE-CHOICE QUESTIONS

1. The actual rent a property brings is called
   a. Contract rent
   b. Economic rent
   c. Effective rent
   d. None of the above

2. In considering gross income for appraisal purposes, which of the following rent schedules is used?
   a. Effective rent
   b. Economic rent
   c. Contract rent
   d. None of the above

3. Effective gross income is determined by
   a. Subtracting a vacancy rate from the gross income
   b. Adding a vacancy rate to the gross income
   c. Subtracting contract rent from economic rent
   d. None of the above

4. Net income is determined by
   a. Subtracting fixed expenses from gross income
   b. Subtracting fixed expenses, operating expenses, and reserves from gross income
   c. Subtracting fixed expenses, operating expenses, and reserves from effective gross income
   d. None of the above

5. Real property taxes fall into which of the following expense categories?
   a. Operating expenses
   b. Fixed expenses
   c. Reserves for replacement
   d. None of the above

6. Management expenses fall into which of the following expense categories?
   a. Fixed expenses
   b. Reserves for replacement
   c. Operating expenses
   d. All of the above

7. Accounting expenses fall into which of the following expense categories?
   a. Fixed expenses
   b. Operating expenses
   c. Indirect expenses
   d. None of the above

8. Expenses that are incurred yearly with relatively little change are
   a. Operating expenses
   b. Fixed expenses
   c. Direct expenses
   d. Indirect expenses

9. When discussing income-producing properties, a broker's net usually differs from the appraiser's net income estimate in which of the following ways?
   a. The broker's net does not consider gross income.
   b. The broker's net does not allow for vacancy and rent loss.

c. The broker's net does not allow for reserves for replacement.
d. Both b and c

10. A prudent buyer would be well advised to consider the value estimate of an income property by a competent, honest, objective, appraiser over the average broker because
   a. The broker's net is usually higher than the appraiser's estimate of net income.
   b. The appraiser's estimate is based on anticipated future expenses and income.
   c. The broker's net reflects an optimistic analysis of the property for use as a sales tool in the brokerage business.
   d. All of the above

11. A summary of income and expenses prepared by an appraiser is called
   a. An appraisal
   b. An estimate of value
   c. A preliminary estimate of value
   d. A reconstructed operating statement

12. A vacancy and rent loss percentage estimate by an appraiser normally falls between
   a. 15 and 25 percent
   b. 10 and 15 percent
   c. 2 and 10 percent
   d. None of the above

13. For appraisal purposes, when contract rent exceeds economic rent the appraiser should consider
   a. Contract rent
   b. Economic rent
   c. Neither a nor b
   d. Both a and b

14. For appraisal purposes, when economic rent exceeds contract rent the appraiser should consider
   a. Contract rent
   b. Economic rent
   c. Neither a nor b
   d. Both a and b

15. Reserves for replacement as an expense item affect which of the following?
   a. Components that are an integral part of the building
   b. Chattels normally included in the sale and lease of the real property
   c. Furniture and kitchen appliances
   d. All of the above

Chapter 14

INCOME APPROACH: CAPITALIZATION THEORY AND TECHNIQUES

Body of Knowledge Topics

- *Direct Capitalization*

- *Gross Rent Multiplier*

At the beginning of Chapter 13, we said that the income approach measures the present worth of the net income a property will produce during its remaining economic life. The process of estimating the present worth of a property based on its anticipated income is *capitalization*. There are several methods of capitalizing net income; the method discussed in this chapter is *direct* capitalization. Annuity methods of capitalization, such as the Ellwood Compound Interest Tables and the Hoskold Sinking Fund, have a limited application and therefore are not discussed in this book. There are also capitalization methods based on equity yield and mortgage terms. These methods, such as the Ellwood Tables, are best reserved for studies in advanced appraising or investment property analysis.

Capitalization is a discounting process. A sum of $1,000 payable 2 years hence is not worth $1,000 today. The expected income of $1,000 must be discounted for the loss of 2 years' interest. Likewise, an anticipated monthly or yearly income from property must be discounted to reflect the current value of the property.

The classic illustration of the change in values over time is the *Six Functions of One Dollar* chart shown in Figure 14–1, which expresses the results of six types of calculations meaningful to investors.

Various tables and mathematical formulas are used in capitalization. We divide the net annual income by the capitalization rate to indicate the value of the property:

Net income/Capitalization rate = Present value

or

1. The value of $1 in 12 months from now—Future Value of $1.
2. The compounded value of a $1 per year investment in an annuity, assuming a fixed interest rate over time—Future Value Annuity $1 per Year.
3. The amount of investment required each year, assuming a fixed rate of interest, to accumulate $1—Sinking Fund Factor
4. The amount of investment required now, assuming a fixed interest rate, in order to realize a return of $1 at the end of a specific period of years—Present Value of $1. This is referred to as *reversion*.
5. The amount of investment required now, assuming a fixed interest rate, in order to receive an annual payment of $1 for a specific period of years—Present Value Annuity of $1 per Year.
6. The annual payment needed to satisfy a loan of $1 for a specific number of years—Installment to Amortize $1. This is an annual, not monthly, amount.

Years	1 Amount of One	2 Amount of One Per Period	3 Sinking Fund Factor	4 Present Worth of One	5 Present Worth One Per Period	6 Partial Payment
1	1.080 000	1.000 000	1.000 000	.925 926	.925 926	1.080 000
2	1.166 400	2.080 000	.480 769	.857 339	1.783 265	.560 769
3	1.259 712	3.246 400	.308 034	.793 832	2.577 097	.388 034
4	1.360 489	4.506 112	.221 921	.735 030	3.312 127	.301 921
5	1.469 328	5.866 601	.170 456	.680 583	3.992 710	.250 456
6	1.586 874	7.335 929	.136 315	.630 170	4.622 880	.216 315
7	1.713 824	8.922 803	.112 072	.583 490	5.206 370	.192 072
8	1.850 930	10.636 628	.094 015	.540 269	5.746 639	.174 015
9	1.999 005	12.487 558	.080 080	.500 249	6.246 888	.160 080
10	2.158 925	14.486 562	.069 029	.463 193	6.710 081	.149 029
11	2.331 639	16.645 487	.060 076	.428 883	7.138 964	.140 076
12	2.518 170	18.977 126	.052 695	.397 114	7.536 078	.132 695
13	2.719 624	21.495 297	.046 522	.367 698	7.903 776	.126 522
14	2.937 194	24.214 920	.041 297	.340 461	8.244 237	.121 297
15	3.172 169	27.152 114	.036 830	.315 242	8.559 479	.116 830
16	3.425 943	30.324 283	.032 977	.291 890	8.851 369	.112 977
17	3.700 018	33.750 226	.029 629	.270 269	9.121 638	.109 629
18	3.996 019	37.450 244	.026 702	.250 249	9.371 887	.106 702
19	4.315 701	41.446 263	.024 128	.231 712	9.603 599	.104 128
20	4.660 957	45.761 964	.021 852	.214 548	9.818 147	.101 852
21	5.033 834	50.422 921	.019 832	.198 656	10.016 803	.099 832
22	5.436 540	55.456 755	.018 032	.183 941	10.200 744	.098 032
23	5.871 464	60.893 296	.016 422	.170 315	10.371 059	.096 422
24	6.341 181	66.764 759	.014 978	.157 699	10.528 758	.094 978
25	6.848 475	73.105 940	.013 679	.146 018	10.674 776	.093 679
26	7.396 353	79.954 415	.012 507	.135 202	10.809 978	.092 507
27	7.988 061	87.350 768	.011 448	.125 187	10.935 165	.091 448
28	8.627 106	95.338 830	.010 489	.115 914	11.051 078	.090 489
29	9.317 275	103.965 936	.009 619	.107 328	11.158 406	.089 619
30	10.062 657	113.283 211	.008 827	.099 377	11.257 783	.088 827
31	10.867 669	123.345 868	.008 107	.092 016	11.349 799	.088 107
32	11.737 083	134.213 537	.007 451	.085 200	11.434 999	.087 451
33	12.676 050	145.950 620	.006 852	.078 889	11.513 888	.086 852
34	13.690 134	158.626 670	.006 304	.073 045	11.586 934	.086 304
35	14.785 344	172.316 804	.005 803	.067 635	11.654 568	.085 803
36	15.968 172	187.102 148	.005 345	.062 625	11.717 193	.085 345
37	17.245 626	203.070 320	.004 924	.057 986	11.775 179	.084 924
38	18.625 276	220.315 945	.004 539	.053 690	11.828 869	.084 539
39	20.115 298	238.941 221	.004 185	.049 713	11.878 582	.084 185
40	21.724 521	259.056 519	.003 860	.046 031	11.924 613	.083 860
41	23.462 483	280.781 040	.003 561	.042 621	11.967 235	.083 561
42	25.339 482	304.243 523	.003 287	.039 464	12.006 699	.083 287
43	27.366 640	329.583 005	.003 034	.036 541	12.043 240	.083 034
44	29.555 972	356.949 646	.002 802	.033 834	12.077 074	.082 802
45	31.920 449	386.505 617	.002 587	.031 328	12.108 402	.082 587
46	34.474 085	418.426 067	.002 390	.029 007	12.137 409	.082 390
47	37.232 012	452.900 152	.002 208	.026 859	12.164 267	.082 208
48	40.210 573	490.132 164	.002 040	.024 869	12.189 136	.082 040
49	43.427 419	530.342 737	.001 886	.023 027	12.212 163	.081 886
50	46.901 613	573.770 156	.001 743	.021 321	12.233 485	.081 743
51	50.653 742	620.671 769	.001 611	.019 742	12.253 227	.081 611
52	54.706 041	671.325 510	.001 490	.018 280	12.271 506	.081 490
53	59.082 524	726.031 551	.001 377	.016 925	12.288 432	.081 377
54	63.809 126	785.114 075	.001 274	.015 672	12.304 103	.081 274
55	68.913 856	848.923 201	.001 178	.014 511	12.318 614	.081 178
56	74.426 965	917.837 058	.001 090	.013 436	12.332 050	.081 090
57	80.381 122	992.264 022	.001 008	.012 441	12.344 491	.081 008
58	86.811 612	1072.645 144	.000 932	.011 519	12.356 010	.080 932
59	93.756 540	1159.456 755	.000 862	.010 666	12.366 676	.080 862
60	101.257 064	1253.213 296	.000 798	.009 876	12.376 552	.080 798

$$S^n = (1 + i)^n \qquad S_{\overline{n}|} = \frac{S^n - 1}{i} \qquad 1/S_{\overline{n}|} = \frac{i}{S^n - 1} \qquad V^n = \frac{1}{S^n} \qquad A_{\overline{n}|} = \frac{1 - 1/S^n}{i} \qquad \frac{1}{A_{\overline{n}|}} = \frac{i}{1 - 1/S^n}$$

FIGURE 14–1   Six Functions of One Dollar—8.0 % annual interest rate, base 1.08.

If any two factors of this formula are known, the third can be computed. If present value and net income are known, the capitalization rate can be computed as follows: $I/V = R$. To compute net income when value and rate are known, the formula $R \times V = I$ is used. This is the process of direct capitalization.

CAPITALIZATION RATES

The rate used in the capitalization of income is the annual rate of return from a property that an investor demands before he or she will purchase that property. Capitalization rate is a composite of the interest rate (return *on* an investment) and the recapture rate (return *of* an investment). If income is produced by land only, capitalization rate and interest rate are synonymous. When buildings or other improvements contribute to the production of income, an allowance must be made for recapture of the value of the improvements. Structural improvements have a limited economic life, while land may be used indefinitely.

A buyer who will pay $1 million for a property yielding an annual net income of $90,000, is indicating willingness to purchase the property at a 9 percent capitalization rate. If a number of sellers and buyers are willing to transfer similar property on the same terms, the capitalization rate indicated for this particular type of property is 9 percent. We apply these data to the capitalization process: an annual net income of $90,000 divided by the capitalization rate of 9 percent indicates a property value of $1 million:

$$\$90,000/0.09 = \$1,000,000$$

In some capitalization techniques, net income from a property is segregated between land and improvements. Income to the land is capitalized at the interest rate and income to the improvements is capitalized at a rate that combines the interest rate and an annual recapture rate. The recapture rate is computed by dividing the remaining economic life of the improvements into 100 percent. The annual recapture rate for a building with an estimated remaining life of 50 years would be 2 percent:

$$100\%/50 = 2\%$$

The recapture rate for a building with a remaining economic life of 40 years would be 2.5%:

$$100\%/40 = 2.5\%$$

Real estate competes with all other types of investment for available investment funds. When estimating the rate of return (capitalization rate) demanded by investors, the appraiser must consider many characteristics of the investment (which is individual property, in this case). The main items are described here.

1. *Reliability of net income.* The appraiser must evaluate certainty of future income and expenses. A property on a long-term net lease to a responsible lessee is more desirable and would probably attract capital funds at a lower rate than a similar property on a month-to-month tenancy.

2. *Liquidity.* An investment that can be readily sold, such as stocks and bonds, is usually preferable to an asset like real estate or machinery that may require weeks or months to sell. Similarly, an investment that can be acquired in relatively small denominations has a much wider market of prospective purchasers than a larger investment.

3. *Burden of management.* In this case, we mean general supervision and care of the investment, not management of the type that would be deducted from the income as an operating expense. Investment assets require different degrees of management. Bonds and mortgages require virtually none. A real property under a long-term net lease requires less management than a property under a month-to-month tenancy.

4. *Probability of increase or decrease in value.* The probability of a change in value varies with the type of investment and individual asset. Bonds and mortgages are likely to remain stable in capital value. Real estate and corporate stocks often increase or decrease in value. If the buyers and sellers anticipate an increase in the capital value of an asset, the present yield rate will be less than the rate for an asset of stable or decreasing value.

5. *Taxation.* The income tax treatment of anticipated future benefits from an investment can influence the capitalization rate. Tax-free municipal bonds are purchased at a lower yield rate than similar taxable bonds. Real estate may benefit from a depreciation allowance for improvements. Investment in real estate and corporate stocks may also be preferred because a gain at the time of sale will be treated as a capital gain.

6. *Hypothecation.* Being able to use a capital asset as collateral for borrowing money is an advantage. Assets that fluctuate rapidly in value do not normally serve as good collateral.

Let us compare real estate with other forms of investment. Real estate does not have the liquidity of stocks and bonds. Most real estate involves greater risk as to the reliability of net income than most bonds and mortgages. The burden of management is usually greater for real estate than for other investments. One of the most important characteristics of real estate and of corporate common stocks is their potential appreciation in value as a hedge against inflation. Real estate owners benefit from preferential income tax treatment more than owners of most other investments. Real estate is one of the best assets as collateral for loans.

Just as real estate competes with other investments for capital funds, each parcel of real estate competes with every other parcel. Capitalization rates for real property vary with the type, age, and condition of the property, location and surrounding development, and existing economic conditions. The more secure the future net income, the lower the capitalization rate. A lower rate would be used in capitalizing the income from an apartment house in a well-maintained and stable neighborhood than in an area of declining economic conditions. The difference in capitalization rates would reflect people's judgment of the quality of the properties in relation to the features we listed for a good investment. In an undesirable neighborhood, the capitalization rate might be higher because the reliability of income is poorer, the probability of appreciation in value is less, and the burden of management is greater.

The age, condition, and construction of the buildings on improved properties have a direct effect on the capitalization rate. Capitalization rate is a combination of interest rate and recapture rate. The value of improvements must be recaptured during their remaining economic life. The shorter the future economic life of the improvements, the greater the annual allowance for recapture. The value of a building with an estimated future economic life of 50 years must be recaptured at a rate of 2 percent per year. The value of a building with an estimated future economic life of 20 years must be recaptured at a rate of 5 percent per year. Usually, the older the building, the cheaper the construction, or the poorer the condition, the shorter will be the estimated future economic life and the greater will be the annual recapture rate.

SELECTION OF CAPITALIZATION RATES

Selecting the capitalization rate is one of the most important parts of the capitalization process. A minor change in the rate will cause a substantial difference in property value. A rate increase from 8 to 9 percent will result in an 11 percent decrease in value. For example, capitalizing a net income of $60,000 per year at 8 percent indicates a value of $750,000:

$$\$60,000/0.08 = \$750,000$$

Capitalizing the same income at a 9 percent rate indicates a value of $666,670:

$$\$60,000/0.09 = \$666,670$$

There are three basic types of rates used in the direct capitalization process. *Interest rate* is the return on an investment necessary to attract capital funds. The interest rate is applicable only to the net income from the land. A *capitalization rate* consisting of the interest rate plus an annual allowance for recapture of improvement value is applicable only to the net income from improvements. A *composite capitalization rate* providing in one rate a return on the investment and a return of the investment value is applicable to the net income from the improved property.

The type of capitalization rate selected depends on the capitalization technique used. All capitalization rates consist of an interest rate and a recapture rate. The appraiser attempts to select a capitalization rate that reflects the actions of buyers and sellers for the particular type and class of property.

Three methods have been developed to aid the appraiser in selecting a capitalization rate:

1. Comparative sales method

2. Band-of-investment method

3. Summation method

Comparative Sales Method

Selection of a capitalization rate from comparative sales involves a direct analysis of transactions between buyers and sellers in the market. The capitalization rate indicated by a sale is determined by dividing the sale price into the net income from the property. A sales price of $600,000 for a property with an annual net income of $57,000 would indicate a capitalization rate of 9.5 percent for that particular transaction:

$$\$57,000 / \$600,000 = 9.5\%$$

Sales of several similar properties must be analyzed in the same manner and the indicated rates correlated into one.

Selection of a capitalization rate by the comparative sales method is considered the most appropriate method, since it directly reflects the capitalization rates at which properties are bought and sold. The mathematics of this method are simple; however, the application has many hazards. The appraiser must use good judgment in selecting a capitalization rate. Before accepting a rate estimated by the comparative sales method, several factors must be considered:

1. The comparative sales should be recent. Capitalization rates change with general economic conditions.

2. The net income imputed to the sale properties must be derived in the same way as that of the subject property. If applicable, the same type of expenses must be deducted from the gross income of the sale parcel as from the gross income of the subject property. Often, the same ratio of gross income to net income as was estimated for the subject property is used for the sale property.

3. The sale property should be located in the same neighborhood

as the subject property or in a neighborhood considered equally desirable.

4. The improvements of the sale property should be similar to those of the subject property in type or class, age and condition, size, construction, and ratio of building to land.

In appraisal practice, it is often difficult to obtain sufficient sales data to derive a capitalization rate directly applicable to the subject property. It may be necessary to adjust the capitalization rates indicated by the sales to the rate proper for the subject property. Adjustment of rates indicated by other sales and correlation of these rates to select a capitalization rate for the subject property involve the appraiser's judgment.

As we said before, differences in capitalization rates reflect the quality of the properties in relation to the features of a good investment. If a sale property indicates a rate of 11 percent, any features of the sale property that are superior to the subject property indicate a rate higher than 11 percent for the subject. Conversely, features of the subject property that are superior to the sale property indicate a rate lower than 11 percent for the subject. A capitalization rate from a comparative sale may be adjusted up or down for any number of differences; however, the more adjustments necessary, the less reliable the indicated capitalization rate.

Capitalization rates derived from properties with structural improvements include both an interest rate and a recapture allowance. If you want to know only the interest rate, you can compute it by deducting the building recapture rate from the overall, or composite, rate. Since the recapture portion of the capitalization rate applies only to the income attributable to the improvements, you must segregate land and building values for the sale property.

Estimate the remaining economic life of the building. Multiply the annual recapture rate by the building value to determine the annual recapture in dollars. Deduct this figure from the net income to determine net income after recapture. Dividing the sale price into the net income after recapture yields the interest rate. Assume the figures are as follows:

Sale price		$800,000
Building value		$600,000
Remaining life of building	50 years	
Annual net income		$72,000

You would compute the interest rate by the comparative sales method as follows:

Net income		72,000
Recapture of building		
(2% × $600,000)		−12,000
Net income after recapture	=	$60,000
Interest rate	$ 60,000 =	7.50%
	$800,000	

Estimating a capitalization rate by the comparative sales method is the most practical method. In practice, the appraiser keeps abreast of current capitalization rates by a continual analysis of property sales and listings and by discussions with informed buyers and sellers.

Band-of-Investment Method

The band-of-investment method combines the mortgage interest rate available to the property and the equity rate of return necessary to attract investors. A weighted average, based on the percentage and rate of the mortgage and equity, is computed to indicate an interest rate for use in the capitalization process. Assume a mortgage, or deed of trust, is available for 70 percent of the property value at 11 percent interest and that the equity rate, which would be 30 percent of the property value, demands a 12 percent return. The interest rate by the band-of-investment method would be computed as shown in Table 14–1.

The ratio of loan to property value and the interest rate available to the subject property can be learned from local lending institutions. However, the buyer's credit standing and the business relationship between buyer and lending institution may substantially affect the terms of a loan. The equity rate is even more difficult to establish than the mortgage rate. Most people agree that the equity position involves greater risk than the mortgage position and therefore necessitates a higher rate of return. However, the return to the investor includes the annual net income plus the anticipated appreciation in property value that will be realized when the property is sold. If the investor requires an overall return of 14 percent to purchase an income-producing property, this yield may be provided by a 9 percent annual rate of return (capitalization rate) and a 5 percent annual anticipated increase in property value. If the total return anticipated from the purchase of real property is greater than the mortgage interest rate, the investor can potentially increase the investment return by reducing the down payment (equity) and borrowing funds against the property. During periods of increasing real estate values, required equity returns will usually be less than mortgage rates. The most realistic method of esti-

TABLE 14–1   Interest rate computed by the band-of-investment method

	Percent of value		Rate		Product
First mortgage	70	×	11%	=	7.7%
Equity	30	×	7%	=	2.1%
Interest rate indicated					9.8%

mating the equity rate of return demanded for a particular investment is from an analysis of comparative sales.

The basic premise of the band-of-investment method is that the mortgage loan available to a property reflects current economic conditions and various qualities of the property that influence the rate of return demanded by investors. For instance, the best first mortgage available on an older apartment house may be 60 percent of value at 12 percent interest. A loan on a newer apartment may be available for 75 percent of value at 11 percent interest. The difference in terms between the two loans reflects the lending institution's rating of the risk and quality of the two properties.

The rate indicated by the band-of-investment method is an interest rate only. A recapture rate must be added for capitalizing income from improved properties. An overall capitalization rate can be developed by the band-of-investment method to include both interest and recapture. The method is similar to that discussed above, except that instead of the interest rate from a mortgage, the total annual payment rate for both interest and amortization of the loan is used. In effect, this substitutes the amortization rate of the loan for the recapture rate of the improvements. The rationale of this method is that a lending institution will not normally extend the loan period beyond the expected economic life of the improvements. The shorter the future economic life, the less the loan period, and therefore the higher the amortization rate.

Assume a first mortgage loan for 70 percent of value, 11 percent interest rate, and 25-year term. The combined annual interest and amortization (principal or recapture) rate, derived from a mortgage payment schedule, is 11.76 percent. For example, a loan of $400,000 with annual payment of $47,040 would yield an interest and amortization rate of 11.76 percent. The capitalization rate would be computed as shown in Table 14–2.

There is some justification for relating capitalization interest rates to current mortgage rates. Capitalization rates and mortgage rates tend to fluctuate in the same direction; however, the *direct* relationship between mortgage rate and capitalization rate for a particular property is questionable. The band-of-investment method can be used as a check on the comparative sales method or as a means of estimating a capitalization rate when sufficient sales data are not available.

TABLE 14–2 Capitalization rate computed by band of investment

	Percent of value		Rate		Product
First mortgage	70%	×	11.76%	=	8.2%
Equity	30%	×	7.0%	=	2.1%
Capitalization rate	100%		10.3%		

Summation Method

The summation method establishes a safe rate for an investment and adds or subtracts from this basic rate according to the proper interest rate for the subject property. The safe rate chosen is usually that of a risk-free investment, such as savings deposits or government bonds. Additions or subtractions are made by percentages for investment characteristics considered more or less desirable than the safe-rate investment. The six characteristics to be considered in evaluating an investment, discussed earlier in this chapter, are:

1. Reliability of net income

2. Liquidity

3. Burden of management

4. Probability of increase or decrease in value

5. Taxation

6. Hypothecation

Those are the major characteristics of any investment. The relative importance of any particular characteristic depends on the type of investment being evaluated. Although other investment characteristics might be added to the list, enlarging it would result in overlapping of elements or including items of minor importance. For instance, risk is a major consideration in an investment. However, risk is considered with both the reliability of net income and the probability of increase or decrease in value.

The appraiser prepares a chart, such as the one that follows, that shows how the subject property differs in investment characteristics from the safe rate investment.

Safe rate	8.0%
Adjustments	
Reliability of net income	+ 2.0%
Liquidity	+ 1.5%
Burden of management	+ 1.0%
Probability of increase	
in value (appreciation)	−4.0%
Indicated interest rate	8.5%

The rate derived by the summation method is an interest rate. Any allowance necessary for the recapture of improvement cost must be added to this rate.

Estimating a capitalization rate by the summation method requires considerable subjective judgment on the part of the appraiser. For this reason, it is best to use this method only as a check against one of the other available methods.

CAPITALIZATION TECHNIQUES

We have discussed the direct capitalization of income. The capitalization formula $I/R = V$ is basic to the income approach.

I Net annual income

R Interest, or capitalization, rate

V Property value

Assume that a vacant parcel of land is rented for use as an automobile sales lot. The net income to the owner is $24,000 per year. The interest rate applicable to this type of property is 8 percent. The value of the property is indicated by the income approach as follows:

$$\$24,000/8\% = \$300,000 \quad \text{or} \quad \$24,000/.08 = \$300,000$$

In valuing the land at $300,000, we assume that the net income of $24,000 per year will continue indefinitely. In fact, however, the net income will probably increase or decrease at some future date. What we are actually measuring is a ratio between income and value as reflected by the market. If we analyze comparative sales and find that the rate of return required by buyers of similar land suitable for automobile sales lots is 8 percent, we assume that the subject property will also sell based on an 8 percent return. The possible future increase or decrease in net income has already been taken into consideration by buyers and sellers in the market; it is reflected in the interest rate estimated for the subject property.

The productive life of land usually continues indefinitely. Land use may change, buildings may be constructed, and land value may increase or decrease. However, land is perpetual and normally capable of producing income continuously. Buildings, on the other hand, have a limited life. Income from improved property is produced by both the land and the building. Income attributable to the building is limited by the remaining economic life of the building. The value of the building must be recaptured over its remaining economic life. Income attributable to the land is perpetual.

We provide for recapture of building value in equal annual installments. This method is called *straight-line recapture.* There are other recapture methods, but they need not concern us in this book. The three techniques we shall use in capitalization of income from improved property differ only in the provision for recapture of improvement value. They are all called *residual techniques,* since the capitalization is to the residual net income attributable to the land, building, or property, as a whole. The three techniques are:

1. Property residual technique

2. Building residual technique

3. Land residual technique

Which technique is selected depends on the validity of market data available for use in estimating the capitalization rate and substantiating land or building value of the individual subject property. The capitalization process begins with the same net income figure regardless of the technique used.

Property Residual Technique

The property residual technique is the simplest and most direct method of capitalizing the net income from improved property. The method is the same one used for capitalizing the income from vacant land, except that instead of capitalizing with an interest rate only, a composite rate of interest and recapture is used. If net income to the property is $90,000 per year and the overall capitalization rate is estimated to be 12 percent, the property value indicated by the income approach would be computed as follows:

$$\$90,000/0.12 = \$750,000 \text{ (property value)}$$

The most important element in the property residual technique is selection of the capitalization rate. The rate should be developed by the comparative sales method. We have discussed the selection of a proper capitalization rate. The comparative sales must be similar to the subject property in location and improvements and in the manner in which net income is estimated.

Building Residual Technique

The building residual technique is used when the land value is known and the building value is unknown. This technique allocates the net income from the property between land and improvements. In applying the technique, you must first estimate the value of the subject land (see Chapter 7). Multiply the land value by the applicable interest rate to determine the income attributable to the land. Deduct income to the land from net income to determine income attributable to improvements. Capitalize income to the improvements at the interest rate plus recapture rate to derive improvement value. Add land value to improvement value to indicate property value by the building residual technique. For example, assume the following figures:

Annual net income from property	$ 80,000
Land value	$200,000
Interest rate	7%
Recapture rate (based on remaining economic life of 25 years)	4%

Valuation by the building residual technique is computed as follows:

Net income	$ 80,000
Income to land	
$200,000 × 7%	$ 14,000
Income to improvements	$ 66,000
Capitalization rate: 11%	
(7% + 4%)	
Indicated improvement value	
$66,000/11%	$600,000
Land value	$200,000
Property value indicated by building residual technique	$800,000

The building residual technique is used primarily to value property in cases where the improvements show substantial depreciation, especially functional and/or economic obsolescence. In such cases it is often difficult to find enough sales of property similar to the subject property to develop the overall, or composite, capitalization rate necessary for the property residual technique. The building residual technique may be used any time land value can be substantiated and an overall capitalization rate cannot readily be developed from sales.

Land Residual Technique

The land residual technique is used when the building value is known and the land value is unknown. The land residual technique is similar to the building residual technique, except that the improvement value must be estimated, rather than the land value. The improvement value is multiplied by the applicable building capitalization rate (interest rate recapture) to indicate income attributable to improvements. Income to improvements is deducted from net income to indicate income attributable to land. Income to the land is capitalized at the interest rate to indicate land value. Improvement value is added to land value to derive property value by the land residual technique.

Assume the same figures we used in the building residual technique example, except that improvement value is $600,000 and land value is unknown. Valuation by the land residual technique is computed as follows:

Net income	$80,000
Income to improvements	
$600,000 × 11%	$66,000
Income to land	$14,000
Indicated land value	
($14,000/7%)	$200,000
Improvement value	$600,000
Property value indicated by land residual technique	$800,000

The land residual technique may be used when the estimated improvement value can be substantiated. The improvements should be relatively new and should represent the highest and best use of the land. Like the building residual technique, the land residual technique is normally used only when an overall capitalization rate is not readily available from comparative sales.

The land residual technique may also be used to check the economic feasibility of a proposed building development. A comparison between the capitalized value of the land, indicated by the land residual approach, and the asking price or land value, indicated by sales, may be used to justify the economic feasibility of the building construction.

GROSS RENT MULTIPLIER

At the beginning of this chapter, we discussed the difficulty of relating home ownership amenities to dollar income. The appraisal of a single-family residence is not adapted to the theory of the income approach. Since more than one of every five single-family residences in California is occupied on a rental basis, we should give some consideration to income potential in appraising the single-family home, especially when the subject property is tenant occupied.

In single-family residence appraisal, the gross rent multiplier (sometimes called gross income multiplier) is applied through the income method of valuation. The gross rent multiplier is also used in appraising multiple-family residential and commercial properties, but is included as part of the market data approach.

The gross rent multiplier is a factor of the ratio between gross rent and sales price. The gross rent multiplier for the subject property is estimated on the basis of an analysis of the ratio between the sale price and gross rent for a number of comparable properties. The sale price of a property is divided by its gross monthly rent to determine a gross rent multiplier factor. The rent multipliers of several comparable sales should be determined and analyzed to estimate the proper gross rent multiplier for the subject property.

To Det. gross rent mult.

Let us derive a gross rent multiplier from an analysis of five comparable sales, shown in Table 14–3.

The rent multipliers range from 122 to 133. We must analyze the sale properties and select a gross rent multiplier to be applied to the subject property. The rent multipliers are ratios between price and rent *at the time of sale,* and no adjustments are necessary. The five considerations in analyzing the sale properties follow:

1. The sales should be recent. Rent multipliers may change with economic conditions.

TABLE 14–3   Analysis of five comparable sales

Property	Monthly rent	Sale price	Rent multiplier
A	$800	$104,000	130
B	740	94,000	127
C	900	110,000	122
D	800	106,000	133
E	760	100,000	132

2. The sale properties should be located in the same or equal neighborhoods as the subject property.

3. The sale properties should be reasonably similar to the subject in all essential physical elements.

4. The rent for the sale properties must be their fair market rent at the time of sale.

5. The ratio of expenses to rent should be similar for sale property and subject.

Properties A, B, and C in Table 14–3 are comparable to the subject property in all these respects. We find that the rent for property D was established years ago and was not considered to be the fair market rent at the time of sale. Property E is an older sale, located in a better neighborhood than the subject property. Based on our analysis, we narrow the rent multiplier range and estimate a reasonable gross rent multiplier of 130 for the subject property. If the present rent and the economic rent for the subject property are $800 per month, we derive the value for the property as follows:

$$\$800 \times 130 = \$104,000$$

Gross rent multipliers for single-family residences, duplexes, and small apartment houses are usually expressed as a monthly multiplier factor. Multipliers applicable to large apartment houses and commercial properties are expressed on a yearly income basis. You can convert a monthly multiplier to a year factor by dividing by 12. A monthly multiplier of 130 would be the same as a yearly multiplier of 10.8.

The gross rent multiplier is a reliable method of valuation only when sufficient sales data are available. As with the income approach, the gross rent for the subject property must be estimated from or substantiated by comparable rents in the area. Many investors in small residential income properties, such as duplexes and fourplexes, rely strongly on a gross rent multiplier in purchasing property.

LIMITATIONS OF THE INCOME APPROACH

1. Generally is not applicable to more expensive single-family residences.

2. When used on single-family or multiple-family residential income property, the gross income (rent) multiplier is most often employed in the real estate industry. This becomes, in essence, a market approach that considers only gross income and may not properly account for differences in operating expenses, management, maintenance, and reserve accounts, which might have a dramatic effect on *net* income.

3. Requires a proper determination of capitalization rates with knowledge of how these rates relate to borrowed capital, both first and secondary financing; safe investment (bank savings accounts, etc.); risk factor of property; management; nonliquidity; tax benefits, such as depreciation and capital gains. Also requires knowledge of hypothecation (lending ability) possibilities of property along with general national, state, regional, and local economic conditions that may affect the appreciation or depreciation of the property.

4. Requires an estimate of future vacancy rates.

5. Requires an estimate of future economic rent.

6. Requires an estimate of future expenses, both fixed and operating.

7. Requires an estimate of future reserve requirements.

8. In determining the rate of return by the comparative sales method it is sometimes difficult to obtain proper income and expense information of comparable properties.

SUMMARY

The income approach measures the present value of a property based on its expected future income. Properties purchased primarily for their income production are most suited to valuation by the income approach.

The first step of the income approach is to develop an economic rent schedule for the subject property. The rent schedule is based on the existing rents and rental data from similar properties in the neighborhood. Any other income attributable to the property is included to determine annual gross income.

An allowance for vacancy and rent loss is deducted from gross income to indicate effective gross income. The vacancy and rent loss allowance is the estimated average annual loss in income during the future productive life of the property.

An estimate of expenditures necessary for the production of income is deducted from effective gross income to determine net income. Expenditures are classified as (1) fixed expenses, (2) operating expenses, and (3) reserves for replacement.

The appraiser prepares a reconstructed operating statement—logically arranged estimate of income, expenses, allowances, and reserves—to determine the estimated net income attributable to the property.

Net income is capitalized, or discounted, to indicate the present value of the property. The capitalization method we discussed is direct capitalization. A capitalization rate applicable to the subject property must be selected for use in processing the net income to a property value. A capitalization rate is a composite of interest *on* an investment and recapture *of* an investment. There are three methods of selecting a capitalization rate: (1) comparative sales method, (2) band-of-investment method, and (3) summation method. Selection of the capitalization rate by comparative sales is the most reliable method, if sufficient sales data are available.

We discussed the three processes—called residual techniques—of capitalizing income: (1) property residual technique, (2) building residual technique, and (3) land residual technique. The proper residual technique to be used depends on available market data and the subject property. The property residual technique is the method most commonly used.

In appraising a single-family residence, the gross rent multiplier is normally used in place of the standard income approach. In valuing income-producing properties, the gross rent multiplier is used as part of the market data approach.

A rent multiplier is a factor of the ratio between sales price and rent, obtained by dividing the monthly gross rent from a sale property into the sale price. Rent multipliers are determined for several sale properties similar to the subject property. A gross rent multiplier applicable to the subject property is selected from the sales data and multiplied by the estimated monthly economic rent for the subject property to indicate the property value.

DISCUSSION QUESTIONS

1. Discuss the theory of capitalization.

2. Define the term *capitalization rate.*

3. What are the main characteristics of investments, as they relate to real estate?

4. What are the main considerations in selecting a capitalization rate?

5. What are the three methods that can be used in selecting a capitalization rate?

6. What are the three types of residual techniques used in the capitalization process?

7. What is a gross rent multiplier?

8. Discuss the basic considerations in analyzing sale properties when estimating a gross rent multiplier.

9. How is a capitalization rate derived by the comparative sales method? Why is this method considered the most appropriate?

MULTIPLE-CHOICE QUESTIONS

1. The appraisal process of estimating the present worth of a property based on its anticipated income is
   a. Band-of-investment method

    b. Capitalization
    c. Summation method
    d. All of the above

2. If income = rate × value, which of the following is true?
    a. $R = I/V$
    b. $V = I/R$
    c. $I = R \times V$
    d. All of the above

3. The capitalization rate consists of
    a. Recapture rate plus interest rate
    b. Interest rate minus the recapture rate
    c. Bank rate plus the capital rate
    d. None of the above

4. In appraising, the recapture rate is determined by
    a. Multiplying the number of years of remaining economic life by 100 percent
    b. Dividing the number of years of remaining economic life by 100 percent
    c. Dividing the number of years of remaining economic life into 100 percent
    d. None of the above

5. Real estate as an investment is superior to stocks and bonds in which of the following ways?
    a. Highly liquid
    b. Less risk
    c. Less management burden
    d. Hedge against inflation

6. Being able to use a capital asset, such as real estate, as collateral for borrowing money is known as
    a. Liquidity
    b. Capitalization
    c. Collateralization
    d. Hypothecation

7. The lower the capitalization rate used
    a. The less secure the future income
    b. The more secure the future income
    c. The lower the value result
    d. None of the above

8. The higher the capitalization rate used
    a. The higher the value result
    b. The lower the value result
    c. The more indication there is of a lower economic neighborhood
    d. Both b and c

9. The shorter the remaining economic life
    a. The higher the recapture rate

b. The lower the recapture rate
c. The lower the capitalization rate
d. None of the above

10. The determination of the capitalization rate by the process of dividing the net income by the selling price is
a. The comparative-sales method
b. The band-of-investment method
c. The summation method
d. None of the above

11. The method of capitalization rate determination that combines the mortgage interest rate available with the equity rate necessary to attract investors is
a. The band-of-investment method
b. The comparative-sales method
c. The summation method
d. None of the above

12. The method of capitalization rate determination that combines the safe rate, reliability of net income, tax benefits, hypothecation, and other variables is
a. The band-of-investment method
b. The summation method
c. The comparative-sales method
d. All of the above

13. Which of the following methods of capitalization rate determination is the most theoretical and therefore of the least value?
a. Summation method
b. Comparative-sales method
c. Band-of-investment method
d. Market sales method

14. In a property residual capitalization approach, what is the value of an improved property with a net income of $80,000 per year, an interest rate of 8 percent, and a recapture rate of 2 percent?
a. $1,000,000
b. $800,000
c. $400,000
d. None of the above

15. In a building residual capitalization approach, what is the value of an improved property with a net income of $80,000 per year, a remaining economic life of the building of 50 years, a land value of $200,000, and an interest rate of 8 percent?
a. $1,000,000
b. $1,080,000
c. $840,000
d. $880,000

Chapter 15

RECONCILIATION AND FINAL VALUE ESTIMATE

Body of Knowledge Topics

• *Valuation Process—Reconciliation and Final Value Estimate*

• *Appraisal Statistical Concepts*

We have discussed three approaches to valuing real estate: the cost approach, the income approach, and the market data approach. They are the three standard approaches for real estate appraisal. Each of the three approaches indicates a value for the subject property. *Reconciliation* is the term that describes the process of bringing together the values indicated by each approach so that the appraiser can form an opinion about the value of the subject property.

All data used in real estate appraising come from the market; therefore, there should be some reciprocal relationship among the three approaches. The values indicated by each approach form what we call a *range of value* for the subject property. Our final estimate of value should be within this range. The values indicated by the three approaches should not usually differ more than 10 percent. If the spread in values exceeds 10 percent, the approaches should be reexamined and possibly adjusted to narrow the difference.

The term *weight* is often used by appraisers. The appraiser weighs specific data before making a judgment, gives more weight to one sale than to another, or weighs the consequence of a certain action in the market. The term *weigh* implies that the appraiser judges the importance, influence, or authority of the specific data being considered.

Throughout the entire appraisal process, we correlate and weigh data to form conclusions. In reaching an indicated value from the market data approach, we weigh and correlate sales and listings of properties similar to the subject. In the cost approach, we correlate data from the market to arrive at estimates of cost new and items of depreciation. Estimating the economic rentals, expenses, and capitalization rates used in the income approach also involves correlating and weighing data from the market. Just as we have made judgments and correlations throughout the entire appraisal process, we estimate the final value of the subject property on the basis of logical reasoning and analysis of the available data.

To reconcile the values indicated by the three approaches, we must judge and weigh the data that led to each value conclusion. We review the data and approaches to value in relation to the following factors:

1. Type of property being appraised

2. Data available

3. Intended use of appraisal

These three factors form the guidelines by which we judge each of the approaches in reconciling a final value estimate.

TYPE OF PROPERTY APPRAISED

The type of property being appraised often dictates a heavier weighing of one or two of the three approaches to value. Single-family residences are generally purchased for the amenities of home ownership, not for the production of income. Home buyers predicate the price they are willing to pay on the sale prices of comparable houses or on the cost of constructing a similar house. Thus, the market data approach and cost approach are the most appropriate methods of valuing a newer house. As the age of the house increases, the validity of the cost approach decreases because of the difficulty of estimating depreciation.

Properties purchased primarily for their income, such as apartment houses, are normally valued with the greatest emphasis on the income approach. However, the cost and market approaches should also be given full consideration. Usually, the older an apartment house, the less significant are the market data and cost approaches, because of both the lessening of similarity between properties with age and the difficulty of accurately estimating depreciation.

Data Available

What data are available to the appraiser is probably the most important aspect of reconciliation. Regardless of which approach is most applicable to a particular type of property, if adequate data are not available, a reliable value estimate cannot be developed by that approach.

All data used in appraising come directly or indirectly from the market. Sales of property similar to the subject are directly compared by the market data approach. The same sales may also be used in estimating gross rent multiplier, capitalization rate, land value, or accrued depreciation. A direct market investigation may be used in estimating an economic rent schedule or the construction cost of a building.

When we talk of the availability of data, we mean both quantity and quality. Quantity is the amount of data. Quality refers to the reliability of the data and their relevance to the particular appraisal problem. Information that cannot be verified and substantiated is not dependable for use in making an appraisal. The relevance of the appraisal data to the subject property is of the utmost importance. It is better to have a limited amount of pertinent data than an abundance of information of questionable applicability.

Intended Use of Appraisal

The intended use of the appraisal may have bearing on the weight given to any of the three approaches. If the appraisal is to be used in an eminent domain trial, sales of similar properties are usually considered the best demonstrative evidence of value. Likewise, evidence of value to be presented to persons unfamiliar with appraisal practices for purchase, sale, taxation, and so on, is often more understandable presented in the form of comparable sales.

In appraising investment properties for loan purposes, the lending institution wants to be sure that the income from the property will cover all expenses and repay the loan debt. In making loans on properties where improvements are to be constructed, the lending institution is concerned that the total value of the improved property be in relation to the cost of the improvements.

Appraising for insurance purposes requires primary consideration of the cost approach. Replacement cost less accrued depreciation is usually the basis for settlement of claims for destroyed or damaged real property.

Review of Approaches to Value

We have established as guidelines for judging the appraisal process (1) the type of subject property, (2) the data available, and (3) the proposed use of the appraisal. Let us now review the three approaches in an attempt to narrow their indicated range of value. Although a spread of 10 percent is acceptable, the closer the range, the more reliable the final estimate of value. Assume that the mathematical computations are correct and that the approaches have been properly applied. Our discussion deals with the judgment involved in each approach, which is crucial to real estate appraising.

Cost Approach

The three major estimates made in the application of the cost approach are:

1. Market value of land

2. Reproduction, or replacement, cost of improvements

3. Accrued depreciation to improvements

The most satisfactory method of valuing the land is to use sales and listings of similar parcels. The land sales must be analyzed, adjusted, and correlated to estimate the value for the subject land. Judgments must be made of the comparability of the sale properties for time, location, and physical characteristics. The degree of similarity between the sale properties and the subject property influences the reliability and accuracy of the estimated land value.

In residential properties, where land might represent approximately one-fourth of the value of the total improved property, a judgment error of 20 percent on land value will result in an error of only 5 percent for an improved property.

The validity of the reproduction, or replacement, cost estimate depends largely on the reliability of the data used in making the estimate. As we stated earlier, bids from several contractors for a specified improvement may vary from 5 to 10 percent. If the appraiser's estimate is within 5 percent of the actual cost of an improvement, it is considered accurate. An improvement similar to others presently being constructed in the neighborhood can normally be estimated more accurately. Known costs of recently completed structures similar to the subject improvement are good evidence as to cost. If the appraiser hires a reliable building contractor to estimate the cost of an improvement, or if the appraiser has had personal experience in construction and cost estimating, the cost estimate will be more reliable. If the improvements are relatively new and the original construction cost is known, greater weight may be placed on the cost estimate.

The cost estimate of accrued depreciation can be reasonably accurate for improvements under 20 years old that show no indications of substantial functional or economic obsolescence. The older the building, the more difficult it is to estimate physical depreciation, and the more likely it is that the property suffers from functional deficiencies.

The condition of the improvements is important as the basis for the appraiser's estimate of effective age. In estimating depreciation, the appraiser should always use effective age rather than actual physical age. Depreciation of a building begins with its construction. After the building is 2 or 3 years old, some depreciation will always be recognized, and it should be measured. A 10-year-old residence, no matter how well maintained, is not equal to an identical *new* residence as far as the structure is concerned.

Market Data Approach

The reliability of the market data approach depends mainly on the availability of sales similar to the subject property. The more dissimilarities between the sale properties and the subject property, the more adjustments necessary, and therefore the greater the probability of errors in judgment. If the necessary adjustments can be confined to readily measurable items with which the appraiser has had experience, the adjusted sale prices will be more indicative of the value for the subject property. During times of rapid change in real property values, the more recent sales and listings of property should be given greater consideration. In using listings, remember that asking prices may not be indicative of the value of the property. Consummated sales are the most reliable indications of value by the market data approach. Properties often sell for less than their original asking prices.

Generally, the larger the geographical area of properties similar to the subject, the greater is the number of comparable sales. In appraising a residence within a subdivision of 200 or 300 homes patterned after three or four basic models, the appraiser is usually assured of finding an adequate number of recent comparable sales.

Confirmation of sales with the real estate broker or one of the principals in the transaction is important. To make a meaningful comparison with the subject property, the appraiser should attempt to gather as many data on a sale property as possible. In addition to learning the sale price and other factual data, the appraiser should determine whether any circumstances of the transaction might discredit the validity of that sale as an indication of value. Physical condition of a property is important to a prospective purchaser. Improvements may have been made to a sale property by the new owner at the time of the appraiser's inspection. The appraiser should be aware of recent improvements, such as painting, roof covering, and landscaping, to establish and verify the actual condition of the property at the time of sale.

In appraising investment properties, the appraiser may have analyzed many units of comparison, such as sale price per room, per living unit, or per square foot of building or the gross rent multiplier. The appraiser should choose the unit or units of comparison that form a pattern of conformity among the sale properties. For instance, if the annual rent multipliers from the sales range from 7.7 to 8.1, a gross rent multiplier could probably be estimated that would indicate the value of the subject property. However, if the sale prices per living unit are $50,000, $60,000, and $70,000, the range in price per living unit would be too great and the pattern too illogical for the appraiser to make a meaningful estimate of a per-unit value for the subject property. If more than one unit of comparison is used, the indicated values for the subject property must be reconciled to one value.

Income Approach

The danger of the income approach is that an error in estimating income or expenses is multiplied many times over in the indicated value. For instance, with an overall capitalization rate of 9 percent, a change of $1,000 in income or expense results in a difference of over $11,000 in value. The income approach consists of a series of estimates, all subject to error: gross income, vacancy allowance, expenses, and reserves for replacement. The basis of support for these estimates should be reexamined, as we said in Chapter 13. At best, the appraiser can anticipate that the minor errors will offset each other.

Estimation of the capitalization rate is one of the most difficult and important aspects of the income approach. Income and expense estimates can be substantiated by the actual history of the subject property. The selection of the capitalization rate, however, depends largely on the judgment and experience of the appraiser. A small change in the capitalization rate will result in a considerable change in value. For instance, an increase in the rate from 8 to 9 percent will result in a decrease in value of 11 percent. The reliability of the capitalization rate selected must be judged by the appraiser on the basis of the data used and his or her familiarity with the rates of return demanded for similar investment properties.

The techniques used in capitalizing the net income from the property depend on the selection of the capitalization rate and the substantiation of the improvement or land value. Regardless of which of the three techniques are used, the indicated values should be within a reasonably close range.

In appraising single-family residences, the gross rent multiplier is used in place of the standard income approach. The accuracy of the estimated gross rent multiplier depends largely on the number of tenant-occupied sale properties found. The sale properties used in estimating the gross rent multiplier need not be as similar to the subject property as those used in the market data approach. Differences between the sale properties and the subject property are compensated for by the properties' respective rents.

The appraiser must analyze enough sales to make a meaningful estimate of a gross rent multiplier applicable to the subject property. Rental data for properties similar to the subject must be available to substantiate the present rental for the subject as a fair rent, or to establish an economic rent for the subject if it is not tenant occupied.

FINAL VALUE ESTIMATE

Most definitions of market value refer to *a price* or *the price* a property is worth. The courts require the appraiser to testify as to *one value* for a particular property. Appraisal clients expect the appraiser to advise them of *the value* of the subject property. Theoretically, a property has one value—the price it will sell for in the open market. In theory, each of the three approaches should indicate the same value, if the appraiser has all of the pertinent data and executes the processes properly. In theory, all buyers and sellers are fully knowledgeable in real estate transactions. But as we learned earlier, theory often differs from reality.

As appraisers, we know that the market does not operate on a theoretical basis. Buyers and sellers of property are not always knowledgeable. Some properties sell for more or less than their actual value. It is not our role to correct or perfect the market. Our job is to report and analyze the happenings in the market and to give our opinion of the probable selling price of a particular property in an imperfect real market.

A more reasonable approach to valuing property would be for the appraiser to indicate a range of values within which the selling price of the subject property would probably fall. However, in present appraisal practice we must express our opinion of market value as a dollar figure. Therefore, reconciliation of the three approaches into a single value estimate is necessary. It is generally conceded that a value estimate within 5 percent of the actual value of most properties is as accurate as can reasonably be expected.

STATISTICAL CONCEPTS

Mathematical Calculation of Market Data or Sales Comparison Approach

Most computerized form programs for appraisers have automatic mathematical calculation capability for comparable property adjustments, and often for computing the average of the adjusted sales prices of the comparables. Here, it is important to distinguish between the *mean*, or average, the *median*, and the *mode*.

Mean   This is the average of the sales prices, when added together and divided by the number of sales used.

Median   This is the "middle" price, based on the number of sales used. If the number of sales used is three, the price between the highest and the lowest is the median. If four sales are used, the median is the average of the two "middle" prices.

Mode   This is the price that occurs most often.

When calculating the sales comparison approach market value, an appraiser may use the median, or the mode price, if the comparable properties are very similar. If there are greater variations, the appraiser may choose the mean price, as this would tend to smooth the differences. If a particular comparable sale is most like the subject, the appraiser will use this to otherwise *weight* his or her evaluation of the estimated value.

Final Valuation

In practice, reconciliation is the process of selecting one of the three standard approaches as the most significant for a specific appraisal problem. The final value estimate is never computed by a mathematical averaging of the values indicated by the three approaches. The final value of the subject property is usually the value indicated by the approach that the appraiser feels best reflects the actions of the market. We have discussed the guidelines for selecting one particular approach based on the type of property being appraised, the data available, and the intended use of the appraisal. If, after reviewing the three approaches, two of the approaches can be considered equally valid, the appraiser may properly compromise between those two value indications to determine a final value estimate.

The greatest reliance is usually placed on only one approach in arriving at a final value estimate. The other approaches are used to check on and to substantiate the value indicated by the most valid approach. In some appraisal assignments it may not be deemed necessary to use all three approaches. The final value estimate may be based on two approaches or, in some cases, on only one approach to value.

In the appraisal of residential properties valued at less than $100,000, the final value estimate should be rounded to the nearest $250 or $500. For properties valued over $100,000 the value estimate may be rounded to the nearest $500 or $1,000.

SUMMARY

Each approach has certain applications and certain limitations. Upon performing the proper approaches it then becomes necessary to reconcile these approaches and to determine a value of the property being appraised. This reconciliation takes into account the type of property being appraised, the data available, and the intended use of the appraisal. Upon weighing all of the pertinent available facts, the appraiser then makes a judgment based principally on one specific approach (the one most applicable) and utilizes the other two approaches, where necessary, as a verification of the estimate of valuation.

DISCUSSION QUESTIONS

1. Explain the term *reconciliation* as it is used in real estate appraising.

2. What three factors form the guidelines by which we judge each of the valuation approaches in reconciling a final value estimate?

3. In the reconciliation process, we refer to the availability of data. Define the terms *quantity* and *quality* as they are used in relation to the availability of data.

4. In reviewing the cost approach, what are the major factors the appraiser should examine?

5. What is the major danger in the application of the income approach?

6. Discuss the major consideration in substantiating the reliance of the gross rent multiplier.

7. In testing the reliability of the market data approach, what should be the appraiser's main consideration?

8. In the market data approach, why is the confirmation of comparable sales important?

MULTIPLE-CHOICE QUESTIONS

1. The term *reconciliation* as used in appraising means
   a. The process of determining value by referring to the highest sales that have occurred in the neighborhood
   b. The process of bringing together all of the sales in the area and analyzing them
   c. The process of bringing together the values indicated by each approach so that the appraiser can form an opinion about the value of the subject property
   d. The process of analyzing comparable rental properties and establishing a gross rent multiplier

2. In the appraisal of a single-family residence, the most weight is normally given to
   a. The cost approach   c. The income approach
   b. The market approach   d. Both a and c

3. In the appraisal of a new, detached, single-family residence, a proper weighting would include
   a. The market approach   c. The income approach
   b. The cost approach   d. Both a and b

4. The cost approach loses its validity in appraising which of the following types of properties?
   a. A condominium   c. A duplex
   b. A single-family detached residence   d. None of the above

5. In theory, each of the three approaches should indicate
   a. Values within 5 percent   c. The same value
   b. Values within 10 percent   d. None of the above

6. The best way to arrive at a final value estimate is
   a. By mathematical averaging of all three value estimates
   b. By extrapolating a mean average
   c. By relying on the approach deemed most valid by the appraiser, with one or two other approaches used as a check or substantiation of the most valid approach
   d. Both b and c

Chapter 16

WRITING THE REPORT

Body of Knowledge Topic

- *Report Writing*

USPAP defines an appraisal report as: "any communication, written or oral, of an appraisal, review, or consulting service that is transmitted to the client upon completion of an assignment."

Standard Rule 2 of USPAP directs that: "In reporting the results of a real property appraisal an appraiser must communicate each analysis, opinion, and conclusion in a manner that is not misleading."

The appraisal report represents both the appraiser and the appraiser's opinion of value. The report should be prepared in anticipation that, in most instances, it will be the only opportunity the appraiser will have to demonstrate the reliability of his or her opinion of the value of a particular property.

TYPES OF REPORTS

In July, 1994, USPAP Standards Rule 2-2 was amended, requiring that all reports be categorized into one of three types, and that the type designation be prominently stated on each report, indicating to the reader how the appraisal is reported. In communicating the results of an appraisal, the appraiser must choose one of the following formats: Self-Contained Appraisal Report (Standards Rule 2-2[a], Summary Appraisal Report (Standards Rule 2-2[b]), or Restricted Appraisal Report (Standards Rule 2-2[c]).

As indicated in the USPAP Standards Rule 2-2 Report Comparison Chart (p. 290), the essential difference between the three report options is in the use and application of the terms *describe, summarize,* and *state*. *Describe* is used to connote a comprehensive level of detail in the presentation of information, most often found in narrative reports. *Summarize* is used to connote a more concise presentation of information, as in a URAR, Condominium, 2–4 Small Income, or Land form report. *State* is used to connote the minimal presentation of information, as may be provided in Limited reports, such as drive-by and other types of restricted appraisal reports.

USPAP Standards Rule 2–2 Report Comparison Chart

The essential difference among the three options is in the use and application of the terms describe, summarize and state. **DESCRIBE** is used to connote a comprehensive level of detail in the presentation of information. **SUMMARIZE** is used to connote a more concise presentation of information. **STATE** is used to connote the minimal presentation of information.

a) Self-Contained Appraisal Report	b) Summary Appraisal Report	c) Restricted Appraisal Report
i. identify and describe the real estate being appraised	i. identify and provide a summary description of the real estate being appraised	i. identify the real estate being appraised
ii. **state** the real property interest being appraised	ii. **state** the real property interest being appraised	ii. **state** the real property interest being appraised
iii. **state** the purpose and intended use of the appraisal	iii. **state** the purpose and intended use of the appraisal	iii. **state** the purpose and intended use of the appraisal
iv. define the value to be estimated	iv. define the value to be estimated	iv. **state** and reference a definition of the value to be estimated
v. **state** the effective date of the appraisal and the date of the report	v. **state** the effective date of the appraisal and the date of the report	v. **state** the effective date of the appraisal and the date of the report
vi. **state** the extent of the process of collecting, confirming and reporting data	vi. **summarize** the extent of the process of collecting, confirming and reporting data	vi. **describe** the extent of the process of collecting, confirming and reporting data
Comment: The full extent of the process should be apparent to the reader in the contents of the report.	*Comment:* The full extent of the process may not be apparent to the reader in the contents of the report.	*Comment:* The full extent of the process will not be apparent to the reader in the contents of the report.
vii. **state** all assumptions and limiting conditions that affect the analyses, opinions, and conclusions	vii. **state** all assumptions and limiting conditions that affect the analyses, opinions, and conclusions	vii. **state** all assumptions and limiting conditions that affect the analyses, opinions and conclusions
viii. **describe** the information considered, the appraisal procedures followed, and the reasoning that supports the analyses, opinions, and conclusions	viii. **summarize** the information considered, the appraisal procedures followed, and the reasoning that supports the analyses, opinions, and conclusions	viii. **state** the appraisal procedures followed, state the value conclusion and reference the existence of specific file information in support of the conclusion
ix. **describe** the appraiser's opinion of the highest and best use of the real estate, when such an opinion is necessary and appropriate	ix. **summarize** the appraiser's opinion of the highest and best use of the real estate, when such an opinion is necessary and appropriate	ix. **state** the appraiser's opinion of the highest and best use of the real estate, when such an opinion is necessary and appropriate
x. explain and support the exclusion of any of the usual valuation approaches	x. explain and support the exclusion of any of the usual valuation approaches	x. **state** the exclusion of any of the usual valuation approaches
xi. **describe** any additional information that may be appropriate to show compliance with, or clearly identify and explain permitted departures from, the specific guidelines of Standard 1	xi. **summarize** any additional information that may be appropriate to show compliance with, or clearly identify and explain permitted departures from, the specific guidelines of Standard 1	xi. contain a prominent use restriction that limits reliance on the report to the client and warns that the report cannot be understood properly without additional information in the workfile of the appraiser, and clearly identifies and explain any permitted departures from the specific guidelines of Standard 1
xii. include a signed certification in accordance with Standards Rule 2–3	xii. include a signed certification in accordance with Standards Rule 2–3	xii. include a signed certification in accordance with Standards Rule 2–3

Explanatory Comments have not been included in this chart, except for excerpt of Comment on vi.

SFR -
URAR form

Computerized form reports are the most common method of reporting residential property appraisals. The most often requested appraisal is for a single-family residence, which is typically reported on the Uniform Residential Appraisal Report (URAR) form, approved for use on Fannie Mae and Freddie Mac transactions, and is the de facto industry standard form for this type of appraisal. The latest version of this form is dated June 1993.

There are standardized forms for condominiums, two to four small income properties, vacant land, review appraisals, employee relocations, and many, many more. Sample reports for the most common residential appraisals—URAR, condominium, two to four small income, and vacant land, are provided in the supplement to this textbook.

The most recent forms to appear are those designed to be used under the USPAP departure provision for conducting "less than complete" appraisals, which have been promulgated by the major change in the *de minis*, or threshold level. This threshold is the transaction dollar value under which an appraisal may be made for lending purposes without a licensed or certified appraiser, or the appraisal may be less than the full appraisal required under the USPAP standards. The forms for these appraisals are generally intended as "drive-by" appraisals: however, there are versions that provide for a complete interior inspection, as well. A sample of a Limited Appraisal Report is included in the supplement.

Note that some states have laws requiring that all appraisals for lending purposes must be made by licensed or certified appraisers, regardless of transaction value, while other states allow unlicensed appraisers to participate in this market. Fannie Mae and Freddie Mac may still require complete appraisals, compliant with USPAP standards. Over time, the rules do change, and appraisers need to maintain an awareness of the authorized forms.

For narrative reports, there is no special style or design for an appraisal report. We shall discuss here the essential elements to be included in the most common type of report, the types of reports used by appraisers, and the general format they have developed for appraisal reports.

Appraisal reports are usually directed to business people. Like all business correspondence, appraisal reports should be concise and neat. Only data pertinent to the appraisal should be included. Wording should be brief, with technical terms avoided or defined when used. All types of reports should be printed on good-quality bond paper, suitable for either the form or the narrative. The client should receive the original of the appraisal report and the number of legible copies requested.

ESSENTIAL ELEMENTS OF AN APPRAISAL REPORT

Standard 2 of USPAP defines the required elements of an appraisal report, as follow:

Rule 2–1: Each written or oral real property appraisal report must:
  a. clearly and accurately set forth the appraisal in a manner that will not be misleading;
  b. contain sufficient information to enable the (Client) who receives or relies on the report to understand it properly;
  c. clearly and accurately disclose any extraordinary assumptions or limiting condition that directly affects the appraisal and indicate its impact on value.

Rule 2–2: Each written real property appraisal report must:
  1. identify and describe the real estate being appraised
  2. identify the real property interest being appraised
  3. state the purpose of the appraisal
  4. define the value to be estimated
  5. set forth the effective date of the appraisal and the date of the report
  6. describe the extent of the process of collecting, confirming, and reporting data
  7. set forth all assumptions and limiting conditions that affect analyses, opinions, and conclusions
  8. set forth information considered, the appraisal procedures followed, and the reasoning that supports the analyses, opinions, and conclusions
  9. set forth the appraiser's opinion of the highest and best use of the real estate, when appropriate
  10. explain and support the exclusion of any of the usual valuation approaches.
  11. set forth any additional information that may be appropriate to show compliance with, or clearly identify and explain permitted departure from, the requirements of Standard 1.
  12. a signed certification in accordance with Standard Rule 2–3.

There are other, practical elements that may be included in a report, such as:

1. Name of the party for whom the appraisal is made

2. Name of borrower and/or owner

3. Appraiser lender-approval identification number

4. Supplemental forms required by lenders

Note that most form reports have all of these essential elements covered, plus options for additional data.

TYPES OF APPRAISAL REPORTS

Four basic types of reports are used by appraisers:

1. Form report

2. Letter report

3. Narrative report

4. Oral

The type of report the appraiser uses depends largely on the wants and needs of the client. An institution or government agency that processes many appraisals of similar type properties may require the use of a standardized form to facilitate reporting and reviewing appraisal data.

Letter reports are often used in place of the full narrative report because of their lower cost to the client. A complete narrative report usually requires one or two days to prepare after completion of the field work. In contrast, a letter report can be written in half a day. For single-family residence appraisals, most clients prefer a letter, or an abbreviated narrative report, over a full narrative report, especially when the client is familiar with the property and does not require a full description of the city, neighborhood, site, improvements, utilities, and so forth.

Full narrative reports are most often required by agencies acquiring property for public use under the right of eminent domain. Pertinent data must be included in the report to enable the agency to review the appraisal, ensuring that the value conclusion is reasonable with respect to the data available. Detailed data that support the appraiser's opinion of value are also necessary for the agency to negotiate meaningfully with the property owner to acquire the property. Lenders, purchasers, and others who are not familiar with the area of the subject property may deem the expenditure for a complete narrative report worthwhile.

The basic difference between a letter report and a narrative report is the format and amount of supporting data included. Letter reports, at one time merely the appraiser's written opinion of a property's value, have become more or less a short form of the narrative report.

Regardless of the type of report to be submitted, the appraiser should make a complete appraisal of the property. No opinion of value should be rendered without the supporting data and knowledge necessary for such an appraisal. Any value estimate without adequate supporting data should be termed a preliminary estimate of value rather than an appraisal. A permanent work file containing all data gathered by the appraiser should be retained in the event that information other than that submitted in the report is needed to substantiate or explain the appraiser's opinion of value.

There is no fixed manner of writing an appraisal report. It may be a hybrid, or combination, of the three types of reports discussed on the following pages. However, most appraisals of fee appraisers, banks, savings and loans, and FHA, VA, and other government agencies rely on the form report and narrative report formats presented in the supplement to this textbook.

FORM REPORT

The form report has taken on many forms in the past 30 years. In June 1993 representatives of FHA, VA, FNMA, and many other aspects of the primary and secondary mortgage market agreed to modify the original URAR form that had been in use since 1989. This form is identified as Freddie Mac Form 70 6–93 and Fannie Mae Form 1004 (6/93). Freddie Mac and Fannie Mae have become the common names used for the Federal Home Loan Mortgage Corporation (FHLMC) and the Federal National Mortgage Association (FNMA).

Although many banks, savings and loan associations, FHA and VA offices, appraisal offices, and professional appraisal groups have had their own forms in the past, use of this new URAR is universally accepted.

Form Report Format

On the first two pages, the form provides for a description of the subject, neighborhood, site, improvements, interior, and automobile storage and for a room list, comments, the cost approach, accrued depreciation, sales comparison analysis, and conclusions (see Figure 16–1).

The third page is for additional comparable properties, if included.

The fourth and fifth pages include the USPAP-compliant definition of market value and the appropriate Certification and Statement of Limiting Conditions.

The sixth page is a Sketch Addendum, to be used for the floor plan and building dimensions.

The seventh page is the Plat Map Addendum, showing the county plat of the property.

The eighth page is the Location Map addendum showing the locale and the comparable properties in relationship to the subject.

The ninth page, a photograph addendum, provides for 35mm color photos of the front and rear of the *subject* property and a street scene. Digital imaging systems that link to computers now can provide both color and black and white images that replace traditional photos.

The tenth page includes another photograph addendum for photographs of the three *comparables,* all 35mm color photos.

Often, a cover page and an invoice accompany the report.

Any number of pages can be added to provide for additional information, such as copies of building permits in the event there have been additions made to the residence, geological reports, engineering studies, or other information deemed pertinent by the appraiser.

Many lending institutions and government agencies require three copies of the report with duplicate original photos in each copy.

The main advantages in the use of a standardized form report over a letter or narrative report are

1. The form report can be completed by the appraiser in a relatively short time.

* * * * *

UNIFORM RESIDENTIAL APPRAISAL REPORT   File No. **Blank**

Property Description

SUBJECT		
Property Address	City	State Zip Code
Legal Description		County
Assessor's Parcel No.	Tax Year R.E. Taxes $	Special Assessments $
Borrower	Current Owner	Occupant ☐ Owner ☐ Tenant ☐ Vacant
Property rights appraised ☐ Fee Simple ☐ Leasehold Project Type ☐ PUD ☐ Condominium (HUD/VA only)		HOA$ /Mo.
Neighborhood or Project Name	Map Reference	Census Tract
Sale Price $ Date of Sale	Description and $ amount of loan charges/concessions to be paid by seller	
Lender/Client	Address	
Appraiser Kathleen Gallagher - AL019620	Address	

NEIGHBORHOOD

Location	☐ Urban	☐ Suburban	☐ Rural	Predominant occupancy	Single family housing		Present land use %	Land use change
					PRICE $(000)	AGE (yrs)		
Built up	☐ Over 75%	☐ 25-75%	☐ Under 25%				One family ___	☐ Not likely ☐ Likely
Growth rate	☐ Rapid	☐ Stable	☐ Slow	☐ Owner	Low		2-4 family ___	☐ In process
Property values	☐ Increasing	☐ Stable	☐ Declining	☐ Tenant	High		Multi-family ___	To: ___
Demand/supply	☐ Shortage	☐ In balance	☐ Over supply	☐ Vacant (0-5%)	Predominant		Commercial ___	
Marketing time	☐ Under 3 mos.	☐ 3-6 mos.	☐ over 6 mos.	☐ Vacant (over 5%)			___	

Note: race and the racial composition of the neighborhood are not appraisal factors.

Neighborhood boundaries and characteristics: ___

Factors that affect the marketability of the properties in the neighborhood (proximity to employment and amenities, employment stability, appeal to market, etc.): ___

Market conditions in the subject neighborhood (including support for the above conclusions related to the trend of property values, demand/supply, and marketing time -- such as data on competitive properties for sale in the neighborhood, description of the prevalence of sales and financing concessions, etc.): ___

PUD

Project Information for PUDs   (If applicable -- Is the developer/builder in control of the Home Owner's Association (HOA)?   ☐ Yes ☐ No

Approximate total number of units in the subject project ___   Approximate total number of units for sale in the subject project ___

Describe common elements and recreational facilities: ___

SITE

Dimensions ___	Topography ___
Site area ___ Corner Lot ☐ Yes ☐ No	Size ___
Specific zoning classification and description ___	Shape ___
Zoning compliance ☐ Legal ☐ Legal nonconforming (Grandfathered use) ☐ Illegal ☐ No Zoning	Drainage ___
Highest & best use as improved: ☐ Present use ☐ Other use (explain)	View ___

Utilities	Public	Other	Off-site Improvements	Type	Public	Private		
Electricity	☐	☐	Street		☐	☐	Landscaping	___
Gas	☐	☐	Curb/gutter ___		☐	☐	Driveway Surface	___
Water	☐	☐	Sidewalk ___		☐	☐	Apparent easements	___
Sanitary sewer	☐	☐	Street lights ___		☐	☐	FEMA Special Flood Hazard Area ☐ Yes ☐ No
Storm sewer	☐	☐	Alley ___		☐	☐	FEMA Zone ___ Map Date ___
							FEMA Map No. ___	

Comments (apparent adverse easements, encroachments, special assessments, slide areas, illegal or legal nonconforming zoning use, etc.): ___

DESCRIPTION OF IMPROVEMENTS

GENERAL DESCRIPTION	EXTERIOR DESCRIPTION	FOUNDATION	BASEMENT	INSULATION
No. of Units ___	Foundation ___	Slab ___	Area Sq. Ft. ___	Roof ___ ☐
No. of Stories ___	Exterior Walls ___	Crawl Space ___	% Finished ___	Ceiling ___ ☐
Type (Det./Att.) ___	Roof Surfaces ___	Basement ___	Ceiling ___	Walls ___ ☐
Design (Style) ___	Gutters & Dwnspts. ___	Sump Pump ___	Walls ___	Floor ___ ☐
Existing/Proposed ___	Window Type ___	Dampness ___	Floor ___	None ___ ☐
Age (Yrs.) ___	Storm/Screens ___	Settlement ___	Outside Entry ___	Unknown ___ ☐
Effective Age (Yrs.) ___	Manufactured House ___	Infestation ___		

ROOMS	Foyer	Living	Dining	Kitchen	Den	Family Rm.	Rec. Rm.	Bedrooms	# Baths	Laundry	Other	Area Sq. Ft.
Basement												
Level 1												
Level 2												

Finished area above grade contains: ___ Rooms;   ___ Bedroom(s);   ___ Bath(s);   ___ Square Feet of Gross Living Area

INTERIOR	Materials/Condition	HEATING		KITCHEN EQUIP.		ATTIC		AMENITIES		CAR STORAGE	
Floors	___	Type	___	Refrigerator	☐	None	☐	Fireplace(s) # ___ ☐		None ☐	
Walls	___	Fuel	___	Range/Oven	☐	Stairs	☐	Patio ___		Garage # of cars	
Trim/Finish	___	Condition	___	Disposal	☐	Drop Stair	☐	Deck ___		Attached ___	
Bath Floor	___	COOLING		Dishwasher	☐	Scuttle	☐	Porch ___		Detached ___	
BathWainscot	___	Central	___	Fan/Hood	☐	Floor	☐	Fence ___		Built-In ___	
Doors	___	Other	___	Microwave	☐	Heated	☐	Pool ___		Carport ___	
		Condition	___	Washer/Dryer	☐	Finished	☐			Driveway ___	

Additional features (special energy efficient items, etc.): ___

COMMENTS

Condition of the improvements, depreciation (physical, functional, and external), repairs needed, quality of construction, remodeling/additions, etc.: ___

Adverse environmental conditions (such as, but not limited to, hazardous wastes, toxic substances, etc.) present in the improvements, on the site, or in the immediate vicinity of the subject property.: ___

Freddie Mac Form 70 6-93   ClickFORMS Real Estate Appraisal Software by Bradford and Robbins (800) 622-8727   Fannie Mae Form 1004 (6-93)

FIGURE 16–1   Uniform Residential Appraisal Report.

UNIFORM RESIDENTIAL APPRAISAL REPORT   File No.   **Blank**

Valuation Section

COST APPROACH

ESTIMATED SITE VALUE . . . . = $ _____	Comments on Cost Approach (such as, source of cost estimate,
ESTIMATED REPRODUCTION COST-NEW-OF IMPROVEMENTS:	site value, square foot calculation and for HUD, VA and FmHA, the
Dwelling _____ Sq. Ft. @ $ _____ = $ _____	estimated remaining economic life of the property): _____
_____ Sq. Ft. @ $ _____ = _____	
= _____	
Garage/Carport _____ Sq. Ft. @ $ _____ = _____	
Total Estimated Cost New . . . . = $ _____	
Less Physical Functional External	
Depreciation _____ = $ _____	
Depreciated Value of Improvements . . . . = $ _____	
"As is" Value of Site Improvements . . . . = $ _____	Site Value: area x $ _____ = _____
INDICATED VALUE BY COST APPROACH . . . . = $ _____	Est Rem Econ Life: _____ yrs

SALES COMPARISON ANALYSIS

ITEM	SUBJECT	COMPARABLE NO. 1	COMPARABLE NO. 2	COMPARABLE NO. 3
Address				
Proximity to Subject				
Sales Price	$	$	$	$
Price/Gross Liv. Area	$	$	$	$
Data and/or				
Verification Source				

VALUE ADJUSTMENTS	DESCRIPTION	DESCRIPTION	+(-)$ Adjustment	DESCRIPTION	+(-)$ Adjustment	DESCRIPTION	+(-)$ Adjustment
Sales or Financing							
Concessions							
Date of Sale/Time							
Location							
Leasehold/Fee Simple							
Site							
View							
Design and Appeal							
Quality of Construction							
Age							
Condition							
Above Grade	Total / Bdrms / Baths	Total / Bdrms / Baths		Total / Bdrms / Baths		Total / Bdrms / Baths	
Room Count							
Gross Living Area	Sq. Ft.	Sq. Ft.		Sq. Ft.		Sq. Ft.	
Basement & Finished							
Rooms Below Grade							
Functional Utility							
Heating/Cooling							
Energy Efficient Items							
Garage/Carport							
Porch, Patio, Deck,							
Fireplace(s), etc.							
Fence, Pool, etc.							
Net Adj. (total)		☐ + ☐ - $ 0		☐ + ☐ - $ 0		☐ + ☐ - $ 0	
Adjusted Sales Price							
of Comparable		$		$		$	

Comments on Sales Comparison (including the subject property's compatibility to the neighborhood, etc.): _____

ITEM	SUBJECT	COMPARABLE NO. 1	COMPARABLE NO. 2	COMPARABLE NO. 3
Date, Price and Data				
Source, for prior sales				
within year of appraisal				

Analysis of any current agreement of sale, option, or listing of the subject property and analysis of any prior sales of subject and comparables within one year of the date of appraisal.

INDICATED VALUE BY SALES COMPARISON APPROACH . . . . $ _____

INDICATED VALUE BY INCOME APPROACH (If Applicable) Estimated Market Rent $ _____ /Mo.x Gross Rent Multiplier _____ =$ _____

This appraisal is made ☐ "as is" ☐ subject to the repairs, alterations, inspections or conditions listed below ☐ subject to completion per plans and specifications.

Conditions of Appraisal: _____

Final Reconciliation: _____

RECONCILIATION

The purpose of this appraisal is to estimate the market value of the real property that is subject to this report, based on the above conditions and the certification, contingent and limiting conditions, and market value definition that are stated in the attached Freddie Mac Form 439/Fannie Mae Form 1004B (Revised _____).

I (WE) ESTIMATE THE MARKET VALUE, AS DEFINED, OF THE REAL PROPERTY THAT IS THE SUBJECT OF THIS REPORT, AS OF _____

(WHICH IS THE DATE OF INSPECTION AND THE EFFECTIVE DATE OF THIS REPORT) TO BE $ _____

APPRAISER:	SUPERVISORY APPRAISER (ONLY IF REQUIRED):	
Signature	Signature	☐ Did ☐ Did Not
Name Kathleen Gallagher - AL019620	Name	Inspect Property
Date Report Signed	Date Report Signed	
State Certification # _____ State	State Certification # _____	State
Or State License # _____ State	Or State License # _____	State

Freddie Mac Form 70 6-93   ClickFORMS Real Estate Appraisal Software by Bradford and Robbins (800) 622-8727   Fannie Mae Form 1004 (6-93)

FIGURE 16–1 Continued

EXTRA COMPARABLES 4-5-6   File No. _____ Blank _____

Borrower	
Property Address	
City County State Zip Code	
Lender/Client Client or Client Firm Name Address	

These recent sales of properties are most similar and proximate to subject and have been considered in the market analysis. The description includes a dollar adjustment, reflecting market reaction to those items of significant variation between the subject and comparable properties. If a significant item in the comparable property is superior to, or more favorable than, the subject property, a minus (-) adjustment is made, thus reducing the indicated value of subject; if a significant item in the comparable is inferior to, or less favorable than, the subject property, a plus (+) adjustment is made, thus increasing the indicated value of the subject.

ITEM	SUBJECT	COMPARABLE NO. 4		COMPARABLE NO. 5		COMPARABLE NO. 6	
Address							
Proximity to Subject							
Sales Price	$	$		$		$	
Price/Gross Liv. Area	$	$		$		$	
Data and/or Verification Source							
VALUE ADJUSTMENTS	DESCRIPTION	DESCRIPTION	+(-)$ Adjustment	DESCRIPTION	+(-)$ Adjustment	DESCRIPTION	+(-)$ Adjustment
Sales or Financing Concessions							
Date of Sale/Time							
Location							
Leasehold/Fee Simple							
Site							
View							
Design and Appeal							
Quality of Construction							
Age							
Condition							
Above Grade	Total Bdrms Baths	Total Bdrms Baths		Total Bdrms Baths		Total Bdrms Baths	
Room Count							
Gross Living Area	Sq. Ft.	Sq. Ft.		Sq. Ft.		Sq. Ft.	
Basement & Finished Rooms Below Grade							
Functional Utility							
Heating/Cooling							
Energy Efficient Items							
Garage/Carport							
Porch, Patio, Deck, Fireplace(s), etc.							
Fence, Pool, etc.							
Net Adj. (total)		+ - $	0	+ - $	0	+ - $	0
Adjusted Sales Price of Comparable		$		$		$	

(left margin: SALES COMPARISON ANALYSIS)

Comments on Comparables: _____

ITEM	SUBJECT	COMPARABLE NO. 4	COMPARABLE NO. 5	COMPARABLE NO. 6
Date, Price and Data Source, for prior sales within year of appraisal.				

(left margin: COMMENTS)

ClickFORMS Real Estate Appraisal Software by Bradford and Robbins (800) 622-8727

FIGURE 16–1   Continued

DEFINITION OF MARKET VALUE: The most probable price which a property should bring in a competitive and open market under all conditions requisite to a fair sale, the buyer and seller, each acting prudently, knowledgeably and assuming the price is not affected by undue stimulus. Implicit in this definition is the consummation of a sale as of a specified date and the passing of title from seller to buyer under conditions whereby: (1) buyer and seller are typically motivated; (2) both parties are well informed or well advised, and each acting in what he considers his own best interest; (3) a reasonable time is allowed for exposure in the open market; (4) payment is term of cash in U. S. dollars or in terms of financial arrangements comparable thereto; and (5) the price represents the normal consideration for the property sold unaffected by special or creative financing or sales concessions* granted by anyone associated with the sale.

*Adjustments to the comparables must be made for special or creative financing or sales concessions. No adjustments are necessary for those costs which are normally paid by sellers as a result of tradition or law in a market; these costs are readily identifiable since the seller pays these costs in virtually all sales transactions. Special or creative financing adjustments can be made to the comparable property by comparisons to financing terms offered by a third party institutional lender that is not already involved in the property or transaction. Any adjustment should not be calculated on a mechanical dollar for dollar cost of the financing or concession but the dollar amount of any adjustment should approximate the market's reaction to the financing or concessions based on the appraiser's judgment.

STATEMENT OF LIMITING CONDITIONS AND APPRAISER'S CERTIFICATION

CONTINGENT AND LIMITING CONDITIONS: The appraiser's certification that appears in the appraisal report is subject to the following conditions:

1.   The appraiser will not be responsible for matters of a legal nature that affect either the property being appraised or the title to it. The appraiser assumes that the title is good and marketable and, therefore, will not render any opinions about the title. The property is appraised on the basis of it being under responsible ownership.

2.   The appraiser has provided a sketch in the appraisal report to show approximate dimensions of the improvements and the sketch is included only to assist the reader of the report in visualizing the property and understanding the appraiser's determination of its size.

3.   The appraiser has examined the available flood maps that are provided by the Federal Emergency Management Agency (or other data sources) and has noted in the appraisal report whether the subject site is located in an identified Special Flood Hazard Area. Because the appraiser is not a surveyor, he or she makes no guarantees, express or implied, regarding this determination.

4.   The appraiser will not give testimony or appear in court because he or she made an appraisal of the property in question, unless specific arrangements to do so have been made beforehand.

5.   The appraiser has estimated the value of the land in the cost approach at its highest and best use and the improvements at their contributory value. These separate valuations of the land and improvements must not be used in conjunction with any other appraisal and are invalid if they are so used.

6.   The appraiser has noted in the appraisal report any adverse conditions (such as, needed repairs, depreciation, the presence of hazard wastes, toxic substances, etc.) observed during the inspection of the subject property or that he or she became aware of during the normal research involved in performing the appraisal. Unless otherwise stated in the appraisal report, the appraiser has no knowledge of any hidden or unapparent conditions of the property or adverse environmental conditions (including the presence of hazardous wastes, toxic substances, etc.) that would make the property more or less valuable, and has assumed that there are no such conditions and makes no guarantees or warranties, express or implied, regarding the condition of the property. The appraiser will not be responsible for any such conditions that do exist or for any engineering or testing that might be required to discover whether such conditions exist. Because the appraiser is not an expert in the field of environmental hazards, the appraisal report must not be considered as an environmental assessment of the property.

7.   The appraiser obtained the information, estimates, and opinions that were expressed in the appraisal report from sources that he or she considers to be reliable and believes them to be true and correct. The appraiser does not assume responsibility for the accuracy of such items that were furnished by other parties.

8.   The appraiser will not disclose the contents of the appraisal report except as provided for in the Uniform Standards of Professional Appraisal Practice.

9.   The appraiser has based his or her appraisal report and valuation conclusion for an appraisal that is subject to satisfactory completion, repairs, or alterations on the assumption that completion of the improvements will be performed in a workmanlike manner.

10. The appraiser must provide his or her prior written consent before the lender/client specified in the appraisal report can distribute the appraisal report (including conclusions about the property value, the appraiser's identity and professional designations, and references to any professional appraisal organizations or the firm with which the appraiser is associated) to anyone other than the borrower; the mortgagee or its successors and assigns; the mortgage insurer; consultants; professional appraisal organizations; any state or federally approved financial institution; or any department, agency, or instrumentality of the United States or any state or the District of Columbia; except that the lender/client may distribute the property description section of the report only to data collection or reporting service(s) without having to obtain the appraiser's prior written consent. The appraiser's written consent and approval must also be obtained before the appraisal can be conveyed by anyone to the public through advertising, public relations, news, sales, or other media.

Freddie Mac Form 439 (6-93)   ClickFORMS Real Estate Appraisal Software by Bradford and Robbins (800) 622-8727   Fannie Mae Form 1004B   (6-93)

FIGURE 16–1   Continued

APPRAISER'S CERTIFICATION: The Appraiser certifies and agrees that:

1.   I have researched the subject market area and have selected a minimum of three recent sales of properties most similar and proximate to the subject property for consideration in the sales comparison analysis and have made a dollar adjustment when appropriate to reflect the market reaction to those items of significant variation. If a significant item in a comparable property is superior to, or more favorable than, the subject property, I have made a negative adjustment to reduce the adjusted sales price of the comparable and, if a significant item in a comparable property is inferior to, or less favorable than the subject property, I have made a positive adjustment to increase the adjusted sales price of the comparable.

2.   I have taken into consideration the factors that have an impact on value in my development of the estimate of market value in the appraisal report. I have not knowingly withheld any significant information from the appraisal report and I believe, to the best of my knowledge, that all statements and information in the appraisal report are true and correct.

3.   I stated in the appraisal report only my own personal, unbiased, and professional analysis, opinions, and conclusions, which are subject only to the contingent and limiting conditions specified in this form.

4.   I have no present or prospective interest in the property that is the subject of this report, and I have no present or prospective personal interest or bias with respect to the participants in the transaction. I did not base, either partially or completely, my analysis and/or the estimate of market value in the appraisal report on the race, color, religion, sex, handicap, familiar status, or national origin of either the prospective owners or occupants of the subject property or of the present owners or occupants of the properties in the vicinity of the subject property.

5.   I have no present or contemplated future interest in the subject property, and neither my current or future employment nor my compensation for performing this appraisal is contingent on the appraised value of the property.

6.   I was not required to report a predetermined value or direction in value that favors the cause of the client or any related party, the amount of the value estimate, the attainment of a specific result, or the occurrence of a subsequent event in order to receive my compensation and/or employment for performing the appraisal. I did not base the appraisal report on a requested minimum valuation, a specific valuation, or the need to approve a specific mortgage loan.

7.   I performed this appraisal in conformity with the Uniform Standards of Professional Appraisal Practice that were adopted and promulgated by the Appraisal Standards Board of The Appraisal Foundation and that were in place as of the effective date of this appraisal, with the exception of the departure provision of those Standards, which does not apply. I acknowledge that an estimate of a reasonable time for exposure in the open market is a condition in the definition of market value and the estimate I developed is consistent with the marketing time noted in the neighborhood section of this report, unless I have otherwise stated in the reconciliation section.

8.   I have personally inspected the interior and exterior areas of the subject property and the exterior of all properties listed as comparables in the appraisal report. I further certify that I have noted any apparent or known adverse conditions in the subject improvements, on the subject site, or on any site within the immediate vicinity of the subject property of which I am aware and have made adjustments for these adverse conditions in my analysis of the property value to the extent that I had market evidence to support them. I have also commented about the effect of the adverse conditions on the marketability of the subject property.

9.   I personally prepared all conclusions and opinions about the real estate that were set forth in the appraisal report. If I relied on significant professional assistance from any individual or individuals in the performance of the appraisal or the preparation of the appraisal report, I have named such individual(s) and disclosed the specific tasks performed by them in the reconciliation section of this appraisal report. I certify that any individual so named is qualified to perform the tasks. I have not authorized anyone to make a change to any item in the report; therefore, if an unauthorized change is made to the appraisal report, I will take no responsibility for it.

SUPERVISORY APPRAISER'S CERTIFICATION: If a supervisory appraiser signed the appraiser report, he or she certifies and agrees that: I directly supervise the appraiser who prepared the appraisal report, have reviewed the appraisal report, agree with the statements and conclusions of the appraiser, agree to be bound by the appraiser's certifications numbered 4 through 7 above, and am taking full responsibility for the appraisal and the appraisal report.

ADDRESS OF PROPERTY APPRAISED: _____

APPRAISER:

Signature: _____
Name: _____ Kathleen Gallagher - AL019620 _____
Date Signed: _____
State Certification #: _____
or State License #: _____
State: _____
Expiration Date of Certification or License: _____

SUPERVISORY APPRAISER   (only if required)

Signature: _____
Name: _____
Date Signed: _____
State Certification #: _____
or State License #: _____
State: _____
Expiration Date of Certification or License: _____
☐ Did   ☐ Did Not Inspect Property

Freddie Mac Form 439 6-93   ClickFORMS Real Estate Appraisal Software by Bradford and Robbins (800) 622-8727   Fannie Mae Form 1004B 6-93

FIGURE 16–1   Continued

SKETCH ADDENDUM   File No.   Blank

Borrower
Property Address
City   County   State   Zip Code
Lender/ClientClient or Client Firm Name   Address

ClickFORMS Real Estate Appraisal Software by Bradford and Robbins (800) 622-8727

FIGURE 16–1   Continued

PLAT MAP   File No. <u>Blank</u>

Borrower
Property Address
City   County   State   Zip Code
Lender/Client Client or Client Firm Name   Address

ClickFORMS Real Estate Appraisal Software by Bradford and Robbins (800) 622-8727

FIGURE 16–1   Continued

LOCATION MAP ADDENDUM   File No.   __Blank__

Borrower			
Property Address			
City	County	State	Zip Code
Lender/Client Client or Client Firm Name	Address		

ClickFORMS Real Estate Appraisal Software by Bradford and Robbins (800) 622-8727

FIGURE 16–1   Continued

SUBJECT PHOTO ADDENDUM   File No.   Blank

Borrower
Property Address
City   County   State   Zip Code
Lender/Client Client or Client Firm Name   Address

**FRONT OF
SUBJECT PROPERTY**

Address

Sale Date
Sale Price

Site
View
Design/Appeal
Const. Quality
Age
Square Feet
Total Rooms
Bedrooms
Bathrooms
Basement
Garage
Fireplace

**REAR OF
SUBJECT PROPERTY**

STREET SCENE

FIGURE 16–1   Continued

COMPARABLES 1-2-3 PHOTO ADDENDUM   File No._____**Blank**_____

Borrower
_____
Property Address
_____
City   County   State   Zip Code
_____
Lender/Client Client or Client Firm Name   Address
_____

COMPARABLE SALE 1

Address

Sale Date
Sale Price

Site
View
Design/Appeal
Const. Quality
Age
Square Feet
Total Rooms
Bedrooms
Bathrooms
Basement
Garage
Fireplace

COMPARABLE SALE 2

Address

Sale Date
Sale Price

Site
View
Design/Appeal
Const./Quality
Age
Square Feet
Total Rooms
Bedrooms
Bathrooms
Basement
Garage
Fireplace

COMPARABLE SALE 3

Address

Sale Date
Sale Price

Site
View
Design/Appeal
Const. Quality
Age
Square Feet
Total Rooms
Bedrooms
Bathrooms
Basement
Garage
Fireplace

FIGURE 16–1   Continued

APPRAISAL INVOICE

Date: Date Report Signed   File No.: Blank

Prepared for:

Attn: (Name of Person Ordering Appraisal)
Client or Client Firm Name
Street Address
City, State, Zip Code
Phone and Fax numbers

Property Appraised:

Subject Property Street Address
City, State, Zip Code
Borrower Name

Work Performed:

Appraisal - URAR	Fee
Inspection Date: XX-XX-XX	
Total Amount Due:	Fee

Please make checks payable to:

Appraiser or Appraisal Firm Name
Mailing Address
Phone and Fax numbers

FIGURE 16–1 Continued

2. Portions of the report can be completed while inspecting the subject property.

3. The form, used as a checklist, avoids inadvertent omission of pertinent data.

4. The uniform format allows a more efficient review and processing of the appraisal report.

5. Features of the subject property can be readily compared with minimum standards of acceptance.

6. Typing is reduced because of the printed headings.

7. Allows for ease of review in the secondary mortgage market.

8. Is easily adapted for computer use.

Major disadvantages of the form report are

1. The form may be too rigid, making no provision for additional pertinent data.

2. The form does not usually allow for an analysis of the data or for the appraiser's reasoning as to value conclusions.

3. Some of the items in the form may not be applicable to the property being appraised.

4. The form report may not allow the appraiser to report the data in the order or manner that seems most appropriate for a particular appraisal problem.

LETTER REPORT

The letter report conveys appraisal data in the form of a business letter. The format should conform with the rules and standards of business correspondence. The appraiser's letterhead may be used for the initial page. Typing should be single spaced, with adequate margins.

The eight essential elements of an appraisal report should be included in the letter report. In addition, the appraiser usually includes a brief description of the improvements, such as type, number of rooms, size, construction, and condition, and some factual data supporting value conclusions. The supporting data are often summarized as a list of the sale properties with pertinent sales data, a reconstructed operating statement and capitalization process, or a depreciated cost study. A brief discussion should follow relating the appraiser's estimate of value to the supporting data.

The letter report can vary from 2 to 10 pages or more in length, up to 15 to 20 pages. Exhibits, such as property or improvement plats and pictures, are often attached to and incorporated as part of the letter report. The letter report is very flexible as to format and what data are included.

NARRATIVE REPORT

The narrative appraisal report is the best way for an appraiser to relate to the client the data gathered, the analysis of the data, and the reasons for the value estimate. Over years of report writing, a logical presentation of appraisal data in narrative report form has been developed. Although most appraisers follow this general framework, each appraiser develops a particular style and mode of writing a report. *The important part of report writing is to include all pertinent data in a clear, logical sequence to convince the reader of your conclusions.* A model narrative report is included in the supplement to this textbook.

Demonstration narrative reports are prepared by students and by candidates for membership in appraisal organizations to show their competence in gathering, processing, and analyzing appraisal data, applying appraisal techniques, and preparing an appraisal report. The model narrative report in the supplement is not intended to be representative of all narrative reports prepared by professional appraisers, but is included to show an acceptable method of reporting various aspects of appraisal data.

Demonstration narrative reports substantiate the appraiser's knowledge of appraisal techniques and practices. A professional narrative report conveys appraisal data and conclusions for a particular property. While professional appraisers may make authoritative estimates of building cost, sale adjustments, capitalization rate, and so on, based on their knowledge and experience, writers of demonstration reports must provide support for their judgments and illustrate their understanding of appraisal techniques.

Narrative Report Format

The narrative appraisal report should give the appearance of a professionally prepared document. A slovenly report suggests an inferior appraisal. We offer some suggestions as to the physical format of an appraisal report.

1. *Cover.* A durable cover of heavy paper, plastic, or leather should bind the report. Identification of the property and the appraiser can be typed, printed, or embossed on the cover.

2. *Paper.* Quality bond paper, $8\frac{1}{2}$ by 11 inches is most acceptable. Larger sheets for maps, charts, and so forth, should be folded and bound into the report.

3. *Envelopes.* Large envelopes may be cut to $8\frac{1}{2}$ by 10 inches and bound into the report to hold folded maps or other exhibits.

4. *Typing.* Typing may be single or double spaced.

5. *Margins.* The following approximate margins are recommended:
   a. 1 inch at right side of paper
   b. $1\frac{1}{2}$ inches at left side of paper
   c. $1\frac{1}{4}$ to $1\frac{1}{2}$ inches at top of page
   d. $1\frac{1}{4}$ inches at bottom of page

6. *Headings.* Headings differentiating subjects or topics should be underlined or emphasized in some other manner. Sections of the report may be separated by title pages.

Outline of Report

Appraisal reports vary in content and arrangement, with three major divisions:

1. Introduction

2. Description, analysis, and conclusions

3. Addenda

Within these three divisions, the appraiser tailors the report to fit the particular appraisal problem. We give here a detailed outline satisfactory for, and adaptable to, most appraisal assignments. The report follows the general order of the appraisal process, discussed in Chapter 4.

I. Introduction
    1. Title page
    2. Letter of transmittal
    3. Table of contents
    4. Summary of salient facts and conclusions

II. Description, analysis, conclusions
    5. Identification of property
    6. Purpose of appraisal
    7. Description of city and neighborhood
    8. Site data
    9. Zoning
    10. Highest and best use
    11. Assessed value and taxes
    12. Description of improvements
    13. Approaches to appraisal
    14. Site valuation
    15. Cost approach
    16. Market data approach
    17. Income approach
    18. Reconciliation and final value estimate
    19. Certificate of appraisal

III. Addenda
    20. Photographs of subject property
    21. Improvement plats, floor plan, and plot plan of subject property
    22. Sale data sheets
    23. Comparable sales map
    24. Any statistical or supporting data not included elsewhere
    25. Assumptions and limiting conditions
    26. Qualifications of appraiser

Note: Items 25 and 26 are sometimes inserted in the front of the report.

Title Page

The first page of the report is the title page. It should identify the subject property and the appraiser. If this information is given on the cover of the report, a flyleaf should be used instead of a title page.

Letter of Transmittal

The letter of transmittal formally presents the appraisal report to the client. The letter may be addressed to the client, or to another person as directed, and should be prepared in compliance with standard business correspondence. The transmittal letter should contain the following elements:

1. Date of letter

2. A statement that the appraiser was requested to make the appraisal and the name of the person requesting the appraisal

3. Identification of the property appraised

4. Purpose of the appraisal and the property rights appraised

5. A statement that the appraiser has made the necessary investigation and analysis to arrive at an opinion of value for the subject property

6. A reference that the letter is transmitting the report; the number of pages in the report

7. The valuation date

8. The estimate of value

9. The appraiser's signature

The letter of transmittal may contain other pertinent data the appraiser wishes to include, such as a brief description of the subject property, the certification, assumptions made in the appraisal, or limiting conditions. The demonstration report in the supplement contains an acceptable letter of transmittal.

Table of Contents

The table of contents lists the subject matter as it appears in the report and indicates the page numbers on which particular data can be found. The table of contents permits quick reference to specific appraisal data. It is normally divided into three major parts:

1. Introduction

2. Description, analysis, and conclusions

3. Addenda

Subject matter is listed by headings as it appears in the report.

Summary of Salient Facts and Conclusions

The summary of salient facts and conclusions is a convenient one-page reference, stating briefly the pertinent appraisal data. The data usually included in the summary, when applicable to the subject property, are:

1. Ownership of the subject property

2. Location of the property

3. Date of the appraisal and date of report

4. Type of property (for example, single-family residence, 20-unit apartment house)

5. Size of subject parcel

6. Size of improvements (square footage, number of rooms, and so forth)

7. Age of improvements

8. Zoning

9. Present use

10. Highest and best use

11. Site value

12. Value indicated by cost approach

13. Value indicated by market data approach

14. Value indicated by income approach

15. Reconciliation and final value estimate

The appraiser includes in the summary whatever information he or she considers important to the particular appraisal assignment. This may include data concerning property rights, type of value, or a brief description of the improvements. In the case of partial takings, the value of the property taken, property value before and after the taking, severance damages, and special benefits should be included in the summary.

REPORT ELEMENTS

The elements for both form and narrative reports are basically the same, however, in a narrative, the descriptive work is generally more extensive. Some of the most important elements are discussed below.

Identification of Property

The subject property should be identified clearly to enable the client to locate the property and to avoid confusion with any other parcel of real estate. Improved properties are usually identified by street address and legal description. If the legal description of the subject property is short, it should be included in the body of the report. If the legal description is more than one-fourth of a page, it should be included in the addenda, with a reference in this portion of the report.

If the subject property is unimproved, the parcel should be identified by street frontage and distance to intersecting street as well as by legal description; for example, "the west side of Ninth Street, 150 feet north of Vine Avenue." Town or county and state should be included in the identification of the property.

Purpose of Appraisal

The statement of purpose of the appraisal should include the following three elements:

1. The property rights being appraised

2. The definition of the value being estimated

3. The specific date on which the valuation applies (valuation date)

The statement of purpose should be brief and direct, for example:

> The purpose of this appraisal is to estimate the market value of the unencumbered fee estate of the subject property as of June 10, 19–. Market value is defined as the most probable price estimated in terms of money that a property should bring if exposed for sale in the open market, allowing a reasonable time to find a purchaser who buys with knowledge of all the uses to which it is adapted and for which it is capable of being used.

Description of City and Neighborhood

We discussed physical, economic, political, social, city, and neighborhood data in Chapter 4. The intended use of the appraisal report determines what information is included in this section. A report prepared for an out-of-town prospective purchaser might include a greater amount of city and neighborhood data than a report for a local client. Normally, only neighborhood data having a direct influence on the subject property are included in the report. The data should be analyzed and discussed in relation to their effect on the subject property, not merely included as statistics. If the appraiser feels that a considerable amount of statistical data may be of interest or importance to a client, the data should be included in the addenda of the report, with a reference to such data made at this point. Better yet, Chamber of Commerce–type material may be sent to the client under separate cover.

It may be desirable to include a map of the subject area in the addenda, noting and relating area features to the subject property. The following data should be considered in analyzing a residential neighborhood:

1. Proximity of the subject property to amenities such as shopping, schools, and parks

2. Encroachment of heterogeneous uses or nuisances

3. Life stage and trend of neighborhood

4. Percentage of tenant occupancy and vacancy

5. Adequacy of public transportation, traffic control, and police and fire protection

6. Conformity of use and maintenance of properties

7. Socioeconomic status of neighborhood

Site Data

Site data describe the physical subject parcel exclusive of on-site improvements. The following characteristics of the site should be discussed:

1. *Lot size and shape.* In addition to a narrative description of the dimensions and area of the lot, a plat of the site is usually included in the addenda, and referred to at this point.

2. *Street improvements.* The width and improvement of streets bounding or affecting the subject property should be noted.

3. *Topography and soil conditions.* The slope of the site and such features as creeks, ravines, or hillsides are described. Any problem or potential problem with soil stability, erosion, or drainage should be discussed.

4. *Public utilities.* The availability and ownership of public utilities, such as water, sanitary sewer, gas, and electricity, should be noted. Any problem with reliability or availability of utilities should be discussed in relation to the utility of the subject site.

Appraisers should be cautious in the factual statements they make regarding availability of utilities. This will avoid merely stating that "all necessary public utilities are available to the subject property," only to find out later from the client that sewage is disposed of by a septic tank on the site rather than by a public sanitary sewer system. Likewise, appraisers should not make positive statements they cannot substantiate regarding subsoil conditions. If problems with soil stability or drainage are evident, the appraiser should recommend, or rely on, the opinion of a soils engineer.

Zoning

The appraiser should identify both the municipality that has jurisdiction over the subject property and the precise zoning classification of the parcel. The discussion of zoning should include not only the uses permitted under the zoning regulations but also other restrictions affecting the subject parcel, such as minimum building setback line, parking requirement, height and density regulations, and so forth. Any private building regulation or restrictions affecting the subject property should also be discussed.

If the subject parcel is unimproved, zoning and building regulations are usually more important than if it is already improved. Copies of zoning regulations pertinent to the subject parcel may be included in the addenda. If the subject property is improved, the appraiser should note whether the existing improvements conform to the zoning regulations. Any items of nonconformity should be specifically mentioned.

Highest and Best Use

Appraisers should state their *opinions* of the highest and best use of the subject property and discuss the supporting evidence on which they have based those opinions. If an opinion of the highest and best use indicates a change in zoning, the appraiser should document the probability of such a zoning change with such evidence as the master land use plan for the subject area, similar surrounding uses or zoning, and statements from a staff member of the planning department that has jurisdiction over the subject property. If the highest and best use differs from the present use of the subject property, the appraiser should include a detailed discussion in support of that opinion.

Assessed Value and Taxes

The assessed value and taxes for the subject property should be given based on the latest roll available. This information can be obtained from the county tax collector's office. The appraiser may discuss the probability of a change in the amount of taxes or compare the subject area tax rate with surrounding areas.

Refer to Chapter 1 for further discussion of assessed value and property tax.

Description of Improvements

The appraiser includes in this section a description of the subject improvements. The description may be detailed or it may be a brief summary of the more important factors. If the description is in narrative form, it should be included in this section. If a detailed list of construction data is to be included, it should be placed in the addenda and referred to in this section.

In addition to the description of the physical improvements, physical depreciation and any items of functional or economic obsolescence should be discussed. The items that should be discussed in this section are:

1. Construction detail

2. Mechanical equipment

3. Size of improvements

4. Number of rooms, units, etc.

5. Condition of improvements

6. Quality of construction

7. Items of obsolescence

8. Landscaping

Photographs, improvement plats, and floor plans of the subject property are often included in the addenda, with a reference to them in this section of the report.

Approach to Appraisal, or Rationale

In the approach-to-appraisal section, appraisers have the opportunity to explain the process by which they have valued the subject property. For a client unfamiliar with real estate appraising, the appraiser may briefly describe the three approaches to value and may also explain why a particular approach is not applicable to this appraisal assignment. This section introduces the valuation portion of the appraisal report.

Site Valuation

In this section, appraisers present supporting data and justify their valuation of the subject land. (We discussed the methods of site valuation in Chapter 7.) If the subject property includes structural improvements, site valuation is normally considered as part of the cost approach. Site valuation may be a separate section of the report or may be incorporated into the cost approach section. If the valuation of the site is an important, substantial part of the appraisal, it is usually better to make site valuation a separate section.

In Chapter 7, we presented four methods of site valuation. In residential property appraisal, the analysis of land sales (market or comparative approach) is by far the best and most common method of site valuation.

A summary and analysis of pertinent sales data in comparison with the subject site should be included in the body of the report. In addition, the addenda usually contain a sales data sheet for each sale parcel, listing recording and factual data, description of parcel, availability of utilities, plat, and so forth.

Sales information and analysis in the body of the appraisal report are usually presented in a narrative style but may appear in chart form. The narrative report in the supplement includes an example of sales data presented in narrative form, with a chart for adjustment of the sales. The body of the report should include the following sales data:

1. Names of buyer and seller

2. Location

3. Date of sale

4. Description of site

5. Size of parcel

6. Sale price

7. Terms of sale

8. Price per square foot

Appraisers should explain their analysis and adjustments of the sale parcels for time, location, and physical characteristics.

Cost Approach

Estimated cost new of improvements and estimated depreciation are usually itemized. Supporting data and explanations are keyed to this itemized list. Any itemized supporting data, such as a breakdown of replacement cost of improvements, should be placed in the addenda if over one page in length.

Market Data Approach

The comparable sales may be presented in summary form or narrative style. The basic data to be included in the appraisal of a single-family residence are:

1. Name of buyer and seller

2. Address

3. Date of sale

4. Lot size

5. Description of residence
   a. Size
   b. Rooms

    c. Age

    d. Construction

    e. Any item to be compared and adjusted to the subject property

6. Sale price

7. Terms of sale

In reporting sales of multiple-family residences, the appraiser should include the following data in addition to the preceding:

8. Number of units

9. Sale price per unit, per room, and/or per square foot

10. Gross income

11. Gross rent multiplier

Comparability between the sale properties and the subject property should be discussed. A chart indicating the adjustments may be included in the report.

A sales data sheet for each sale parcel, giving information such as recording and factual data, description of parcel and improvements, photograph of property, and so forth, and a comparable sales map are usually included in the addenda and referred to in this section.

Income Approach

The reconstructed operating statement and account of the capitalization process should be presented in an itemized form similar to that for the cost approach. Supporting data and explanations are also keyed to the itemized list.

In single-family residence appraisal, the gross rent multiplier is presented as the income approach. Comparable rentals should be described and compared with the subject property, and the estimated rent for the subject justified. Sales developed as the basis for estimating the gross rent multiplier should be narratively described to provide pertinent data, or they may be set forth in an itemized or chart form. A gross rent multiplier is correlated from the sales and applied to the estimated rental to indicate the value of the subject property.

Reconciliation and Final Value Estimate

With the narrative discussion, the appraiser logically leads the reader to a final value estimate based on the data that has been presented. After reviewing briefly the indicated values from each of the approaches used in the appraisal, if necessary, the appraiser should discuss the applicability of each approach to the subject property and the reliability of the data used to arrive at the indicated values. The

appraiser should justify the method of arriving at the final value estimate and discuss the weight given to each approach, relative to the
estimated value.

Certification and Limiting Conditions of Appraisal

The certification and statement of limiting conditions required under
USPAP are shown in Figure 16–1, and are used in a typical form report.

Photographs of Subject Property

A minimum of three photographs are normally included in the report of a single-family residence appraisal: a front view of the residence, a rear yard view, and a view showing the subject property
and neighboring properties along the street. Photographs are usually
placed one or two to a page, with captions to indicate the subject and
the direction in which the picture was taken.

The number of photographs included often depends on the intended use of the appraisal. In an appraisal for condemnation use,
for demonstration purposes, or for an out-of-town prospective purchaser, photographs of all exterior siding and interior views of the
residence may be desirable. The appraiser should include in each appraisal assignment as many photographs as the client might need.
Aerial photographs often help the client see particular features of the
parcel or visualize the subject property in relation to the surrounding area.

Improvement Sketch and Plat Map

The appraiser should prepare and include in the addenda any
sketches or plans that would help convey the appraisal data to the
client. A plat showing the exterior dimensions of the improvements
and a diagram of the subject parcel should always be included in the
report. A plot plan showing the improvements in relation to the total
parcel, and an interior floor plan can also be included.

Sketches or plats should be drawn to scale and must be legible.
Paper $8\frac{1}{2}$ by 11 inches in size is preferred for narrative reports.
Larger-sized plats or plans should be folded and bound into the re-
port or inserted in an envelope.

Sales Data Sheets

The addenda should include a sheet of pertinent recording and factual data for each comparable sale or listing used in the appraisal.
Sales are numbered in consecutive order. Pictures of the improved
sale parcels or plats of the land sale parcels are often attached to the
bottom of the sale sheets.

Location Map

A sales map, numbered to correspond with the sale sheets, should follow the sale sheets or be inserted in an envelope at the end of the report. The subject property should be outlined and identified on the sales map. Sale parcels should be outlined in a different color from the subject parcel.

Qualifications of Appraiser

The appraiser's license or certification number, state of issue, and expiration date, along with qualifications should be listed in the report. The list should be in a summary form, limited to two or three pages. In addition to the appraiser's name, address, and business affiliation, the following information should be given:

1. Formal education (degrees granted)

2. Technical training and education

3. Experience in real estate (type and years)

4. Licenses or certificates in the real estate field (e.g., real estate broker's license, contractor's license)

5. Business and professional memberships (including offices held)

6. Types of properties appraised

7. Representative list of appraisal clients

8. Courts in which appraiser has qualified as an expert witness

9. Published articles or books by the appraiser related to the real estate field

ORAL REPORTS

USPAP Standard Rule 2–4 allows for oral reporting of appraisal assignments. It states that:

> To the extent that it is both possible and appropriate, each oral real property appraisal report (including expert testimony) must address the substantive matters set forth in Standard Rule 2–2.

This means that the same type and quality of information as required for written reports applies for oral reports. Note that FIRREA, however, does not recognize oral reports for federally related transactions.

SUMMARY

The report, written concisely and neatly, should include all of the essential elements and comply with USPAP regulations. It should be attractive and tasteful and represent the appraiser in a professional and articulate manner.

DISCUSSION QUESTIONS

1. Why is it important that appraisers be able to express and substantiate their opinions of value in a written report?

2. What are the essential elements of an appraisal report?

3. Name the three basic types of appraisal reports.

4. What are the main advantages and disadvantages of the form appraisal report?

5. What is the main advantage of the letter form of appraisal?

6. Name and describe the three major divisions of a narrative appraisal report.

7. What is the purpose of a letter of transmittal? What information should it contain?

8. What three elements should the purpose of appraisal contain?

9. What does the appraiser certify in the certificate of appraisal, as used in an appraisal report?

10. What is the purpose of assumptions and limiting conditions in an appraisal report?

MULTIPLE-CHOICE QUESTIONS

1. Appraisal reports, as all business correspondence, should be
   a. Extensive and wordy
   b. Neat and wordy
   c. Brief and neat
   d. All of the above

2. The most commonly used type of appraisal report is
   a. The form report
   b. The letter report
   c. The narrative report
   d. Both b and c

3. Government institutions and banks rely mostly on
   a. Letter reports
   b. Form reports
   c. Narrative reports
   d. Both a and c

4. In which of the following types of appraisal reports is the cost approach not considered?
    a. Form report
    b. Letter report
    c. Narrative report
    d. None of the above

5. The section of the report containing statements to protect the appraiser is
    a. The reconciliation and final value estimate section
    b. The certificate of appraisal
    c. The assumptions and limiting conditions
    d. All of the above

Chapter 17

COMPUTERIZATION OF THE APPRAISAL PROCESS

In today's computerized environment of mortgage processing and underwriting, appraisal production and reviewing has become high tech, using state-of-the-art technology. Computers are the standard mode of operation, and for residential appraising, computerized forms are the standard form of appraisal report. Automated data gathering, from on-line and CD-ROM services, plus modem access to multiple-listing information, make an appraiser's job much more efficient, and allows appraisers to produce reports faster and with more accurate data than ever before.

In addition, digital imaging techniques have progressed to replace traditional photography in the appraisal report, producing color or black-and-white pictures of the subject and comparable properties. With database-driven software, these images can be stored in the computer and used for subsequent reports or for additional copies of the original report. This digitizing of the photos facilitates the delivery of appraisals over the telephone lines, via computer modem, using industry standard Electronic Data Interchange (EDI) formats.

There are numerous software providers, offering a wide range of program packages, including sketch and map programs. Rapid technology changes require appraisers to continue to update their basic understanding of computerized systems. The following basic and maximized system examples are provided to refresh and enhance a working appraiser's computer systems knowledge.

HARDWARE CONSIDERATIONS

Minimum System Requirements

In order to operate any of today's software programs, an appropriate computer system is needed, with adequate working memory, fixed-disk storage capacity, and associated peripherals, such as a color monitor and, for most programs, a laser printer. The basic platform for most of today's appraisal software programs is a 386, 25-MHz (Intel 80386 microprocessor with a clock speed of 25 MHz) IBM-compatible personal computer. Most of the software providers recommend a 486 machine, as this processor has a more efficient operating environment and has an on-board math coprocessor.

While there are several software suppliers offering programs for the Apple environment, we will not discuss these in any detail, as the vast majority of programs are written for the IBM world.

In selecting a software package, program "overhead," or the amount of fixed disk space required to store the program, is only one of the important memory considerations. Adequate "free" fixed-disk space for temporary program storage, as well as adequate operating memory, or RAM (random access memory), is required.

Storage memory capacity can be a limiting factor in selecting software, unless your system is up-gradable for a larger-capacity fixed-disk drive, or unless your current operating system can support data compression, making more space available on your existing fixed-disk drive.

Operating memory, or RAM, capacity is a consideration. Although most basic appraisal software programs will operate on 2 Megabytes of RAM, most suppliers recommend 4 Megabytes, minimum. This ensures optimized processing of program data.

Basic Computer System Composition

The following outline lists basic computer system components, including various peripherals, and a representation of typical personal computer system memory requirements.

Minimum System Configuration

a. Computer: IBM PC or compatible AT

b. CPU (processor): 80286, min. or PS/2
   1. Clock Speed: 20 Megahertz, min.

c. Operating system
   1. Single user: PC DOS. MS DOS 3.0 and higher
   2. Network: Most UNIX and derivatives
   3. Shell Compatibility: Microsoft Windows—Some programs run under Windows, and some may be accessed through Windows, but actually run outside of Windows. Some programs only run outside of Windows.

d. Operating memory
   1. RAM: 2 Megabytes, min.
   2. ROM: 128 Kilobytes, min.
   3. Fixed-disk operating space: 5 Megabytes, min.
   4. Windows requires additional swap file memory

e. Disk drives
   1. Fixed-disk capacity: 20 Megabytes, min.
   2. Removable disk capacity: $3\frac{1}{2}$ in. 1.4 Megabyte
   3. Optional drives
      a. Removable drive: $5\frac{1}{4}$ in. 1.2 Megabyte
      b. CD-ROM: Used for various data and maps services
      c. Tape drive: Used for system and file backup

f. I/O ports
    1. Parallel port (Centronics): 1 used for most printers
    2. Serial ports (RS232): 2, min: 1 used for mouse; 1 for optional devices

g. Expansion slots: Optional

h. Keyboard: 101-key standard

i. Monitor: Color, EGA or higher (VGA and SVGA are higher)

j. Mouse: Compatible with operating system

k. Modem: Optional

l. Networks supported: Most novel; limited others

m. Printers: Some programs use letter-quality dot matrix, or an ink jet printer, however, most programs require a laser printer. Color digital imaging programs for photographs require color laser printers, and black-and-white imaging uses standard laser printers.

Maximized System

In order to take advantage of all of the state-of-the-art technology available to appraisers, and to fully utilize the various data and information services, additional system capability may be required. For example, in order to use Metroscan or some of the DataQuick services, a CD-ROM disk drive is required, as well as additional hard-disk storage capacity. For the on-line DataQuick services, and for multiple-listing services, a modem is required. For some color photo imaging, an expansion slot for the special adapter card is required, along with 8 Megabytes (MB) of RAM. A typical system configuration supporting a CD-ROM drive, plus color photo imaging would require the following:

1. Memory requirements: Assumes a 80386 CPU, or higher
    a. Operating memory requirements
        1. RAM: 8 Megabytes, minimum, 16 MB is recommended
        2. ROM: over 580 Kilobytes
        3. Fixed-disk operating space: 15 Megabytes
    b. Storage memory requirements
        1. Program storage: 20–25 Megabytes
            a. Major forms program: 8 MB
            b. Sketch program: 3 MB
            c. Metroscan: 2 MB
            d. DataQuick: 2 MB
            e. Photo imaging: 5 MB

2. System options
    a. Printers: A single laser printer will be adequate for most applications, however, additional memory may be required by individual programs to accommodate soft fonts or other for-

matting features. A total of 2 MB of RAM is recommended. This same printer may be used for black-and-white photo imaging; however, a separate, color printer is required for color photo imaging.

b. CD-ROM drives: A single CD-ROM drive may be used by either Metroscan or DataQuick, but must be at least 680-MB capacity.

c. Digital imaging systems: Today, most color photo imaging systems require an add-in card, inserted in an expansion slot. Black-and-white systems, using a digital camera, may require only the use of a serial port. This means that at least two serial ports are needed if a mouse is also used.

d. Modems: Most multiple-listing services are available via modem, and such services as DataQuick and other regional offerings, as well as training and support services from the Appraisal Institute and other organizations offer on-line access, as well. Modems can be internal or external, and most systems support "Hayes" compatibility. Some modems are combined with Fax capabilities, allowing for double duty as a facsimile machine.

INFORMATION AND DATA RESOURCES SERVICES

Multiple-Listing Services

Multiple-listing services (MLS) are established by regional realty boards for the purpose of facilitating property sales by providing access to listing and sales data for a given area. In the past year, major changes have occurred in many areas, consolidating boards and information resources, and providing appraisers access to active listings and pending sales, restricted in the past, unless the appraiser was also a licensed realtor. These services are in two forms, on-line via modem or as monthly published booklets. The on-line services provide varying degrees of data, generally offering the following:

1. An MLS log or tracking number, assigned by the board at the time a listing is created.

2. Detailed information regarding configuration and amenities of listed properties.

3. List and sale prices.

4. Search capability under a number of selectable variables, providing detailed sales analysis data.

Each board offering an on-line MLS will have specific requirements for signing on to the system and may dictate which modem access program is required.

Most MLS offerings are billed quarterly, with a one-time initiation fee and annual board membership dues. Rates and fees vary widely around the country, and in certain areas it may be necessary to belong to multiple boards or even boards in adjoining states to have adequate coverage.

CD-ROM Compact Disk Media

DataQuick and Metroscan are two examples of compact disk technology used effectively in the real estate industry. Both companies offer extensive data services, on a monthly subscription basis, including sales histories, comparable property searches, automated comparable selection, plat maps, flood zone data, and a plethora of other useful information.

```
    D A T A Q U I C K    I N F O R M A T I O N    N E T W O R K

========  11/22/9  ======  DATABASE MENU  ======  7:14 am  =========

A.  Real Estate Data            J.  Western Flood Data
B.  Statewide Searches          K.  Foreclosure Data
C.  Title Plant Access          L.  Property History / Doc # Search
D.  Verifacts                   N.  REO/USA
E.  BusinessLink                O.  Demographic/Trend Report
F.  COMPS                       P.  Demographic Marketing System
G.  New Homes/New Owners        Q.  PHO PeopleTracker
H.  CMDC (Members Only)
I.  Mortgage Leads

1.  Help * *2400bd,etc* *       4.  Pricing Info.
2.  End Session                 5.  California Assessor Updates
3.  DQ Software

Note:  For detailed database information, choose option #1.

=======================================================================
```

On-Line Information Services

DataQuick offers the most extensive example of on-line services, including the sales histories and comparable search capabilities of the CD-ROM services, plus much more. The preceding menu shows the current available services.

Options: Regional Considerations

Today, both Metroscan and DataQuick are region and state limited; however, both companies plan nationwide expansion over the next few years. The examples of services shown above demonstrate the type of data that may be available to supplement the county records. Other data services may be available in various parts of the country, offering similar services.

Cost Effectiveness

Generally, on-line services such as DataQuick are billed by the minute or by a flat rate per item or items selected. These fees will vary with monthly usage. The CD-ROM service is billed on a per county basis, at a flat rate per month, based on the number of counties subscribed.

The on-line services offer flexibility, where an appraiser crosses many county or regional board lines, plus offers a variety of services under one program. A CD-ROM drive is required, however, for maps.

The CD-ROM service offers extensive data, more quickly accessible, for a given county, and can be used without incurring phone charges as well as on-line minutes.

Some appraisers find both systems valuable, while others select one or the other. Certainly, both types of systems may be valuable, depending on the users' individual needs and the areas served.

SOFTWARE PROGRAMS

Forms

There are over 20 computerized appraisal forms software suppliers including some value-added suppliers who resell others' products. There is variation among suppliers in terms of ease of use, database capability, interactivity with sketch and photo imaging programs, and other features. In addition, hardware requirements for use of programs varies widely.

1. *Minimum Compliance Requirements:* Today, most appraisal forms suppliers are aware of the federal regulations for appraisal standards and make a point of compliance with the appropriate agencies. The binding federal regulations are dictated by USPAP, and further interpreted for residential appraisers, by Fannie Mae and Freddie Mac. The following summarizes these issues:

   a. FIRREA: This document demands that appraisals be written, in compliance with USPAP standards.

   b. USPAP compliance: The document provides that appraisals may be written in narrative format, or on a form, as long as they are sufficiently descriptive.

   c. Fannie Mae and Freddie Mac compliance: In the residential milieu, these companies create forms for their ultimate use, which become "industry standards," or approve forms designed by others for their use.

   d. Lender preferences: Various lending institutions may have special requirements that may mean modification of existing forms, or addition of special comments or addendums to appraisal reports. Software package customization features or formatting may be a selection criteria.

2. *Regional Considerations:* Software packages are written, for the most part, by people familiar with a particular region of the country, and the names of various forms or headers may vary from east to west, north to south. The capability for a program to allow for custom headers or labels for pages in a form set may be a valuable feature.

CAD Sketch Programs

There are only a handful of drawing programs on the market for appraisers, however, there are a vast number of CAD programs that could be used to generate sketches. The few sketch programs for appraisers are designed for automatic calculation of square footage, and can usually be integrated into some of the major forms software packages. A sample sketch created using a CAD program is shown in Figure 17–1.

MAP Programs

Due to the large amount of data required to produce and store map information, most programs are for limited geographic areas. Some of these programs are "stand-alone," and some may be integrated with a forms set. Figure 17–2 shows an example of a map generated from a regional program.

STATE-OF-THE-ART TECHNOLOGY

As computers become faster, smaller, and more powerful, the number and type of potential applications continues to grow. Interactivity and connectivity via telephone lines further expand the horizons for computerized information access and dissemination. Today, the hot button for appraisers is digital imaging to replace traditional photography for providing pictures of the subject and comparable properties. The figures bantied about the industry predict that photo imaging can produce color photos on plain white paper for approximately a dime per photo, and black-and-white photos for substantially less. These numbers are easily justified by a potentially significant decrease in photo processing expenses, while increasing productivity. The potential for ultimate cost savings resulting from more efficient use of time and resources, coupled with the concept of sending the entire appraisal to a lender over the phone, make this an attractive option.

Digital Imaging

Photo imaging is the digitizing of photographs, making them electronically available to a computer for storage, manipulation, and printing.

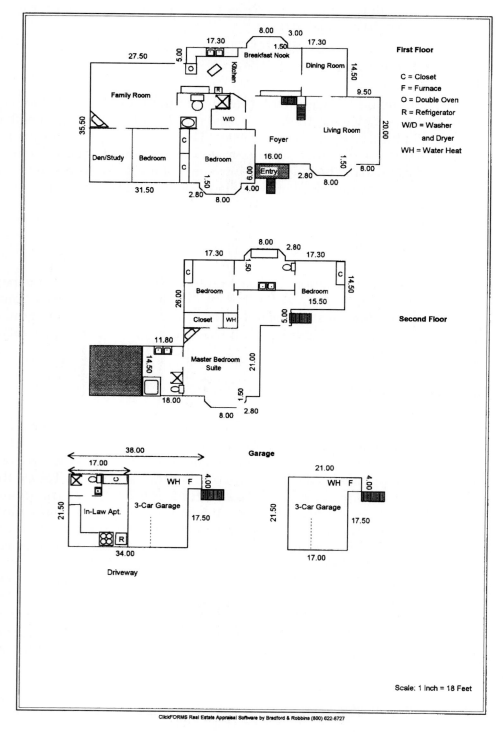

FIGURE 17–1 Sample sketch addendum: 2-story, trilevel home with 3-car garage and in-law quarters in basement.

SKETCH ADDENDUM   File No. 1969VINE

Borrower   Goodman, Herbert & Janet
Property Address   1969 Vinehill Circle
City Fremont   State Alameda   Country CA   Zip Code 94539
Lender/Client   California First Mortgage   Address

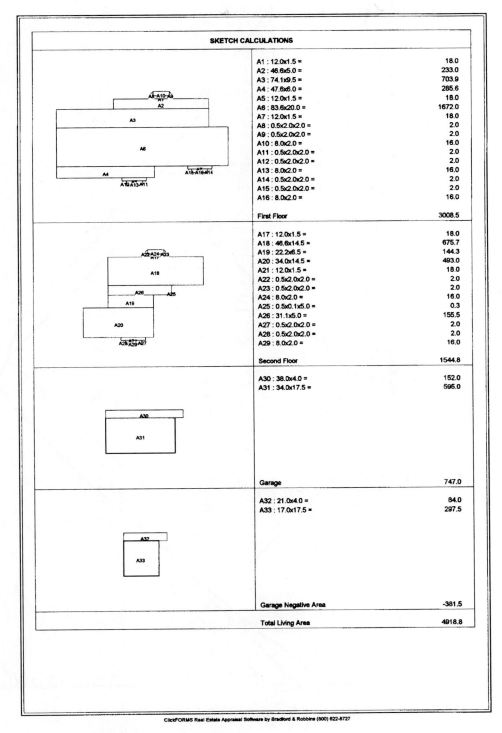

SKETCH CALCULATIONS	
A1 : 12.0x1.5 =	18.0
A2 : 46.6x5.0 =	233.0
A3 : 74.1x9.5 =	703.9
A4 : 47.6x6.0 =	285.6
A5 : 12.0x1.5 =	18.0
A6 : 83.6x20.0 =	1672.0
A7 : 12.0x1.5 =	18.0
A8 : 0.5x2.0x2.0 =	2.0
A9 : 0.5x2.0x2.0 =	2.0
A10 : 8.0x2.0 =	16.0
A11 : 0.5x2.0x2.0 =	2.0
A12 : 0.5x2.0x2.0 =	2.0
A13 : 8.0x2.0 =	16.0
A14 : 0.5x2.0x2.0 =	2.0
A15 : 0.5x2.0x2.0 =	2.0
A16 : 8.0x2.0 =	16.0
First Floor	**3008.5**
A17 : 12.0x1.5 =	18.0
A18 : 46.6x14.5 =	675.7
A19 : 22.2x6.5 =	144.3
A20 : 34.0x14.5 =	493.0
A21 : 12.0x1.5 =	18.0
A22 : 0.5x2.0x2.0 =	2.0
A23 : 0.5x2.0x2.0 =	2.0
A24 : 8.0x2.0 =	16.0
A25 : 0.5x0.1x5.0 =	0.3
A26 : 31.1x5.0 =	155.5
A27 : 0.5x2.0x2.0 =	2.0
A28 : 0.5x2.0x2.0 =	2.0
A29 : 8.0x2.0 =	16.0
Second Floor	**1544.8**
A30 : 38.0x4.0 =	152.0
A31 : 34.0x17.5 =	595.0
Garage	**747.0**
A32 : 21.0x4.0 =	84.0
A33 : 17.0x17.5 =	297.5
Garage Negative Area	**-381.5**
Total Living Area	**4918.8**

FIGURE 17–1   Continued

LOCATION MAP ADDENDUM

FIGURE 17–2

1. Color: Most color systems today require a color video camera, a special "grabber" adapted card inserted in the computer and a special color printer. Some systems require a scanner device, as well.

2. Black and white: Note that Fannie Mae requires only black-and-white photos, so that this less expensive option may be attractive to some appraisers. Also, a regular laser printer can print the photos, and a standard serial port is the only "internal" requirement.

Electronic Data Interchange (EDI)

The ability to send an entire appraisal report to a lender, over the phone, required that standard formats and transmission protocols be established. These standards provide the means to decrease the turnaround time, from appraisal order to receipt of the completed report, potentially reducing the loan approval cycle time. EDI is another technological step in the constant process of improving communications between appraisers and their clients.

Future Technology—Applications and Products

Planning your computer system to be both expandable in terms of memory and storage capacity, as well as upgradable in terms of CPU and software will allow for maximum advantage when new products and services become available. Computers are an integral part of our business lives, and care should be taken when selecting both hardware and software.

SUMMARY

Use of computer systems is commonplace in today's appraisal business, and as technology continues to advance, interconnectivity with lending institutions and other real estate-related businesses will continue to improve. Basic computer system hardware, and a wide variety of software packages, are available to appraisers to compete efficiently and effectively in a fast-paced high-volume business environment.

Chapter 18

CONSIDERATIONS IN APPRAISING OTHER TYPES OF SINGLE-FAMILY RESIDENCES

Body of Knowledge Topic

- *Legal Considerations in Appraisal—Forms of Property Ownership*

So far, we have discussed primarily the valuation of standard single-family, *detached* residences. Over the past three decades, other forms of single-family residential ownership have grown increasingly popular. Potential home buyers have for many reasons sought smaller, more economical residential units to satisfy their residential buying needs. Among the increasingly popular forms of single-family residential ownership are:

1. Mobile homes

2. Nonmobile homes

3. Townhouses

4. Rowhouses

5. Condominiums

6. Cooperative apartments

7. Community apartment projects

8. Cluster homes

9. Modular, manufactured, and kit homes (factory built)

10. Patio homes and Duet homes (zero lot line)

11. Compact homes

12. Planned unit development (PUD)

13. Time shares

MOBILE HOMES

The term *mobile home* was originally used for homes that were truly mobile—small units that could be readily hitched to an automobile and driven to a different location. Today, however, the term is somewhat misleading; the newer single units are often 12 feet by 60 feet. They are usually set up in double units (24 feet by 60 feet or 26 feet by 66 feet—some states limit highway hauling of units to the smaller size), either in a mobile home park on rented or leased space or on a single-family residential lot (assuming local zoning and private deed restrictions allow) never to be moved again. In the latter case, the mobile home sometimes becomes real property.

California law permits real estate licensees to handle mobile home resales. The popularity of the mobile home in California continues, especially in some resort areas and in smaller towns and communities on the outskirts of urban areas. Some mobile home parks can still be found in urban areas, such as Los Angeles and Santa Clara counties. However, the increase in land value occasioned by the influx of high-tech and related industrial and commercial development indicates that few such mobile home parks will be able to survive, as buyers and developers continue to bid the land value up, encouraging many owners of mobile home parks to sell out. Some communities, realizing the threat to mobile home residents, have enacted some controls on owners of mobile home parks to ensure that the parks continue to be operated as mobile home parks.

The appraisal student, licensee, or even potential mobile home park resident is advised that there are both advantages and disadvantages to mobile home park living.

Some of the advantages are:

1. Cost per living unit is lower.

2. Annual property taxes are lower. (The mobile home is usually treated as personal property unless it is part of real estate.)

3. The living unit is smaller and more compact, with less wasted space.

4. Heating and air-conditioning costs are lower.

5. Water costs are lower. (Yards are smaller.)

6. Less yard maintenance is required.

7. More conveniences, such as club house, swimming pool, spas, exercise rooms, recreational rooms, laundry facilities, libraries, and recreational vehicle and boat storage are provided.

8. One entrance, many times electronically controlled or guarded (especially in large, good-quality mobile home parks), provides a sense of security for residents, especially those who like to travel and feel their homes and belongings are safe.

9. Good Neighborhood Watch programs are possible because many parks do not allow street parking, which makes the presence of any nonresident readily apparent. (Most mobile home parks have private streets for such control.)

10. Many have guest parking areas to eliminate the need for street parking.

11. There are strict rules to control pets, noise, and maintenance of yards and mobile home exteriors.

Some of the disadvantages are:

1. Generally, the mobile home owner has no ownership of the land but only leases the space for the mobile home. This means that rents can rise with little control in the hands of the resident. It also means that, if the owner of the mobile home park wishes to sell the park, for whatever reason, the mobile home resident might be faced with having to move, should the new owner wish to develop the land for another use.

2. If faced with having to move the mobile home from the park, the mobile home owner may have difficulty finding another park in the area that will accommodate the mobile home. This is especially true if the mobile home is an older one. If this is the case, the market value of the mobile home can be greatly reduced.

3. There is usually no appreciation of a mobile home, unless it is situated in a quality mobile home park. Away from its site, the mobile home becomes personal property and generally depreciates to a small percentage of its original cost.

4. Some people feel confined and regimented by the restrictions and rules in effect in most quality mobile home parks.

Appraisers must consider the advantages and disadvantages of mobile homes and the needs and desires of their potential buyers.

When appraising mobile homes as *personal* property, the appraiser must note the unit, the services provided by the park, and the location and care of the park—all factors that are important in relating one unit's value to another. Units are generally compared with sales of others in the same park, with consideration given to differences in location, utility, time, and terms of sale. The mobile home park manager or a local mobile home sales specialist can often furnish an expert comparison.

Mobile homes may be placed on a mobile home park pad directly on the property line to create a larger courtyard or garden area (compare Figures 18–1 and 18–2). The side of the unit on the property line would then have opaque windows and skylights to provide light only and to create more privacy for both the unit and the neighbor's unit. This zero lot line arrangement provides one larger usable

FIGURE 18–1 Mobile home park with standard side yards.

yard rather than two smaller, relatively limited side yards. The garage or carport may be at the front of the unit as shown in the illustration. Such an arrangement is desirable because of overall privacy and good use of the available yard space, even allowing for a small swimming pool, spa, or hot tub in some slightly wider lots.

NONMOBILE HOMES

Although many so-called mobile homes remain relatively immobile once they are placed on a pad in a mobile home park, they are still usually considered personal property. However, there has been a move toward permanent placement of a factory-built mobile home on a concrete or other permanent foundation; features such as wood or masonry fascia exterior siding and a wood shingle gabled roof can be included. The result is a relatively compact, inexpensive, single-family detached home. These units may be placed on standard sized lots and are quite similar to the modular home placed on a separate site, since both are primarily factory built, then transported to the site

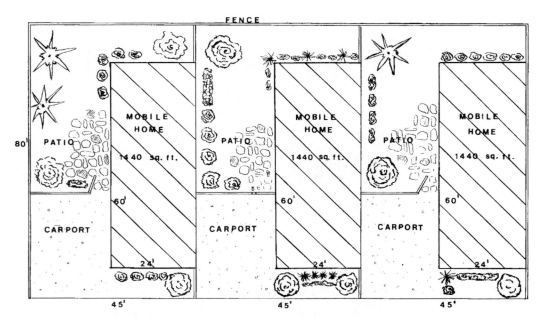

FIGURE 18–2   Mobile homes with zero lot line placement.

where additions and refinements are added. A fine example of such a home can be seen in Figure 18–3.

When appraising a mobile home that has been placed on a permanent foundation on an individually owned lot, the appraiser must treat the residence as a single-family detached home. Such a unit is legally classified as real estate, having all the physical characteristics of a modular (or factory-built) home placed on a lot. In appraising such a mobile home the appraiser should use the same market ap-

FIGURE 18–3   Nonmobile home. Example of good quality double-width mobile home, with a concrete foundation and exterior rustic treatment, placed on a separate lot.

proach as for a standard site-built home. He or she should consider comparable sales that are as similar as possible in the following:

market approach

Location
Utility
Time
Terms of sale

With the cost approach, care should be taken to determine replacement cost, including:

Cost approach

Cost of unit at factory
Delivery cost of unit to site
Site preparation
Foundation and other concrete work
Cost of placing unit on foundation and of other finishing work
Cost of all utilities
Accrued depreciation (subtract)
Value of land including off-site improvements (add)

With either approach, the appraiser should determine whether the improvement is legal—that is, whether it complies with local zoning ordinances and private deed restrictions.

TOWNHOUSES, ROWHOUSES, CONDOMINIUMS, COOPERATIVE APARTMENTS, COMMUNITY APARTMENT PROJECTS, AND CLUSTER HOMES

Although the terms *townhouse, rowhouse, condominium, cooperative apartment,* and *cluster home* refer to slightly different types of single-family residences, all such residences are appraised in basically the same way. We shall define each term and then explain appraisal methods.

Townhouses

A townhouse or townhome is a single-family residence where the ownership of the land and the unit are one. It can have one, two, or more stories and has common walls with one or more similar residences.

According to California State Department of Real Estate, *townhouse* is not a legal term; the term describes a residential development in which individual dwellings are in very close physical proximity, sometimes separated only by party walls. It is conceivable that a residential development using the townhouse design could be legally structured as a condominium. For the most part, however, this is not done.

Townhouse developments are normally planned developments. Each individual owner has fee title to the structure and the land underlying it. Ownership in common with others is usually confined to the land that does not underlie the residential structure, frequently including private streets, sidewalks, green areas, and a separate parcel improved with recreational facilities. For examples of townhouses, see Figures 18–4 to 18–7.

All three approaches can be used in appraising townhouses; however, the market approach is generally most reliable. The same guidelines apply to the use of the market approach as were given in Chapter 12. If the property is income property, apply the income approach as described in Chapter 13. The cost approach is normally the least reliable approach in the appraisal of townhouses. The determination of land value is rather difficult because the land includes not only that underlying the residence, in the case of a townhouse but also land owned in common with other parties together with the improvements thereon.

One way to use the cost approach is to treat the unit being appraised as a unit by itself, and apply a replacement cost less depreciation to the residence and garage. Then take a *proportionate* replacement cost new less depreciation of the common area improvements including walkways, driveways, lawns, swimming pool, and so on.

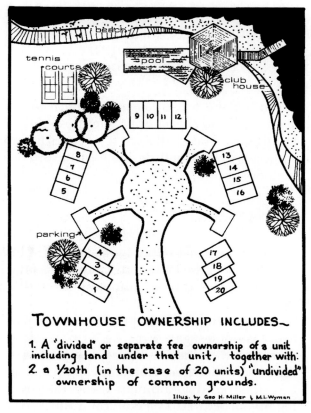

FIGURE 18–4   Overhead view of beach townhouse development.

FIGURE 18–5   Typical townhouse elevations. Note the common walls and private patios.

FIGURE 18–6   A mountain townhouse.

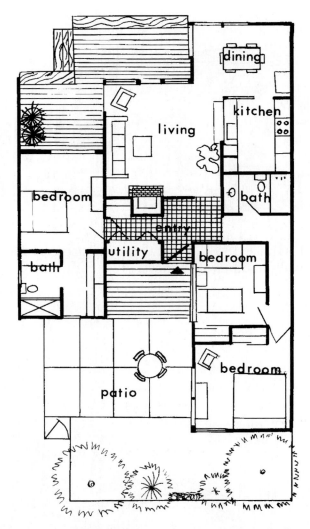

FIGURE 18–7   Floor plan of townhouse. Note the deck and patio for maximum privacy and outdoor living in minimal space.

Add to this the estimated value of the land, calculated either from the assessor's land value or by assigning the land a percentage of the whole property value.

In some cases, the townhouse complex has so many living units (and perhaps two or more swimming pools and other improvements) that a proper allocation of the value of the improvements in common ownership becomes virtually impossible. In these cases, one can only *estimate* the proportionate cost of other improvements and their relationship to the unit being appraised.

The market value of townhouses depends not only on the recreational and other facilities available to unit owners but also on the care that the managing organization, whether a homeowners' group or other entity, provides for the common areas. The appraiser must judge the quality of the management from observations and discussions with other owners.

Rowhouses

A *rowhouse* is physically similar to a townhouse, except that a rowhouse generally has its garage in a *tandem* arrangement on the ground or basement level. (That is, the garage has room for two cars, one parked ahead of the other.) Rowhouses can be found in many of the major cities in the United States, including New York, Philadelphia, Baltimore, and San Francisco. The design originated in England and was brought to the United States by early settlers in the 1700s. Since the rowhouse is usually built in city areas where land is at a premium, rowhouse lots are often only 25 feet wide. Amenities associated with later townhouse developments, such as wide garages, walkways, recreational areas, and swimming pools, are not normally part of rowhouse ownership. Typical rowhouses are shown in Figures 18–8 to 18–10.

All three approaches can be used in appraising rowhouses. In the market approach, the appraiser should be sure to compare similar rowhouses and similar locations. The cost and income approaches should be applied as appropriate.

Condominiums — market approach

According to the California Civil Code (Section 783), a *condominium* consists of "an undivided interest in common in a portion of a parcel of real property together with a separate interest in space, such as an apartment, office or store." Most condominium owners acquire a fee simple interest in a cubicle of air space and the interior surfaces of the

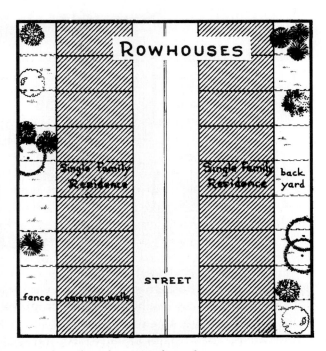

FIGURE 18–8   Overhead view of rowhouses.

FIGURE 18–9   San Francisco rowhouse elevations. Usually built on 25-foot-wide lots. Garages generally provide space for parking two cars in tandem (one behind the other). These homes, unlike the Eastern rowhouses, are equipped with garages because most families in California cities must rely on private automobiles. Quality of construction shown is good.

walls, floors, ceilings, windows, and so forth that define the air space. The underlying land and virtually all of the rest of the structure that houses the condominium unit, along with any common ground, lawns, recreational facilities, and the like are owned in tenancy in common with other owners in the development. (See Figure 18–11.)

FIGURE 18–10   Eastern rowhouse elevations. Usually built on 20-foot-wide lots. These rowhouses range from the fair quality construction, shown above, to excellent quality in the fine old residential urban areas. They do not usually have garages since they are generally located near public transportation.

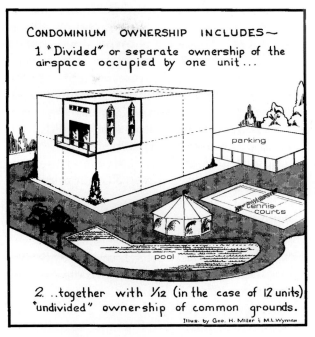

FIGURE 18–11 Condominium ownership.

The condominium makes possible the individual ownership, alienation, and mortgaging of a portion of *air space* occupied by an apartment or living unit situated on any floor of the building. The principal point to remember is that, in the ownership of a condominium unit, it is possible for the owner of that unit to have a separately owned unit either above or below, or both.

A condominium unit is appraised much the same as a townhouse, except that there is no specific lot value applicable to the condominium unit: All of the land is in common ownership. Because of this, the cost approach is not practical; the market approach is the only reliable method. In the case of multistory condominiums, it is difficult to compute the replacement cost of individual units because there are so many common improvements in the structure itself: hallways, stairs, elevators, and the like. As in townhouses, the market value of condominiums depends not only on the recreational and other facilities available to unit owners but also on the care that the managing organization, whether a homeowners' group or other entity, provides for the common areas. The appraiser must judge the quality of the management from observations and discussions with other unit owners.

Cooperative Apartments

According to the California Department of Real Estate Reference Book a *cooperative apartment* is "a form of apartment ownership, ownership of shares in a cooperative venture which entitles the owner to use, rent, or sell a specific apartment unit. The corporation usually reserves the right to approve certain actions such as a sale or improvement." This form of ownership is not considered as real estate.

The cooperative apartment in effect differs from a condominium in that any charges or debts attached to any units can become the obligation of the other units or shareholders. Another difference is that approval must be received from the other shareholders before a unit can be sold, rented, gifted, or leased or any other similar action can be taken.

Physically, the cooperative apartment might resemble any other apartment building or even a condominium.

Community Apartment Project

Community apartment projects are typically operated, maintained, and controlled by a governing board elected by the owners of the fractional interests. The California Civil Code Business and Professions Code Sections 11004 and 11004.5 states that "the purchaser receives an undivided interest in the land, together with the right of exclusive occupancy of an apartment located thereon."

Purchasers generally receive a *leasehold* interest in the community apartment, while in a condominium, the purchaser customarily receives a *fee* interest in the unit. For a cooperative apartment, the purchaser receives shares of stock and the right to occupy a specific unit.

Physically, community apartment projects, cooperative apartments, and condominiums are similar. The appraiser must review the transfer documents in order to determine the differences.

Cluster Homes

A *cluster home* is built as a detached single-family residence on a separate lot, adjoining an open space or recreation area owned in common by single-family residential lot owners in the cluster. The cluster home concept originated in areas where zoning restricted density of development per acre. For example, suppose a developer wished to develop a 40-acre parcel of land zoned for one-acre-minimum lots. However, suppose that 20 acres of the parcel were either too steep to develop or contained a stream or creekbed with natural growth that would enhance the development if left in its natural state. The best solution would be to cluster 40 homes on the remaining 20 acres, on one-half-acre sites, with the scenic 20 acres left in perpetuity as open space, horse trails, bicycle trails, or other recreational area for the express enjoyment of the owners of the cluster homes. In this way the integrity of the one-acre-minimum zoning would be maintained for the entire 40-acre parcel, since the undeveloped land would remain undisturbed. In some areas, the cluster home concept can be groups of homes clustered close together, even with common walls, while the recreational or common areas surround the clusters of homes. Compare Figures 18–12 and 18–13.

The cluster home is appraised like a standard single-family residence, except by the market approach. In using this approach, the appraiser should examine only sales of other homes in the *same* cluster development, if possible.

MODULAR, MANUFACTURED, AND KIT HOMES (FACTORY BUILT)

A *modular home* is built substantially at a factory or somewhere else away from the site, transported to the site in one piece or in parts, and placed on a foundation by a large crane or other heavy equipment. Sometimes called a factory-built home, it differs from the standard detached single-family residence that is usually built at the site piece by piece, and referred to as a site-built home.

There are many modular home factories in the United States, offering several basic plans and qualities of material. Most factory-built homes are state-inspected at the factory. (Modular homes cannot cross state lines, kit homes can.) They can generally be placed anywhere in that state, subject to local zoning restrictions, such as setbacks and height limitations, and subject to private deed restrictions, such as minimum house square footage and architectural approval.

Most modular homes are built in a standard module, for exam-

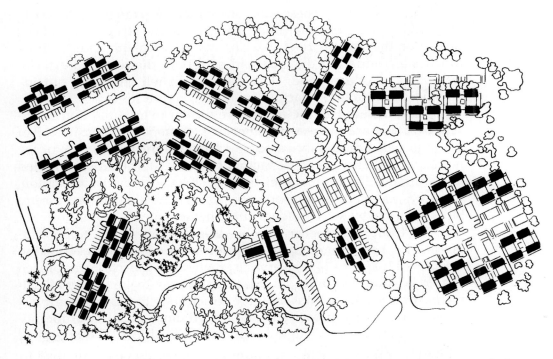

FIGURE 18–12 Overhead view of large development of cluster homes showing open space and recreational areas *interspersed* among the homes.

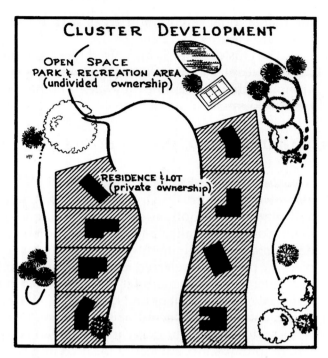

FIGURE 18–13   Overhead view of cluster homes of small development showing separate common area in one location, allowing for individual single-family residential lots in a separate location.

ple, 12 feet by 24 feet. These components can be arranged in a variety of ways to form particular floor plans. Once the structure has been placed on the site, the roof, exterior rustic treatment, and finishing touches are added. If the type and quality of the roof and exterior treatment are very good, it is difficult to tell from the outside whether the structure is factory-built. (See Figure 18–14.)

Manufactured, or kit, homes are similar to modular homes, except that they are not assembled prior to transport to the site. All of the materials are prefabricated and labeled, and in the case of log homes, are assembled at the factory to check fit, then disassembled and shipped. The kit includes boards, sheet rock, nails, insulation, windows, cabinets, fixtures, plumbing, etc. The kits are then assembled at the site by local builders or the homeowner.

All three approaches can be used in appraising a modular home. The market and income approaches are used as described in Chapters 12, 13, and 14. The appraiser who uses the market approach should be careful to find comparable sales or to make proper adjustments for sales that do not compare structurally to the unit being appraised. The cost approach should be used much the same as for mobile homes placed on single-family residential lots. The appraiser determines the following:

Replacement cost of the unit at the factory
Cost of delivery to the site

FIGURE 18–14   Modular home, average quality.

Cost of site preparation
Cost of placing the unit on the foundation and finishing it
Cost of installing all utilities
Subtract accrued depreciation
Add the value of the land, including off-site improvements

PATIO HOMES AND DUETS (ZERO LOT LINE)

A patio home, also called a garden home, is a single-family residence on an individual lot that is generally much smaller than a standard residential lot. If the residence is positioned on the side lot line so that there is in effect no side yard setback, it is referred to as a zero lot line. Special zoning must generally be instituted for such homes. If the residence is on the side lot line, it has only a backyard or patio area. Adjoining residences are sometimes built with a common wall on their common lot line, with the remainder of each lot being the patio or backyard area. Such homes can be built on lots of 4,500 square feet, even on as little as 3,000 square feet, whereas the minimum lot in many suburban and urban areas is 6,000 square feet. (See Figures 18–15 and 18–16.) These adjoining residences are often referred to as "duets."

All three approaches can be used in appraising a patio home. The most reliable approach is generally the market approach, providing there are sufficient recent sales of comparable properties. To apply the cost approach, the appraiser must determine proper construction costs. The value of the land is usually estimated by one of the methods other than the comparable sales method, since there are generally no lot sales. The cost approach is normally only a backup to the market approach or the income approach.

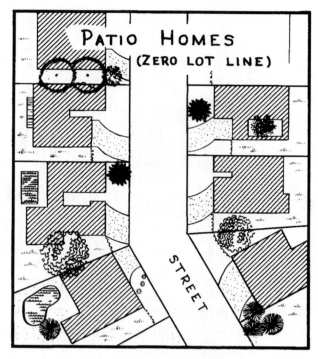

FIGURE 18–15   Patio homes or garden homes (zero lot line).

COMPACT HOMES

A *compact home* has a smaller area than the average single-family detached home, which runs between 1,300 and 1,800 square feet. The compact home, between 900 and 1,200 square feet, appeals to people who want more privacy than townhouses or condominiums afford, yet do not want the expense and upkeep of a standard sized home. The compact home is essentially a slightly smaller version of the fair-quality home illustrated in Chapter 8, Figure 8–8. It usually has two bedrooms and one and a half or two baths and lacks a fireplace, dishwasher, and some other amenities that standard sized homes might have. Most compact homes have only a one-car garage. The lot is usually a bit smaller than the standard lot. The compact home combines the privacy of a single-family home with some of the economies of the townhouse; in addition, the original cost of the compact home and the cost of its operation are less than those of a larger home.

Since the compact home exhibits all the physical characteristics, on a reduced scale, of the standard single-family home, the standard appraisal approaches may be used. Comparable sales data should be limited to similar compact homes because of the unique characteristics of this type of residence.

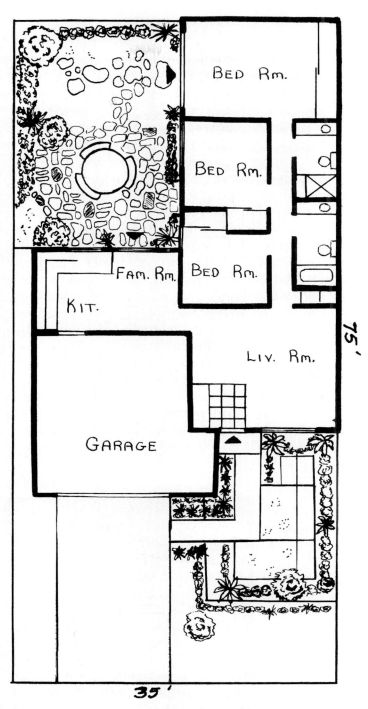

FIGURE 18–16 Floor plan of patio home (zero lot line). Notice the two patios for maximum privacy and outdoor living in minimal space.

PLANNED UNIT DEVELOPMENT (PUD)

Planned unit developments are becoming more popular as prospective homeowners adopt, and builders try to satisfy, a changing life style. This type of development is very similar to the "common green" concept of community development. The PUD is a community of clustered single-family detached residences, townhouses, garden apartments, and other types of residences, with ample open space, community recreational facilities, and sometimes local shopping and employment centers. (See Figure 18–17.)

In appraising residences in such a development, the appraiser should follow the guidelines set forth in this chapter for each respective residence type. In the market approach, the appraiser should be certain to limit any comparable market sales data to the confines of the planned unit development under consideration. The main reason for limiting the range of comparables is that the market value of homes in these developments, as with townhouses and condominiums, is dependent not only on the recreational and other facilities available but also on the quality of care that the managing organization provides for the common areas. The appraiser must judge management of common areas from observation and from discussions with unit owners. Some lenders require appraisers to select one comparable from the subject development and two comparables from outside the development in new (less than 2 years old) PUDs or two comparables from the subject development and one comparable from outside on older more established PUDs.

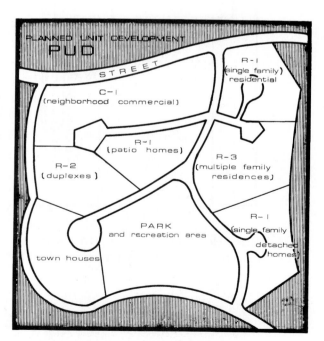

FIGURE 18–17   Planned unit development.

TIME SHARES

According to West's Annotated California Codes 1987, page 139, Business and Professions Code Section 11003.5:

> (a) A "time-share project" is one in which a purchaser receives the right in perpetuity, for life, or for a term of years, to the recurrent exclusive use or occupancy of a lot, parcel, unit, or segment of real property, annually or on some other periodic basis, for a period of time that has been allotted from the use or occupancy periods into which the project has been divided.
> (b) A "time-share estate" is a right of occupancy in a time-share project which is coupled with an estate in the real property.
> (c) A "time-share use" is a license or contractual or membership right of occupancy in a time-share project which is not coupled with an estate in the real property.

Time shares have been sold throughout the world, generally involving recreation-type properties including apartments, hotels, motels, condominiums, townhouses, private campgrounds, and recreational vehicle parks.

Stated simply, a time-sharing program involves long-term rights to use and occupy real property for short-term use periods into which the property has been divided (for example, the right to use a dwelling unit for 2 weeks of each year for the next 10 years). In some cases, a time-share purchaser acquires an undivided interest in the real property (a time-share estate) as well as the periodic use right. In others, the purchaser acquires only a right to use (time-share use). In either case, the right to use may be specified (for example, the first 2 full weeks in July each year) or it may be on a first-reserved, first-served basis.

The student appraiser or licensee is advised that, in our opinion, the best way to establish the fair market value of such offerings is, if at all possible, to gather recent market sales of time shares other than those sold at the initial stage of offering, at which time intense promotional activities are sometimes used to sell such shares. The *resales* activity, in our opinion, is a better indicator of the marketability of such interest in real estate.

SUMMARY

In this chapter, we have discussed most of the major types of residences found in the marketplace that require appraisal knowledge out of the ordinary. There are some other variations, and no doubt there will be more, that will demand additional considerations. The appraiser must be up to the challenge.

DISCUSSION QUESTIONS

1. What is the major difference between condominium ownership and townhouse ownership?

2. What is the primary identifying characteristic of a patio home or garden home?

3. Is there any difference between a townhouse and rowhouse? If so, what is it?

4. How might a mobile home become part of the realty (real estate)?

5. Do you think that the modular home concept will become more popular? Why or why not?

6. In what way are a modular home and a mobile home similar?

MULTIPLE-CHOICE QUESTIONS

1. Generally, a major disadvantage to ownership of a mobile home located in a mobile home park is
    a. Lower annual real estate taxes
    b. Owner of the mobile home is subject to possible sale of the park for another use requiring mobile home to be moved
    c. Strict rules to control pets, noise, and maintenance
    d. Smaller living unit

2. Generally, a major advantage to ownership of a mobile home located in a mobile home park is
    a. Security
    b. Ease of maintenance
    c. Availability of low-interest loans
    d. Ease of moving a mobile home

3. A nonmobile home, mobile home, and modular home have which of the following in common?
    a. They are appraised exactly the same way.
    b. They are all real property.
    c. They are all factory-built.
    d. They are all taxed only on the land.

4. A cooperative apartment building and a condominium building have which of the following in *common*?
    a. Each building has more than one owner.
    b. Owners are responsible only for debts to their own individual units.
    c. There are no restrictions for selling one's unit.
    d. Anyone who has the money can buy a unit that is for sale.

5. A townhouse and a condominium differ in which of the following ways?

a. One has common owned areas.
b. One has ownership of the land beneath the unit.
c. One has homeowner association dues.
d. There is no difference between the two.

6. Which approach is the least reliable in appraising a condominium?
   a. Market approach
   b. Comparable approach
   c. Cost approach
   d. None of the above

7. A rowhouse is closest in construction and ownership concept to
   a. A cooperative apartment
   b. A condominium
   c. A townhouse
   d. A mobile home

8. "An undivided interest in common in a portion of a parcel of real property together with a separate interest in space, such as an apartment, office, or store" best describes
   a. A cooperative apartment
   b. A townhouse
   c. A rowhouse
   d. A condominium

9. One major difference between a rowhouse and townhouse is
   a. A townhouse does not have common walls.
   b. A townhouse does not have common areas.
   c. A rowhouse does not have common areas.
   d. There are no differences.

10. The cluster-home concept would provide what major benefit to the community?
    a. Low-priced housing
    b. Privately owned roads
    c. Retention of common areas in their natural state
    d. All of the above

11. Which of the following homes is built at the site?
    a. Custom home
    b. Modular home
    c. Mobile home
    d. Nonmobile home

12. One noticeable difference between a western rowhouse and a townhouse is
    a. Type of roof
    b. Location of the patio
    c. Location of the garage
    d. There are no differences

13. In which of the following is it possible to have a separately owned unit either above or below another unit?
    a. Townhouse
    b. Rowhouse
    c. Cluster home
    d. Condominium

14. Which of the following employs the concept of zero lot line construction?
    a. Compact homes
    b. Patio homes
    c. Cluster homes
    d. Modular homes

15. Which of the following is an advantage that an occupant of a compact home would have over an occupant of a condominium or townhouse?
    a. More square footage of home
    b. More bedrooms
    c. Lower payments
    d. More privacy

Chapter 19

SPECIAL-PURPOSE APPRAISING

Body of Knowledge Topic

- *Valuation of Partial Interests*

A residential real estate appraiser is occasionally confronted with an appraisal problem that cannot be solved by conventional means. Although many types of valuation problems can arise in the appraisal of residential real estate, we shall concern ourselves in this chapter with a few of the more common types of special problems.

Throughout most of this text, we have discussed primarily the valuation of whole properties—the fee title including the entire bundle of rights. Sometimes, however, we must value only a portion of a property, perhaps a physical division of the real estate, such as a part take, or one of the bundle of rights, such as a leasehold. The following discussion is only an introduction to some of these problems, not an attempt to cover completely the entire field of special-purpose appraising.

LEASE INTERESTS

Some special appraisal problems are normally not encountered in residential real estate as often as they are in commercial or industrial real estate. Notable in this category is the appraisal of lease interests. Seldom is a residential property, single or multiple family, encumbered with a lease exceeding one year. Most tenant-occupied residential properties are rented on a month-to-month basis, with an occasional rent agreement drawn up for a period of a year. These rent agreements, sometimes termed leases, seldom exceed a year. A commercial property, such as a service station, might have a 25-year lease to a major tenant. The valuation of this lease at any time before its expiration is a problem that can best be solved by an expert in this field. Property owned by the federal government, notably national forest land, is sometimes leased for 50 or 99 years to citizens who build vacation homes. Private owners in portions of the Hawaiian islands have also long been leasing land for residential use; their leases usually run for 50 years, but some extend to 99 years. Even in some areas on the mainland, especially in recreational areas, private landowners are leasing land for residential development.

The basic approach to appraising a lease interest, or leasehold, is to value as of a certain date all the future benefits, if any, to be realized by the lease holder (lessee). In no case can the value of the leasehold together with the underlying fee exceed the value of the whole property.

Since the proper valuation of a leasehold requires knowledge of annuity capitalization, a topic covered in advanced appraisal courses, we shall not attempt to present such an analysis here. This discussion should merely alert the student or the appraiser to the occasional need for a separate valuation of the leasehold interest. Additional study is necessary to learn how to appraise a leasehold interest properly.

EASEMENTS

Broadly speaking, an easement is a right held by one person or entity over, in, or under the property of another. An easement can be overhead, for example, a power line easement enjoyed by a private electric company. It can be underground, for example, a pipeline easement enjoyed by a utility company. Or it can be on the surface, for example, a road easement held by one person over land owned by another.

Underground Easements

Underground easements lie below the surface of the ground. They include pipeline easements of all types, such as storm drainage, sewer, water, and underground conduits for electrical cable.

An easement is valued in proportion to the value loss suffered by the whole property because of the existence of that easement. Underground easements often do not unduly restrict the use of the surface for residential purposes. For example, a subdivider or developer grants most underground utility easements along the rear or side line of a residential lot, so that the utility company may provide service to that and other lots. These easements, usually only 5 feet wide on each lot, do not unduly restrict the use of the lot, since most residential lots have setback lines that preclude the building of any structure within a certain distance of the property line. The owner can usually grow small trees and shrubs and enjoy such easement-encumbered land in a normal manner. However, if an underground easement is needed after a lot has been developed for residential purposes, the general rule is that the easement is valued as a percentage of the total value of the land under which it lies. This percentage can range from 10 to 100 percent of fee value, depending on the restrictions imposed on the use of the land. For example, an underground easement for a pipeline running diagonally across a backyard, restricting the building of a swimming pool, could possibly be valued at 100 percent of fee value of the land needed for the easement. In addition, there would no doubt be some allowance for severance damage (discussed later in this chapter).

Surface Easements

The most common type of surface easement is the road easement. Easements for roads, or for any other purpose that uses the land surface—flood control channels, drainage ditches, and so on—are generally valued at 100 percent of fee value of the area occupied by the easement. The land surface is usually the most usable portion of the property.

Overhead Easements

The most common type of overhead easement is the power line easement. Values for this type of easement range from 10 to 100 percent of fee, depending on restrictions imposed on the use of the fee. For example, an easement for a power line that diagonally crossed the backyard of a good-quality residence, possibly restricting the growing of trees or the construction of a swimming pool, would be valued at 100 percent of fee for the easement area, plus probable severance damage. Although it might seem unusually restrictive to prohibit construction of a swimming pool because of an overhead power line, people have been electrocuted when the extended handle of a vacuum cleaner they were using to clean a pool contacted a high-voltage line. In addition, occasional interference with radio and television reception decreases the value of the property. These problems must be considered when the appraiser is valuing the easement and the possible effects of the facilities to be placed in the easement area on the total property value.

AIR RIGHTS

A subject of increasing importance as urban areas become more crowded is air rights—the rights to the air over a parcel of land. Some buildings in New York, Chicago, and other densely populated areas are built on air rights above railroad tracks and streets. Air rights include, of course, the right to provide the usual foundation or support material for each particular structure. A practical approach to the valuation of air rights would be to subtract from the market value of the underlying fee the estimated total cost of providing additional foundation and support structures needed to realize the practical use of the air above an existing structure.

The air rights referred to in this discussion apply to the air immediately above a parcel of land that can be practically used for construction of buildings or other structures; they do not include the air *space* above a certain height controlled by the U.S. government for military, commercial, and private aircraft use. (Refer to Chapter 2.)

SOLAR RIGHTS

Although most single-family residences enjoy reasonable rights to light and air, a subject of probable increasing concern will be the rights of a residence to solar rays. More and more homes are being constructed with solar collectors for solar heating of space and water and for other augmentation of existing home energy systems. The question of the rights of a single-family residence to receive the sun's rays, especially during the winter months when the sun strikes all areas of the United States at a severe slant, will require some definitive law regarding proper appraisal of these solar rights and their limitation. An encroachment of solar rights could come about, for example, if a home equipped with solar collector units relying on the rays of the sun, especially from the south during the winter months, was denied such rays because of the construction of a two-story home or the planting of fast growing trees on the adjoining lot to the south. This would, in effect, render such a system useless during the winter months.

PLOTTAGE, OR ASSEMBLAGE

Plottage denotes an increase in value when two or more parcels of land are combined with the result that the total value of the combined parcels in the "after" situation exceeds the sum of the individual parcel values in the "before" situation. Plottage is the difference between the total value of the separate parcels and the total value of the parcels after combination.

Although the principle can be applied to all types of land, we shall illustrate its application to single-family residential land. Suppose two vacant residential lots, A and B, are located next to one another (see Figure 19–1).

Suppose that the minimum legal lot size is 6,000 square feet, and that a 6,000-square-foot lot is worth $120,000 or $20 per square foot. Lot A, even though it consists of 10,000 square feet, is still only one site worth, for example, $150,000 or $15 per square foot. Lot B, at 2,000 square feet, is too small for a separate site; by itself it has little or no value. However, the owner of lot B is asking the maximum price of $20 per square foot, or $40,000.

It would probably be worthwhile for the owner of lot A to buy lot B and redefine two separate lots, with the diagonally striped 40-foot strip of lot A added to lot B to create two building sites of 6,000 square feet each from the total 12,000-square-foot combined parcel.

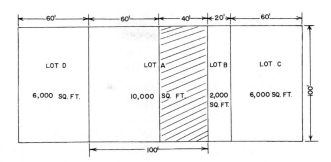

FIGURE 19–1   Plottage.

The before valuation would have been as follows:

Lot A	10,000 square feet	$150,000
Lot B	2,000 square feet	40,000
Total	12,000 square feet	$190,000

The after valuation would be as follows:

Lot A	6,000 square feet	$120,000
Lot B	6,000 square feet	$120,000
Total	12,000 square feet	$240,000

Even if the owner of lot A pays top dollar, or $20 per square foot, for lot B, it is still economically worthwhile. The few minor title and engineering costs to effect this plottage would normally be under $10,000. The entrepreneur still makes a profit of $40,000.

Plottage, then, is the combining of two or more parcels of land with the result that the total value of the combined parcels (in our example $240,000) in the after situation exceeds the value of the sum of the individual parcels ($190,000) in the before situation. In our example, the amount of plottage, or assemblage, is $50,000.

The same basic plottage principle can be applied to multiple residential or any other type of land.

THE PART TAKE

An appraiser may be asked to provide an estimate of the value of a part take, or a portion of a real property. This usually happens when a local condemning authority has taken action to acquire a portion of that particular property or a group of properties. The land is often needed for a road improvement, the widening or extension of a city, county, or state road or freeway. However, the land may be needed for other public purposes, such as flood control ditches, power lines, or water mains. Under some conditions, the condemning agency acquires the whole property. Under others, it needs only a small part of the property.

The decision to buy only a part of the property is usually made by the chief right-of-way agent or chief real estate agent, or by an attorney or engineer serving in this capacity. The commonsense rule is that a whole take will not be considered unless there is a potential substantial loss in value to the remaining property because of a part take. If a part take is decided on, it is necessary to value the part taken and also the effect the take will have on the part not taken, or what is referred to as the remainder.

The rule for the value estimate of a part take is that the owner should be compensated enough that he or she will not lose economically in the transaction. For example, if an owner's residence is worth $240,000 in the before situation, an agency needs a portion of the land, and the agency's value estimate is $12,000 for this portion, then the remainder of property should be worth $228,000. The net effect is to leave the owner "whole" in an economic sense. Ideally, the owner should neither gain nor lose from the transaction.

Let us illustrate further. Assume that we are dealing with a 10-year-old single-family residence of 1,600 square feet, with three bedrooms and two baths, located on a city lot 70 feet wide by 100 feet deep, as shown in Figure 19–2. The city requires 10 feet of the backyard for a four-lane expressway. The property in the before situation is worth $240,000, of which the lot represents $56,000. A logical valuation of the part take would be as follows:

Land	$5,600
10 × 70 feet = 700 square feet @ $8	1,400
Improvements	
Fencing—70 lineal feet @ $10	700
Trees—4 shade trees @ $500	2,000
Miscellaneous shrubs and flowers	2,000
Relocate portion of walkway	
and sprinkler system	1,700
Total value of the take	$12,000

The value of the take, $12,000, plus the remainder value, $228,000, equals $240,000, the value of the whole property before the take.

Sometimes the original property value has been reduced beyond the value of the part take; that is, there has been an additional

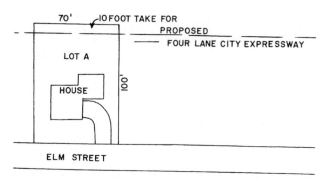

FIGURE 19–2   Part take for expressway.

loss in value to the remainder other than that considered in the part take appraisal. This additional loss is called severance damage.

SEVERANCE DAMAGE

Suppose that, in our example, the remainder value of the property after the take is estimated to be only $200,000. If this estimate is a true indication of remainder value, then an additional $28,000 in severance damage must be added to the valuation of the part take so that the property owner is made whole. The computations would then be as follows:

Value of whole before the take		$240,000
Value of part take	12,000	
Severance damage	28,000	40,000
Value of the remainder		$200,000

Severance damage is the damage, or loss in value, accruing to the remainder of a property because of the taking of a portion of the property. Many people incorrectly believe that all properties suffer severance damage if part of them is taken, but this is not necessarily so. In many cases, there is no additional damage. In fact, in some cases involving raw acreage, value can be added by a projected freeway or road that provides access to the land. Each case must be considered separately.

In estimating the remainder value in a part take, it is useful to study market sales of properties similar to the remainder property. If the subject property in the before situation had a 30-foot backyard bounded by a creek, and in the after situation the backyard is only 20 feet deep and is bounded by a city expressway, the appraiser must find recent sales of property with the same age, size, quality, utility, and neighborhood as the remainder property. Sale properties, in addition to those similarities, should also back up to a comparable expressway and have 20-foot backyards. If no recent comparable sales exist, the appraiser must make a reasonable estimate of the subject property remainder value.

Sometimes the agency may not need to physically acquire any property, but only to acquire a right in that property to restrict direct access to an expressway or freeway. Access rights are sometimes taken by means of payment of some consideration to the property owner.

ACCESS RIGHTS

Let us consider again the property shown in Figure 19–2. Suppose that the city did not need any land from lot A but only wanted to ensure that the lot would not have direct access to the proposed expressway. Almost all properties adjoining public roads are entitled to access rights, subject, of course, to local police power authority to control openings and driveways. The access rights plus the value of the remainder of property are valued in much the same way as other partial takes; that is, the value of the access rights plus the value of the remainder of the property rights must equal the value of the whole property in the before situation. This procedure can be applied to commercial and industrial property as well as to residential property.

In the case of our single-family residential property (Figure 19–2), the value of the access rights would probably be minimal. Since access to lot A will continue to be by Elm Street in the front of the house, the taking of the direct access rights to the expressway in the rear should have no detrimental effect on the after value of lot A. The value of the rear yard access rights of lot A would probably be a nominal $100.

Sometimes, however, the taking of access rights can completely destroy the value of a property. For example, consider an operating service station pumping 100,000 gallons of gas per month, with direct access to a major city street. If the city requires access rights to convert the street into an expressway, it must obviously purchase the whole property, because without direct automobile access, the service station would be economically useless. The cost of the access rights in this case might exceed $1 million if no after use could be found in the sale of the remainder service station property to owners of adjoining property.

CONSIDERATIONS IN APPRAISING SINGLE-FAMILY RESIDENTIAL PROPERTIES CLOSE TO PUBLIC FACILITIES

Because of its proximity to a public facility, a residence often will reflect a higher or lower relative value compared to similar residences not so located. There are several considerations in such cases. The concern about proximity to electromagnetic fields discussed in Chapter 6 is an example of a negative influence. Although our discussion focuses on single-family residential units, the same or similar considerations apply to appraising multiple-family residential units.

Freeways, Expressways, and Major City Streets

A subject of increasing importance, especially in space-deprived urban areas, is the effect of freeways and expressways on residential real estate. To value properly the economic effect on residences of a nearby freeway, expressway, or other major traffic artery, the appraiser should consider recent sales of comparable properties, oriented and located similarly to the property under question. From an analysis of these sales, he or she should be able to make a reasonable estimate of the traffic artery's effect on property value.

Sometimes, however, there are not enough sales of comparable properties. The appraiser must then make value estimates, independent of supporting sales data. The major factors to consider are:

1. Closeness of residence to traffic artery

2. Elevation of traffic artery (whether road is depressed or raised)

3. Amount and type of traffic (for example, heavy truck traffic)

4. Quality and size of residence (the more expensive the residence, the greater the damage)

5. Attitudes of inhabitants and prospective buyers toward existence of traffic artery (Will it be a detriment?)

6. If a major city street, whether it runs in *front* of residence or in *back* (A heavily traveled city street located in front of a residence might restrict street parking or make pulling out of the driveway hazardous. If so, its negative effect on value would be more pronounced than if it were located in *back* of the residence.)

7. If a major city street, whether there is a busy intersection close by (If so, a city street could have a greater negative effect than a freeway because of the noise of cars, trucks, and other vehicles decelerating and accelerating.)

The closeness, elevation, and type and amount of traffic certainly will affect the livability of the residence. If the freeway is 40 feet from the residence, its damage to property value will be more severe than if it is 150 feet from the residence. Also, the elevation of the freeway will have a noticeable effect. Generally, the lower (more below grade) the freeway, the less the damage to value; conversely, the higher (more above grade) the freeway, the more the damage. Some freeways or arteries are major truck routes, and these large vehicles can create annoying noise.

The attitudes of local residents and prospective buyers toward such arteries are obviously of major importance to the appraiser when considering values of residential properties close to major traffic arteries. Some people are not bothered much by closeness to a freeway, while others are extremely bothered by it. Appraisers can measure these attitudes by analyzing sales of similar properties. When no such similar sales exist, they must use judgment and objectivity to estimate the freeway's effect.

A rough rule is that residences usually lose from 10 to 20 percent or more in value because of closeness to a major freeway. A $150,000 residence might lose $15,000 in value, but a $400,000 residence might lose $50,000 or more. Generally, the more expensive the residence, the more the loss in value *and* the greater the percentage loss in value.

Other Public Facilities such as Schools, Parks, and Libraries

Residents' and potential buyers' attitudes toward proximity to a facility such as a public school vary a great deal, depending on the family situation of the buyer and the public facility itself. Major appraisal points relative to close proximity to a public school or community college (city college) include the following:

1. What type of school is it—grammar school, junior high, high school, or city or community college?

2. Does the school have good facilities? Are its recreational and educational facilities available summers and evenings for use by local residents?

3. Is it well maintained and supervised?

4. Does it have a good local reputation as an educational institution?

5. Are the students generally well behaved? Do they respect individual property rights?

6. If it is a junior high, high school, or community college, are there outdoor evening activities, such as football games, that might attract large, noisy, unruly crowds?

7. Will financing be difficult to obtain because of proximity to such a school?

8. Does the school generally contribute to or detract from the pride of property maintenance exhibited by neighborhood occupants?

9. Does the school generate objectionable traffic?

10. Is there sufficient off-street parking for school staff?

11. If it is a high school, community college, or city college, is there sufficient off-street parking for students who drive their cars to school?

12. Is the school architecturally and aesthetically in harmony with surrounding residences?

In addition to the items listed above, additional considerations apply in case of close proximity to state colleges and universities:

1. Is the neighborhood surrounding the state college or university in transition from single-family residential to multiple-family residential? If so, the property may have a higher and better use as a rooming house, boarding house, or conversion to apartments.

2. Does the college or university offer educational programs at night and throughout the year, including summer school? This is important for year-round rental income.

3. Are there enough nonlocal students to generate demand for housing in close proximity to campus?

4. If it is a state-supported college or university, are there plans for expansion of facilities that might require eminent domain action against adjoining private properties?

5. If it is a private institution, are there plans for expansion? Private speculation in adjoining properties might precede such expansion.

The close proximity of a public park can have a positive or negative effect on a piece of residential property. The astute appraiser should consider the following points:

1. Is the park generally used by local residents?

2. Are the people who use the park responsible?
If not, are they properly supervised?

3. Does the park have facilities that are worthwhile for local residents, and are these facilities well maintained?

4. Does the close proximity of the park add to or subtract from the general pride of property upkeep exhibited by local residents?

The following considerations apply to proximity to a library.

1. Is the library useful to local residents?

2. Is the structure aesthetically and architecturally in harmony with surrounding residences?

3. If the library brings in nonlocal users, is there sufficient offstreet parking?

Shopping Centers—Regional, Community, and Neighborhood

Residences located in close proximity to shopping centers are subject to a wide variety of value variations. The appraiser should consider the following points:

1. Are public access roads and streets sufficient to provide free flow of traffic to and from the shopping center, so that such traffic will not affect local residents?

2. Is off-street parking sufficient for cars for all the activities taking place at the center?

3. If the center is open at night, are the lights or noise objectionable to surrounding occupants in close proximity?

4. Is the center maintained properly?

SUMMARY

Special-purpose appraising may require specialized knowledge, though in some cases the appraiser can reason out such problems with a commonsense approach. Whatever the residential appraisal problem, even after most factors have been considered, the final estimate must be a judgment by the appraiser. This judgment can be reliable only when all pertinent information has been analyzed objectively and completely.

DISCUSSION QUESTIONS

1. Why is an underground easement, such as an easement for a water pipeline, usually valued less than a surface easement for road purposes?

2. Define the term *plottage*.

3. Define the term *severance damage*.

4. Define *easement*.

5. Why are air rights becoming more important?

6. Do freeways always decrease the value of abutting properties? Explain your answer.

7. Are access rights always valued on a nominal basis?

8. In your opinion, do properties in close proximity to schools or colleges gain or lose value? Why?

9. In your opinion, will solar rights become an area of more importance in the future? Why?

MULTIPLE-CHOICE QUESTIONS

1. Which of the following types of appraisal problems requires advanced appraisal knowledge?
    a. Appraisal of lease interests
    b. Appraisal of plottage or assemblage
    c. The part take
    d. All of the above

2. Severance damage can be associated only with
    a. Plottage
    b. Assemblage
    c. Solar rights
    d. Part take

3. Which of the following best describes the taking of access rights by the public body?
    a. To restrict direct entrance to and exit from a freeway

b. A part take of land
c. Splitting a parcel in the middle
d. All of the above

4. Which of the following statements is false?
   a. The close proximity of a freeway will have a higher percentage detrimental effect on a larger, more expensive home than on a smaller, less expensive home.
   b. Having a major city street in front of a home will have a more pronounced detrimental effect on a home than having a major city street in the back of the home.
   c. A home will suffer less damage in value if a freeway is at ground level than if it is depressed.
   d. An elevated freeway will cause more loss in value to a home than a freeway at ground level.

5. Generally, a home in close proximity to which of the following would suffer the most in loss of market value?
   a. Park
   b. Grammar school
   c. College
   d. Major city street

Chapter 20

PROFESSIONAL OPPORTUNITIES IN REAL ESTATE APPRAISING

As more and more people compete for the available land in California, the need to understand real estate values becomes more important. California is physically no larger today than it was at the start of the gold rush in 1849. Its population, however, has increased manyfold; by the mid-1990s more than 30 million people resided in the state. Most population projections predict a population of over 31 million residents for California by the year 2000.

As available land becomes increasingly scarce, more specialization will be required to analyze properly the multiple forces acting to create demand and their effect on value. One person can no longer practically handle all the facets of a real estate transaction including title search, surveying, description writing, appraising, selling, mortgage brokering, deed preparation, recording, guarantee of title, and all the necessary forms and correspondence. Most of these functions are handled today by experts in each particular field.

Appraising is no exception. Because of the increased sophistication of the whole real estate industry, it has become so complex that most written appraisals today are performed by specially trained and experienced experts. This is especially true in California, where more laws and regulations have been enacted to control the operations of the real estate industry than in almost any other state.

The continued need for trained, licensed and certified real estate appraisers becomes more apparent when we realize that the average California single-family residential property changes ownership approximately every 7 years, requiring an appraisal. In addition, as interest rates fluctuate, owners will refinance, requiring another appraisal. Appraisals are also made for divorce settlements, death of an owner, establishment of living trusts, estate planning, and in preparation of financial statements. This is equivalent to an appraisal for *each* property in California approximately every 3 to 4 years (exclusive of assessor's office appraisals).

In this chapter we shall study career opportunities under three general headings: salaried and nonsalaried, professional organizations and designations, and the future of the appraising profession.

SALARIED OPPORTUNITIES

Organizations of all types that are involved with real estate are becoming increasingly aware of the need for qualified appraisers on their staffs. Such positions range from appraiser trainee in a lending institution or government office to vice president and chief appraiser of the lending institution or head assessor in a metropolitan county assessor's office.

A 4-year college degree is a minimum qualification for beginning positions on most appraisal staffs. An educational background in economics, business, accounting, finance, engineering, or law is generally sufficient for entrance into a training position. However, more and more California organizations are requiring basic knowledge in all aspects of real estate—in the form of a real estate certificate or a bachelor's degree with a major in real estate—as a measure of proficiency prior to employment. This is especially true of civil service or government positions, where rigid minimum standards are set in addition to the passing of a civil service examination prior to employment.

Salaried positions generally provide specific on-the-job training in addition to a monthly or yearly salary, with opportunities for advancement for employees who show increasing proficiency. These positions sometimes serve as training grounds for individuals who want eventually to go into independent appraising.

Private Employment

In California, most private organizations with appraisers on their real estate department staffs fall into one of the following six categories:

1. Lending institutions, such as banks, savings and loan companies, life insurance companies, pension funds, and others that lend money on real estate, must make *realistic* appraisals to protect their position.

2. Investment organizations, such as land development companies, industrial and commercial specialists, and even life insurance companies deciding to enter the real estate business directly instead of lending money for someone else's venture, stake their livelihood on proper appraisals prior to their investments.

3. Private utilities, including electric, gas, water, and telephone companies, usually have appraisal staffs for buying needed properties, easements, and rights of way. The major private utility companies in California are Pacific Gas and Electric, operating in the northern two-thirds of the state, and Southern California Edison and San Diego Light and Power, operating in the southern portion. Pacific Bell is the state's major telephone com-

pany. Many private water companies in various sections of the state employ trained personnel in their real estate departments. Even though these organizations have the power of eminent domain, they still must pay fair market value for property acquired for their needs. Since these acquisitions are subject to litigation, complete narrative reports are often needed to substantiate any offer to purchase. Trained appraisal personnel are required who know not only appraising but also condemnation law, title search, deed and contract preparation, and many other facets of the real estate industry.

4. National oil companies, national and statewide grocery and drugstore chains, department stores, take-out food operations, and other retail merchandising operations often require constant appraisal and purchase of properties to present their products to consumers. Such organizations usually have their own real estate staffs, specializing in site selection for their particular purpose. The life of these organizations depends on proper site selection and appraisal.

5. Many national hotel and motel chains have on staff real estate experts who are constantly in the field, studying new freeway routes and interchanges and appraising and buying quality sites.

6. Private universities and nonprofit organizations, such as churches, sometimes have a real estate appraiser either on retainer or on staff. For example, Stanford University, which owns hundreds of acres of partially developed light industrial and residential land in the Palo Alto foothills, has a real estate manager who handles the leasing of university properties to numerous national firms, on a 51-year basis, for construction of sophisticated light industrial plants. The real estate manager must be expert in appraising industrial sites to determine the proper value of leases.

Besides using staff appraisers, many private organizations engage independent fee appraisers for appraisals requiring a particular expertise, for example, the appraisal of raw land for commercial development or the appraisal of service station sites. Many independent appraisers specializing in particular properties are kept busy by their clientele.

Government Employment

In addition to the variety of private salaried appraisal positions, many salaried positions with the government are available to qualified persons. These positions include employment with federal, state, county, city, and district offices in a wide range of appraisal functions. The various government agencies with appraisal departments include:

1. Federal government agencies, such as General Services Administration, which does much of the appraising and buying of land needed by the Interstate Highway System and for parks, national forests, military bases, national defense sites, and so on.

   The federal government also guarantees FHA and VA (GI) loans. Staff appraisers generally make the appraisals required to qualify a residential property for a loan from a bank or other lending institution. Although private funds are extended for the loan, a federal agency guarantees the loan in the event of nonpayment by the buyer.

2. The State of California Division of Transportation, California Veterans' Home and Farm Loans, and the state General Services Administration all have full-time staff members ranging from appraisers and right-of-way agent trainees to chief appraiser and headquarters right-of-way agent in Sacramento. Although a college degree is normally required for such positions, the Division of Transportation (Cal trans), for example, the state's largest real estate purchaser for many years, has an extensive in-service training program called the right-of-way academy where trainees are drilled in appraisal techniques, negotiations, condemnations, and property management in order to be properly prepared to purchase the thousands of parcels of real property required for the continued expansion of one of the world's largest, most modern freeway systems.

   The state General Services Administration appraises and acquires property for all state purposes other than freeways, such as beaches and parks, state hospitals, state college and university expansions, and prison farms. A complete staff of appraisers is needed to accomplish this function.

3. The largest single group of salaried appraisers in the state is concentrated in the various county assessors' offices. It is not unusual for a large metropolitan county, such as Los Angeles, to employ more than 500 appraisers to keep up with the job of constantly maintaining property valuations for local tax assessment purposes. Los Angeles County, with the largest population of the state's 54 counties, has over a million separate properties that must be constantly reassessed. Even a smaller county, such as Santa Clara County in northern California, employs more than 60 full-time appraisers who keep up with its more than a quarter of a million separate properties. Most large counties run in-service training programs that, together with the strict state certification qualifications and entrance examinations, constantly assure qualified appraisal personnel. State certification by the California State Board of Equalization, the result of Assembly Bill 80 of 1966, applies only to appraisers who

work for county assessors' offices. It does not apply to certification or licensing of appraisers in general. See Chapter 21 for a further discussion of state licensing and certification of appraisers.

Other county government functions that require appraisal personnel are those that provide land for county expressways, roads, airports, parks, boat harbors, prison farms, boys' and girls' rehabilitation ranches, civic center expansions, and countywide mass transit systems.

4. City real estate departments serve functions similar to those of county real estate departments. San Francisco, whose city and county boundary lines are the same, is referred to as the City and County of San Francisco. In addition to the functions listed for county real estate departments, San Francisco's real estate department manages the metropolitan airport and boat harbor. Some cities, such as Oakland, have autonomous authority to operate port and other facilities. These special functions require specially trained appraisers in addition to other real estate personnel. Some cities even provide their citizens with utilities such as gas and electricity, usually purchased from large private companies at wholesale rates and provided to the residents in conjunction with other services such as water, sewage, and garbage disposal. Again, trained staff appraisers are employed by the larger cities to provide the necessary appraisal vices.

5. School districts usually hire independent appraisers on a per diem basis, and sometimes they use staff appraisers on loan from city or county. Seldom do they require the services of a full-time staff appraiser.

6. Special districts for flood control, water, sewers, storm drainage, and rapid transit usually have staffs of appraisers and other real estate personnel to appraise and buy the needed land, rights of way, and easements for dams and lakes, transmission pipelines, storage reservoirs, distribution pipelines, filtering plants, pumping stations, sewer lines, digestion tanks, flood control channels, train tracks, bus and train depots, percolation ponds, reservoirs, and so on.

An example is the Bay Area Rapid Transit District (BART), formed in the mid-1960s to provide a much-needed rapid transit system for several San Francisco Bay Area counties. Many appraisers were engaged on a salary basis for a crash land-acquisition program that covered more than 5 years.

These salaried government positions are mostly civil service jobs requiring a written examination and an oral examination before a review board. They offer a variety of fringe benefits, invaluable in-service training programs, and experience for those advancing to the top, whether they remain in government work or become independent appraisers.

NONSALARIED OPPORTUNITIES (INDEPENDENT)

Nonsalaried appraisers are commonly called independent fee appraisers. Included in this category are inheritance tax referees. The term *independent* is used because these appraisers are in business for themselves, and the word *fee* because they generally charge a fee on the basis of a complete contract or appraisal assignment, or on a per diem basis (a daily dollar charge).

Education and Experience

Independent appraisers often hold a college degree in finance, business, economics, accounting, or a related field, with extensive additional studies in appraising and advanced appraising at the college or professional appraisal level. Or they may have many years' experience in various aspects of real estate, including developing, building, and selling real property. To be entirely competent, they should take specific courses to prepare properly for such a specialized field, although no state licensing or testing is presently required for qualification as a fee appraiser. The independent appraiser may or may not be a member of a professional organization. He or she has generally had some appraisal experience at one of the salaried positions we have discussed, either on a variety of appraisal assignments for many years, or on relatively simple appraisal assignments for only one year.

It is difficult to imagine a completely qualified appraiser without extensive education and experience.

Fee Schedule

Most qualified independent appraisers charge a minimum of $250 to $500 per appraisal for their services. In the larger metropolitan and certain resort areas, fees may be higher. Consultation fees may be charged on an hourly, or daily basis, with hourly rates of $100, and daily rates between $600 and $800. These charges cover actual work performed on an appraisal assignment, any consultations, and any court testimony. Most good appraisers have all the work they can handle; many of them work 6 days a week to keep up with their clients' demands. However, since the appraisers are self-employed and usually must hire a secretary and rent a completely equipped office, their fees are really not net income.

Anticipated Expenses

The appraiser should have certain basic office equipment: a computer system with appraisal software and a modem, printer, desks, chairs, an electric typewriter, dictating machine, letter copying machine, map racks, file cabinets, and telephones. All of these are a drain on resources. The appraiser must also have a car and must allow for extensive expenses for gas, oil, and maintenance.

If the appraiser has an office outside the home, payments for a secretary and allowance for vacation, sick leave, medical insurance, holidays, and other fringe benefits must be considered. Most appraisers starting their businesses should plan to spend about $5,000 per month for constant expenses that would amount to $60,000 per year. For the undertaking to be financially worthwhile, the appraiser must bring in a minimum gross annual income of about $160,000. At $640 a day, this means working 250 days a year, or an average 5-day week. The beginning independent appraiser is sometimes not fully employed and may have uncollectible accounts; it is easy to see why some appraisers must charge higher rates to make their venture worthwhile.

Larger private appraisal offices employ salaried appraisers to work under the direction of a principal appraiser, for less money than what clients pay for the services of the office. In this way, one or several salaried appraisers can multiply the effectiveness of the principal appraiser, increasing the economic productivity of the office. For example, assume that a fee appraiser hires two salaried appraisers. The total cost per day for each of these salaried appraisers, including salaries, office expenses, and fringe benefits, might be less than $250 apiece, or about $500 per day. However, if they are experienced and capable, they can bring $1,000 per day into the office. The principal appraiser still signs the appraisals, prepared under his or her direct supervision. Much of the detail work (legwork) can be handled by the salaried appraisers. The principal appraiser can also work on other appraisals, testify in court, and consult with clients. This arrangement is similar to an architectural or engineering firm, where subordinates work on a project that is eventually approved and signed by the principal architect or engineer.

The principal appraiser who is successful can build the operation into a larger organization, but must be careful, however, not to expand so much that the organization becomes unwieldy and economically worthless.

The Appraisal Corporation

A group of qualified appraisers, either principal or former salaried appraisers, sometimes join together to form an appraisal corporation. In this way several appraisers, each expert in a particular field, can provide a more complete service to prospective clients. The corporation aspect also distributes office expenses and affects other economies, making each principal a more productive unit.

Other Independent Appraisers

Not all independent appraisers are necessarily fee appraisers. Many investors in real estate act as their own appraisers. These people, who have been investing successfully in a particular type of real estate, usually become expert after several years or many investment ventures.

Some real estate brokers and salespeople may advise clients on value to give the client a more complete real estate service. A real estate salesperson or broker who has been active in a particular area or type of real estate usually becomes expert in estimating the value of that particular type of property in the area in which he or she is active.

The largest single group of nonprofessional appraisers are the people in all walks of life who every day are comparing one property with another before renting or buying a residence. They are making informal appraisals—forming an opinion or estimate of value. Most of them have no formal appraisal training, but they often become surprisingly expert during the time they are in the market for a residence.

PROFESSIONAL ORGANIZATIONS

Several national professional appraisal organizations are active throughout the United States. These groups bestow their particular designation on qualified members, in addition to the appraiser's state license or certification. Prior to licensing, these designations comprised the "qualification" system for the appraisal profession, however, each organization had somewhat different requirements. The national licensing and certification requirements standardize the basic skills levels, and the designations, today, provide optional additional commodation and accreditation for appraisers.

The most common master designations and their respective bestowing organizations are:

1. C.A.—Certified Appraiser (American Association of Certified Appraisers, Inc.)

2. C.A.E.—Certified Assessment Evaluator (International Association of Assessing Offices)

3. C.R.A.—Certified Review Appraiser (National Association of Review Appraisers and Mortgage Underwriters)

4. C.R.E.A.—Certified Real Estate Appraiser (National Association of Real Estate Appraisers)

5. I.F.A.—Independent Fee Appraiser (National Association of Independent Fee Appraisers)

6. Appraisal Institute designations: M.A.I.—Member Appraisal Institute; S.R.A.—Senior Residential Appraiser

7. M.G.A.—Master Governmental Appraiser (Society of Governmental Appraisers)

8. C.A.R.E.A.—California Association of Real Estate Appraisers

Other appraisal organizations are:

1. S.A.A.—Society of Auditor Appraisers

2. A.A.A.—American Appraisal Association

3. National Society of Real Estate Appraisers, Inc.

Each of these organizations has qualifications for membership, and all subscribe to the USPAP code of ethics and rules of conduct. They require of candidates certain education and a certain number of years of appraisal experience. Most also require the successful completion of at least one comprehensive written examination. Some have subdesignations that indicate partial fulfillment of the master designation.

The C.A.R.E.A. is the newest professional appraisal organization in California, open to all levels of licensed and certified appraisers. This group, formed in 1993, is dedicated to representing the appraiser's political interests in both California and at the national level. The organization provides affordable continuing education, dissemination of information on legislative and regulatory issues and changes, industry data resources, and offers networking with other California appraisers.

The National Association of Review Appraisers, which bestows the designation of C.R.A. (R.R.A. in Canada), was formed in 1975, not to compete with the other appraisal organizations, but to further the appraisal profession by enlisting those who have served in a managerial, executive, educational, governmental, or administrative appraisal capacity relative to the review and approval of real estate appraisals for various private, governmental, and educational purposes. Members of the N.A.R.A. are many times also members of one or more other appraisal organizations, and these members include private and governmental appraisers, corporate executives and administrators, presidents and executive officers of their own real estate investment and appraisal companies, educators, and others interested in maintaining the highest standards of appraisal review practice.

Each organization has its own requirements, and as these requirements are constantly changing, the prospective applicant for membership should contact the organization directly for the latest information about membership or candidacy. The addresses of the national headquarters for some of the appraisal organizations follow:

American Association of Certified Appraisers, Inc. (C.A.)
No. 7 Edwin Drive
Greenhills Shopping Plaza
Cincinnati, OH 45218

Appraisal Institute
430 N. Michigan Avenue
Chicago, IL 60611

California Association of Real Estate Appraisers
P. O. Box 576648
Modesto, CA 95357

International Association of Assessing Offices (C.A.E.)
1313 E. 60th Street
Chicago, IL 60637

National Association of Independent Fee Appraisers (I.F.A.)
Executive Office
7501 Murdoch
St. Louis, MO 73119

National Association of Real Estate Appraisers (C.R.E.A.)
8715 Via De Commercio
Scottsdale, AZ 85258

National Association of Review Appraisers and
Mortgage Underwriters (C.R.A.)
8715 Via De Commercio
Scottsdale, AZ 85258

National Society of Real Estate Appraisers, Inc.
1025 Vermont Avenue NW, Suite 1111
Washington, D.C. 20005

Society of Government Appraisers (S.G.A.)
536 Cedar Berry Lane
San Rafael, CA 94903

Society of Real Estate Appraisers (S.R.E.A.)
7 South Dearborn Street
Chicago, IL 60603

Another appraisal-related organization that is very active is:

The American Right-of-Way Association (A.R./W.A.)
3727 West 6th Street, Suite 504
Los Angeles, CA 90005

The A.R./W.A. consists primarily of appraisers and land acquisition specialists, most of whom are employed by the various state divisions of transportation, private oil companies, utility companies, title companies, city and county real estate departments, and railroad companies.

This list, although not complete, does identify those organizations that are most active in the United States. These and other organizations are constantly striving to attain greater professionalism in appraising and related facets of the entire real estate industry.

THE FUTURE OF APPRAISING AS A PROFESSION

Webster's Dictionary defines a profession as "the occupation, if not commercial, mechanical, agricultural, or the like, to which one devotes oneself; a calling, as, the profession of arms, of teaching, the three professions or learned professions of theology, law and medicine. The body of persons engaged in a calling." Formerly only three callings were commonly accepted as professions. However, today, because many fields are technologically advanced, increased training is necessary to prepare for a calling in our complex society. More occupations are recognized as professions; for example, teaching, engineering, architecture, psychology, dentistry, and others that require extensive education and training.

The licensing and certification of appraisers, nationwide, has elevated the appraisal profession to new levels.

Characteristics of a Profession

A profession requires the following characteristics of its members:

1. Extensive education

2. Practical training or experience

3. Constant study to keep abreast of changes

4. Service to a practical community need

5. Aims that have the respect of the community

6. A code of ethics

7. An understanding of responsibility

8. An understanding of accountability

Real estate appraising encompasses all of these aspects, and more. Its future as a profession depends on its continued ability to attract bright, dedicated people to the calling, dedicated to following the USPAP rules and regulations of practice and conduct, and on the continued support by the various organizations in maintaining these standards and practices. The future *need* for appraising is obvious, and responsible organizations and individuals must ensure its future by adherence to the rules and guidelines.

RESPONSIBILITIES OF THE APPRAISER

In addition to the ethics provisions under USPAP, appraisers should be aware of the grave responsibilities placed upon them as they perform their work. Lenders will commit funds (many times funds belonging to others) for many years; investors will commit their own funds (many times hard earned), also for many years; and finally buyers, especially home buyers, might invest their life savings and commit themselves to high payments for 30 years or more (truly a lifetime) on property that hopefully was purchased at a *market* price.

It should not be difficult to imagine the relative financially destructive effect on an individual or a family if that individual or family purchases a home or commits to pay for that home and the home is overpriced.

Therefore, to most fairly perform, the appraiser should adhere to the following:

1. Treat all parties fairly and equally.

2. Gather all available pertinent facts before rendering a value estimate.

3. Report any conflicts of interest that may be involved in an appraisal.

4. Be aware of all laws that might affect the value of a parcel of real estate.

5. Constantly keep abreast of the latest laws, procedures, and information affecting the appraisal of real estate.

6. Constantly give independent, honest, and objective opinions relating to the appraisal of real estate.

7. Maintain and improve professional standards of appraisers.

LIABILITIES OF THE APPRAISER

The savings and loan crisis that precipitated FIRREA and USPAP created a higher level of liability than previously existed for appraisers. USPAP requires binding compliance with certain rules and regulations, and has specific remedies for errors and omissions made by appraisers. The penalties may range from license suspension and monetary fines to possible imprisonment for severe offenses.

In those cases affecting the valuation of real estate, whether it be commercial, industrial apartment buildings, or even single-family residential homes, recent court actions and decisions are placing more and more liability on those responsible for estimating the market value of properties. In many cases, this liability can partly be placed on the appraiser. Many professional appraisal organizations and many lenders now require that their members, or those who appraise real estate on their behalf, carry liability insurance such as "errors and omissions" insurance.

This has been inevitable, since in some cases, a few appraisers seeking to please their clients or employers were not at all professional and performed appraisals that bore little resemblance to *market value.* Hopefully, those few appraisers, and others responsible for grossly *overvaluing* real estate in order to earn exorbitantly high fees, will either see the error of their ways and change or be forced out of the appraisal profession altogether.

The truly professional appraiser should not accept assignments or contracts to appraise property unless the employer or client allows the appraiser to act independently, objectively, and honestly and to treat all parties fairly. Licensed and certified appraisers are expressly prohibited, under USPAP, from accepting an assignment based on a specific valuation of the property. Chapter 21 discusses further professional licensing and certification requirements.

SUMMARY

Appraising is becoming more and more specialized and accepted as a profession. The opportunities range from salaried positions, both private and governmental, to nonsalaried independent fee appraising. For competent, hard-working individuals many opportunities are available. Many nationally recognized professional organizations provide professional training and designations for the interested and qualified prospective member. With the increasing need for competent appraisals in an active real estate economy, the future, for those interested and qualified, continues to look bright.

DISCUSSION QUESTIONS

1. Discuss the increasing importance in the real estate industry of the professional real estate appraiser.

2. What do you think are the advantages and disadvantages of working for a government organization in the appraisal field?

3. What do you think are the advantages of pursuing a career in real estate appraising? The disadvantages?

4. What do you think would be the advantages of a salaried position in appraisal over an independent position? The disadvantages?

5. Name two distinct advantages of an appraisal corporation formed by two or more principal appraisers.

Chapter 21

LICENSE AND STATE EXAMINATION REQUIREMENTS, LENDER APPRAISAL GUIDELINES, AND COMMON ERRORS AND OMISSIONS

When Title XI of the Financial Institutions Reform, Recovery and Enforcement Act (FIRREA) became effective in 1989, each state was mandated to establish an authority to regulate appraisal activities, using the federal guidelines as a basis. The requirement that all "federally related real estate appraisals" be conducted only by state-licensed and certified appraisers was originally targeted for July 1, 1991, but was extended until January 1, 1993.

Federally related transactions include all those involving federal insurance or assistance, such as federally insured loans, and any transactions in which a federally related agency or institution participates. This covers the majority of real estate transactions that occur in the United States.

In preparation for accommodation of these federal regulations, California enacted the *Appraisal Law* in 1990, creating the Office of Real Estate Appraisal (OREA), a division of the Business, Transportation, and Housing Agency. OREA was chartered with establishing appraisal standards, setting qualifications, monitoring appraisers' professional activities, and discipline within the guidelines. This directive set the minimum qualification levels as those that meet or exceed the levels created by the Appraiser Qualification Board, a subcommittee of the Appraisal Foundation, and set the minimum standards as those set forth in the Uniform Standards of Professional Appraisal Practice (USPAP), developed by the Appraisal Foundation.

The pertinent text of Title XI is provided under Appendix I, with USPAP Standards provided under Appendix II.

In November of 1992, California adopted the USPAP Standards and set licensing requirements to be consistent with the federal guidelines.

STATE LICENSING

License Levels

As briefly outlined in Chapter 5, there are four levels of license in California, as follow:

Category	Scope
Trainee License	Appraisal of properties only under supervision of a licensed or certified appraiser, up to the level of that licensed or certified appraiser.
Licensed	Appraisal of 1- to 4-unit residential property up to transaction value of $1 million if noncomplex, and up to $250,000 if complex in nature. Appraisal of nonresidential property up to a transaction value of $250,000. This includes the appraisal of vacant land where the highest and best use is for 1- to 4-unit residential purposes.
Certified Residential	Appraisal of 1- to 4-unit residential property without regard to transaction value or complexity. Appraisal of nonresidential property up to $250,000. This includes the appraisal of vacant or unimproved land where the highest and best use is for 1- to 4-unit residential purposes.
Certified General	Appraisal of all real estate without regard to transaction value or complexity.

It is important to note the definitions of *transaction value* and *complexity*. Transaction value is defined as the amount of the loan, sale, lease, etc. It is not the appraised value. Complexity is a judgment of the lending institution. A transaction may be determined to be complex if the property is atypical or if the form of ownership or market conditions are atypical. Examples of possibly complex factors could include:

- Atypical ownership rights, such as life estates, residences constructed on leased land, subterranean or air rights, unusual deed restrictions, easements, encroachments, etc.

- Changes in neighborhood characteristics suggesting that the highest and best use has changed.

- Actual or suspected environmental hazards.

Education and Experience Requirements

The licensing requirements are of two types—a minimum number of experience hours; and coverage of the topics required for the appropriate license level. The educational requirements are based on a *Body of Knowledge,* presented in detail in Appendix III. This was developed by the Appraisal Foundation for states to standardize testing requirements. The specific topics required, and the minimum hours for each level are summarized below:

Requirements	Train.	Licen.	Cert. Resid.	Cert. Genrl.
Total number of experience hours	None	2,000	2,000	2,000
Time period	N/A	None	24 mo.	24 mo.
Total minimum educational hours	75	75	120	165
(Number of above hours on USPAP)	15			
Educational Topics				
Influences on real estate value	X	X	X	X
Legal considerations in appraisal	X	X	X	X
Types of value	X	X	X	X
Economic principles	X	X	X	X
Real estate markets and analysis	X	X	X	X
Valuation process	X	X	X	X
Property description	X	X	X	X
Highest and best-use analysis	X	X	X	X
Sales comparison approach	X	X	X	X
Site value	X	X	X	X
Cost approach	X	X	X	X
Income approach				
Gross rent multiplier	X	X	X	X
Estimation of income expense	X	X	X	X
Operating expense ratios	X	X	X	X
Direct capitalization			X	X
Cash flow estimates				X
Measures of cash flow				X
Discounted cash flow analysis				X
Valuation of partial interests			X	X
Appraisal standards and ethics	X	X	X	X
Narrative report writing				X

There is a state license examination given in order to test competency in these topics. Upon passing this test, and paying the appropriate fees, a license or certificate is issued.

Term of License

The expiration date for all licenses and certificates (except trainee licenses) is the fifth birthday after the date of issuance. All initial terms, except at the trainee level, are for 4 years.

Continuing Education Requirements

The requirement for continuing education ensures that appraisers participate in programs to maintain and increase their skills, knowledge, and competency in the appraising profession. In California, appraisers must complete a total of 40 hours of accredited continuing education during the term of their license or certificate. Appraisers may acquire these education hours at any time during the term of the license or certificate.

LENDER APPRAISAL GUIDELINES FOR SINGLE-FAMILY RESIDENCES

Supplementing the USPAP Standards and regulations, major lenders have additional guidelines that must be followed when appraising for these institutions. Freddie Mac, Fannie Mae, FSLIC, and mortgage insurers have established these requirements to enhance the veracity and depth of the appraisal. The appraiser is responsible for incorporating any lender-specific items into a report made for a specific lender, provided that they do not conflict with the USPAP binding restrictions. The general, basic requirements for these major lenders are:

1. Every sale used in an appraisal report must be confirmed, including confirmation of the date of sale and close as well as the terms of sale. Pending sales are not acceptable.

2. Any conversions, remodeling, and/or additions must be disclosed.

3. Permits must be verified for additions, conversions, and/or remodeling; no permit, no value.

4. Comparable sales should be within the same tract or immediate neighborhood and of similar age, size, and quality; in similar condition; and have similar room count and yard improvements.

5. No sales over 6 months old should be used.

6. Any obvious water or structural damage to the structure must be disclosed.

7. Any settling on the site, including major (not hairline) cracks in foundations, walks, driveways, and patios must be disclosed.

8. If property is in a geological hazard area, slide area, or flood zone, this must be disclosed.

9. Any economic obsolescence (such as any use other than single-family) adjacent to or near the subject property must be disclosed.

10. Any illegal and/or nonconforming uses, such as an additional rental on the site, must be disclosed.

COMMON ERRORS AND OMISSIONS BY APPRAISERS AND HOW TO AVOID THEM

Most professional appraisers carry E&O (errors and omissions) insurance to protect themselves against honest errors and omissions. Most 90 to 95 percent loans can be reviewed by two or three underwriters and two or three review appraisers. Generally speaking, the appraisal is reviewed a minimum of four times. The 95 percent loan has a 95 percent chance of being field reviewed; the 90 percent loan, a 25 to 50 percent chance; and the 80 percent loan, a 10 to 25 percent chance. These field reviews can be done by the primary lender, the investor, Fannie Mae, or Freddie Mac, if the loan is sold to one of them, and by the mortgage insurance company if insurance is necessary. The appraiser has little or no margin of error available today.

Following are some common appraiser errors and omissions found on the Fannie Mae–Freddie Mac Uniform Residential Appraisal Report form, along with some recommendations review appraisers have made for avoiding them.

Neighborhood Description

Inadequate neighborhood description; rewrite.

Neighborhood makeup is inadequate/incorrect.

Explain economic conditions.

Comment on other-than-single-family-residential (SFR) use adjacent to or near the subject.

Comment on distances to schools, shopping, and employment centers. Comment on proximity of other-than-SFR use and its effect on value and marketability.

Explain why the subject's value differs from the predominant value.

Explain why the subject's age differs from the predominant age.

Explain fair and/or poor ratings.

Elaborate on changing land use. How will this affect the subject's value and marketability.

Comment on other properties that are not receiving proper maintenance and the effect, if any, on the subject.

Improvements

Recheck age of property. Does not coincide with market data section.

Subject appears older or newer than indicated. Effective age is not supported; explain.

Recheck materials used for exterior walls; photos don't coincide.

Comment on lack of gutters and downspouts. Does this cause drainage or erosion problems?

Comment on foundation cracks and/or cracks on exterior walls.

Should a structural engineer's report be ordered?

Comment on sloped floors and/or interior cracks in walls and/or ceilings.

Adequately describe basement. Include walls, wiring, heating, plumbing, etc.

Clarify and comment on foundation type (i.e., is it a perimeter, pier, or jack foundation?). Also, acceptability in the market place.

Any evidence of termite or water damage? Is a termite report needed or recommended?

Room List

Room list and room count do not coincide.

Room count, page 1, conflicts with what appears in the market data section.

The house sketch does not coincide with the room list and/or room count. Please clarify.

Gross living area is in conflict with calculations in cost approach and/or market approach.

Basement area does not coincide with sketch and/or calculations.

Site

Correct site dimensions/size.

Recheck zoning. Current use does not, or may not, conform. Clarify zoning and uses allowed under that zoning.

Zoning: is use legal or is it an illegal, nonconforming use?

Subject has guest quarters and/or possible rental. The appraiser must certify that guest quarters are not being used as a rental if zoning apparently does not allow an accessory rental unit. The appraiser should be aware that, if this is misrepresented, civil prosecution against the appraiser could be forthcoming.

Illegal, nonconforming properties are not lendable per FNMA, FHLMC, and the Federal Home Loan Bank Board.

Explain highest and best use; may not be present use.

Septic: when was last time it was checked? is it functioning? Should a septic clearance be required? Are septics common to the area? Comment.

Clarify water source, quality. Is it a continuous supply year-round?

If well, how old? What depth? How many gallons per minute? What is the quality of the water?

Does the water source have a history of problems?

Comment on road maintenance and on the distance to a publicly maintained road.

Comment on private road maintenance agreement, condition of drainage, surface material, storm damage, or any other factors or problems in the neighborhood.

Explain encroachments/setback violations.

Subject may be/is in a geological hazard area. Supply property map with subject site located on same. Explain effect on value and/or marketability.

If the structure is on a slope, does it show evidence of hill creep?

Has area had storm damage, slides, erosion, fires, or the like? Comment.

Expand on drainage; comment. Comment on slippage and/or erosion on the site or on an adjacent site.

Site may be/is influenced by detrimental use adjacent to/close by the site; indicate type, distance from subject, and effect on marketability and value.

Supply flood-hazard map with subject property indicated on same.

Clarify view. Explain in detail. Follow through on market data section.

Plat map and/or pictures indicate other single-family residential use adjacent to the subject.

Please explain and supply additional photographs.

Photos of special improvements/view required.

Interior Finish and Equipment

Kitchen equipment: None shown. If none, so state.

Heat: Type of fuel and/or condition omitted.

Explain condition.

Is this type of heating typical?

Please fill in missing blank or blanks for floors, trim/finish, bath wainscot, walls, bath floor.

Special features: Please state or clarify insulation.

Special features not clearly stated. Omitted on market data section.

Attic: State type of attic.

Car storage: Incomplete/explain.

If garage conversion, when? Were there permits? Is there adequate off-street parking?

Property rating not supported/overstated; omitted, conflicts with ratings under market data approach.

Quality and Condition

Quality of construction.

Condition of improvements.

Room sizes and layout.

Closets and storage.

Insulation—adequacy.

Plumbing—adequacy/condition.

Electrical—adequacy/condition.

Kitchen cabinets—adequacy/condition.

Compatibility to neighborhood.

Overall livability.

Appeal and marketability.

Physical inadequacies: Repairs not covered/fully explained.

Require building permit for addition and/or conversion?

Give approximate dates of refurbishing, remodeling, additions.

Cost Approach

Addition/multiplication on cost approach incorrect; redo.

Inadequate comment on functional or economic obsolescence under cost approach.

Land to improvement ratio: typical or common to the area?

Dollars per square foot inconsistent with quality rating.

Physical, functional, or economic adjustments not supported, understated, overstated, not addressed.

Land value not substantiated, overstated, understated.

Depreciation inconsistent with age, condition and/or functional or economic (external) obsolescence.

Market Data Analysis

Price/living area-comparables exceed 10 percent, not acceptable/replace comparable/explain.

Address incorrect/incomplete. Subject, comparables 1, 2, and 3.

Proximity and direction: missing/incomplete/inaccurate. Location map missing.

Sales price: incorrect/missing. Subject, comparables 1, 2, and 3.

Data source incomplete: Board name, MLS number; agent's name and phone number.

Subject date of sale/date of appraisal: missing/inaccurate.

Date of close not shown. If not, supply closed sale.

Time adjustment: negative/positive; substantiate/delete time adjustment.

Comparable sale, too old, supply newer sale or explain.

Location adjustment: not made/not explained/not supported. Replace comparables 1, 2 and 3. Add comparables 1, 2, and 3 with similar or same location advantage/disadvantage.

Reason(s) comparables located in closer proximity to the subject were not utilized.

Supply current listings—same or similar property in subject development and comment.

Lot sizes: inaccurate/missing. May affect value.

View not stated; may affect value. Expand on view.

Lot size adjustment(s) inconsistent/not applied. Comparables 1, 2, and 3.

Discuss site usability of subject versus that of comparables.

Design/appeal: Comparables 1, 2, and 3 require an adjustment. Substantiate and explain reason for adjustments or lack of same.

Quality of construction: Comparables 1, 2, and 3 require an adjustment. Substantiate and explain reasons for adjustments or lack of same.

Fill in chronological ages of the subject and all comparables. May affect value. If older home, also show effective age—substantiate and correlate with subject under age and condition.

Age adjustment(s) are needed. Comparables 1, 2, and 3.

Adjustments for condition not supported/explained. Comparables 1, 2, and 3.

Replace comparables 1, 2, and 3 with sale(s) of same room count.

Subject new construction: Only 1 comparable can be used from inside the tract.

Size of comparables 1, 2, and 3 exceeds 20 percent of subject: explain, replace, and/or add comparable with same room count, or explain.

Inconsistent adjustment for functional utility. Comparables 1, 2, and 3.

Adjustment for air-conditioning: Omitted, overstated, understated, not supported.

Garage/carport: Adjustment omitted, overstated, understated, correct. Adjustment to cure functional obsolescence is missing.

Yard improvements not properly addressed, not substantiated, overstated, or understated: Support. Explain yard improvements in detail.

Supply additional comparables 1, 2, and 3 with similar improvements/pool.

Special energy items omitted, not addressed, or not substantiated. Burglar alarm, solar, thermal windows, and so forth.

Other (fireplace, kitchen appliances, heating system/remodeling) not addressed, overstated, understated, or not substantiated.

Financing concessions omitted, incomplete, or not properly adjusted for.

How much cash down on comparables 1, 2, 3, 4, 5, and 6? Detailed explanation of all aspects of financing may, or does, require an adjustment.

Addition in market data analysis incorrect for comparables 1, 2, and 3.

Comparables 1, 2, and 3 do not support conclusion to value.

Add 1 or 2, comparables replace comparables 1, 2, and 3.

Comments on market data: Comparables 1, 2, and 3 inadequate. Explain adjustments in detail, and give reasons for same.

Addition on conversion: No permit, no value. Redo appraisal.

Economic rent omitted: Needed on tenant-occupied homes.

    a. Gross rent multiplier omitted

    b. Value by income approach omitted.

Due to condition of property:

    a. Require certification of roof by a state-licensed contractor.

    b. Termite by report Section 1/11 may be/is required (comment on report).

    c. Was a or b taken into consideration in the appraisal process? Explain.

    d. Require installation of an acceptable heating unit and certification by a state licensed contractor.

General

Reconciliation unacceptable/inadequate. Does not support value.

Require completion certificate, Form 442, signed by the appraiser.

Reprinted report must be submitted for a final review with a copy of this review.

Addendum/addenda must be submitted for a final review with a copy of this review.

Reprint form on correct form.

Supply plat map showing measurements of the site and distance to nearest cross street.

Diagram of structure must show interior walls, placements on lot, and distance to fence line sides and rear, walks, patios, and other improvements.

Supply photos of comparable sales.

Photo(s) of special improvements and/or view required.

Supply location map showing subject and comparable sales.

Condo project size missing.

Units per acre incorrect or omitted.

Number of rentals in project not stated: confirm with homeowner's association or management company. State name and phone number.

Give accurate zoning for condo/PUD project.

Recheck if project is a condo or PUD.

Auto storage ratios incorrect. Number of spaces or storage should be rechecked.

New definition of market value, as of July 1, 1986, must be included in report.

Appraiser utilizing inexperienced staff personnel without adequate supervision.

Filling the appraisal with chamber-of-commerce-type data without relating the data to the subject appraisal.

Overall report is too short to adequately cover the property.

TITLE IX FEDERAL INSTITUTIONS REFORM, RECOVERY, AND ENFORCEMENT ACT (FIRREA)

FIRREA, TITLE XI—REAL ESTATE APPRAISAL REFORM AMENDMENTS

¶3101

SEC. 1101. PURPOSE.

The purpose of this title is to provide that Federal financial and public policy interests in real estate related transactions will be protected by requiring that real estate appraisals utilized in connection with federally related transactions are performed in writing, in accordance with uniform standards, by individuals whose competency has been demonstrated and whose professional conduct will be subject to effective supervision.

¶3102

SEC. 1102. ESTABLISHMENT OF APPRAISAL SUBCOMMITTEE OF THE FEDERAL FINANCIAL INSTITUTIONS EXAMINATION COUNCIL.

The Federal Financial Institutions Examination Council Act of 1978 (12 U.S.C. 3301 et seq.) is amended by adding at the end thereof the following new section:

SEC. 1011. ESTABLISHMENT OF APPRAISAL SUBCOMMITTEE.

"There shall be within the Council a subcommittee to be known as the 'Appraisal Subcommittee', which shall consist of the designees of the heads of the Federal financial institutions regulatory agencies. Each such designee shall be a person who has demonstrated knowledge and competence concerning the appraisal profession."

¶3103

SEC. 1103. FUNCTIONS OF APPRAISAL SUBCOMMITTEE.

(a) In General.—The Appraisal Subcommittee shall—

(1) monitor the requirements established by States for the certification and licensing of individuals who are qualified to perform appraisals in connection with federally related transactions, including a code of professional responsibility;

(2) monitor the requirements established by the Federal financial institutions regulatory agencies and the Resolution Trust Corporation with respect to—

    (A) appraisal standards for federally related transactions under their jurisdiction, and

    (B) determinations as to which federally related transactions under their jurisdiction require the services of a State certified appraiser and which require the services of a State licensed appraiser;

(3) maintain a national registry of State certified and licensed appraisers who are eligible to perform appraisals in federally related transactions; and

(4) transmit an annual report to the Congress not later than January 31 of each year which describes the manner in which each function assigned to the Appraisal Subcommittee has been carried out during the preceding year.

(b) MONITORING AND REVIEWING FOUNDATION.—The Appraisal Subcommittee shall monitor and review the practices, procedures, activities, and organizational structure of the Appraisal Foundation.

¶3104

SEC. 1104. CHAIRPERSON OF APPRAISAL SUBCOMMITTEE; TERM OF CHAIRPERSON; MEETINGS.

(a) CHAIRPERSON.—The Council shall select the Chairperson of the subcommittee. The term of the Chairperson shall be 2 years.

(b) MEETINGS; QUORUM; VOTING.—The Appraisal Subcommittee shall meet at the call of the Chairperson or a majority of its members when there is business to be conducted. A majority of members of the Appraisal Subcommittee shall constitute a quorum but 2 or more members may hold hearings. Decisions of the Appraisal Subcommittee shall be made by the vote of a majority of its members.

¶3105

SEC. 1105. OFFICERS AND STAFF.

The Chairperson of the Appraisal Subcommittee shall appoint such officers and staff as may be necessary to carry out the functions of this title consistent with the appointment and compensation practices of the Council.

¶3106

SEC. 1106. POWERS OF APPRAISAL SUBCOMMITTEE.

The Appraisal Subcommittee may, for the purpose of carrying out this title, establish advisory committees, hold hearings, sit and act at times and places, take testimony, receive evidence, provide information, and perform research, as the Appraisal Subcommittee considers appropriate.

¶3107

SEC. 1107. PROCEDURES FOR ESTABLISHING APPRAISAL STANDARDS AND REQUIRING THE USE OF CERTIFIED AND LICENSED APPRAISERS.

Appraisal standards and requirements for using State certified and licensed appraisers in federally related transactions pursuant to this title shall be prescribed in accordance with procedures set forth in section 553 of title 5, United States Code, including the publication of notice and receipt of written comments or the holding of public hearings with respect to any standards or requirements proposed to be established.

¶3108

SEC. 1108. STARTUP FUNDING.

(a) IN GENERAL.—For purposes of this title, the Secretary of the Treasury shall pay to the Appraisal Subcommittee a one-time payment of $5,000,000 on the date of the enactment of this Act. Thereafter, expenses of the subcommittee shall be funded through the collection of registry fees from certain certified and licensed appraisers pursuant to section 1109 or, if required, pursuant to section 1122(b) of this title.

(b) ADDITIONAL FUNDS.—Except as provided in section 1122(b) of this title, funds in addition to the funds provided under subsection (a) may be made available to the Appraisal Subcommittee only if authorized and appropriated by law.

¶3109

SEC. 1109. ROSTER OF STATE CERTIFIED OR LICENSED APPRAISERS; AUTHORITY TO COLLECT AND TRANSMIT FEES.

(a) IN GENERAL.—Each State with an appraiser certifying and licensing agency whose certifications and licenses comply with this title, shall—

(1) transmit to the Appraisal Subcommittee, no less than annually, a roster listing individuals who have received a State certification or license in accordance with this title; and

(2) collect from such individuals who perform or seek to perform appraisals in federally related transactions, an annual registry fee of not more than $25, such fees to be transmitted by the State agencies to the Council on an annual basis.

Subject to the approval of the Council, the Appraisal Subcommittee may adjust the dollar amount of registry fees, up to a maximum of $50 per annum, as necessary to carry out its functions under this title.

(b) USE OF AMOUNTS APPROPRIATED OR COLLECTED.—Amounts appropriated for or collected by the Appraisal Subcommittee under this section shall be used—

(1) to maintain a registry of individuals who are qualified and eligible to perform appraisals in connection with federally related transactions;

(2) to support its activities under this title;

(3) to reimburse the general fund of the Treasury for amounts appropriated to and expended by the Appraisal Subcommittee during the 24-month startup period following the date of the enactment of this title; and

(4) to make grants in such amounts as it deems appropriate to the Appraisal Foundation, to help defray those costs of the foundation relating to the activities of its Appraisal Standards and Appraiser Qualification Boards.

¶3110

SEC. 1110. FUNCTIONS OF THE FEDERAL FINANCIAL INSTITUTIONS REGULATORY AGENCIES RELATING TO APPRAISAL STANDARDS.

Each Federal financial institutions regulatory agency and the Resolution Trust Corporation shall prescribe appropriate standards for the performance of real estate appraisals in connection with federally related transactions under the jurisdiction of each such agency or instrumentality. These rules shall require, at a minimum—

(1) that real estate appraisals be performed in accordance with generally accepted appraisal standards as evidenced by the appraisal standards promulgated by the Appraisal Standards Board of the Appraisal Foundation; and

(2) that such appraisals shall be written appraisals.

Each such agency or instrumentality may require compliance with additional standards if it makes a determination in writing that such additional standards are required in order to properly carry out its statutory responsibilities.

¶3111

SEC. 1111. TIME FOR PROPOSAL AND ADOPTION OF STANDARDS.

Appraisal standards established under this title shall be proposed not later than 6 months and shall be adopted in final form and become effective not later than 12 months after the date of the enactment of this Act.

¶3112

SEC. 1112. FUNCTIONS OF THE FEDERAL FINANCIAL INSTITUTIONS REGULATORY AGENCIES RELATING TO APPRAISER QUALIFICATIONS.

Each Federal financial institutions regulatory agency and the Resolution Trust Corporation shall prescribe, in accordance with sections 1113 and 1114 of this title, which categories of federally related transactions should be appraised by a State certified appraiser and which by a State licensed appraiser under this title.

¶3113

SEC. 1113. TRANSACTIONS REQUIRING THE SERVICES OF A STATE CERTIFIED APPRAISER.

In determining whether an appraisal in connection with a federally related transaction shall be performed by a State certified appraiser, an agency or instrumentality under this title shall consider whether transactions, either individually or collectively, are of sufficient financial or public policy importance to the United States that an individual who performs an appraisal in connection with such transactions should be a State certified appraiser, except that—

(1) a State certified appraiser shall be required for all federally related transactions having a value of $1,000,000 or more; and

(2) 1-to-4 unit, single family residential appraisals may be performed by State licensed appraisers unless the size and complexity requires a State certified appraiser.

¶3114

SEC. 1114. TRANSACTIONS REQUIRING THE SERVICES OF A STATE LICENSED APPRAISER.

All federally related transactions not requiring the services of a State certified appraiser shall be performed by either a State certified or licensed appraiser.

¶3115

SEC. 1115. TIME FOR PROPOSAL AND ADOPTION OF RULES.

As appropriate, rules issued under sections 1113 and 1114 shall be proposed not later than 6 months and shall be effective upon adoption in final form not later than 12 months after the date of the enactment of this Act.

¶3116

SEC. 1116. CERTIFICATION AND LICENSING REQUIREMENTS.

(a) IN GENERAL.—For purposes of this title, the term "State certified real estate appraiser" means any individual who has satisfied the requirements for State certification in a State or territory whose criteria for certification as a real estate appraiser currently meets the minimum criteria for certification issued by the Appraiser Qualification Board of the Appraisal Foundation.

(b) RESTRICTION.—No individual shall be a State certified real estate appraiser under this section unless such individual has achieved a passing grade upon a suitable examination administered by a State or territory that is consistent with an equivalent to the Uniform State Certification Examination issued or endorsed by the Appraiser Qualification Board of the Appraisal Foundation.

(c) DEFINITION.—As used in this section, the term "State licensed appraiser" means an individual who has satisfied the requirements for State licensing in a State or territory.

(d) ADDITIONAL QUALIFICATION CRITERIA.—Nothing in this title shall be construed to prevent any Federal agency or instrumentality under this title from establishing such additional qualification criteria as may be necessary or appropriate to carry out the statutory responsibilities of such department, agency, or instrumentality.

¶3117

SEC. 1117. ESTABLISHMENT OF STATE APPRAISER CERTIFYING AND LICENSING AGENCIES.

To assure the availability of State certified and licensed appraisers for the performance in a State of appraisals in federally related transactions and to assure effective supervision of the activities of certified and licensed appraisers, a State may establish a State appraiser certifying and licensing agency.

¶3118

SEC. 1118. MONITORING OF STATE APPRAISER CERTIFYING AND LICENSING AGENCIES.

(a) IN GENERAL.—The Appraisal Subcommittee shall monitor State appraiser certifying and licensing agencies for the purpose of determining whether a State agency's policies, practices, and procedures are consistent with this title. The Appraisal Subcommittee and all agencies, instrumentalities, and federally recognized entities under this title shall not recognize appraiser certifications and licenses from States whose appraisal policies, practices, or procedures are found to be inconsistent with this title.

(b) DISAPPROVAL BY APPRAISAL SUBCOMMITTEE.—The Federal financial institutions, regulatory agencies, the Federal National Mortgage Association, the Federal Home Loan Mortgage Corporation, and the Resolution Trust Corporation shall accept certifications and licenses awarded by a State appraiser certifying the licensing agency unless the Appraisal Subcommittee issues a written finding that—

(1) the State agency fails to recognize and enforce the standards, requirements, and procedures prescribed pursuant to this title;

(2) the State agency is not granted authority by the State which is adequate to permit the agency to carry out its functions under this title; or

(3) decisions concerning appraisal standards, appraiser qualifications and supervision of appraiser practices are not made in a manner that carries out the purposes of this title.

(c) REJECTION OF STATE CERTIFICATIONS AND LICENSES.—

(1) OPPORTUNITY TO BE HEARD OR CORRECT CONDITIONS.—Before refusing to recognize a State's appraiser certifications or licenses, the Appraisal Subcommittee shall provide that State's certifying and licensing agency a written notice of its intention not to recognize the State's certified or licensed appraisers and ample opportunity to provide rebuttal information or to correct the conditions causing the refusal.

(2) ADOPTION OF PROCEDURES.—The Appraisal Subcommittee shall adopt written procedures for taking actions described in this section.

(3) JUDICIAL REVIEW.—A decision of the subcommittee under this section shall be subject to judicial review.

¶3119

SEC. 1119. RECOGNITION OF STATE CERTIFIED AND LICENSED APPRAISERS FOR PURPOSES OF THIS TITLE.

(a) EFFECTIVE DATE FOR USE OF CERTIFIED OR LICENSED APPRAISERS ONLY.—

(1) IN GENERAL.—Not later than July 1, 1991, all appraisals performed in connection with federally related transactions shall be performed only by individuals certified or licensed in accordance with the requirements of this title.

(2) EXTENSION OF EFFECTIVE DATE.—Subject to the approval of the council, the Appraisal Subcommittee may extend, until December 31, 1991, the effective date for the use of certified or licensed appraisers if it makes a written finding that a State has made substantial progress in establishing a State certification and licensing system that appears to conform to the provisions of this title.

(b) TEMPORARY WAIVER OF APPRAISER CERTIFICATION OR LICENSING REQUIREMENTS FOR STATE HAVING SCARCITY OF QUALIFIED APPRAISERS.—Subject to the approval of the Council, the Appraisal Subcommittee may waive any requirement relating to certification or licensing of a person to perform appraisals under this title if the Appraisal Subcommittee or a State agency whose certifications and licenses are in compliance with this title, makes a written determination that there is a scarcity of certified or licensed appraisers to perform appraisals in connection with federally related transactions in a State leading to inordinate delays in the performance of such appraisals. The waiver terminates when the Appraisal Subcommittee determines that such inordinate delays have been eliminated.

(c) REPORTS TO STATE CERTIFYING AND LICENSING AGENCIES.—The Appraisal Subcommittee, any other Federal agency or instrumentality, or any federally recognized entity shall report any action of a State certified or licensed appraiser that is contrary to the purposes of this title, to the appropriate State agency for a disposition of the subject of the referral. The State agency shall provide the Appraisal Subcommittee or the other Federal agency or instrumentality with a report on its disposition of the matter referred. Subsequent to such disposition, the subcommittee or the agency or instrumentality may take such further action, pursuant to written procedures, it deems necessary to carry out the purposes of this title.

¶3120

SEC. 1120. VIOLATIONS IN OBTAINING AND PERFORMING APPRAISALS IN FEDERALLY RELATED TRANSACTIONS.

(a) VIOLATIONS.—Except as authorized by the Appraisal Subcommittee in exercising its waiver authority pursuant to section 1119(b), it shall be a violation of this section—

   (1) for a financial institution to seek, obtain, or give money or any other thing of value in exchange for the performance of an appraisal by a person who the institution knows is not a State certified or licensed appraiser in connection with a federally related transaction; and

   (2) for the Federal National Mortgage Association, the Federal Home Loan Mortgage Corporation, or the Resolution Trust Corporation to knowingly contract for the performance of any appraisal by a person who is not a State certified or licensed appraiser in connection with a real estate related financial transaction defined in section 1121(5) to which such association or corporation is a party.

(b) PENALTIES.—A financial institution that violates subsection (a)(1) shall be subject to civil penalties under section 8(i)(2) of the Federal Deposit Insurance Act or section 206(k)(2) of the Federal Credit Union Act, as appropriate.

(c) PROCEEDING.—A proceeding with respect to a violation of this section shall be an administrative proceeding which may be conducted by a Federal financial institutions regulatory agency in accordance with the procedures set forth in subchapter II of chapter 5 of title 5, United States Code.

¶3121

SEC. 1121. DEFINITIONS.

For purposes of this title:

(1) STATE APPRAISER CERTIFYING AND LICENSING AGENCY.—The term "State appraiser certifying and licensing agency" means a State agency established in compliance with this title.

(2) APPRAISAL SUBCOMMITTEE; SUBCOMMITTEE.—The terms "Appraisal Subcommittee" and "subcommittee" mean the Appraisal Subcommittee of the Federal Financial Institutions Examination Council.

(3) COUNCIL.—The term "Council" means the Federal Financial Institutions Examinations Council.

(4) FEDERALLY RELATED TRANSACTION.—The term "federally related transaction" means any real estate-related financial transaction which—

   (A) a federal financial institutions regulatory agency or the Resolution Trust Corporation engages in, contracts for, or regulates; and

   (B) requires the services of an appraiser.

(5) REAL ESTATE RELATED FINANCIAL TRANSACTION.—The term "real

estate-related financial transaction" means any transaction involving—

   (A) the sale, lease, purchase, investment in or exchange of real property, including interests in property, or the financing thereof;

   (B) the refinancing of real property or interests in real property; and

   (C) the use of real property or interests in property as security for a loan or investment, including mortgage-backed securities.

(6) FEDERAL FINANCIAL INSTITUTIONS REGULATORY AGENCIES.—The term "Federal financial institutions regulatory agencies" means the Board of Governors of the Federal Reserve System, the Federal Deposit Insurance Corporations, the Office of the Comptroller of the Currency, the Office of Thrift Supervision, and the National Credit Union Administration.

(7) FINANCIAL INSTITUTION.—The term "financial institution" means an insured depository institution as defined in section 3 of the Federal Deposit Insurance Act or an insured credit union as defined in section 101 of the Federal Credit Union Act.

(8) CHAIRPERSON.—The term "Chairperson" means the Chairperson of the Appraisal Subcommittee selected by the council.

(9) FOUNDATION.—The terms "Appraisal Foundation" and "Foundation" means the Appraisal Foundation established on November 30, 1987, as a not for profit corporation under the laws of Illinois.

(10) WRITTEN APPRAISAL.—The term "written appraisal" means a written statement used in connection with a federally related transaction that is independently and impartially prepared by a licensed or certified appraiser setting forth an opinion of defined value of an adequately described property as of a specific date, supported by presentation and analysis of relevant market information.

¶3122

SEC. 1122. MISCELLANEOUS PROVISIONS.

(a) TEMPORARY PRACTICE.—A State appraiser certifying or licensing agency shall recognize on a temporary basis the certification or license of an appraiser issued by another State if—

   (1) the property to be appraised is part of a federally related transaction,

   (2) the appraiser's business is of a temporary nature, and

   (3) the appraiser registers with the appraiser certifying or licensing agency in the State of temporary practice.

(b) SUPPLEMENTAL FUNDING.—Funds available to the Federal financial institutions regulatory agencies may be made available to the Federal Financial Institutions Examination Council to support the council's functions under this title.

(c) PROHIBITION AGAINST DISCRIMINATION.—Criteria established by the Federal financial institutions regulatory agencies, the Federal National Mortgage Association, the Federal Home Loan Mortgage Corporation, and the Resolution Trust Corporation for appraiser qualifications in addition to State certification or licensing shall not exclude a certified or licensed appraiser for consideration for an assignment solely by virtue of membership or lack of membership in any particular appraisal organization.

(d) OTHER REQUIREMENTS.—A corporation, partnership, or other business entity may provide appraisal services in connection with federally related transactions if such appraisal is prepared by individuals certified or licensed in accordance with the requirements of this title. An individual who is not a State certified or licensed appraiser may assist in the preparation of an appraisal if—

    (1) the assistant is under the direct supervision of a licensed or certified individual; and

    (2) the final appraisal document is approved and signed by an individual who is certified or licensed.

(e) STUDIES.—

    (1) STUDY.—The Appraisal Subcommittee shall—

        (A) conduct a study to determine whether real estate sales and financing information and data that is available to real estate appraisers in the State is sufficient to permit appraisers to properly estimate the values of properties in connection with federally related transactions; and

        (B) study the feasibility and desirability of extending the provisions of this title to the function of personal property appraising and to personal property appraisers in connection with Federal financial and public policy interests.

    (2) REPORT.—The Appraisal Subcommittee shall—

        (A) report its findings to the Congress with respect to the study described in paragraph (1)(A) no later than 12 months after the date of the enactment of this title, and

        (B) report its findings with respect to the study described in paragraph (1)(B) to Congress not later than 18 months after the date of the enactment of this title.

Appendix II

UNIFORM STANDARDS OF PROFESSIONAL APPRAISAL PRACTICE (USPAP)

**UNIFORM STANDARDS OF PROFESSIONAL
APPRAISAL PRACTICE (USPAP)**

We have been granted permission by The Appraisal Foundation to publish excerpts from the USPAP text. Please note that the excerpts are only portions of the text, and that the USPAP regulations and standards are revised from time to time. The complete annual edition and current revisions of the USPAP is available and may be purchased from The Appraisal Foundation, 1029 Vermont Avenue, N.W., Suite 900, Washington, D.C. 20005.

Excerpts Selected
Preamble
Ethics Provision
Competency Provision
Departure Provision
Statement 7—Changes to the Departure Provision
Definitions
Standard 1—Real Property Appraisal
Standard 2—Real Property Appraisal, Reporting

PREAMBLE

It is essential that a professional appraiser arrive at and communicate his or her analysis, opinions, and advice in a manner that will be meaningful to the client and will not be misleading in the marketplace. These Uniform Standards of Professional Appraisal practice reflect that current standards of the appraisal profession.

The importance of the role of the appraiser places ethical obligations on those who serve in this capacity. These Standards include explanatory comment and begin with the Ethics Provisions setting forth the requirements for integrity, objectivity, independent judgment, and ethical conduct. In addition, these Standards include a Competency Provision which places an immediate responsibility on the appraiser prior to acceptance of an assignment. The Standards contain binding requirements, as well as specific guidelines to which a Departure Provision may apply under certain limited conditions. Definitions applicable to these Standards are also included.

These Standards deal with the procedures to be followed in performing an appraisal, review or consulting service and the manner in which an appraisal, review or consulting service is communicated. . . .

These Standards are for appraisers and the users of appraisal services. To maintain the highest level of professional practice, appraisers must observe these Standards. The users of appraisals should demand work performed in conformance with these Standards.

ETHICS PROVISION

Because of the fiduciary responsibilities inherent in professional appraisal practice, the appraiser must observe the highest standards of professional ethics. This Ethics Provision is divided into four sections: Conduct, Management, Confidentiality, and Record Keeping.

Conduct

An appraiser must perform ethically and competently in accordance with these standards and not engage in conduct that is unlawful, unethical, or improper. An appraiser who could reasonably be perceived to act as a disinterested third party in rendering an unbiased appraisal, review, or consulting service must perform assignments with impartiality, objectivity, and independence and without accommodation of personal interests.

Management

The acceptance of compensation that is contingent upon the reporting of a predetermined value or a direction in value that favors the cause of the client, the amount of the value estimate, the attainment of a stipulated result, or the occurrence of a subsequent event is unethical.

The payment of undisclosed fees, commissions, or things of value in connection with the procurement of appraisal, review, or consulting assignments is unethical.

Advertising for or soliciting appraisal assignments in a manner which is false, misleading or exaggerated is unethical. . . .

Confidentiality

An appraiser must protect the confidential nature of the appraiser-client relationship.

Record Keeping

An appraiser must prepare written records of appraisal, review, and consulting assignments—including oral testimony and reports—and retain such records for a period of at least five (5) years after preparation or at least two (2) years after final disposition of any judicial proceedings in which testimony was given, whichever period expires last.

COMPETENCY PROVISION

Prior to accepting an assignment or entering into an agreement to perform any assignment, an appraiser must properly identify the problem to be addressed and have the knowledge and experience to complete the assignment competently; or alternatively:

1. disclose the lack of knowledge and/or experience to the client before accepting the assignment; and

2. take all necessary or appropriate steps to complete the assignment competently; and

3. describe the lack of knowledge and/or experience and the steps taken to complete the assignment competently in the report.

DEPARTURE PROVISION

This provision permits limited exceptions to sections of the Uniform Standards that are classified as *specific guidelines* rather than *binding requirements*. The burden of proof is on the appraiser to decide before accepting a limited assignment that the result will not confuse or mislead. The burden of disclosure is also on the appraiser to report any limitations.

An appraiser may enter into an agreement to perform an assignment that calls for something less than, or different from, the work that would otherwise be required by the specific guidelines, provided that prior to entering into such an agreement:

1. the appraiser has determined that the assignment to be performed is not so limited in scope that the resulting appraisal, review, or consulting service would tend to mislead or confuse the client, the users of the report, or the public; and

2. the appraiser has advised the client that the assignment calls for

something less than, or different from, the work required by the specific guidelines and that the report will state the limited or differing scope of the appraisal, review, or consulting service.

Exceptions to (certain) requirements are not permitted. . . .

STATEMENT 7—REVISION TO DEPARTURE PROVISION

This Statement, effective July 1, 1994, amends the Departure Provision, as follows:

An appraiser may enter into an agreement to perform an assignment that calls for something less than. . . . provided that prior to entering into such an agreement:

1. (Same as above)

2. (Same as above)

3. The client has agreed that the performance of a limited appraisal or consulting service would be appropriate.

Exceptions to (certain) requirements are not permitted. . . .

This Statement established classifications of reporting, as follows:

1. *Self-Contained Appraisal Report*

2. *Summary Appraisal Report*

3. *Restricted Appraisal Report*

DEFINITIONS

[Note: The following are excerpts from the USPAP *Definitions*]

Appraisal (noun) the act or process of estimating value; an estimate of value; (adj.) of or pertaining to appraising and related functions; e.g., appraisal practice, appraisal services.

Appraisal Practice the work or services performed by appraisers, defined by three terms in these standards: appraisal, review, and consulting.

Binding Requirement All or part of a standard rule of USPAP from which departure is not permitted.

Cash Flow Analysis a study of the anticipated movement of cash into or out of an investment.

Client any party for whom an appraiser performs a service.

Complete Appraisal the act or process of estimating value or an estimate of value performed without invoking the Departure Provision.

Consulting the act or process of providing information, analysis or real estate data, and recommendations or conclusions on diversified problems in real estate, other than estimating value.

Limited Appraisal   The act or process of estimating value or an estimate of value performed under and resulting from invoking the Departure Provision.

Market Analysis   a study of real estate market conditions for a specific type of property.

Market Value   market value is the major focus of most real property appraisal assignments. Both economic and legal definitions of market value have been developed and refined. The current economic definition agreed upon by agencies that regulate federal financial institutions in the United States of America is:

The most probable price which a property should bring in a competitive and open market under all conditions requisite to a fair sale, the buyer and seller each acting prudently and knowledgeably, and assuming the price is not affected by undue stimulus. Implicit in this definition is the consummation of a sale as of a specified date and the passing of title from seller to buyer under conditions whereby:

1.   buyer and seller are typically motivated;

2.   both parties are well informed or well advised, and acting in what they consider their best interests;

3.   a reasonable time is allowed for exposure in an open market;

4.   payment is made in terms of cash. . . .

5.   the price represents the normal consideration for the property sold unaffected by special or creative financing or sales concessions. . . .

Personal Property   identifiable portable and tangible objects which are considered by the general public as being "personal," e.g., furnishings, artwork, . . . , machinery, and equipment; all property that is not classified as real estate.

Report   any communication, written or oral, of an appraisal, review, or consulting service that is transmitted to the client upon completion of an assignment.

   Self-Contained Appraisal Report   A written report prepared under Standards Rule 2–2(a) of a Complete or Limited Appraisal performed under Standard 1.

   Summary Appraisal Report   A written report prepared under Standards Rule 2–2(b) of a Complete or Limited Appraisal performed under Standard 1.

   Restricted Appraisal Report   A written report prepared under Standard Rule 2–2(c) of a Complete or Limited Appraisal performed under Standard 1.

Review   the act or process of critically studying a report prepared by another.

Specific Guideline   All or part of a standard rule of USPAP from which departure is permitted under certain limited conditions.

STANDARD 1

In developing a real property appraisal, an appraiser must be aware of, understand, and correctly employ those recognized methods and techniques that are necessary to produce a credible appraisal.

Standards Rule 1–1

In developing a real property appraisal, an appraiser must:

(a)   be aware of, understand, and correctly employ those recognized methods and techniques that are necessary to produce a credible appraisal;

(b)   not commit a substantial error of omission or commission that significantly affects an appraisal;

(c)   not render appraisal services in a careless or negligent manner, such as a series of errors that considered individually, may not significantly affect the results of an appraisal, but which when considered in the aggregate, would be misleading.

Standards Rule 1–2

In developing a real property appraisal, an appraiser must:

(a)   adequately identify the real estate, identify the real property interest, consider the purpose and intended use of the appraisal, consider the extent of the data collection process, identify any special limiting conditions, and identify the effective date of the appraisal;

(b)   define the value being considered; if the value to be estimated is market value, the appraiser must clearly indicate whether the estimate is the most probable price:
    (i) in terms of cash
    (ii) in terms of financial arrangements equivalent to cash
    (iii) in such other terms as may be precisely defined. . . .

(c)   consider easements, restrictions, encumbrances, leases, reservations, covenants, contracts, declarations, special assessments, ordinances, or other items of similar nature;

(d)   consider whether an appraised fractional interest, physical segment, or partial holding contributes pro rata to the value of the whole;

(e) identify and consider the effect on value of any personal property, trade fixtures, or intangible items that are not real property but are included in the appraisal.

Standards Rule 1–3

In developing a real property appraisal, an appraiser must observe the following specific appraisal guidelines:

(a) consider the effect on use and value of the following factors: existing land use regulations, reasonably probable modifications of such land use regulations, economic demand, the physical adaptability of the real estate, neighborhood trends, and the highest and best use of the real estate;

(b) recognize that land is appraised as though vacant and available for development to its highest and best use and that the appraisal of improvements based on their actual contribution to the site. . . .

Standards Rule 1–4

In developing a real property appraisal, an appraiser must observe the following specific appraisal guidelines, when applicable:
(Not excerpted)

Standards Rule 1–5

In developing a real estate appraisal, an appraiser must:

(a) consider and analyze any current Agreement of Sales, option, or listing of the property being appraised, if such information is available to the appraiser in the normal course of business;

(b) consider and analyze any prior sales of the property being appraised that occurred within the following time periods:
(i) one year for one-to-four family residential property; and
(ii) three years for all other property types.

(c) consider and reconcile the quality and quantity of data available and analyzed within the approaches used and the applicability or suitability of the approaches used.

STANDARD 2 (AS MODIFIED BY STATEMENT 7, JULY 1994)

In reporting the results of a real property appraisal an appraiser must communicate each analysis, opinion, and conclusion in a manner that is not misleading.

Standards Rule 2–1

Each written or oral real property appraisal report must:

(a) clearly and accurately set forth the appraisal in a manner that will not be misleading;

(b) contain sufficient information to enable the person(s) who are expected to receive or rely on the report to understand it properly;

(c) clearly and accurately disclose any extraordinary assumptions or limiting condition that directly affects the appraisal and indicate its impact on value.

Standards Rule 2–2

Each written real property appraisal report must be prepared under one of the following three options and prominently state which option is used: Self-Contained Appraisal Report, Summary Appraisal Report, or Restricted Appraisal Report.

(a) The Self-Contained Appraisal Report must:
- (i) identify and describe the real estate being appraised;
- (ii) state the real property interest being appraised;
- (iii) state the purpose and intended use of the appraisal;
- (iv) define the value to be estimated;
- (v) state the effective date of the appraisal and the date of the report;
- (vi) state the extent of the process of collecting, confirming, and reporting data;
- (vii) state all assumptions and limiting conditions that affect the analysis, opinions, and conclusions;
- (viii) describe the information considered, the appraisal procedures followed, and the reasoning that supports the analysis, opinions, and conclusions;
- (ix) describe the appraiser's opinion of the highest and best use of the real estate . . .
- (x) explain and support the exclusion of any of the usual valuation approaches;
- (xi) describe any additional information that may be appropriate to show compliance with, or clearly identify and explain permitted departures from the specific guidelines of Standard 1;
- (xii) include a signed certification in accordance with Standards Rule 2–3.

(b) The Summary Appraisal Report must:
- (i) identify and provide a summary description of the real estate being appraised;

    (ii) state the real property interest being appraised;

   (iii) state the purpose and intended use of the appraisal;

   (iv) define the value to be estimated;

    (v) state the effective date of the appraisal and the date of the report;

   (vi) summarize the extent of the process of collecting, confirming, and reporting data;

  (vii) state all assumptions and limiting conditions that affect the analysis, opinions, and conclusions;

 (viii) summarize the information considered, the appraisal procedures followed, and the reasoning that supports the analysis, . . .

   (ix) summarize the appraiser's opinion of the highest and best use . . .

    (x) explain and support the exclusion of any of the usual valuation approaches;

   (xi) summarize any additional information . . . to show compliance with . . . or . . . permitted departure from the specific guidelines . . .

  (xii) include a signed certification. . . .

(c)   The Restricted Appraisal Report must:

    (i) identify the real estate being appraised;

   (ii) state the real property interest being appraised;

  (iii) state the purpose and intended use of the appraisal;

  (iv) state and reference a definition of the value to be estimated;

   (v) state the effective date of the appraisal and the date of the report;

  (vi) describe the extent of the process of collecting, confirming, and reporting data;

  (vii) state all assumptions and limiting conditions that affect the analysis, opinions, and conclusions;

 (viii) state the appraisal procedures followed, state the value conclusion and reference the existence of specific file information in support of the conclusion;

  (ix) state the appraiser's opinion of the highest and best use. . . .

   (x) state the exclusion of any of the usual valuation approaches;

  (xi) contain a prominent use restriction that limits reliance on the report to the client and warns that the report cannot be understood properly without additional information in the workfile of the appraiser, and identify and explain any permitted departures from the specific guidelines of Standard 1;

  (xii) include a signed certification. . . .

BODY OF KNOWLEDGE

The California Office of Real Estate Appraisers (OREA) has, in compliance with Federal regulations, prepared a Body of Knowledge outlining the specific topics covered in the state license examinations. These topics are required for various license levels, as described in Chapter 21.

BASIC EDUCATION TOPICS

Required for State of California Licensing Examinations
- I. Influences on Real Estate Value
  - A. Physical and environmental
  - B. Economic
  - C. Governmental and legal
  - D. Social
- II. Legal Consideration in Appraisal
  - A. Real estate vs. real property
  - B. Real property vs. personal property
    1. Fixtures
    2. Trade fixtures
    3. Machinery and equipment
  - C. Limitations on real estate ownership
    1. Private
       a. Deed restrictions
       b. Leases
       c. Mortgages
       d. Easements
       e. Liens
       f. Encroachments
    2. Public
       a. Police power
          1. Zoning
          2. Building and fire codes
          3. Environmental regulations
       b. Taxation
          1. Property tax
          2. Special assessments
       c. Eminent domain
       d. Escheat

   D. Legal rights and interests
    1. Fee simple estate
    2. Life estate
    3. Leasehold interest
    4. Lease fee interest
    5. Other legal interests
     a. Easements
     b. Encroachment
   E. Forms of property ownership
    1. Individual
    2. Tenancies and undivided interests
    3. Special ownership forms
     a. Condominiums
     b. Cooperatives
     c. Timesharing
   F. Legal descriptions
    1. Metes and bounds
    2. Government survey
   G. Transfer of title
    1. Basic types of deeds
    2. Recordation
  III. Types of Value
   A. Market value or value in exchange
   B. Price
   C. Cost
   D. Investment value
   E. Value in use
   F. Assessment value
   G. Insurable value
   H. Going concern value (general, only)
  IV. Economic Principles
   A. Anticipation
   B. Balance
   C. Change
   D. Competition
   E. Conformity
   F. Contribution
   G. Increasing and decreasing returns
   H. Substitution
   I. Supply and demand
   J. Surplus productivity
   K. Opportunity cost (general, only)
  V. Real Estate Markets and Analysis
   A. Characteristics of real estate markets
    1. Availability of information
    2. Changes in supply vs. demand
    3. Immobility of real estate
    4. Segmented markets
    5. Regulations
   B. Absorption analysis

      1. Demographic data
      2. Competition
      3. Absorption
      4. Forecasts
      5. Existing space inventory (general, only)
      6. Current and projected space surplus (general, only)
      7. New space (general, only)
   C. Role of money and capital markets
      1. Competing investments
      2. Sources of capital
   D. Real estate financing
      1. Mortgage terms and concepts
         a. Mortgagor
         b. Mortgagee
         c. Principal and interest
      2. Mortgage payment plans
         a. Fixed rate, level payment
         b. Adjustable rate
         c. Buydown
         d. Other
      3. Types of mortgages
         a. Conventional
         b. Insured
VI. Valuation Process
   A. Definition of the problem
      1. Purpose and use of the appraisal
      2. Interests to be appraised
      3. Type of value to be estimated
      4. Date of value estimate
      5. Limiting conditions
   B. Collection and analysis of data
      1. National and regional trends
      2. Economic base
      3. Local area and neighborhood
         a. Employment
         b. Income
         c. Trends
         d. Access
         e. Locational convenience
      4. Site and improvements
   C. Analysis of highest and best use
   D. Applications and use of each approach to value
      1. Sales comparison
      2. Cost
      3. Income capitalization
   E. Reconciliation and final value estimate
   F. The appraisal report
VII. Property Description
   A. Site description
      1. Utilities

  2. Access

  3. Topography

  4. Size

 B. Improvement description

  1. Size

  2. Condition

  3. Utility

 C. Basic construction and design

  1. Techniques and materials

   a. Foundations

   b. Framing

   c. Finish (exterior and interior)

   d. Mechanical (general, only)

  2. Functional utility

VIII. Highest and Best-Use Analysis

 A. Four tests

  1. Physically possible

  2. Legally permitted

  3. Economically feasible

  4. Maximally productive

 B. Vacant site, or as if vacant

 C. As improved

 D. Interim use

IX. Appraisal Statistical Concepts

 A. Mean

 B. Median

 C. Mode

 D. Standard deviation

 E. Range

 F. Compound interest concepts—Six functions of $1 (general, only)

  1. Future value of $1

  2. Present value of $1

  3. Future value of an annuity of $1 per period

  4. Present value of an annuity of $1 per period

  5. Sinking fund factor

  6. Installment to amortize $1 (loan constant)

X. Sales Comparison Approach

 A. Research and selection of comparables

  1. Data sources

  2. Verification

  3. Units of comparison—Data sources

   a. Income

    1. Potential gross income multiplier

    2. Effective gross income multiplier

    3. Overall rate (general, only)

   b. Size

    1. Square feet

    2. Acres

    3. Other

  c. Utility (examples, only)
   1. Rooms (general for motels and apartments)
   2. Seats (general for theater seats)
   3. Other
 B. Elements of comparison
  1. Property rights conveyed
   a. Leased fee/leasehold
   b. Easements
   c. Mineral rights (general, only)
   d. Other
  2. Financing terms
   a. Loan payment
   b. Loan balances
  3. Conditions of sale
   a. Arms-length sale
   b. Personalty
  4. Market conditions at time of contract and closing
  5. Location
  6. Physical characteristics
  7. Tenant improvements (general, only)

XI. Site Value
 A. Sales comparison
 B. Land residual
 C. Allocation
 D. Extraction
 E. Plottage and assemblage
 F. Ground rent capitalization (general, only)
 G. Subdivision analysis:
  1. Development cost—direct and indirect
  2. Contractor's overhead and profit
  3. Forecast absorption and gross sales
  4. Entrepreneurial profit
  5. Discount value conclusion

XII. Cost Approach
 A. Steps in the cost approach
  1. Reproduction vs. replacement cost
   a. Comparative unit method
   b. Unit-in-place method
   c. Quality service method
   d. Cost service index
  2. Accrued depreciation
   a. Types of depreciation
    1. Physical deterioration
     a. Curable
     b. Incurable
     c. Short-lived
     d. Long-lived
    2. Functional obsolescence
     a. Curable
     b. Incurable

         3. External obsolescence
           a. Locational
           b. Economic
      b. Methods of estimating depreciation
         1. Age-life method
         2. Breakdown method and sequence of deductions
         3. Market extraction of depreciation
  B. Application of the cost approach
XIII. Income Approach
  A. Estimation of income and expenses
    1. Gross market income
    2. Effective gross income
      a. Vacancy
      b. Collection loss
    3. Operating expenses
      a. Fixed expenses
      b. Variable expenses
      c. Reserve for replacements
    4. Net operating income
  B. Operating expense ratios
    1. Operating expense ratio
    2. Net income ratio
    3. Break-even ratio
  C. Gross rent multiplier
  D. Direct capitalization
    1. Relevance and limitations
    2. Overall capitalization rate
    3. Gross income multiplier and net income ratio
    4. Band of investment (mortgage equity) techniques
    5. Residual techniques
      a. Land (building value given)
      b. Building (land value given)
      c. Equity (mortgage value given)
  E. Cash flow estimates (before tax, only)
    1. Operating years
      a. Estimating NOI with a change in NOI
      b. Estimating NOI using lease information
      c. Cash flow (NOI less mortgage payments)
    2. Reversion
      a. Estimating resale with a change in value
      b. Estimating resale with a terminal capitalization rate
      c. Cash flow (sale price less mortgage balance)
      d. Deductions for costs of sale and legal fees to arrive at a net reversion
  F. Measure of cash flow
    1. Equity dividend rate (cash on cash rate)
    2. Debt coverage ratio
  G. Discounted cash flow analysis (DCF)
    1. Relevance and limitations
    2. Potential gross income and expense estimate

   a. Market vs. contract rents

   b. Vacancy and lease commissions

   c. Tenant improvements and concessions

  3. Discount rates and yield rates (definition and concept, but no calculation of yield rates)

  4. Discounting cash flows (from operations and reversion where all cash flows projected in dollar amounts)

XIV. Valuation of Partial Interests

 A. Partial interests

  1. Life estates

  2. Undivided interest in commonly held property

  3. Easements

  4. Timeshares

  5. Cooperatives

 B. Interests created by a lease

  1. Leased fee estate

  2. Leasehold estate

  3. Subleasehold (general, only)

  4. Renewal options (general, only)

  5. Tenant improvements (general, only)

  6. Concessions (general, only)

 C. Lease provisions

  1. Overage rent

  2. Expense stops

  3. Net leases

  4. Minimum rent

  5. Percentage rent

  6. CPI adjustments

  7. Excess rent

 D. Valuation considerations

  1. Identifying the cash flows to the different interests, including turnover ratios

  2. Discount rate selection for different interests

  3. Relationship between the values of the interests

XV. Appraisal Standards and Ethics (Must have covered USPAP)

XVI. Appraisal Report Writing

 A. Narrative appraisal reports

 B. Form appraisal reports

Appendix IV

ANSWERS TO CHAPTER QUESTIONS

CHAPTER 1

Answers to Questions

1. Objective.

2. This question asks the student's opinion on the local assessor's estimate of value of a particular property.

3. Generally within 5 percent.

4. Visual comparison appraisal.

5. It is simple.

6. Because fire does not destroy land.

7. Should vary between 1 percent and 1.25 percent of full market value.

8. If the appraisal is too low, the prospective seller will not list with the broker. If it is too high, the property will not sell.

9. The right of the public body to buy private property for public purposes.

10. This question calls for student's opinion.

Answers to Multiple-choice Questions

1. c

2. d

3. b

4. a

5. d

CHAPTER 2

Answers to Questions

1. Property is anything capable of being owned.

2. Real estate.

3. Fee simple absolute.

4. The intention of the person affixing the personal property to the land.

5. This question provides a good opportunity for a classroom discussion in which the students and teacher can elucidate the necessity of the five basic government controls on private real estate.

Answers to Multiple-choice Questions

1. c
2. d
3. a
4. b
5. b
6. b
7. c
8. d

CHAPTER 3

Answers to Questions

1. Highest and best use is the use that will give the maximum net return or benefits to the property. Refer to text for example of its application in appraising.

2. No one will pay more for a property than the cost of an equally desirable substitute property, if time is not a major problem. Refer to text for example of its application in appraising.

3. This question concerns a particular area and should be answered in classroom discussion.

4. This question concerns a particular area and should be answered in classroom discussion.

5. The effect would probably be a loss in value (regression) to the 4,000-square-foot residence with a possible slight rise in value to abutting 2,000-square-foot residences.

6. The effect would probably be a rise in value (progression) to the 1,500-square-foot residence with a possible slight loss in value to abutting 3,000-square-foot residences.

7. The principle of consistent use.

8. Labor, management, capital, and land. They are usually satisfied in this order. Refer to text for more complete discussion.

Answers to Multiple-choice Questions

1. d
2. a
3. b
4. d
5. d
6. b
7. c
8. a
9. b
10. d

CHAPTER 4 5

Answers to Questions

1. The lot and block method of writing legal descriptions is used most often because of its simplicity.

2. The income approach involves more estimates than the other two.

3. Because of odd shape.

4. Because the value of real estate is constantly changing.

5. To preclude any misunderstanding.

6. It is difficult to interpret.

Answers to Multiple-choice Questions

1. c
2. a
3. b
4. c
5. b
6. c
7. d
8. d
9. a
10. b

CHAPTER 5 4

Answers to Questions

1. Lenders of money seek the greatest return. When demand is higher in one region of the United States, lenders will lend money in that area.

2. The federal government also affects local economic conditions by expanding or contracting government defense contracts.

3. Increased mobility because of the extensive use of the automobile. People can live thirty miles or more from their place of business.

4. A sound economic base resulting in full employment allows continued activity in the local real estate market to adjust to supply and demand.

5. In the event of the shutdown or drastic curtailment of activity of a major industry, the economic effect on local real estate values can be very severe.

6. By employing teachers, bringing research and industry into an area, and creating a desirable cultural climate to attract technically trained personnel.

7. An object's value depends on the attitudes of those who desire that object. Single-family residential property values are directly related to the attitudes of buyers and sellers and how their attitudes are expressed in dollar amounts.

8. This question requires classroom discussion, since it relates to any number of geographical areas.

9. Generally, climate and natural environmental features are the most important physical forces affecting local single-family residential real estate values.

10. Representative government responsive to community needs. This includes zoning as well as other political forces.

11. A neighborhood generally consists of a fairly homogeneous group of homes whose occupants are fairly alike in economic status. Sometimes, however, natural or artificially constructed boundaries, such as rivers or roads, separate one neighborhood from another.

12. They virtually do not differ at all.

13. Youth, maturity, and old age.

14. a. Economic condition of residents.
    b. Attitudes of residents.
    c. Quality of construction.
    d. Local economic conditions.

Answers to Multiple-choice Questions

1. b

2. c

3. c

4. d

5. a

CHAPTER 6

Answers to Questions

1. This answer requires review and analysis of the advantages and disadvantages of corner lots, as reflected in the attitudes of buyers in a particular area, and therefore is recommended for classroom discussion.

2. This answer lends itself to classroom discussion of the attitudes of local buyers toward cul-de-sac lots.

3. This answer lends itself to classroom discussion. The principle is that of increasing and decreasing returns.

4. This answer depends on the local situation and is excellent material for classroom discussion.

5. A suggested answer is that a maximum amount of space can usually be efficiently used in a parcel of land close to a square

shape. This is not always true, but it is a generally accepted rule for residential, commercial, and industrial lots.

6. This answer depends on the local situation and is recommended for classroom discussion.

7. This question should be answered in class discussion; it provides an opportunity for learning about lot value.

8. Answers to this question may vary, since different neighborhoods in the same city may reflect different values because of the availability or lack of public transportation.

9. This question calls for students' opinions.

Answers to Multiple-choice Questions

1. c
2. d
3. d
4. b
5. a
6. b
7. b
8. a
9. b
10. c
11. d
12. d
13. b
14. a
15. d

CHAPTER 7

Answers to Questions

1. If there are sufficient market data, the market approach is the best method of site valuation.

2. The difficulty of finding a sufficient number of comparable sales.

3. The five tests of comparability are
    a. Similar location.
    b. Similar utility or use.
    c. Similar time (sale occurring within reasonable time prior to date of appraisal).
    d. Voluntary sale (not under undue pressure).
    e. An actual market sale (not fabricated or contrived).

4. Generally, listings to sell set the upper limit of value and offers to buy set the lower limit of value.

5. Seldom is a single-family residential lot purchased with potential rental income as the basis for development.

Answers to Multiple-choice Questions

1. c
2. a
3. a
4. d
5. b
6. c
7. b
8. b
9. b
10. b

CHAPTER 8

Answers to Questions

1. Because of the wide range of climate differences and the availability of a wide range of materials.

2. The shake is thicker.

3. Because it is strong, durable, relatively inexpensive, available, and adaptable and because the heavy work of pouring can be done mechanically.

4. Metal acts as a conductor of heat. Tile acts as an insulator.

5. Depends on the area.

6. Because of its beauty and durability and insulation qualities.

7. It automatically disengages the electrical power, should an overload occur.

Questions 8, 9, 10, and 11 ask for discussions concerning specific area differences, customs, likes, and dislikes and can be answered only by classroom discussion.

Answers to Multiple-choice Questions

1. c
2. d
3. b
4. d
5. d
6. a
7. c
8. c
9. c
10. d
11. c
12. b
13. a
14. c
15. a
16. a
17. c
18. b
19. b
20. d
21. a
22. a
23. a
24. d
25. b

CHAPTER 9

Answers to Questions

1. Advantage of flat roof: least expensive to install. Disadvantages of flat roof:
   a. Less insulation (house is cooler in winter, hotter in summer).
   b. Aesthetically less appealing than other styles.
   c. Subject to leaking, since water tends to collect on top.

2. Advantage of gable roof:
   a. More insulation qualities (house is warmer in winter, cooler in summer).
   b. Aesthetically more appealing than flat roof.
   c. Readily sheds water.

   Disadvantage of gable roof: more expensive than flat roof.

3. It is generally not as important, since most people do not plan on living permanently in multiple residential units. (The exception to this would be the condominium or owner-occupied multiple unit.)

4. A two-story house provides twice the living area on the same size foundation and with the same roof area as does a single-story house.

5. a. Conservation of fuel for heating and cooling, since the secondary story acts as an insulator.
   b. Less land required for the same amount of living area of house.

6. a. Does the addition or remodeling increase the utility of the residence to potential buyers?
   b. Does the addition or remodeling architecturally fit the existing structure and neighborhood?
   c. Are the neighboring residences of sufficient size and utility so that the house does not suffer by regression?
   d. Does the addition or remodeling conform to local building codes?

7. Sometimes lenders and loan insurers may not approve a loan if there is no garage.

Answers to Multiple-choice Questions

1. c

2. d

3. a

4. b

5. d

6. c

7. c

8. a

9. d

10. d

11. a

12. a

13. b

14. a

15. a

CHAPTER 10

Answers to Questions

1. a. Estimate value of land.
   b. Estimate cost of improvements.
   c. Estimate accrued depreciation.
   d. Deduct accrued depreciation from estimated cost of improvements.
   e. Add depreciated improvement cost to land value.

2. Direct costs refer to the labor and material directly associated with construction of the improvements. Indirect costs are expenditures not directly related to the physical construction, but necessary and usual in the development of the property.

3. a. Financing fees for construction loans.
   b. Interest or a return on money expended during the construction period.
   c. Payment for professional services such as legal, accounting, or appraisal fees.
   d. Administrative and management expenses.
   e. Loss in rental.

4. Reproduction cost is the present-cost estimate of constructing an exact replica of the subject improvements. Replacement cost is the present-cost estimate of replacing improvements with those of similar type, utility, and amenities.

5. An appraisal for insurance purposes or an eminent domain action would probably require that greater consideration be given to the reproduction cost of the improvements.

6. a. The quantity survey method.

    b. The unit-in-place method.

    c. The comparative, or square-foot, method.

    d. The index method.

       The comparative method based on a square-foot cost is the method most often used by appraisers.

7. The index method is most applicable to newer buildings whose original construction cost is known.

8. Very few appraisers know enough about construction costs to use the quantity survey method; also, the method is too time-consuming for most appraisal assignments.

9. a. Recent local building construction.

    b. Building contractors.

    c. Published building cost data.

Answers to Multiple-choice Questions

1. c

2. a

3. a

4. c

5. b

6. b

7. d

8. a

9. d

10. a

CHAPTER 11

Answers to Questions

1. Accrued depreciation is the difference between the reproduction cost of the improvements and the value of the improvements, measured at the same date.

2. a. Physical deterioration—actual wearing out of the building through age and use.

    b. Functional obsolescence—because of its design, the building does not function as well as the currently acceptable replacement.

    c. Economic obsolescence—lessening in value caused by factors external to the property.

3. a. Age-life
   b. Observed condition
   c. Cost to cure
   d. Capitalization of rental loss
   e. Sales data

4. Chronological age is the actual age of the improvements; effective age is the estimated age based on the condition of the improvements. Estimated effective age may be greater or less than chronological age, depending on maintenance, modernization, and replacement of building components.

5. Economic life is the estimated number of years of anticipated usefulness of the improvements. Factors other than the physical aspect of the improvements must be considered. The economic life is usually shorter than the physical life of an improvement because of functional and economic conditions.

6. The cost approach is most reliable when the improvements being appraised are relatively new and represent the highest and best use of the land.

7. The most common method of estimating depreciation is the age-life method, based on the ratio of effective age to economic life.

8. Curable physical deterioration is physical damage that should be repaired immediately to make the property presentable, to protect the income capabilities of the property, and to prevent further damage to the building. All other physical deterioration is incurable. The test is not whether it is possible to cure the deficiency, but whether it is economically justified.

9. a. Estimate reproduction cost of improvements for each sale property.
   b. Estimate land value of each sale property.
   c. Deduct estimated land value from sales price, to arrive at the indicated sale price for improvements only.
   d. Deduct indicated sale price of improvements from estimated reproduction cost of improvements.
   e. The result will be the indicated accrued depreciation for each sale property, expressed in total dollars. Dividing the amount of depreciation by the estimated reproduction cost will indicate the ratio of depreciation applicable to the sale improvements.

Answers to Multiple-choice Questions

1. d

2. d

3. a

4. a

5. b

6. c

7. a

8. b

9. d

10. a

CHAPTER 12

Answers to Questions

1. a. Collection of sales data.
    b. Processing of sales data.
    c. Analysis of sales data.
    d. Comparison of sales data with subject property to arrive at value estimate.

2. Comparable sales are usually adjusted for time, location, and physical characteristics. The adjustment for time reflects the change in value between the date of the comparable sale and the valuation date of the subject property. The adjustment for location may include differences in desirability between neighborhoods or between specific locations within a neighborhood. Adjustments for physical characteristics include all physical differences between the sale properties and the subject property.

3. a. As a percentage of sale price.
    b. By a dollar amount.
    c. By pluses or minuses.

4. A person is not justified in paying more for a property than the cost of substitute property of equal utility and desirability.

5. Besides reflecting the direct actions between buyers and sellers in the market, the market data approach is usually reliable because of the availability of necessary sales data caused by the transitory nature of our modern economy.

6. A comparable sales map is used to locate the comparable sales and to enable the appraiser to view the sale parcels in relation to the subject property and other characteristics of the neighborhood.

7. a. Name of seller.
    b. Name of buyer.

    c. Date of sale.

    d. Location of property.

    e. Size and dimensions of parcel.

    f. Description of improvements.

    g. Confirmation (if possible).

    h. Recording index (if available).

    i. Transfer tax stamps (if available).

    j. Sale price.

    k. Terms of sale (if available).

    l. Remarks or comments.

8. Inspection of the comparable sales is necessary so that the appraiser can relate and adjust the sale properties to the subject parcel. Confirmation of the sale is necessary to obtain or verify data pertinent to the sale.

9. a. Sale price.

    b. Terms of sale.

    c. Any extenuating circumstances in the sale.

    d. Description of improvements.

    e. Occupancy status.

    f. Rental, if not owner-occupied.

    g. Condition of property at date of sale.

    h. Personal property included in sale.

    i. Assessments or encumbrances against property at date of sale.

10. a. Square feet of living area.

    b. Per living unit.

    c. Per room.

    d. Gross rent multiplier.

    e. Available amenities.

11. The rating grid, also called comparison chart, enables the appraiser to visualize the differences between the sale properties and the subject property and make a more meaningful comparison.

Answers to Multiple-choice Questions

1. b

2. c

3. d

4. c

5. b

CHAPTER 13

Answers to Questions

1. a. Estimate gross income.
    b. Estimate allowance for vacancy and rent loss.
    c. Subtract the allowance for vacancy and rent loss from the gross income estimate to indicate effective gross income.
    d. Estimate operating expenses and reserves for replacement.
    e. Deduct estimated expenses and reserves for replacement from effective gross income to arrive at net income.
    f. Select a capitalization rate applicable to the subject property.
    g. Capitalize, or discount, the estimated net income to indicate the present value of the property.

2. Contract rent is the actual, or contracted, rent received from the property. Economic rent is the rent the unit should bring in the open market at the date of appraisal.

3. Effective gross income is estimated annual gross income less an allowance for vacancy and rent loss.

4. a. Fixed expenses.
    b. Operating expenses.
    c. Reserves for replacement.

5. A reconstructed operating statement is a summary of income and expense estimates prepared by the appraiser. An operating statement prepared by an accountant includes certain items, such as interest and principal payments on loans, book depreciation, and other items, that may be considered expenses for tax purposes but are not legitimately used in estimating the net income attributable to the property. Some expense items included by the appraiser, such as management expense for an owner-managed property, will not be included in an accounting statement.

6. a. Utilities.
    b. Administration.
    c. Maintenance and repairs.

7. The income approach attempts to measure directly the present value of property based on its expected future benefits. The expected benefits from ownership of single-family residences include not only the basic utility of housing but also pride of ownership, stability, prestige, freedom of use, and the like. These intangible benefits of home ownership are called amenities. Home ownership amenities cannot be readily expressed in dollars and therefore cannot be accurately measured by the income approach.

8. An annual reserve for replacement allowance is estimated for building components and chattels having a life shorter than the future economic life of the property. This allowance is deducted

from the property's income to arrive at a net income. An allowance is made for short-lived items that are an integral part of the building, chattels (which are normally included in the sale and lease of the real property), and furniture.

Answers to Multiple-choice Questions

1. a
2. b
3. a
4. c
5. b
6. c
7. b
8. b
9. d
10. d
11. d
12. c
13. b
14. b
15. d

CHAPTER 14

Answers to Questions

1. Capitalization is the process of estimating the present worth of a property based on its anticipated income. A sum of $1,000 payable in two years is not worth $1,000 today but must be discounted for the loss of two years' interest. Likewise, an anticipated monthly or annual income from property must be discounted to reflect the current value of the property. In this book, we have used the direct capitalization process and the following formula:

$$\frac{\text{Net Income}}{\text{Capitalization Rate}} = \text{Present Value}$$

$$\left(\frac{I}{R} = V\right)$$

2. Capitalization rate is the annual rate of return from a property that investors (as a group) require before they will purchase that property.

3. a. Reliability of net income.
   b. Liquidity.
   c. Burden of management.
   d. Probability of increase or decrease in value.
   e. Taxation.
   f. Hypothecation.

4. A parcel of real estate is in competition with other investments and with other parcels of real estate for capital funds. Capitalization rates vary depending on the type, age, and condition of the property, location and surrounding development, and existing economic conditions.

5. a. Comparative sales.
   b. Band of investment.
   c. Summation.

6. a. Property residual.
   b. Building residual.
   c. Land residual.

7. The gross rent multiplier is a factor of the ratio between gross rent and estimated value. The gross rent multiplier for a property is estimated from an analysis of the ratio between the sale price for a number of comparable properties and their gross rent.

8. a. The sale should be recent. Rent multipliers may change with economic conditions.
   b. The sale properties should be located in the same neighborhood or in one equal to that of the subject property.
   c. The sale properties should be reasonably similar to the subject in all essential physical elements.
   d. The ratio of expenses to rent should be similar for sale property and subject.

9. A capitalization rate by the comparative sales method is derived from a group of sales by dividing the sales price into one rate applicable to the property being appraised. The comparative sales method is considered the most appropriate method because it directly reflects the capitalization rates at which properties are bought and sold.

Answers to Multiple-choice Questions

1. b

2. d

3. a

4. c

5. d

6. d

7. b

8. d

9. a

10. a

11. a

12. b

13. a

14. b

15. c

CHAPTER 15

Answers to Questions

1. Reconciliation is the process of bringing together the different values from the various approaches to form the appraiser's opinion of the value of the subject property.

2. a. Type of property being appraised.
    b. Data available.
    c. Intended use of appraisal.

3. a. Quantity is the physical amount of data. Quality refers to the reliability of the data and their relevancy to the particular appraisal problem.

4. a. Land value must be adequately supported.
    b. The cost new of improvements must be based on reliable data.
    c. The estimate of accrued depreciation must be reasonably accurate. The older the building, the more difficulty there is estimating depreciation.

5. An error in the income or expense estimate is multiplied many times over in the indicated value.

6. A sufficient number of sales of tenant-occupied properties must be analyzed to enable the appraiser to estimate a meaningful gross rent multiplier applicable to the subject property.

7. Reliability of the market data approach depends mainly on the availability of sales similar to the subject property. The more

dissimilarities between the sales properties and the subject property, the more adjustments necessary, and therefore the greater probability for errors in judgment.

8. The appraiser should attempt to gather as much data on a sale property as is practical to make a meaningful comparison with the subject property. In addition to the sale price and other factual data, the appraiser should inquire about any circumstances of the transaction that might discredit the validity of the sale and the physical condition of the property at the time of sale.

Answers to Multiple-choice Questions

1. c
2. b
3. d
4. a
5. c
6. c

CHAPTER 16

Answers to Questions

1. The appraisal report represents the appraiser and his or her opinion of value. In most instances, the report is the appraiser's only opportunity to demonstrate the reliability of his or her opinion of value for the subject property.

2. Eight elements should be included in all appraisal reports:
   a. Name of party for whom appraisal is made.
   b. Identification of subject property.
   c. Purpose of appraisal.
   d. Date of value.
   e. Assumptions, contingencies, or limiting conditions.
   f. Value estimate.
   g. Certification.
   h. Signature of appraiser.

3. a. Form report.
   b. Letter report.
   c. Narrative report.

4. Advantages of form report:
   a. It can be completed in a relatively short time.
   b. Portions of report can be completed while the appraiser is inspecting property.

    c. The form, used as a checklist, eliminates the accidental omission of pertinent data.

    d. The uniform format allows a more efficient review and processing of the report.

    e. Features of subject property can be readily compared with minimum standards of acceptance.

    f. Typing is reduced because headings are already printed.

Disadvantages of form report:

    a. Form may be too rigid, making no provision for additional pertinent data.

    b. Form does not usually allow for an analysis of the data or for the appraiser's reasoning about value conclusions.

    c. Many items on the form may not apply to the property being appraised.

    d. Form report does not allow the appraiser to report the data gathered in the order or manner he or she feels most appropriate for a particular appraisal problem.

5. The letter report is very flexible as to format and inclusion of appraisal data.

6. The three major divisions of a narrative appraisal report are
   a. Introduction.
   b. Description, analysis, and conclusions.
   c. Addenda.

7. The purpose of the letter of transmittal is to present the appraisal report formally to the client. The transmittal letter should contain the following elements:
   a. Date of letter.
   b. A statement that the appraiser has been requested to make the appraisal, and by whom.
   c. Identification of property.
   d. Purpose of appraisal and property rights appraised.
   e. Statement that appraiser has made an investigation and analysis to arrive at opinion of value.
   f. Fact that letter is transmitting report, and number of pages in report.
   g. Valuation date.
   h. Estimate of value.
   i. Appraiser's signature.

8. The purpose of the appraisal should include the following three elements:
   a. Property rights being appraised.
   b. Definition of value being estimated.
   c. Valuation date.

9. The appraiser certifies the following:
   a. He or she has no present or contemplated interest in the property (or else he or she must disclose any such interest).
   b. He or she has personally inspected the property.

c. Compensation for the appraisal is not contingent on the valuation of the property.

10. The appraiser sets forth any assumptions made in valuing the subject property and any conditions under which he or she disclaims liability.

Answers to Multiple-choice Questions

1. c

2. a

3. b

4. d

5. c

CHAPTER 17

Answers to Questions

1. Condominium ownership includes only ownership of the *space* occupied by the unit. It does not include ownership of the *land* lying underneath the unit. In a condominium, there might be a unit above, below, or both, owned by someone else. In a townhouse, there would be no other unit owned by anyone else above or below one's unit—only on either side.

2. Zero lot line, that is, the edge of the residence can be placed directly on the property line.

3. Usually, *townhouses* are *rowhouses* with additional grounds and recreational facilities in common ownership. Also, a rowhouse usually has a tandem garage.

4. By being placed on, and attached to, a permanent foundation.

5. Asks for personal opinion.

6. Both are predominantly factory built.

Answers to Multiple-choice Questions

1. b

2. a

3. c

4. a

5. b

6. c

7. c

8. d

9. c

10. c

11. a

12. c

13. d

14. b

15. d

CHAPTER 18

Answers to Questions

1. An underground easement generally imposes fewer restrictions on the normal use of the land.

2. Plottage is the combining of two or more parcels of land so that the total value of the combined parcels in the "after" situation exceeds the value of the sum of the individual parcels in the "before" situation.

3. Severance damage is that damage accruing to the remainder of a property because of the taking of a portion of the property and the construction of the improvements as proposed.

4. An easement is a right one person or entity has over, in, or under real property of another.

5. Primarily because there is increasingly less available space, especially in urban areas.

6. No. However, freeways usually decrease the value of abutting residential properties to some degree. The amount of value damage depends on many factors, including proximity of the residence to the freeway, quality of residence, elevation of freeway, and amount and type of traffic. The value of industrial and some special purpose properties is in many cases increased by the introduction of a freeway into an area.

7. Not necessarily. It depends on the actual damage accruing to the remainder property by reason of acquisition of the access rights.

8. This question requires individual opinion and asks for explanation of opinion.

9. Asks for personal opinion and explanation.

Answers to Multiple-choice Questions

1. d
2. d
3. a
4. c
5. d

CHAPTER 19

Answers to Questions

1. In the increasingly complex business world, the valuation of real estate becomes more complex and requires more professionally prepared appraisers.

2. This question requires the personal opinions of each student; what is an advantage to some might be a disadvantage to others. The class discussion should be interesting and informative.

3. This question asks for personal opinion.

4. This question also asks for the personal opinion of the student.

5. The following are two distinct advantages of principal appraisers joining together:
   a. They can provide a more complete service through specialization.
   b. They can effect economies of operation, including office, secretarial, and clerical expenses.

GLOSSARY OF RESIDENTIAL APPRAISAL TERMINOLOGY*

Abatement of nuisance Extinction or termination of a nuisance.

Absolute ownership *See* Fee simple estate.

Absorption period The estimated time period required to sell, lease, begin designated use, or trade the subject property in its marketing area at current prices or rental rates.

Abstract of judgment A condensation of the essential provisions of a court judgment.

Abstract of title A summary or digest of all transfers, conveyances, legal proceedings, and any other facts relied on as evidence of title, showing continuity of ownership, together with any other elements of record that may impair title.

Abstraction method A method of valuing vacant land. The indicated value of the improvement is deducted from the sale price. Also called the *allocation method.*

Abut To border on, touch, as contiguous lots along a border or with a projecting part.

Accelerated cost recovery system (ACRS) The system for figuring depreciation (cost recovery) for depreciable real property acquired and placed into service after January 1, 1981.

Accelerated depreciation A method

of cost write-off in which depreciation allowances are greater in the first few years of ownership than in subsequent years. This permits an earlier recovery of capital and a faster tax write-off of an asset.

Acceleration clause A condition in a real estate financing instrument giving the lender the power to declare all sums owing lender immediately due and payable upon the happening of an event, such as sale of the property, or a delinquency in the repayment of the note.

Acceptance The act of agreeing or consenting to the terms of an offer, thereby establishing "the meeting of the minds" that is an essential element of a contract.

Accessibility Ability to be approached.

Accession An addition to property through the efforts of man or by natural forces.

Access right The right of an owner to have ingress to and egress from owner's property over adjoining property.

Accretion Accession by natural forces, e.g., alluvium.

Accrued depreciation *See* Depreciation, accrued.

Accrued items of expense Those incurred expenses that are not yet

---

*All terms listed in this glossary may not have been used in this text. They are included here in order to provide additional resource material.

payable. The seller's accrued expenses are credited to the purchaser in a closing statement.

Acknowledgment A formal declaration made before an authorized person, e.g., a notary public, by a person who has executed an instrument stating that the execution was his or her free act.

Acoustical tile Blocks of fiber, mineral, or metal, with small holes or rough-textured surface to absorb sound, used as covering for interior walls and ceilings.

Acquisition The act or process by which a person procures property.

Acre A measure of land equaling 160 square rods, or 4,840 square yards, or 43,560 square feet, or a tract about 208.71 feet square.

Actual age *See* Age, actual.

Actual authority That authority an agent has or believes that he or she has because of an intentional, unintentional, or careless act of a principal.

Actual fraud An act intended to deceive another, e.g., making a false statement, making a promise without intending to perform it, or suppressing the truth.

Adjacent Lying near, close, or contiguous; neighboring, bordering; juxtaposed. This term is often used as a synonym for adjoining; however, it can mean either *near* or *adjoining*.

Adjoining Contiguous; in contact with, abutting on, or lying next to, especially in actual contact along a line.

Adjustments A means by which characteristics of a residential property are regulated by dollar amount or percentage to conform to similar characteristics of another residential property. In the *sales comparison* approach, a dollar amount or percentage that is added to or subtracted from the sale price of a comparable property to account for a feature that differentiates it from the subject property.

Administrator A person appointed by the probate court to administer the estate of a deceased person who died intestate.

Adobe brick A brick made from adobe clay soil, dried in the sun. These bricks are generally much larger than the standard red brick.

Adobe soil Earth from which unburned bricks are made; hence, any alluvial or playa clay in desert or semi-desert regions.

Ad valorem Literally, "according to the value"; especially of a duty or charge levied on goods at a certain percent of their invoiced value. This term is most often used to indicate property taxed according to its value.

Ad valorem tax Duty or charge levied on goods at a certain percent of their invoiced value; most often associated with real estate taxes.

Advance Transfer of funds from a lender to a borrower in advance on a loan.

Advance commitment The institutional investor's prior agreement to provide long-term financing upon completion of construction; also known as a "take-out" loan commitment.

Advance fee A fee paid in advance of any services rendered. Sometimes unlawfully charged in connection with the illegal practice of obtaining a fee in advance for the advertising of property or businesses for sale, with no obligation to obtain a buyer, by persons representing themselves as real estate licensees or representatives of licensed real estate firms.

Adverse possession The open and notorious occupation of real property without the permission of the owner.

Affiant One who makes an affidavit or gives evidence.

Affidavit A statement or declaration reduced to writing sworn to or affirmed before some officer who has authority to administer an oath or affirmation.

Affidavit of title A statement, in writing, made under oath by seller or grantor, acknowledged before a notary public in which the affiant identifies himself or herself and affiant's marital status certifying that since the examination of title on the contract date there are no judgments, bankruptcies, or divorces; no unrecorded deeds, contracts, unpaid repairs or improvements, or defects of title known to affiant and that affiant is in possession of the property.

Affirm To confirm, to aver, to ratify, to verify. To make a declaration.

AFLB Accredited farm and land broker.

Age, actual The number of years elapsed since a structure's construction; also called physical age, real age, or chronological age.

Age, effective The number of years indicated by the condition of a structure.

Age-life method A method of computing depreciation based on the ratio of the effective age to the projected economic life of a structure.

Agency The relationship between the principal and the principal's agent that arises out of a contract, either expressed or implied, written or oral, wherein the agent is employed by the principal to do certain acts dealing with a third party.

Agent One who acts for, and with authority from, another called the *principal.*

Agent in production Any of the factors—labor, management, capital, or land—used to produce wealth or income (products or services that can be sold for money). Also called *factors in production.*

Agreement An exchange of promises, a mutual understanding or arrangement; a contract.

Agreement of sale A written agreement or contract between seller and purchaser in which they reach a meeting of minds on the terms and conditions of the sale. The parties concur, are in harmonious opinion.

Air rights The rights in real property to the reasonable use of the air space above the surface of the land.

Alienation The transferring of property to another; the transfer of property and possession of lands, or other things, from one person to another.

Alienation clause A clause in a contract giving the lender certain rights in the event of a sale or other transfer of mortgaged property.

Alley A relatively narrow way that serves as a secondary means of access to a property.

Allocation method *See* Abstraction method.

Allodial tenure A real property ownership system where ownership may be complete except for those rights held by government. Allodial is in contrast to feudal tenure.

Alluvium The gradual increase of the earth on a shore of an ocean or bank of a stream resulting from the action of the water.

ALTA (American Land Title Association) owner's policy of title insurance An owner's extended coverage policy that provides buyers and owners the same protection the ALTA policy gives to lenders.

ALTA title policy A type of title insurance policy issued by title insurance companies that expands the risks normally insured against under the standard type policy to include unrecorded mechanic's liens, unrecorded physical easements, facts a physical survey would show, water and mineral rights, and rights of parties in possession, such as tenants and buyers under unrecorded instruments.

Amenities   Satisfaction of enjoyable living to be derived from a home; conditions of agreeable living or a beneficial influence from the location of improvements, not measured in monetary considerations, but rather as tangible and intangible benefits attributable to the property and often causing greater pride in ownership.

AMO   Accredited Management Organization.

Amortization   The liquidation of a financial obligation on an installment basis; also recovery, over a period, of cost or value.

Amortize   To provide for the gradual extinction of a future obligation in advance of maturity, especially by periodical contributions to a sinking fund adequate to discharge a debt or replace equipment, etc., when necessary. To pay in full, including principal and interest.

Amortized loan   A loan to be repaid, interest and principal, by a series of regular payments that are equal or nearly equal, without any special balloon payment prior to maturity. Also called a *level payments loan.*

Annual percentage rate   The relative cost of credit as determined in accordance with Regulation Z of the Board of Governors of the Federal Reserve System for implementing the Federal Truth in Lending Act.

Annuity   An amount, especially of money, payable yearly or, by extension, at other regular intervals; the return from an investment of capital, in a series of periodic payments that consist of both interest and a partial return of capital.

Annuity capitalization method   An income capitalization method of estimating present value of a property based on its future income over a specific number of years. Also called *yield capitalization.*

Anticipation, principle of   Affirms that value is created by anticipated benefits to be derived in the future.

Apartment   A suite of rooms, especially one occupied as a dwelling.

Appellant   A party appealing a court decision or ruling.

Appraisal   An estimate or opinion of the value of property as of a certain date, resulting from an analysis of facts about the property.

Appraisal Foundation, The   An organization created by the appraisal industry to regulate and monitor its own profession. It was chartered by the Financial Institutions Reforms, Recovery, and Enforcement Act (FIRREA) of 1989, to set minimum standards and qualifications for performing appraisals in federally related transactions.

Appraisal process   A systematic procedure used by appraisers to arrive at an opinion or estimate of value.

Appraised value   Value set on property.

Appraiser   One who appraises; specifically, one who is qualified by education, training, and experience to estimate the value of real or personal property.

Appraiser, independent   In real estate appraising, generally one who contracts and estimates value on his or her own. Commonly called a *fee appraiser.*

Appreciation   The action of appreciating; a favorable critical estimate; a rise in value, as opposed to depreciation, or loss in value.

Appropriation of water   The taking, impounding, or diversion of water flowing on the public domain from its natural course and the application of the water to some beneficial use personal and exclusive to the appropriator.

Appurtenance That which belongs to something else; adjunct; something incident to a chief or principal thing, as a right-of-way to land.

APR *See* Annual percentage rate.

Architectural style The appearance and character of a building's design and construction.

Area A space or size of an area defined by a set of boundaries.

Arm's-length transaction A transaction in which neither party has or can gain an advantage at the expense of the other party.

Articles of incorporation An instrument setting forth the basic rules and purposes under which a private corporation is formed.

ASA American Society of Appraisers.

Assemblage *See* Plottage.

Assessed value A valuation or official estimate of property for the purpose of taxation.

Assessment Act of assessing; amount or value assessed.

Assessor The official who has the responsibility of determining assessed values.

Assignment A transfer to another of any property in possession or in action, or of any estate or right therein. A transfer by a person of that person's rights under a contract.

Assignment of rents A provision in a deed of trust (or mortgage) under which the beneficiary may, upon default by the trustor, take possession of the property and collect income from the property and apply it to the loan balance and the costs incurred by the beneficiary.

Assignor One who assigns or transfers property.

Assigns, assignees Those to whom property or interests therein shall have been transferred.

Association agreement Set of conditions, covenants, and restrictions (CC&Rs) applying to all properties in a planned unit development, condominium, or other community project.

Assumption agreement An undertaking or adoption of a debt or obligation primarily resting upon another person.

Assumption fee A lender's charge for changing over and processing new records for a new owner who is assuming an existing loan.

Assumption of mortgage The taking of a title to property by a grantee wherein the grantee assumes liability for payment of an existing note secured by a mortgage or deed of trust against the property, becoming a co-guarantor for the payment of a mortgage or deed of trust note.

Attachment The process by which real or personal property of a party to a lawsuit is seized and retained in the custody of the court for the purpose of acquiring jurisdiction over the property, compelling an appearance before the court, or furnishing security for a debt or costs arising out of the litigation.

Attest To affirm to be true or genuine; an official act establishing authenticity.

Attorney in fact One who is authorized by another to perform certain acts for another under a power of attorney; power of attorney may be limited to a specific act or acts or be general.

Avulsion A sudden and perceptible loss of land by the action of water, as by a sudden change in the course of a river.

Axial growth City growth that occurs along main transportation routes. Usually takes the form of star-shaped extensions outward from the center.

Backfill   The replacement of excavated earth into a hole or against a structure.

Balance   *See* Principle of surplus productivity, balance, and contribution.

Balance sheet   A statement of the financial condition of a business at a certain time, showing assets, liabilities, and capital.

Balloon payment   An installment payment on a promissory note—usually the final one for discharging the debt—that is significantly larger than the other installment payments provided under the terms of the promissory note. In Article 7, Chapter 3, of the Real Estate Law a balloon payment is defined as an installment that is greater than twice the amount of the smallest installment under the promissory note.

Band of investment   Method of estimating interest and capitalization rates based on a weighted average of the mortgage interest rate (cost of borrowed funds) and the rate of return on equity required.

Bargain and sale deed   Any deed that recites a consideration and purports to convey the real estate; a bargain and sale deed with a covenant against the grantor's act is one in which the grantor warrants that grantor has done nothing to harm or cloud the title.

Base and meridian   Imaginary lines used by surveyors to find and describe the location of private or public lands. In government surveys, base lines run due east and west, meridians run due north and south; they are used to establish township boundaries.

Baseboard   A finishing board placed against the wall around a room next to the floor.

Base line   A government survey line running due east and west, bisecting a principal meridian, from which township lines are established.

Base material   The ground beneath a structure from which that structure draws its support.

Base molding   Molding used at top of baseboard.

Base rent   The fixed minimum amount paid under a percentage lease.

Base shoe   Molding used at junction of baseboard and floor. Commonly called a carpet strip.

Basement   *See* Story.

Basis

1. *Cost basis.* The dollar amount assigned to property at the time of acquisition under provisions of the Internal Revenue Code for the purpose of determining gain, loss, and depreciation in calculating the income tax to be paid upon the sale or exchange of the property.

2. *Adjusted cost basis.* The cost basis after the application of certain additions for improvements, etc., and deductions for depreciation, etc.

Bath   A full bath contains a tub or shower, a lavatory and a water basin. A half bath contains a lavatory and a water basin.

Bearing wall   A wall or partition that supports a part of a building, usually a roof or floor above; also called load-bearing wall.

Benchmark   Definite identification characteristics familiar to the appraiser and relied upon in his or her further analysis of a property. Also a location indicated on a durable marker by surveyors.

Beneficiary   One entitled to the benefit of a trust; one who receives profit from an estate, the title of which is vested in a trustee; the lender on the security of a note and deed of trust.

Bequeath   To give or hand down by will; to leave by will.

Bequest   That which is given by the terms of a will.

Betterment   An improvement upon property that increases the property value and is considered as a capital asset as distinguished from repairs or replacements where the original character or cost is unchanged.

Bill of sale   A written instrument given to pass title of personal property from vendor to the vendee.

Binder   An agreement to consider a down payment for the purchase of real estate as evidence of good faith on the part of the purchaser. Also, a notation of coverage on an insurance policy issued by an agent and given to the insured prior to issuing of the policy.

Blacktop   Asphalt paving used in streets and driveways.

Blanket mortgage   A single mortgage that covers more than one piece of real property.

Blighted area   A district affected by detrimental influences of such extent or quantity that real property values have seriously declined as a result of adverse land use and/or destructive economic forces; characterized by rapidly depreciating buildings, retrogression and no recognizable prospects for improvement. However, renewal programs and changes in use may lead to resurgence of such areas.

Blockbusting   The practice on the part of unscrupulous speculators or real estate agents of inducing panic selling of homes at prices below market value, especially by exploiting the prejudices of property owners in neighborhoods in which the racial makeup is changing or appears to be on the verge of changing.

Board foot   A unit of measurement of lumber, one foot wide, one foot long, and one inch thick; 144 cubic inches.

Bona fide   In good faith; without fraud or deceit; authentic.

Bond   An obligation under seal. A real estate bond is a written obligation issued on security of a mortgage or trust deed.

Book depreciation   *See* Depreciation.

Book value   The current value, for accounting purposes, of an asset expressed as original cost plus capital additions minus accumulated depreciation.

Bracing   Framing lumber nailed at an angle in order to provide rigidity.

Bracketing   Selection of market data, when using the sales comparison approach, so that the subject is contained within a range of data.

Breach   The breaking of a law or failure of duty, either by omission or commission.

Breezeway   A covered porch or passage, open on two sides and connecting house and garage or two parts of the house.

Bridging   Small wood or metal pieces used to brace floor joists.

Broker   A person employed for a fee by another to carry on any of the activities listed in the license-law definition of *broker*.

Broker–salesperson relationship agreement   A written agreement, required by the regulations of the real estate commissioner, setting forth the material aspects of the relationship between a real estate broker and each salesperson and broker performing licensed activities in the name of the supervising broker.

Btu   British thermal unit; the quantity of heat required to raise the temperature of one pound of water one degree Fahrenheit at or near its maximum density.

Building   A structure erected to stand more or less permanently.

Building code   A systematic regulation of construction of buildings within a municipality established by ordinance or law.

Building components   Parts of a building.

Building line   A line, established by ordinance, beyond which a building, or any part thereof, cannot be constructed.

Building, market value of   The sum of money that the presence of the structure adds to, or subtracts from, the value of the land it occupies. Land value on the basis of highest and best use.

Building paper   A heavy waterproofed paper used as sheathing in wall or roof construction as a protection against air passage and moisture.

Building residual technique   A method of property value estimation based on capitalization of the income attributable to the building.

Building restrictions   Zoning, regulatory requirements, or provisions in a deed limiting the type, size and use of a building.

Built-in   Cabinets or similar features built as part of the house.

Bundle of rights   All of the legal rights incident to ownership of property, including rights of use, possession, encumbering, and disposition.

Bureau of Land Management   A federal bureau within the Department of the Interior that manages and controls certain lands owned by the United States.

Business opportunity   The assets for an existing business enterprise, including its goodwill. As used in the real estate law, the term includes "the sale or lease of the business and goodwill of an existing enterprise or opportunity."

Buyer's market   The condition that exists when a buyer is in a more commanding position as to price and terms because real property offered for sale is in plentiful supply in relation to demand.

Bylaws   Rules for the conduct of the internal affairs of corporations and other organizations.

Cal Vet Program   A program administered by the State Department of Veterans Affairs for the direct financing of farm and home purchases by eligible California veterans of the armed forces.

Capital   Accumulated wealth; usually the accumulated pay for labor, that which is saved from previous wages.

Capital assets   Assets of a permanent nature used in the production of an income, such as land, buildings, machinery, and equipment. Under income tax law, it is usually distinguishable from inventory, which comprises assets held for sale to customers in the ordinary course of the taxpayer's trade or business.

Capital gain   At resale of a capital item, the amount by which the net sale proceeds exceed the adjusted cost basis (book value). Used for income tax computations. Gains are called short- or long-term, based on length of holding period after acquisition. Usually taxed at lower rates than ordinary income.

Capitalization   In appraising, determining value of property by considering net income and percentage of reasonable return on the investment. The value of an income property is determined by dividing annual net income by the capitalization rate.

Capitalization rate   The rate of interest considered a reasonable return on the investment and used in the process of determining value based upon net income. It may also be described as the yield rate necessary to attract the money of the average investor to a particular kind of investment. In the case of land improvements that depreciate, to this yield rate is added a factor to take into consideration the annual amortization factor necessary to recapture the initial investment in improvements. This amortization factor can be determined in various ways: (1) straight-line depreciation method, (2) Ellwood tables, and (3) Hoskold tables.

Capitalize To convert into capital, or to use as capital; hence, to make use of for the sake of profit or advantage. To compute the present value of a periodical payment; to convert (an income, annuity, etc.) into a single payment or an equivalent capital sum. To furnish with capital; to provide capital for the operation of; as, to capitalize a business.

Capitalized income method of depreciation Method for estimating depreciation by comparing the subject's capitalized value to its replacement cost new.

Capitalized value The value indicated by use of the capitalization approach.

Carport A roofed space having at least one side open to the weather.

Casement windows Frames of wood or metal that swing outward.

Cash flow (1) The periodic income or loss generated from an investment; (2) the net income generated by a property before depreciation and other non-cash expenses.

Cash-on-cash Based on actual cash invested, cash flow as a percentage or ratio to equity; investment return to cash equity.

Cash return to equity Equity dividend; cash flow to equity.

Catastrophe damage Damage that occurs to a property by an "act of God," an act over which the property owner has no control.

Caveat emptor Let the buyer beware. The buyer must examine the goods or property and buy at his or her own risk, absent misrepresentation.

CBD Central business district.

CC&Rs Covenants, conditions, and restrictions. The basic rules establishing the rights and obligations of owners (and their successors in interest) of real property within a subdivision or other tract of land in relation to other owners within the same subdivision or tract and in relation to an association of owners organized for the purpose of operating and maintaining property commonly owned by the individual owners.

CCIM Certified commercial investment member.

Central tendency The numeric value that is suggested as a typical value in a statistical sample.

Certificate of Eligibility Issued by the government, bearing evidence of an individual's eligibility to obtain a Veterans Administration (GI) loan.

Certificate of Reasonable Value (CRV) The Federal Veterans' Administrative appraisal commitment of property value.

Certificate of Taxes Due A written statement or guaranty of the condition of the taxes on a certain property made by the county treasurer of the county wherein the property is located. Any loss resulting to any person from an error in a tax certificate shall be paid by the county that such treasurer represents.

Certification A signed and dated statement included in an appraisal report that the appraiser has performed an appraisal in an unbiased and professional manner and that all assumptions and limiting conditions are set forth in the report.

Certified real estate appraiser An appraiser certified by the appropriate state to value real estate.

Chain A unit of measurement used by surveyors. A chain consists of 100 links, equal to 66 feet.

Chain of title A history of conveyances and encumbrances affecting the title from the time the original patent was granted, or as far back as records are available, used to determine how title came to be vested in the current owner.

Change, principle of Holds that it is the future, not the past, that is of prime importance in estimating value. Change is largely result of cause and effect.

Characteristics Distinguishing features of a (residential) property.

Chattel mortgage A claim on personal property (instead of real property) used to secure or guarantee a promissory note. *See also* Security agreement and Security interest.

Chattel real An estate related to real estate, such as a lease on real property.

Chattels Goods or every species of property movable or immovable that are not real property. Personal property.

Chose in action A personal right to something not presently in the owner's possession, but recoverable by a legal action for possession.

Chronological age The number of years elapsed since a structure was built; actual age; physical age.

Circuit breaker An electrical device that automatically interrupts an electric circuit when an overload occurs; may be used instead of a fuse to protect each circuit and can be reset; in property taxation, a method for granting property tax relief to the elderly and disadvantaged qualified taxpayers by rebate, tax credits or cash payments. Usually limited to homeowners and renters.

Civil rights Basic rights of freedom and liberty guaranteed to United States citizens by the 13th and 14th amendments to the Constitution and by certain federal laws.

Clapboard Boards, usually thicker at one edge, used for siding.

Closing costs The numerous expenses buyers and sellers normally incur in the transfer of ownership of real property.

Closing statement An accounting of funds made to the buyer and seller separately. Required by law to be made at the completion of every real estate transaction.

Cloud on title A claim, encumbrance, or condition that impairs the title to real property until disproved or eliminated as, for example, through a quitclaim deed or a quiet title legal action.

Code of ethics A set of rules and principles expressing a standard of accepted conduct for a professional group and governing the relationship of members to each other and to the organization.

Collar beam A beam that connects the pairs of opposite roof rafters above the attic floor.

Collateral The property subject to the security interest; anything of value a borrower pledges as security.

Collateral security A separate obligation attached to a contract to guarantee its performance; the transfer of property or of other contracts, or valuables, to ensure the performance of a principal agreement.

Collusion An agreement between two or more persons to defraud another of rights by the forms of law or to obtain an object forbidden by law.

Color of title That which appears to be good title but is not title in fact.

Combed plywood A grooved building material used primarily for interior finish.

Commercial acre A term applied to the remainder of an acre of newly subdivided land after the area devoted to streets, sidewalks, and curbs, etc., has been deducted from the acre.

Commercial loan A personal loan from a commercial bank, usually unsecured and short-term, for other than mortgage purposes.

Commercial paper Bills of exchange used in commercial trade.

Commission An agent's compensation for performing the duties of the agency; in real estate practice, a percentage of the selling price of property, percentage of rentals, etc. A fee for services.

Commitment A pledge or a promise or firm agreement to do something in the future, such as a loan company giving a written commitment with specific terms of mortgage loan it *will* make.

Common law The body of law that grew from customs and practices developed and used in England.

Common stock That class of corporate stock to which there is ordinarily attached no preference with respect to the receipt of dividends or the distribution of assets on corporate dissolution.

Community Part of a metropolitan area, a number of neighborhoods that tend toward common interests and problems.

Community property Property acquired by husband and/or wife during a marriage when not acquired as the separate property of either spouse. Each spouse has equal rights of management, alienation, and testamentary disposition of community property.

Compaction Whenever extra soil is added to a lot to fill in low places or to raise the level of the lot, the added soil is often too loose and soft to sustain the weight of the buildings. Therefore, it is necessary to compact the added soil so it will carry the weight of buildings without the danger of their tilting, settling or cracking.

Comparable sales Sales that have characteristics similar to those of the subject property and are used for analysis in the appraisal process. Commonly called comparables, they are recent selling prices of properties similarly situated in a similar market.

Comparative square foot method Method of estimating construction costs using typical square foot costs for the type of construction being estimated.

Comparison approach A real estate comparison method that compares a given property with similar or comparable surrounding properties; also called *market comparison*.

Competent Legally qualified.

Competition, principle of Holds that profits tend to breed competition and excess profits tend to breed ruinous competition.

Component One of the features making up the whole property.

Composite rate A capitalization rate composed of interest and recapture in separately determined amounts.

Compound interest Interest paid on original principal and also on the accrued and unpaid interest that has accumulated as the debt matures.

Conclusion The final estimate of value, realized from facts, data, experience, and judgment, set out in an appraisal; appraiser's certified conclusion.

Concrete An artificial building material made by mixing cement and sand with gravel, broken stone, or another aggregate, and enough water to cause the cement to set and bind the entire mass.

Concrete, reinforced A method of placing reinforcing steel rods in the wet concrete mixture to add strength and rigidity to the dry finished product.

Condemnation Act of taking property for public use, under the right of eminent domain. Also the police power of disallowing the use of a structure in order to protect the health, safety, and welfare of individuals.

Condition A qualification of an estate granted that can be imposed only in conveyances. They are classified as conditions precedent and conditions subsequent.

Condition precedent A qualification of a contract or transfer of property, providing that unless and until a given event occurs, the full effect of a contract or transfer will not take place.

Condition subsequent A condition attached to an already-vested estate or to a contract whereby the estate is defeated or the contract extinguished through the failure or nonperformance of the condition.

Conditional commitment A commitment of a definite loan amount for some future unknown purchaser of satisfactory credit standing.

Conditional sale contract A contract for the sale of property stating that delivery is to be made to the buyer, title to remain vested in the seller until the conditions of the contract have been fulfilled. *See also* Security interest.

Conditions, covenants, and restrictions (CC&Rs) Deed restrictions associated with land or property.

Condominium, residential or commercial Individual ownership of space in a single living or business unit in a large residential or business complex, with ownership in common of the undivided areas within the project.

Conduit Usually a metal pipe in which electrical wiring is installed or an artificial or natural channel for conveyance of water or fluids.

Confession of judgment An entry of judgment upon the debtor's voluntary admission or confession.

Confirmation of sale A court approval of the sale of property by an executor, administrator, guardian, or conservator.

Confiscation The seizing of property without compensation.

Conformity, principle of Holds that the maximum of value is realized when a reasonable degree of homogeneity of improvements is present. Use conformity is desirable, creating and maintaining higher values.

Conservation The process of utilizing resources in such a manner that their depletion is minimized.

Consideration Anything of value given or promised by a party to induce another to enter into a contract, e.g., personal services or even love and affection. It may be a benefit conferred upon one party or a detriment suffered by the other.

Consistent use *See* Principle of consistent use.

Constant The percentage that, when applied directly to the face value of a debt, develops the annual amount of money necessary to pay a specified net rate of interest on the reducing balance and to liquidate the debt in a specified time period. For example, a 6 percent loan with a 20-year amortization has a constant of approximately $8\frac{1}{2}$ percent. Thus, a $10,000 loan amortized over 20 years requires an annual payment of approximately $850.

Construction

1. *Adobe.* Walls built of adobe brick.
2. *Brick.* Walls built of wire-cut brick.
3. *Fireproof.* Structure built of materials designed to withstand burn-

ing. The contents of the structure may burn completely without impairment of the soundness of the structure.

4. *Fire-resistive.* Structure built of materials designed to withstand ordinary fire temperatures for at least one hour.

5. *Modular.* A complete unit of a room or rooms is pre-assembled at the factory for placement on the site. Plumbing and wiring are generally installed in the unit at the factory.

6. *Panelized wall.* Complete wall sections prefabricated at the factory for installation at the site.

7. *Prefabricated.* Framing and wall materials precut to a standard size at the factory for installation at the site.

8. *Reinforced concrete.* Major structural members of poured concrete around steel rods for added strength.

9. *Tilt-up-slab concrete.* Generally, reinforced concrete poured in a horizontal mold and erected vertically when dry as part of the walls of a structure.

10. *Unit. See* Construction, modular.

11. *Unitized wall. See* Construction, panelized wall.

12. *Wall bearing.* Support of roof and floors is performed by the walls of the structure. Used to restrict the need for vertical support members, such as posts or columns.

13. *Wood frame.* Major support members of a structure are constructed of wood.

14. *Wood simulated concrete.* Color-treated concrete poured over horizontal rough-hewn wood boards; installed vertically when dry as a building material remarkably resembling wood, with the strength and wearing qualities of concrete. Reinforcing rods

are usually installed in the wet concrete.

Construction classification A system that rates fireproofing of structures according to their relative fire resistance, taking into account the type of frame, walls, and roof. Class A is the most fireproof, descending to Class D, the least fireproof.

Construction loans Loans, usually short-term, made for the construction of homes or commercial buildings with funds disbursed by the lender after periodic inspections.

Constructive eviction Breach of a covenant of warranty or quiet enjoyment, e.g., the inability of a lessee to obtain possession because of a paramount defect in title or a condition making occupancy hazardous.

Constructive fraud A breach of duty, as by a person in a fiduciary capacity, without an actual fraudulent intent, that gains an advantage to the person at fault by misleading another to the other's prejudice. Any act of omission declared by law to be fraudulent, without respect to actual fraud.

Constructive notice Notice given by the public records.

Consummate dower A widow's dower interest, which, after the death of her husband, is complete or may be completed and become an interest in real estate.

Contiguous In actual contact, touching.

Contour The outline of a figure, body, mass, etc.; the line, or lines, representing such an outline, as the contours of a state or a coast.

Contour line A continuous line connecting points of equal elevation on a contour map.

Contract An agreement, either written or oral, to do or not do certain things. In real estate, must have five essentials: competent parties, valuable consideration, offer and acceptance, lawful object, and in writing and signed.

Contract rent   The amount of rent being paid under contractual terms binding owners and tenants.

Contribution, principle of   A component part of a property is valued in proportion to its contribution to the value of the whole; holds that maximum values are achieved when the improvements on a site produce the highest (net) return, commensurate with the investment.

Conventional mortgage   A mortgage securing a loan made by investors without governmental underwriting, i.e., one not FHA or VA guaranteed. The type customarily made by a bank or savings and loan association.

Conversion   Change from one character or use to another, as converting an apartment building to condominium use.

Conveyance   An instrument in writing used to transfer (convey) title to property from one person to another, such as a deed or a trust deed.

Cooperative   A form of legal ownership; each owner holds a stated percentage ownership in the cooperative association, which owns the land and buildings, and grants each owner the permanent right to occupy the specific dwelling unit, as well as the right to the joint use of the common areas.

Cooperative apartment   A form of apartment ownership. Ownership of shares in a cooperative venture that entitles the owner to use, rent, or sell a specific apartment unit. The corporation usually reserves the right to approve certain actions, such as a sale or improvement.

Coordination   An agent of production; management.

Corner influence table   A statistical table that may be used to estimate the added value of a corner lot.

Corporation   A group or body of persons established and treated by law as an individual or unit with rights and liabilities, distinct and apart from those of the persons composing it. A corporation is a creature of law having certain powers and duties of a natural person. Being created by law it may continue for any length of time the law prescribes.

Corporeal rights   Possessory rights in real property.

Correction lines   In the Government Rectangular Survey System, a system for compensating inaccuracies due to the curvature of the earth. Every fourth township line, 24-mile intervals, is used as a correction line on which the intervals between the north and south range lines are remeasured and corrected to a full 6 miles.

Correlate the findings   Interpret the data and value estimates; bring them together to a final conclusion of value.

Correlation   A step in the appraisal process involving the interpretation of data derived from the three approaches to value (cost, market, and income) leading to a single determination of value. Also frequently referred to as reconciliation.

Cosigner   A second party who signs a promissory note together with the primary borrower.

Cost   The amount paid, given, charged, or engaged to be paid or given for something.
1. *Book.* The cost recorded on accounting books.
2. *Cubic foot.* A method of cost determination based on the number of cubic feet in the interior of a building. This method is sometimes used in warehouse storage buildings.

3. *Development.* Generally, the cost to begin an enterprise. In residential real estate, the costs of developing a raw parcel of land into a subdivision with streets, utilities, and prepared sites; includes advertising, filing fees, recording fees, engineering, attorney fees, incorporation fees, etc.

4. *Direct.* Costs directly associated with the labor and materials expended in purchase of land and construction of improvements, such as purchase price of land, commissions, cost of building materials and equipment, roads, and contractors' overhead and profit.

5. *Financing.* Costs associated with acquisition of capital to finance a venture.

6. *Hard.* Same as direct cost except does not include general contractors' overhead and profit.

7. *Historical.* The original cost of construction.

8. *Indirect.* Costs not directly related to land purchase and construction, such as financing charges, legal fees, accounting fees, interest and taxes during construction, and administrative expense of entrepreneur during construction.

9. *Square foot.* The cost per square foot of area of land or a building or other structure; found by dividing the number of square feet of area into the total cost of the structure or land.

Cost approach   One of three methods of appraisal. A value estimate of a property is derived by estimating the replacement cost of the improvements, deducting the estimated accrued depreciation, then adding the market value of the land.

Cost basis   The amount originally paid for a property, plus any additional allowable costs; used to compute gain on a property when sold.

Cost of replacement   The cost of constructing or acquiring an equally desirable substitute property, not an exact replica of the subject property.

Cost of reproduction   The cost of constructing or acquiring a duplicate property as much as possible like the subject property.

Cost-to-cure method of depreciation   Method of estimating accrued depreciation (loss in value) based on the cost to cure or repair observed building defects.

Counterflashing   Flashing used on chimneys at roof line to cover shingle flashing and to prevent moisture entry.

Courtyard home   A zero-lot-line home.

Covenant   An agreement or promise to do or not do a particular act, such as a promise to build a house of a particular architectural style or to use or not use property in a certain way.

CPM   Certified property manager, a designation of the Institute of Real Estate Management.

CRA   Certified review appraiser; designates a member of the National Association of Review Appraisers and National Mortgage Underwriters.

Crawl hole   Exterior or interior opening permitting access underneath building as required by building codes.

CRB   Certified residential broker.

CRE   Counselor of real estate, member of American Society of Real Estate Counselors.

CREA   Certified Real Estate Appraiser: designates a member of the National Association of Real Estate Appraisers.

Credit   A bookkeeping entry on the

right side of an account, recording the reduction or elimination of an asset or an expense or the creation of or addition to a liability or item of equity or revenue.

Cubage The number or product resulting from multiplying the width of a thing by its height and by its depth or length. Cubic content.

Cul-de-sac A passage with only one outlet, as a blind alley, a dead-end street. In residential real estate, the term generally refers to a dead-end street with a circle at the end.

Curable depreciation Items of physical deterioration and functional obsolescence that are customarily repaired or replaced by a prudent property owner; that is, items that are economically worthwhile to repair or replace.

Curtail schedule A listing of the amounts by which the principal sum of an obligation is to be reduced by partial payments and of the dates on which each payment will become payable.

Curtesy The right a husband has in a wife's estate at her death.

Cut The level building site or the space created in areas of sloping land when earth is removed. Unlike fill material, which can be unstable, a building site from a cut is generally a more solid base for structures.

Cyclical movement The sequential and recurring changes in economic activity of a business cycle, moving from prosperity through recession, depression, recovery, and back again to prosperity.

Damages The indemnity recoverable by a person who has sustained an injury, either in his or her person, property, or relative rights or through the act or default of another; loss sustained or harm done to a person or property.

Data plant An appraiser's file of information on real estate.

Debenture Bonds issued without security; an obligation not secured by a specific lien on property.

Debit A bookkeeping entry on the left side of an account, recording the creation of or addition to an asset or an expense or the reduction or elimination of a liability or item of equity or revenue.

Debt That which is due from one person or another; obligation, liability.

Debtor A person who is in debt; the one owing money to another.

Debt service The periodic interest and/or principal payments required in a loan agreement.

Decline phase Third phase in the cycle of a neighborhood, generally marked by delayed repairs and deterioration of buildings.

Declining balance depreciation A method of accelerated depreciation allowed by the IRS in certain circumstances. Double declining balance depreciation is its most common form and is computed by using double the rate used for straight-line depreciation.

Decreasing returns, point of The point at which increases in the agents of production fail to produce a worthwhile net income to an enterprise.

Decree of foreclosure Decree by a court ordering the sale of mortgaged property and the payment of the debt owing to the lender out of the proceeds.

Dedication The giving of land by its owner to a public use and the acceptance for such use by authorized officials on behalf of the public.

Deed Written instrument that, when properly executed and delivered, conveys title to real property from one person (grantor) to another (grantee).

Deed in lieu of foreclosure A deed to real property accepted by a lender from a defaulting borrower to avoid the necessity of foreclosure proceedings by the lender.

Deed of trust *See* Trust deed.

Deed restrictions Limitations in the deed to a property that dictate certain uses that may or may not be made of the property.

Default Failure to fulfill a duty or promise or to discharge an obligation; omission or failure to perform any act.

Defeasance clause The clause in a mortgage that gives the mortgagor the right to redeem the mortgagor's property upon the payment of the mortgagor's obligations to the mortgagee.

Defeasible fee Sometimes called a *base fee* or *qualified fee;* a fee simple absolute interest in land that is capable of being defeated or terminated upon the happening of a specified event.

Defendant A person against whom legal action is initiated for the purpose of obtaining criminal sanctions (criminal defendant) or damages or other appropriate judicial relief (civil defendant).

Deferred maintenance Existing, but unfulfilled, requirements for repairs and rehabilitation. Postponed or delayed maintenance causing decline in a building's physical condition.

Deferred payment options The privilege of deferring income payments to take advantage of statutes affording tax benefits.

Deficiency judgment A judgment given by a court when the value of security pledged for a loan is insufficient to pay off the debt of the defaulting borrower.

Delegation of powers The conferring by an agent upon another of all or certain of the powers that have been conferred upon the agent by the principal.

Demand The desire to possess plus the ability to buy; an essential element of value.

Demography The study of human populations, including size, density, growth rates, etc.

Depletion Act of reduction, or state of being reduced; the reduction of an asset, such as the taking of oil from an underground reservoir.

Deposit receipt A term used by the real estate industry to describe the written offer to purchase real property upon stated terms and conditions, accompanied by a deposit toward the purchase price, which becomes the contract for the sale of the property upon acceptance by the owner.

Depreciated cost method Method of adjusting comparable sales, where adjustments are calculated based on analysis of the depreciated replacement costs for each differentiating feature.

Depreciated value The present value of an asset, generally less than its original value because of physical wear, functional obsolescence, economic obsolescence, etc.

Depreciation A decrease in value, specifically of money; a reduction or loss in exchange value or purchasing power.

1. *Accrued.* Depreciation that has occurred; it is measured by the difference between the replacement cost new as of the date of the appraisal, and the present appraisal value.

2. *Book.* Depreciation that should occur in the future; an amount reserved on records of the owner to provide for the replacement of an asset.

Depreciation rate The percentage at which the economic utility, or usefulness, of a property is exhausted.

Depreciation reserve   An amount of money set aside annually to allow for depreciation. In accounting, an amount recorded on the books to allow for depreciation accruals.

Depression   A phase of the business cycle marked by industrial and commercial stagnation, scarcity of goods and money, low prices, and mass unemployment.

Depth table   A statistical table that may be used to estimate the value of the added depth of a lot.

Desist and refrain order   An order directing a person to desist and refrain from committing an act in violation of the real estate law.

Deterioration   A worsening, impairment, or degeneration.

Determinable fee   An estate that may end on the happening of an event that may or may not occur.

Development cost   *See* Cost, development.

Development method (Land development method)   Method of vacant land valuation where development costs and developer's profits are subtracted from estimated gross sales, resulting in a raw land value estimate.

Development phase   First phase of the life cycle of a neighborhood, consisting of initial construction of improvements on vacant land.

Devise   A gift or disposal of real property by last will and testament.

Devisee   One who receives a gift of real property by will.

Devisor   One who disposes of real property by will.

Diminished utility   *See* Accrued depreciation.

Direct capitalization method   The technique of income capitalization where value is estimated by dividing net operating income by the overall capitalization rate.

Direct cost   *See* Cost, direct.

Direct market comparison approach   *See* Sales comparison approach.

Direct market method   *See* Matched pair method.

Directional growth   The location or direction toward which the residential sections of a city are destined or determined to grow.

Discount   To sell a promissory note before maturity at a price less than the outstanding principal balance of the note at the time of sale. Also an amount deducted in advance by the lender from the nominal principal of a loan as part of the cost to the borrower of obtaining the loan.

Discretionary powers of agency   Those powers conferred upon an agent by the principal that empower the agent in certain circumstances to make decisions based on the agent's own judgment.

Disintermediation   The relatively sudden withdrawal of substantial sums of money savers have deposited with savings and loan associations, commercial banks, and mutual savings banks. This term can also be considered to include life insurance policy purchasers borrowing against the value of their policies. The essence of this phenomenon is financial intermediaries losing billions of dollars within a short period of time, as owners of funds held by those institutional lenders exercise their prerogative of taking them out of the hands of these financial institutions.

Disposal income   The after-tax income a household receives to spend on personal consumption.

Dispossess   To deprive one of the use of real estate.

Documentary transfer tax   A state enabling act allows a county to adopt a documentary transfer tax to apply on all transfers of real property located in the county. Notice of payment is entered on the face of the deed or on a separate paper filed with the deed.

Documents   Legal instruments, such

as mortgages, contracts, deeds, options, wills, and bills of sale.

Donee   A person who receives a gift.

Donor   A person who makes a gift.

Door

1. *Double.* Two doors side by side at the entrance to a residence, one opening to the left, the other to the right. This type of door adds a feeling of spaciousness to the entrance; it also facilitates the entrance of large pieces of furniture, such as a grand piano.

2. *Hollow.* A door that is not solid; that is, it has no center. It is usually made of plywood sheets on all sides of an air space.

3. *Milled.* A solid wood door with ornamentation grooved into the wood; usually made of a hardwood.

4. *Pocket.* A door that slides into a wall, completely out of the way when not in use so that an uncluttered opening exists between two rooms. It is unlike a folding door, which opens and closes in accordion fashion. Folding doors are often used for aesthetic appeal, decorated with louvres or another ornamental design. Pocket doors are mostly functional.

5. *Sliding glass.* A large window-like door that slides horizontally to permit access to the out-of-doors; usually used adjacent to a patio.

Dormer window   *See* Window, dormer.

Double declining balance depreciation   *See* Declining balance depreciation.

Double-hung window   *See* Window, double-hung.

Double pitch roof   *See* Roof, double pitch.

Dower   The right a wife has in her husband's estate at his death.

Dual agency   An agency relationship in which the agent acts concur-

rently for both of the principals in a transaction.

Due on sale clause   An acceleration clause granting the lender the right to demand full payment of the mortgage upon a sale of the property.

Duress   Unlawful constraint exercised upon a person whereby he or she is forced to do some act against his or her will.

Dwelling   A place to live.

Earnest money   Down payment made by a purchaser of real estate as evidence of good faith; a deposit or partial payment.

Earnings   *See* Income.

Easement   A right, privilege, or interest limited to a specific purpose that one party has in the land of another.

Eaves   The lower part of a roof projecting over the wall.

Ecology   The relationship between organisms and their environment.

Economic base   The portion of its economic production that is sold or exported outside of a defined geographic area.

Economic life   The period over which a property will yield a return on the investment over and above the economic or ground rent due to land. *See also* Life, economic.

Economic obsolescence   A loss in value due to factors external to the subject property but adversely affecting the value of the subject property.

Economic rent   The reasonable rental expectancy if the property were available for renting at the time of its valuation. *See also* Rent, economic.

Economics   The science that deals with the production, distribution, and consumption of wealth.

Economic trend   Pattern of related changes in some aspect of the economy.

Effective age of improvement The number of years of age that is indicated by the condition of the structure; distinct from chronological age.

Effective date of value The specific day the conclusion of value applies.

Effective gross rent Gross rent minus an allowance for vacancy and credit loss.

Effective income *See* Income, effective.

Effective interest rate The percentage of interest that is actually being paid by the borrower for the use of the money; distinct from nominal interest.

Effective life *See* Life, effective.

Elements of value Utility, scarcity, demand, and transferability are the four prerequisites that must be present for an object to have value.

Ellwood technique A mortgage/equity method of capitalization, expressed in tables.

Emblements Crops produced annually by labor and industry as distinguished from crops that grow naturally on the land.

Eminent domain The right of the government to acquire property for necessary public or quasi-public use by condemnation; the owner must be fairly compensated. The right of the government to do this and the right of the private citizen to get paid is spelled out in the Fifth Amendment to the Constitution.

Enamel A paint that flows out to a smooth coat when applied.

Encroachment An unlawful intrusion onto another's adjacent property by improvements to real property, e.g., a swimming pool built across a property line.

Encumbrance That which encumbers or impedes action; a claim or lien on an estate. In real estate, any liens, easements, deeds of trust, etc., affecting title to a property.

Entrepreneur One who assumes the risk and management of business; enterpriser.

Environment Surroundings; all the external conditions and influences affecting the life and development of an organism, for example, human behavior, society.

Environmental impact report (EIR) A formal report assessing the results or impact of a proposed activity or development upon the environment.

Environmental obsolescence *See* Economic obsolescence.

Epoxy A thick liquid that dries to a hard resin; used as a glue to hold many different materials.

Equity The interest or value an owner has in real estate over and above the liens against it. Branch of remedial justice by and through which relief is afforded to suitors in courts of equity.

Equity buildup The increase of owner's equity in property due to mortgage principal reduction and value appreciation.

Equity capitalization rate The equity cash flow divided by the equity value; a factor used to estimate the value of the equity in the equity residual technique of capitalization.

Equity of redemption The right to redeem property during the foreclosure period, such as a mortgagor's right to redeem within either 3 months or 1 year, as may be permitted after foreclosure sale.

Equity residual technique Technique of income capitalization; the net income remaining to the equity position (after mortgage payments) is capitalized into an estimate of the value of the equity.

Erosion The wearing away of land by the act of water, wind, or glacial ice.

Escalation The right reserved by the tender to increase the amount of the payments and/or interest upon the happening of a certain event.

Escalator clause A clause in a contract providing for the upward or downward adjustment of certain items to cover specified contingencies; usually tied to some index or event; often used in long-term leases to provide for rent adjustments to cover tax and maintenance increases.

Escheat Reversion of land to the crown (to the state, in the United States) by failure of persons to be legally entitled to hold that land; to revert, lapse, or pass by escheat; the reversion of land to the state when a property owner dies intestate, or without a will or known heirs.

Escrow The deposit of instruments and/or funds, with instructions, with a third neutral party to carry out the provisions of an agreement or contract.

Escrow agent The neutral third party holding funds or something of value in trust for another or others.

Estate As applied to real estate, the term signifies the quantity of interest, share, right, equity, of which riches or fortune may consist in real property; the degree, quantity, nature and extent of interest which a person has in real property.

Estate at sufferance An estate arising when the tenant wrongfully holds over after the expiration of the term. The landlord has the choice of evicting the tenant as a trespasser or accepting such tenant for a similar term and under the conditions of the tenant's previous holding; also called a *tenancy at sufferance.*

Estate at will The occupation of lands and tenements by a tenant for an indefinite period, terminable by one or both parties.

Estate for life A possessory, free-hold estate in land held by a person only for the duration of his or her life or the life or lives of another.

Estate for years An interest in lands by virtue of a contract for the possession of them for a definite and limited period of time. May be for a year or less. A lease may be said to be an estate for years.

Estate from period to period An interest in land where there is no definite termination date but the rental period is fixed at a certain sum per week, month, or year; also called a periodic tenancy.

Estate of inheritance An estate that may descend to heirs. All freehold estates are estates of inheritance, except estates for life.

Estimate A preliminary opinion of value. Appraise; set a value.

Estimated remaining life The period of time (years) it takes for improvements to become valueless.

Estoppel A legal theory under which a person is barred from asserting or denying a fact because of that person's previous acts or words.

Ethics That branch of moral science, idealism, justness, and fairness that treats of the duties a member of a profession or craft owes to the public, clients, or partner and to professional brethren or members; accepted standards of right and wrong; moral conduct, behavior or duty.

Eviction Dispossession by process of law. The act of depriving a person of the possession of lands in pursuance of the judgment of a court.

Excess A surplus.

Excess condemnation Excess taking; the acquisition of private property by a public body in excess of the public body's need.

Excess income *See* Income, excess.

Excess rent The amount by which

the total contract rent exceeds market rent; an unreasonable amount of rent.

Exchange   A means of trading equities in two or more real properties, treated as a single transaction through a single escrow.

Exclusive agency listing   A listing agreement employing a broker as the sole agent for the seller of real property under the terms of which the broker is entitled to a commission if the property is sold through any other broker but not if a sale is negotiated by the owner without the services of an agent.

Exclusive right to sell listing   A listing agreement employing a broker to act as agent for the seller of real property under the terms of which the broker is entitled to a commission if the property is sold during the duration of the listing, whether through another broker or by the owner without the services of an agent.

Execute   To complete, to make, to perform, to do, to follow out; to execute a deed, to make a deed, including especially signing, sealing, and delivering. To execute a contract is to perform the contract, to follow out to the end, to complete.

Executor   One named in a will to carry out its provisions as to the disposition of the estate of a deceased person.

Executory contract   A contract in which something remains to be done by one or both of the parties.

Expansible house   Home designed for further expansion and additions in the future.

Expansion joint   A bituminous fiber strip used to separate units of concrete to prevent cracking due to expansion as a result of temperature changes.

Expenditures   Laying out of money,

disbursement; that which is expended.

Expense ratio   *See* Operating expense ratio.

Expenses   Outlay; the costs incurred in an enterprise.

Expert testimony   Testimony given in a court trial by a person qualified by the court as an expert on a particular subject, for example, as an expert witness on real estate values.

Expert witness   One qualified to give expert testimony in a court of law on a particular subject, such as medicine, engineering, or real estate appraising.

Expired life   Life that is used up.

Expressway   Generally, a highway having controlled access, with signaled intersections and grade crossings instead of the interchanges and separated crossings typical of freeways.

External obsolescence   *See* Economic obsolescence.

Facade   Front of a building.

Fair market value (Replaced by Market value, effective June 1993)   The amount of money that would be paid for a property offered on the open market for a reasonable period of time with both buyer and seller knowing all the uses to which the property could be put and with neither party being under pressure to buy or sell.

Fair price   An asking or selling price that represents an equitable amount of money.

Fair rental value   *See* Rent, economic.

Fannie Mae   An acronymic nickname for Federal National Mortgage Association (FNMA).

Farmers Home Administration (FHmA)   An agency of the Department of Agriculture whose primary responsibility is to provide financial assistance for farmers and others living in rural areas where financing is not available on reasonable terms from private sources.

Federal Deposit Insurance Corporation (FDIC)   Agency of the federal government that insures deposits at commercial banks and savings banks.

Federal Home Loan Bank (FHLB)   A district bank of the Federal Home Loan Bank System that lends only to member savings and loan associations.

Federal Home Loan Bank Board (FHLBB)   The administrative agency that charters federal savings and loan associations and exercises regulatory authority over the FHLB system.

Federal Housing Administration (FHA)   An agency of the federal government that insures mortgage loans.

Federal Land Bank System   Federal government agency making long-term loans to farmers.

Federally related transaction   Any real estate transaction involving federal insurance or assistance. *See* FIRREA.

Federal National Mortgage Association (FNMA)   "Fannie Mae," a quasi-public agency converted into a private corporation whose primary function is to buy and sell FHA and VA mortgages in the secondary market.

Federal Reserve System   The federal banking system of the United States under the control of a central board of governors (Federal Reserve Board) involving a central bank in each of twelve geographical districts with broad powers in controlling credit and the amount of money in circulation.

Federal Savings and Loan Association   An association chartered by the FHLBB in contrast to a state-chartered savings and loan association.

Federal Savings and Loan Insurance Corporation (FSLIC)   An agency of the federal government that insures savers' accounts at savings and loan associations.

Fee   A fixed charge for certain services or privileges; compensation for professional service.

Fee ownership   The unrestricted right of ownership in real property.

Fee simple absolute   A legal term meaning, in effect, the most complete degree of ownership of real property.

Fee simple defeasible   An estate in fee subject to the occurrence of a condition subsequent whereby the estate may be terminated.

Fee simple estate   The greatest interest that one can have in real property, an estate that is unqualified, of indefinite duration, freely transferable, and inheritable.

Feudal tenure   A real property ownership system where ownership rests with a sovereign who, in turn, may grant lesser interests in return for service or loyalty; in contrast to allodial tenure.

Feuds   Grants of land.

Fidelity bond   A security posted for the discharge of an obligation of personal services.

Fiduciary   A person in a position of trust and confidence, as between principal and broker; broker as fiduciary owes certain loyalty that cannot be breached under the rules of agency.

Fiduciary duty   That duty owed by an agent to act in the highest good faith toward the principal and not to obtain any advantage over the latter by the slightest misrepresentation, concealment, duress, or pressure.

Fill   Earth used to raise the existing ground level; in residential real estate, base material that is borrowed from another source and is not generally as stable as a cut, for example.

Filtering   The process whereby higher priced properties become available to lower income buyers.

Financial Institutions Reform, Recovery, and Enforcement Act (FIRREA)   A federal law passed in 1989 to regulate financial institutions, including appraisal activities.

Financial intermediary   Financial institutions, such as commercial banks, savings and loan associations, mutual savings banks, and life insurance companies, that receive relatively small sums of money from the public and invest them in the form of large sums; a considerable portion of these funds are loaned on real estate.

Financing cost   *See* Cost, financing.

Financing process   The systematic five-step procedure followed by major institutional lenders in analyzing a proposed loan; includes filing of application by a borrower, lender's analysis of borrower and property, processing of loan documentation, closing (paying) the loan, and servicing (collection and record keeping).

Financing statement   The instrument that is filed to give public notice of the security interest and thereby protect the interest of the secured parties in the collateral. *See also* Security interest and Secured party.

Finish floor   Finish floor strips are applied over wood joists, deadening felt, and diagonal subflooring before finish floor is installed. The final covering on the floor, whether it be wood, linoleum, cork, tile, or carpet.

Fire door   A door of fire-resistant material to prevent or retard the spread of fire.

Fireproof construction   *See* Construction, fireproof.

Fire-resistive construction   *See* Construction, fire resistive.

Fire stop   A solid, tight closure of a concealed space placed to prevent the spread of fire and smoke through such a place.

Fire wall   A wall of fire-resistant material to prevent or retard the spread of fire.

FIRREA   *See* Financial Institutions Reform, Recovery, and Enforcement Act.

First mortgage   A legal document pledging collateral for a loan that has first priority over all other claims against the property except taxes and bonded indebtedness; that mortgage superior to any other. *See also* Mortgage.

First trust deed   A legal document pledging collateral for a loan that has first priority over all other claims against the property except taxes and bonded indebtedness; that trust deed superior to any other. *See also* Trust deed.

Fiscal controls   Federal tax revenue and expenditure policies used to control the level of economic activity.

Fiscal year   A business or accounting year as distinguished from a calendar year.

Fixed expenses   Operating costs that are recurring on a regular (generally monthly) basis and that vary little from year to year.

Fixity of location   The physical characteristic of real estate that subjects it to the influence of its surroundings.

Fixtures   Appurtenances that are attached to the land or improvements and that usually cannot be removed without agreement, as they become real property; examples include plumbing fixtures and store fixtures built into the property.

Flashing   Sheet metal or other material used to protect a building from seepage of water.

Flat   A city apartment on one floor of a building.

Flat lease   *See* Straight lease.

Flood plain   An area that is adjacent to a river or water course and is subject to periodic flooding.

Floor joist   Any of the small timbers or beams ranged parallel from wall to wall to support the floor.

Floor load   The weight in pounds per square foot that may be supported safely by a floor.

Footing   The base or bottom of a foundation wall, pier, or column.

Foreclosure   Procedure whereby property pledged as security for a debt is sold to pay the debt in event of default in payments or terms.

Forfeiture   Loss of money or anything of value, due to failure to perform.

Form report   The most common type of written appraisal report, presented on a standardized form.

Foundation   The supporting portion of a structure below the first-floor construction, or below grade, including the footings.

Frame construction   *See* Construction, wood frame.

Franchise   A specified privilege awarded by a government or business firm that awards an exclusive dealership.

Fraud   The intentional and successful employment of any cunning, deception, collusion, or artifice used to circumvent, cheat, or deceive another person whereby that person acts upon it to the loss of property and to legal injury. (*Actual fraud.* A deliberate misrepresentation or representation made in reckless disregard of its truth or its falsity, the suppression of truth, a promise made without the intention to perform it, or any other act intended to deceive.)

Frauds, statute of   *See* Statute of frauds.

Freehold   The holding of a piece of land for life or with the right to pass it on through inheritance; the estate itself.

Freeway   A high-speed, limited-access roadway, generally having separated opposing lanes with elevated interchanges whereby, under normal traffic conditions, free flow of traffic is unrestricted.

Frontage   A term used to describe or identify that part of a parcel of land or an improvement on the land that faces a street; the lineal extent of the land or improvement that is parallel to and facing the street, e.g., a 75-foot frontage.

Front foot   Property measurement for sale or valuation purposes; the property measured by the front linear foot on its street line, each front foot extending the depth of the lot.

Front money   The minimum amount of money necessary to initiate a real estate venture, to get the transaction underway.

Frostline   The depth of frost penetration in the soil. Varies in different parts of the country. Footings should be placed below this depth to prevent movement.

Functional obsolescence   A loss of value, due to adverse factors from within the structure, that affect the utility value, and marketability of the structure.

Functional utility   The degree of adequacy of the interior planning of a structure.

Furring   Strips of wood or metal applied to a wall or other surface to even it, to form an air space, or to give the wall an appearance of greater thickness.

Future benefits   The anticipated

benefits the present owner will receive from the property in the future.

Future value   The estimated value of money or property at a date in the future.

Gable roof   A pitched roof with sloping sides. *See also* Roof, gable.

Gain   A profit, benefit, or value increase.

Gambrel roof   A curb roof, having a steep lower slope with a flatter upper slope above. *See also* Roof, gambrel.

Garage   A building or enclosure primarily designed or used for motor vehicles.
1. *Attached.* A garage having part or all of one or more walls common to the dwelling or to a covered porch attached to the dwelling.
2. *Built-in.* A garage located within the exterior walls of a dwelling; a garage with living quarters above, having one or more walls or portions thereof common to the walls of the dwelling.
3. *Detached.* A garage completely surrounded by open space; a garage connected to the dwelling by an uncovered terrace is defined as a detached garage.

General lien   A lien on all the property of a debtor.

General warranty deed: A deed which conveys not only all the grantor's interests in and title to the property to the grantee, but also warrants that if the title is defective or has a "cloud" on it (such as mortgage claims, tax liens, title claims, judgments, or mechanic's liens against it) the grantee may hold the grantor liable.

Geodetic survey   A U.S. government survey generally used in identifying government lands and coastal areas.

Gift deed   A deed for which the consideration is love and affection and where there is no material consideration.

Girder   A large beam used to support beams, joists, and partitions.

Goodwill   An intangible, but salable, asset of a business derived from the expectation of continued public patronage.

Government National Mortgage Association (GNMA)   An agency of HUD that functions in the secondary mortgage market, primarily in special housing programs; commonly called by the acronymic nickname "Ginnie Mae."

Government survey   A method of specifying the location of parcels of land using prime meridians, base lines, standard parallels, guide meridians, townships, and sections.

Grade   Ground level at the foundation.

Graduated lease   Lease that provides for a varying rental rate, often based on future determination; sometimes rent is based on result of periodical appraisals; used largely in long-term leases.

Graduated payment mortgage   Provides for partially deferred payments of principal at start of loan. (There are a variety of plans.) Usually after the first five years of the loan term, the principal and interest payments are substantially higher to make up the principal portion of payments lost at the beginning of the loan. *See also* Variable interest rate.

Grant   A technical legal term in a deed of conveyance bestowing an interest in real property on another; the words *convey and transfer* have the same effect.

Grant deed   A limited warranty deed using the word *grant*, or like words, that assure a grantee that the grantor has not already conveyed the land to another and that the estate is free from encumbrances placed by the grantor.

Grantee   A person to whom a grant is made; the buyer or recipient.

Grantor   A person who transfers his or her interest in property to another by grant.

Gratuitous agent   A person not paid by the principal for services on behalf of the principal, who cannot be forced to act as an agent, but who becomes bound to act in good faith and obey a principal's instructions once he or she undertakes to act as an agent.

GRI   Graduate, Realtors' Institute.

Grid   A chart used in rating the borrower risk, property, and the neighborhood.

Gross income   Total income from property before any expenses are deducted.

Gross income multiplier (GIM)   The same as gross rent multiplier.

Gross lease   Rental agreement under which the owner pays all expenses.

Gross national product (GNP)   The total value of all goods and services produced in an economy during a given period of time.

Gross rate   A method of collecting interest by adding total interest to the principal of the loan at the outset of the term.

Gross rent multiplier (GRM)   A number that, times the gross income of a property, produces an estimate of value of the property. Example: The gross income from an unfurnished apartment building is $200,000 per annum. If an appraiser uses a gross multiplier of 7 percent, it is said that, based on the gross multiplier, the value of the building is $1,400,000.

Ground lease   An agreement for use of the land only, sometimes secured by improvements placed on the land by the user.

Ground rent   Earnings of improved property credited to earnings of the ground itself after allowance has been made for earnings of improvements; often termed *economic rent*.

Habendum clause   The to-have-and-to-hold clause that may be found in a deed.

Hazard insurance   Protects against damages caused to property by fire, windstorms, and other common hazards.

Header   A beam placed perpendicular to joists and to which joists are nailed in framing for a chimney, stairway, or other opening.

Heat pump   A device that uses electrical energy to move heat from a colder to a warmer location. This is done by *reversing* the flow of refrigerant in an air conditioner to provide heat.

Heir   One who inherits property.

Highest and best use   An appraisal phrase meaning that use that at the time of an appraisal is most likely to produce the greatest net return to the land and/or buildings over a given period of time; that use that will produce the greatest amount of amenities or profit. This is the starting point for appraisal.

Hilly land   *See* Slope, strongly sloping or hilly.

Hip roof   *See* Roof, hip.

Historical cost   *See* Cost, historical.

Holder in due course   One who has taken a note, check or bill of exchange in due course: (1) before it was overdue, (2) in good faith and for value, and (3) without knowledge that it has been previously dishonored and without notice of any defect at the time it was negotiated to him or her.

Holdover tenant   Tenant who remains in possession of leased property after the expiration of the lease term.

Home mortgage loan   A special kind

of long-term loan for buying a house. There are three kinds of mortgage financing for single family homes in the United States—the conventional mortgage; the VA (Veterans Administration), sometimes called the GI, mortgage; and the HUD-insured loan.

Homestead   A statutory protection of real property used as a home from the claims of certain creditors and judgments up to a specified amount.

Homogeneous   Of the same kind or nature; consisting of similar parts or elements; of the same degree or dimensions.

House   A single-family detached residence.

1. *Detached.* A house surrounded by permanent open spaces.
2. *Rowhouse.* A single-family residence, much like a townhouse, with side walls that are common with adjoining row houses. Differs from a townhouse in that the tandem garage and utility area generally occupy the ground floor or basement level and there are generally no common areas of ownership.
3. *Semidetached.* A house with one side a party or lot-line wall.

Housing Financial Discrimination Act of 1977   California Health and Safety Code Section 35800, et seq., designed primarily to eliminate discrimination in lending practices based upon the character of the neighborhood in which real property is located. *See also* Redlining.

HUD   U.S. Department of Housing and Urban Development. The Office of Housing/Federal Housing Administration within HUD insures home mortgage loans made by lenders and sets minimum standards for such homes.

Hundred percent location   A city retail business location that is consid-

ered the best available for attracting business.

Hypothecation   Act or contract by which property is used as security for a loan.

Imperative necessity   Circumstances under which an agent has expanded authority in an emergency, including the power to disobey instructions where it is clearly in the interests of the principal and where there is no time to obtain instructions from the principal.

Impounds   A trust-type account established by lenders for the accumulation of borrowers' funds to meet periodic payment of taxes, FHA mortgage insurance premiums, and/or future insurance policy premiums required to protect their security. Impounds are usually collected with the note payment. The combined principal, interest, taxes, and insurance payments are commonly termed a *PITI* payment.

Improved value   A value placed upon a property when proposed improvements have been completed.

Improvement   State of being improved; especially, enhanced value or excellence. Residence or other structure or appurtenance attached to or part of the land.

Improvements on land   Structures or improvements placed on the site, such as house, garage, driveway, septic tank. Also called *on-site improvements.*

Improvements to land   Structures or improvements placed off the site, such as roads, curbs, and sewers, giving value to the site. Also called *off-site improvements.*

Inchoate right of dower   A wife's interest in the real estate of her husband during his life, which upon his death may become a dower interest.

Income   A monetary return.
1. *Effective.* The anticipated gross income less an amount for vacancies and rent losses.
2. *Excess.* Income in excess of needs.
3. *Gross.* The total income from an enterprise; usually an annual total income.
4. *Net.* Income remaining after allowing for vacancy and uncollectibles, fixed and operating expenses, and reserves for depreciation.
5. *Operating.* Same as net income.
6. *Surplus.* Same as excess income.

Income approach   One of the three appraisal methods, in which the estimated gross income from the subject residence is used as a basis for estimating value along with gross rent multipliers derived from the marketplace.

Income (capitalization) approach One of the three methods of the appraisal process generally applied to income producing property, and involves a three-step process: (1) find net annual income, (2) set an appropriate capitalization rate or present-worth factor, and (3) capitalize the income dividing the net income by the capitalization rate.

Income forecast   Gross or net income estimate.

Income participation loan   A mortgage loan whose terms give mortgagee the right to share in a portion of the mortgaged property's future income.

Income property   Property whose primary purpose is to produce income.

Income stream   Actual or estimate flow of net earnings over time.

Incompetent   One who is mentally incompetent, incapable; any person who, though not insane, is, by reason of old age, disease, weakness of mind, or any other cause, unable, unassisted, to properly manage and take care of self or property and by reason thereof would be likely to be deceived or imposed upon by artful or designing persons.

Incorporeal rights   Non-possessory rights in real estate, such as rents, that arise out of ownership.

Increasing returns   The situation existing when increases to any of the agents of production result in increased net income to the enterprise; as opposed to decreasing returns.

Increment   An increase. Most frequently used to refer to the increase of value of land that accompanies population growth and increasing wealth in the community. The term *unearned increment* is used in this connection since values are supposed to have increased without effort on the part of the owner.

Incumbrance   A right or interest in real property that affects the underlying fee title; the same as *encumbrance.*

Incurable depreciation   Elements of physical deterioration and functional obsolescence that cannot be corrected except at exorbitant cost; that is, elements that are not economically worthwhile to correct.

Indenture   A formal, written instrument made between two or more persons in different interests, such as a lease.

Independent appraiser   *See* Appraiser, independent.

Independent contractor   A person who acts for another but who sells final results and whose methods of achieving those results are not subject to the control of another.

Index method   Method of estimating construction costs, adjusting original costs to the current cost level by using a multiplier obtained from a published cost index.

Indirect cost   *See* Cost, indirect.

Indirect lighting The light is reflected from the ceiling or other object external to the fixture.

Indorsement The act of signing one's name on the back of a check or note, with or without further qualification.

Injunction A writ or order issued under the seal of a court to restrain one or more parties to a suit or proceeding from doing an act deemed to be inequitable or unjust in regard to the rights of some other party or parties in the suit or proceeding.

Input Data, information, and the like, that is fed into a computer or other system.

Installment note A note that provides for a series of periodic payments of principal and interest until the amount borrowed is paid in full. This periodic reduction of principal amortizes the loan.

Installment reporting A method of reporting capital gains by installments for successive tax years to minimize the impact of the totality of the capital gains tax in the year of the sale.

Installment sales contract Commonly called contract of sale or land contract; purchase of real estate wherein the purchase price is paid in installments over a long period of time, title is retained by seller, and upon default by buyer (vendee), the payments may be forfeited.

Institutional financing A loan from a bank, savings and loan association, insurance company, etc.

Institutional lenders A financial intermediary or depository, such as a savings and loan association, commercial bank, or life insurance company, that pools money of its depositors and then invests funds in various ways, including trust deed and mortgage loans.

Instrument A written legal document; created to effect the rights of the parties, giving formal expression to a legal act or agreement for the purpose of creating, modifying, or terminating a right. Real estate lenders' basic instruments are promissory notes, deeds of trust, mortgages, installment sales contracts, leases, and assignments.

Insurable value *See* Value, insurable.

Intangible value *See* Value, intangible.

Interest A portion, share, or right in something; partial, not complete, ownership. The charge in dollars for the use of money for a period of time; in a sense, the rent paid for the use of money.

Interest extra loan A loan in which a fixed amount of principal is repaid in installments along with interest accrued each period on the amount of the then-outstanding principal only.

Interest only loan A straight, non-amortizing loan in which the lender receives only interest during the term of the loan and principal is repaid in a lump sum at maturity.

Interest rate *See* Rate, interest.

Interim loan A short-term, temporary loan used until permanent financing is available, e.g., a construction loan.

Interim value Temporary value of existing improvements until land can be developed after the period of zoning change to a more intense use.

Intermediation The process of pooling and supplying funds for investment by financial institutions called intermediaries. The process is dependent on individual savers placing their funds with these institutions and foregoing opportunities to directly invest in the investments selected.

Internal rate of return The rate of return generated by an investment over the holding period, considering all future benefits, and discounting them to equal the present value.

Interpleader A court proceeding initiated by the stakeholder of property who claims no proprietary interest in it for the purpose of deciding who among claimants is legally entitled to the property.

Intestate The condition of having made no will, or having made one defective in form, at death; in such a case, the estate descends to the heirs at law or next of kin.

Intrinsic value. *See* Value, intrinsic.

Involuntary lien A lien imposed against property without consent of an owner; examples include taxes, special assessments, and federal income tax liens.

Irrevocable Incapable of being recalled or revoked, unchangeable.

Irrigation districts Quasi-political districts created under special laws to provide for water services to property owners in the district; an operation governed to a great extent by law.

Jalousie A slatted blind or shutter like a venetian blind but used on the exterior to protect against rain as well as to control sunlight.

Jamb The side post or lining of a doorway, window, or other opening.

Joint The space between the adjacent surfaces of two components joined and held together by nails, glue, cement, mortar, etc.

Joint appraisal An appraisal made by two or more appraisers working together.

Joint note A note signed by two or more persons who have equal liability for payment.

Joint tenancy Undivided ownership of a property interest by two or more persons, each of whom has a right to an equal share in the inter-

est and a right of survivorship, i.e., the right to share equally with other surviving joint tenants in the interest of a deceased joint tenant.

Joint venture Two or more individuals or firms joining together on a single project as partners.

Joist Any of the small timbers or beams ranged parallel from wall to wall to support the floor, or to support the laths or furring strips of a ceiling; one of a series of parallel beams to which the boards of a floor and ceiling laths are nailed, and that are supported in turn by larger beams, girders, or bearing walls.

Judgment The final determination of a court of competent jurisdiction of a matter presented to it; money judgments provide for the payment of claims presented to the court, or are awarded as damages, etc.

Judgment lien A legal claim on all of the property of a judgment debtor that enables the judgment creditor to have the property sold for payment of the amount of the judgment.

Junior mortgage A mortgage recorded subsequently to another mortgage on the same property or made subordinate by agreement to a later-recorded mortgage.

Jurisdiction The authority by which judicial officers take cognizance of and decide causes; the power to hear and determine a cause; the right and power a judicial officer has to enter upon the inquiry.

Just compensation A fair price paid in an acquisition under threat of condemnation (eminent domain).

Key lot *See* Lot, key.

Laches Delay or negligence in asserting one's legal rights.

Labor An agent of production; cost

of all operating expenses and wages except management costs.

Land   The solid material of the earth and anything affixed permanently to it including buildings, trees, minerals, water flowing on land, and air space above it.

Land contract   A contract used in a sale of real property whereby the seller retains title to the property until all, or a prescribed part, of the purchase price has been paid. Also commonly called a conditional sales contract, installment sales contract, or real property sales contract. *See also* Real property sales contract.

Land and improvement loan   A loan obtained by the builder-developer for the purchase of land and to cover expenses for subdividing.

Landlord   One who rents property to another. The lessor under a lease.

Land residual technique   A technique of the income approach whereby the net income imputable to the land is capitalized to estimate the value of the land. Land value is then added to the value of the improvements to estimate the total value of the property.

Late charge   A charge assessed by a lender against a borrower failing to make loan installment payments when due.

Later date order   The commitment for an owner's title insurance policy that is issued by a title insurance company and covers the seller's title as of the date of the contract. When the sale closes, the purchaser orders the title company to record the deed to the purchaser and bring down their examination to cover this later date to show the purchaser as owner of the property.

Lateral support   The support the soil of an adjoining owner gives to a neighbor's land.

Latex   A rubberized paint that is durable and relatively easy to apply. Brushes can be cleaned easily with warm water and soap.

Lath   A building material of wood, metal, gypsum, or insulating board fastened to the frame of a structure.

Leaching   Draining waste material into the soil by means of percolation.

Lean-to   A temporary structure for protection from the elements.

Lean-to roof   A roof similar to a shed roof.

Lease   A contract by which real estate is conveyed for life, for a term of years, or at will, usually for a specified rent; also, the act of such conveyance, or the term for which it is made. Also, a written document permitting one party—the lessee—possession of land or a building of another party—the lessor. Usually for more than a year.

1. *Net.* A lease under which the lessee pays any one of the following: taxes, insurance, or maintenance.
2. *Net net (double net).* A lease under which the lessee (tenant) pays any *two* of the following: taxes, insurance, or maintenance.
3. *Net net net (triple net).* A lease under which the lessee (tenant) pays all *three* of the following: taxes, insurance, and maintenance. This term is generally used in commercial and industrial leased properties where the lessor (owner) provides the land and capital improvements.

Leasehold estate   A tenant's right to occupy real estate during the term of the lease. This is a personal property interest.

Leasehold value   Market value of the excess of economic rent over contract rent.

Legal description   A land description recognized by law; a description by which property can be definitely located by reference to government surveys or approved recorded maps.

Lessee   One who contracts to rent, occupy, and use property under a lease agreement; a tenant.

Lessor   An owner who enters into a lease agreement with a tenant; a landlord.

Level-payment mortgage   A loan on real estate that is paid off by making a series of equal (or nearly equal) regular payments. Part of the payment is usually interest on the loan, and part of it reduces the amount of the unpaid principal balance of the loan. Also sometimes called an amortized mortgage or an installment mortgage.

Leverage   The use of debt financing of an investment to maximize the return per dollar of equity invested.

Lien   A form of encumbrance that usually makes specific property security for the payment of a debt or discharge of an obligation. Examples include judgments, taxes, mortgages, and deeds of trust.

Life
1. *Economic.* The useful life of a property; that period during which a property will return a profit.
2. *Effective.* Same as economic life.
3. *Expired.* That portion of a property's life that is used up.
4. *Physical.* The length of time a structure will function if normally maintained.

Life estate   An estate or interest in real property that is held for the duration of the life of some certain person. It may be limited by the life of the person holding it or by the life of some other person.

Limitations, statute of   The commonly used identifying term for various statutes that require that a legal action be commenced within a prescribed time after the accrual of the right to seek legal relief.

Limited partnership   A partnership consisting of a general partner or partners and limited partners in which the general partners manage and control the business affairs of the partnership while limited partners are essentially investors taking no part in the management of the partnership and having no liability for the debts of the partnership in excess of their invested capital.

Lintel   A horizontal board that supports the load over an opening such as a door or window.

Liquid assets   Assets that can be promptly converted into cash.

Liquidated damages   A sum agreed on by the parties to be full damages if a certain event occurs.

Liquidated damages clause   A clause in a contract by which the parties by agreement fix the damages in advance for a breach of the contract.

Liquidation price   *See* Price, liquidation.

Liquidity   Holdings in or the ability to convert assets to cash or its equivalent. The ease with which a person is able to pay maturing obligations.

Lis pendens   A notice filed or recorded for the purpose of warning all persons that the title or right to the possession of certain real property is in litigation; literally, "suit pending"; usually recorded so as to give constructive notice of pending litigation.

Listing   An employment contract between principal and agent authorizing the agent to perform services for the principal involving the latter's property; listing contracts are entered into for the purpose of securing persons to buy, lease, or rent property. Employment of an agent by a prospective purchaser or lessee to locate property for purchase or lease may be considered a listing.

Live load   *See* Floor load.

Livery of seisin (seizin)   The appropriate ceremony at common law for transferring the possession of lands by a grantor to a grantee.

Living area   The square-foot area of a residence, measured from the outside, including all rooms that are similarly supplied for year-round living with such things as insulation, heating, cooling, plumbing, and electrical facilities. This generally excludes garages and screened patios or porches ("Florida rooms").

Living units   A house or portion thereof providing complete living facilities for one family, including provisions for living, sleeping, eating, cooking, and sanitation.

Loam   A type of soil consisting of a crumbly mixture of varying proportions of clay, sand, and organic matter.

Loan administration   Also called loan servicing. Mortgage bankers not only originate loans, but also service them from origination to maturity of the loan through handling of loan payments, delinquencies, impounds, payoffs, and releases.

Loan application   The loan application is a source of information on which the lender bases a decision to make the loan. Defines the terms of the loan contract; gives the name of the borrower, place of employment, salary, bank accounts, and credit references; describes the real estate that is to be mortgaged; and stipulates the amount of loan being applied for and the repayment terms.

Loan closing   When all conditions have been met, the loan officer authorizes the recording of the trust deed or mortgage. The disbursal procedure of funds is similar to the closing of a real estate sales escrow. The borrower can expect to receive less than the amount of the loan, as title, recording, service, and other fees may be withheld, or can expect to deposit the cost of these items into the loan escrow. This process is sometimes called funding the loan.

Loan commitment   Lender's contractual commitment to make a loan based on the appraisal and underwriting.

Loan-value ratio   The percentage of a property's value that a lender can, or may, loan to a borrower. For example, if the ratio is 80%, this means that a lender may loan 80% of the property's appraised value to a borrower.

Location   The site, setting, or position of a property or object in relation to other properties or objects.

Lot   A plot of ground.
1. *Corner.* A lot at the confluence or convergence of two streets.
2. *Cul-de-sac.* A lot situated at the end of a dead-end street that has a turn-around area.
3. *Flag.* A lot located so that access can be had only at the side of another lot.
4. *Interior.* A lot situated so that its boundaries touch no more than five lots. Generally it is surrounded by three lots.
5. *Key.* A lot situated so that its boundaries touch six lots or more.

Louver   An opening with a series of horizontal slats set at an angle to permit ventilation without admitting rain, sunlight, or vision.

MAI   Member of the Appraisal Institute; designates a person who is a member of the American Institute of Real Estate Appraisers of the National Association of Realtors.

Maintenance The upkeep of property, equipment, and the like.

Maintenance, deferred Maintenance that has been postponed; accumulated repairs.

Management Act or art of managing, control, direction; judicious use of means to accomplish an end; skillful treatment.

Mansard roof *See* Roof, mansard.

Marginal land Land from which the return or income is barely sufficient to produce a profit.

Margin of security The difference between the amount of the mortgage loan(s) and the appraised value of the property.

Marketable title Title that a reasonable purchaser, informed as to the facts and their legal importance and acting with reasonable care, would be willing, and ought, to accept.

Market data approach One of the three appraisal methods. A means of comparing similar, recently sold residential properties to the subject property.

Market price The price actually paid in the market for a property.

Market value The most probable price in terms of money that a property should bring in a competitive and open market and under all conditions required for a fair sale, i.e., the buyer and seller acting prudently and knowledgeably and neither affected by undue pressures.

Matched pair method Method of adjusting comparable sales where sets of two comparable properties with one differing feature are used to estimate an amount of adjustment for that feature. *See also* Paired sales method.

Material fact A fact that the agent should realize would be likely to affect the judgment of the principal in giving his or her consent to the agent to enter into the particular transaction on the specified terms.

Mature phase Second phase in the cycle of a neighborhood, marked by the stability of the existing buildings and occupants.

Mean Measure of central tendency; the average price or numeric value of a statistical sample.

Mechanic's lien A lien created by statute and that exists against real property in favor of persons who have performed work or furnished materials for the improvement of the real property.

Median The middle value in a statistical sample.

Memory bank Data and information held in storage in a computer.

Meridians Imaginary north-06 south lines that intersect base lines to form a starting point for the measurement of land.

Mesne profits Profits from land use accruing between two periods, as for example moneys owed to the owner of land by a person who has illegally occupied the land after the owner takes title, but before the owner takes possession.

Metes and bounds A term used in describing the boundary lines of land, setting forth all the boundary lines together with their terminal points and angles. Metes (length or measurements) and bounds (boundaries) description is often used when much accuracy is required.

Metropolitan area A large center of population encompassing the adjacent satellite communities.

Mile 5,280 feet.

Milled wood Solid wood that has been manufactured and finished in millwork plants. The term generally refers to special woodwork, such as doors, cabinets, and window and door frames.

Minor All persons under 18 years of age.

Misplaced improvements Improvements on land that do not conform to the most profitable use of the site.

Misrepresentation   A false or misleading statement or assertion.

Mobile home   As defined in Business and Professions Code Section 10131.6(c), "mobile home" means a structure transportable in one or more sections, designed and equipped to contain not more than two dwelling units to be used with or without a foundation system. "Mobile home" does not include a recreational vehicle, as defined in Section 18010.5 of the Health and Safety Code, a commercial coach, as defined in Section 18012 of the Health and Safety Code, or factory-built housing, as defined in Section 19971 of the Health and Safety Code.

Mode   The most frequently occurring price or value in a statistical sample.

Modernization   To render modern; to change to conform to present use, style, taste, etc.

Modular   A system for the construction of dwellings and other improvements to real property through the on-site assembly of component parts (modules) that have been mass produced away from the building site.

Moldings   Usually patterned strips used to provide ornamental variation of outline or contour, such as cornices, bases, and window and door jambs.

Monetary controls   Federal Reserve tools (such as adjusting discount rates and reserve requirements) for regulating the availability of money and credit to influence the level of economic activity.

Monument   A stone or other permanent object to mark a boundary; often a small concrete block with a steel marker indicating a boundary point.

Moratorium   The temporary suspension, usually by statute, of the enforcement of liability of debt.

Mortgage   An instrument, recognized by law, by which property is hypothecated to secure the payment of a debt or obligation; a procedure for foreclosure in event of default is established by statute.

Mortgage banker   A person whose principal business is the originating, financing, closing, selling, and servicing of loans secured by real property for institutional lenders on a contractual basis.

Mortgage contracts with warrants   Warrants make the mortgage more attractive to the lender by providing both the greater security that goes with a mortgage, and the opportunity of a greater return through the right to buy either stock in the borrower's company or a portion of the income property itself.

Mortgagee   One to whom a mortgagor gives a mortgage to secure a loan or performance of an obligation; a lender or creditor. *See also* Secured party.

Mortgage guaranty insurance   Insurance against financial loss available to mortgage lenders from private mortgage insurance companies (PMICs).

Mortgage investment company   A company or group of private investors that buys mortgages for investment purposes.

Mortgage loan disclosure statement   On a form approved by the real estate commissioner, the statement that is required by law to be furnished by a mortgage loan broker to the prospective borrower of loans of a statutorily prescribed amount before the borrower becomes obligated to complete the loan.

Mortgagor   One who gives a mortgage on his or her property to secure a loan or assure performance of an obligation; a borrower. *See also* Debtor.

Multiple listing A listing, usually an exclusive right to sell, taken by a member of an organization composed of real estate brokers, with the provision that all members will have the opportunity to find an interested buyer; a cooperative listing ensuring that owner property will receive a wide market exposure.

Multiple listing service (MLS) An association of real estate agents providing for a pooling of listings and the sharing of commissions on a specified basis.

Multiplier A number that, when multiplied by the income, gives an estimate of value; also called gross income multiplier or gross rent multiplier. *See also* Gross income multiplier.

Mutual savings banks Financial institutions owned by depositors, each of whom has rights to net earnings of the bank in proportion to his or her deposits.

Mutual water company A water company organized by or for water users in a given district with the object of securing an ample water supply at a reasonable rate; stock is issued to users.

NAR National Association of Realtors.

NAREB National Association of Real Estate Brokers.

Narrative appraisal A summary of all factual materials, techniques, and appraisal methods used by the appraiser in setting forth his or her value conclusion.

Negotiable Capable of being negotiated, assignable, or transferable in the ordinary course of business.

Neighborhood A district or section, especially with reference to the condition or type of its inhabitants.

Net income *See* Income, net.

Net income ratio Net income divided by the effective gross income.

Net lease A lease requiring a lessee to pay such charges against the property as taxes, insurance, and maintenance costs in addition to rental payments.

Net listing A listing that provides that the agent may retain as compensation for agent's services all sums received over and above a net price to the owner.

Net net *See* Lease, net net (double net).

Net net net *See* Lease, net net net (triple net).

Net worth The surplus of assets over liabilities.

New money That amount of money, cash or new loans or both, that represents the difference between the selling price of a parcel of real estate and existing loans, if any, that are assumed by the buyer.

Nominal interest rates The percentage of interest that is stated in loan documents.

Nonconforming building An existing building that does not conform to the latest building or zoning codes.

Notary public An appointed officer with authority to take the acknowledgment of persons executing documents, sign the certificate, and affix official seal.

Note A signed written instrument acknowledging a debt and promising payment according to the specified terms and conditions; a promissory note.

Notice

1. *Actual.* Express or implied knowledge of a fact.

2. *Constructive.* A fact, imputed to a person by law, that should have been discovered because of the person's actual notice of circumstances and the inquiry that a

prudent person would have been expected to make.

3. *Legal.* Information required to be given by law.

Notice of nonresponsibility   A notice, provided by law, designed to relieve a property owner from responsibility for the cost of unauthorized work done on the property or of materials furnished therefor; notice must be verified, recorded, and posted.

Notice to quit   A notice to a tenant to vacate rented property.

Novation   The substitution or exchange of a new obligation or contract for an old one by the mutual agreement of the parties.

Nuisance value   *See* Value, nuisance.

Null and void   Of no legal validity or effect.

Observed conditions   The condition of a property, determined by observation.

Obsolescence   Loss in value due to reduced desirability and usefulness of a structure because its design and construction become obsolete; loss because of becoming old-fashioned and not in keeping with modern needs, with consequent loss of income. May be functional or economic.

Occupancy   A taking or holding possession; act of taking possession of an owned thing.

Offer to purchase   The proposal made to an owner of property by a potential buyer to purchase the property under stated terms.

Offset statement   Statement by owner of property or owner of lien against property setting forth the present status of liens against said property.

Open-end mortgage   A mortgage containing a clause that permits the mortgagor to borrow additional money after the loan has been reduced without rewriting the mortgage.

Open housing law   A law passed by Congress in April 1968; prohibits discrimination in the sale of real estate because of race, color, or religion of buyers.

Open listing   An authorization given by a property owner to a real estate agent wherein said agent is given the nonexclusive right to secure a purchaser; open listings may be given to any number of agents without liability to compensate any except the one who first secures a buyer ready, willing, and able to meet the terms of the listing or who secures the acceptance by the seller of a satisfactory offer.

Operating expenses   The costs of operation; generally include fixed expenses of taxes and insurance as well as monthly operating costs of utilities, cleaning, etc.; do not generally include reserves for depreciation.

Operating expense ratio   The ratio of total operating expenses to the effective gross rent in an income property.

Operating income   *See* Income, net.

Operating statement   A written summary of the income, expenses, and profits of an enterprise, usually on an annual basis.

Opinion of title   An attorney's written evaluation of the condition of the title to a parcel of land after examination of the abstract of title.

Optimum use   *See* Highest and best use.

Option   The exercise of the power of choice; a stipulated privilege of buying or selling a stated property, security, or commodity at a given price within a specified time.

Oral contract   A verbal agreement; one that is not reduced to writing.

Orientation   Placing a structure on its lot with regard to its exposure to the rays of the sun, prevailing winds, privacy from the street, and protection from outside noises.

Ostensible authority　That authority a third person reasonably believes an agent possesses because of the acts or omissions of the principal.

Overall rate　*See* Rate, overall.

Overhang　The part of the roof extending beyond the walls, to shade buildings and cover walks.

Over-improvement　An improvement that is not the highest and best use for the site on which it is placed by reason of excess size or cost.

Ownership　The right of one or more persons to possess and use property to the exclusion of all others. A collection of rights to the use and enjoyment of property.

Package mortgage　A type of mortgage used in home financing covering real property, improvements, and movable equipment/appliances.

Paired sales method　*See* Matched pair method.

Panel board　A control panel containing an electric meter, circuit breakers, and a main power switch.

Paramount title　Title that is superior to or foremost among all others.

Parcel　A part, piece; as, a certain piece of land is part and parcel of another piece.

Partial taking　Governmental agency acquiring only a portion of a property through condemnation.

Parquet floor　Hardwood floor laid in squares or patterns.

Participation　Sharing of an interest in a property by a lender. In addition to base interest on mortgage loans on income properties, a percentage of gross income is required, sometimes predicated on certain conditions being fulfilled, such as a minimum occupancy or a percentage of net income after expenses, debt service, and taxes. Also called *equity participation* or *revenue sharing*.

Parties (party)　Those entities taking part in a transaction as a principal, for example, the seller, buyer, or lender in a real estate transaction.

Partition　A division of real or personal property or the proceeds therefrom among co-owners.

Partition action　Court proceedings by which co-owners seek to sever their joint ownership.

Partnership　A decision of the California Supreme Court has defined a partnership in the following terms: "A partnership as between partners themselves may be defined to be a contract of two or more persons to unite their property, labor or skill, or some of them, in prosecution of some joint or lawful business, and to share the profits in certain proportions." A voluntary association of two or more persons to carry on a business or venture on terms of mutual participation in profits and losses.

Party wall　A wall erected on the line between two adjoining properties that are under different ownership, for the use of both properties.

Par value　Market value, nominal value.

Patent　Conveyance of title to government land.

Penalty　An extra payment or charge required of the borrower for deviating from the terms of the original loan agreement. Usually levied for being late in making regular payment (late charges) or for paying off the loan before it is due (prepayment penalties).

Penny　The term, as applied to nails, serves as a measure of nail length and is abbreviated by the letter *d*.

Percentage lease　Lease on the property, the rental for which is determined by amount of business done by the lessee; usually a percentage of gross receipts from the business with provision for a minimum rental.

Percolation   The draining or permeating of water through soil.

Perimeter heating   Baseboard heating, or any system in which the heat registers are located along the outside walls of a room, especially under the windows.

Permeability   Capability of being permeated; penetrability.

Perpetuity   Continuing forever; usually applied to an income or return extending into the future without termination.

Personal property   *See* Property, personal.

Physical assets   Assets of a physical nature, such as real estate, machinery, and equipment.

Physical deterioration   Impairment of condition. Loss in value brought about by wear and tear, disintegration, use, and actions of the elements.

Physical life   *See* Life, physical.

Pier   A column of masonry, usually rectangular in horizontal cross section, used to support other structural members.

Pitch   The incline or rise of a roof.

Plaintiff   In a court action, the one who sues; the complainant.

Planned unit development (PUD)   A land use design that provides intensive utilization of the land through a combination of private and common areas with pre-arranged sharing of responsibilities for the common areas. Individual lots are owned in fee, with joint ownership of the open areas.

Planning commission   An agency of local government charged with planning the development, redevelopment, or preservation of an area.

Plat or plot   An illustration of a small plot of ground; a plan, map, or chart, especially of a town site.

Plate   A horizontal board placed on a wall or supported on posts or studs to carry the trusses of a roof or rafters directly; a shoe, or base member, as of a partition or other frame; a small flat board placed on or in a wall to support girders, rafters, etc.

Pledge   The depositing of personal property by a debtor with a creditor as security for a debt or engagement.

Pledgee   One who is given a pledge or a security. *See also* Secured party.

Pledgor   One who offers a pledge or gives security. *See also* Debtor.

Plottage   A term used in appraising to designate the increased value of two or more contiguous lots when they are joined under single ownership and available for use as a larger single lot. Also called assemblage.

Plottage increment   The appreciation in unit value created by joining smaller ownerships into one large single ownership.

Plottage value   *See* Value, plottage.

Plywood   Wood made of a number of thin veneer sheets glued together, the grain of each layer usually at right angles to the one next to it.

Pocket door   *See* Door, pocket.

Points   Under FHA-insured or VA-guaranteed loans, discounts of points paid to lenders are, in effect, prepaid interest and are used by lenders to adjust their effective interest rate so that it is equal to, or nearly equal to, the prevailing market rate (the rate charged on conventional loans). The discounts are absorbed by the sellers. One point is 1 percent of the loan amount. On FHA-insured and VA-guaranteed loans, buyers may be charged only

1 percent service charge. This restriction does not apply to conventional loans. Under conventional loans, the charge for making a loan at most institutions is usually called a loan fee, service charge, or commitment fee, or it may be referred to as points to the buyer.

Police power   The right of the public body to enact laws and enforce them for the order, safety, health, morals, and general welfare of the public.

Possessory interest   An interest in privately owned improvements on land whose owner is property tax exempt; for example, the renting of a house belonging to the state. The renter may be subject to a possessory interest tax.

Potential value   *See* Value, potential.

Power line right-of-way   A right to use land for a power line. Similar to an easement; however, could denote fee title. *See also* Rights, power line.

Power of attorney   A written instrument whereby a principal gives authority to an agent. The agent acting under such a grant is sometimes called an *attorney in fact.*

Power of sale   The power of a mortgagee or trustee, when the instrument so provides, to sell the secured property without judicial proceedings if a borrower defaults in payment of the promissory note or otherwise breaches the terms of the mortgage or deed of trust.

Prefabricated house   A house manufactured and sometimes partly assembled before delivery to a building site.

Preferred stock   A class of corporate stock entitled to preferential treatment, such as priority in distribution of dividends.

Prepaid items of expense   Prorations of prepaid items of expense that are credited to the seller in the closing escrow statement.

Prepayment   Provision made for loan payments to be larger than those specified in the note.

Prepayment penalty   The charge payable to a lender by a borrower under the terms of the loan agreement if the borrower pays off the outstanding principal balance of the loan prior to its maturity.

Prescription   Obtaining title to property by adverse possession by occupying it for the period determined by law to bar action for recovery.

Present value   The lump sum value today of an annuity. A $100 bill to be paid to someone in one year is worth less than if it were a $100 bill to be paid to someone today. This is due to several things, one of which is that the money has time value. How much the $100 bill to be paid in one year is worth today will depend on the interest rate that seems proper for the particular circumstances. For example, if 6 percent is the appropriate rate, the $100 to be paid one year from now would be worth $94.34 today.

Presumption   A rule of law that courts and judges shall draw a particular inference from a particular fact, or from particular evidence, unless and until the truth of such inference is disproved.

Price   The cost of an object, property, or service.
1. *Forced.* The price paid in a sale made under undue pressure.
2. *Liquidation.* Same as forced price.
3. *Selling.* The price *paid,* for whatever reason.

Pride of ownership   The pride of the owner in his or her property, reflected in the care and maintenance of the property.

Prima facie   Presumptive on its face.

Principal   This term is used to mean the employer of an agent or the amount of money borrowed, or the amount of the loan. Also, one of the main parties in a real estate transaction, such as a buyer, borrower, seller, or lessor.

Principle of agents of production Production or income resulting from the four factors of labor, coordination, capital, and land.

Principle of anticipation Value is the present worth of future benefits, both income and intangible amenities.

Principle of balance See Principle of surplus productivity.

Principle of change Real estate values are constantly changed by social, economic, and political forces in society.

Principle of competition Market demand generates profit; profits generate competition; and competition stabilizes profits.

Principle of conformity Maximum value results when properties in a neighborhood are relatively similar in size, style, quality, use, and/or type.

Principle of consistent use Requires that land and improvements be appraised on the basis of the same use.

Principle of contribution *See* Principle of surplus productivity.

Principle of increasing and decreasing returns Income and other benefits available from real estate may be increased by adding capital improvements only up to the point of balance in the agents of production, beyond which the increase in value tends to be less than the increase in costs.

Principle of progression and regression Lower valued properties generally benefit from close proximity to properties of higher value, and higher valued properties tend to suffer when placed in close proximity with properties of lower value.

Principle of substitution When a property can be easily replaced by another, the value of such property tends to be set by the cost of acquiring an equally desirable substitute property.

Principle of supply and demand Prices and rent levels tend to increase when demand is greater than supply, and tend to decrease when supply exceeds demand.

Principle of surplus productivity, balance, and contribution Income that is available to land after the other economic agents have been paid for is known as the surplus of productivity; a proper balance of the agents maximizes the income available to land; the value of any agent is determined by its contribution to the whole.

Principal note The promissory note that is secured by the mortgage or trust deed.

Priority of lien The order in which liens are given legal precedence or preference.

Prior lien A lien that is senior or superior to others.

Private mortgage insurance (PMI) Mortgage guaranty insurance available to conventional lenders on the first, high-risk portion of a loan.

Privity Mutual relationship to the same rights of property; contractual relationship.

Privity of contract The relationship that exists between the persons who are parties to a contract.

Procuring cause That cause originating from a series of events that, without break in continuity, results in the prime object of an agent's employment producing a final buyer; the real estate agent who first procures a ready, willing, and able buyer for the agreed-upon price and terms and is entitled to the commission.

Production Act or process of producing; devoted to yielding a net return of wealth.

Profits The excess of returns over expenditures in a given transaction or series of transactions; also, the excess of income over expenditure, as in a business, during a given period of time.

Progression, principle of   The worth of a lesser valued residence tends to be enhanced by association with higher valued residences in the same area.

Progress payments   Scheduled, periodic, and partial payment of construction loan funds to a builder as each construction stage is completed.

Promissory note   Following a loan commitment from the lender, the borrower signs a note, promising to repay the loan under stipulated terms. The promissory note establishes personal liability for its payment. The evidence of the debt.

Property   Wealth, goods; something capable of being owned.

1. *Income.* Property from which an income is derived.
2. *Industrial.* Land and/or improvements adapted for industrial use.
3. *Intangible.* Property that lacks a physical form.
4. *Investment.* Property purchased for expected future return.
5. *Personal.* All that is not real property.
6. *Real.* Land and all that is attached thereto.
7. *Tangible.* Property that has a physical form.

Property management   A branch of the real estate business involving the marketing, operation, maintenance, and day-to-day financing of rental properties.

Pro rata   In proportion; according to a certain percentage or proportion of a whole.

Proration   Adjustments of interest, taxes, and insurance, etc., on a pro rata basis as of the closing or an agreed-upon date. Fire insurance is normally paid for three years in advance. If a property is sold during this time, the seller wants a refund on that portion of the advance payment that has not been used at the time the title to the property is transferred. For example, if the property is sold two years later, the seller will want to receive one-third of the advance premium that was paid. Usually done in escrow by the escrow holder at time of closing the transaction.

Proration of taxes   To divide or prorate the taxes equally or proportionately to time of use, usually between seller and buyer.

Proximate cause   That cause of an event that, in a natural and continuous sequence unbroken by any new cause, produced that event and without which the event would not have happened. Also, the procuring cause.

Purchase and installment saleback   Involves purchase of the property upon completion of construction and immediate saleback on a long-term installment contract.

Purchase and leaseback   Involves the purchase of property by a buyer and immediate leaseback to the seller.

Purchase money mortgage or trust deed   A trust deed or mortgage given as part or all of the purchase consideration for real property. The purchase money mortgage or trust deed loan can be made by a seller who extends credit to the buyer of property or by a third-party lender (typically a financial institution) that makes a loan to the buyer of real property for a portion of the purchase price to be paid for the property. There are legal limitations upon mortgagees and trust deed beneficiaries collecting deficiency judgments against the purchase money borrower after the collateral hypothecated under such security instruments has been sold through the foreclosure process. Generally no deficiency judgment is allowed if the collateral property under the mortgage or trust deed is residential property of four units or less with the debtor occupying the property as a place of residence.

Purchase of land, leaseback, and leasehold mortgages   An arrangement whereby land is purchased by the lender and leased back to the developer with a mortgage negotiated on the resulting leasehold of the income property constructed. The lender receives an annual ground rent, plus a percentage of income from the property.

Pyramid roof   *See* Roof, pyramid.

Quantity survey   A highly technical process in arriving at cost estimate of new construction and sometimes referred to in the building trade as the price take-off method. It involves a detailed estimate of the quantities of raw material (lumber, plaster, brick, cement, etc.), used as well as the current price of the material and installation costs. These factors are all added together to arrive at the cost of a structure. It is usually used by contractors and experienced estimators.

Quarter round   A molding that presents a profile of a quarter circle.

Quiet enjoyment   Right of an owner or tenant to the use of property without interference of possession.

Quiet title   A court action brought to establish title, to remove a cloud on the title.

Quitclaim deed   A deed to relinquish any interest in property the grantor may have, without any warranty of title or interest.

Rabbeted   Joined by means of a rabbet, which is a groove or cut made in the edge of a board in such a way that another piece may be fitted into it to form a joint.

Radiant heating   A method of heating, usually consisting of coils or pipes placed in the floor, wall, or ceiling.

Rafter   One of a series of boards of a roof designed to support roof loads. The rafters of a flat roof are sometimes called roof joists.

Range   A strip or column of land six miles wide, determined by a government survey, running in a north-south direction and lying east or west of a principal meridian.

Range lines   A series of government survey lines running north and south at six-mile intervals starting with the principal meridian and forming the east and west boundaries of townships.

Rate   A fixed ratio, proportion; also a charge, payment, or price fixed according to a ratio, scale, or standard. To appraise, value; specifically, to assess the value of, for a tax.

1. *Capitalization.* A rate of return used to determine value. Capitalization rate consists of the interest rate and the recapture rate—that is, return on money borrowed as well as return *of* money borrowed. Similar to payment of principal and interest or total amortization of a loan or debt.

2. *Depreciation.* The degree of lessening in value of an object or property; usually applied on an annual scale.

3. *Interest.* The percentage of a sum of money charged for its use. Rent or charge paid for use of money, expressed as a percentage per month or year of the sum borrowed.

4. *Overall.* A capitalization rate that measures income attributable to both land and improvements, that is, to the whole property.

5. *Recapture.* A rate (expressed as a

percentage) to allow for future replacement of a wasting asset. Return of principal.

6. *Split*. A separate capitalization rate attributable to a portion of a property, such as land or improvements but not both: each has a different rate.

Ratification The adoption or approval of an act performed on behalf of a person without previous authorization, such as the approval by a principal of previously unauthorized acts of an agent after the acts have been performed.

Ratio Fixed or approximate relation, as between things, in number, quantity, or degree; rate; proportion.

Ready, willing, and able buyer One who is fully prepared to enter into the contract, really wants to buy, and unquestionably meets the financing requirements of purchase.

Real estate Lands, tenements, and hereditaments; freehold interests in landed property; property in houses and land. In California the same as real property; land and all that is attached thereto.

Real estate board A group of people active in the real estate brokerage business who have joined together to further the goals of professionalism in the industry.

Real Estate Certificate Institute (RECI) Designates a member of the institute who has completed a minimum program of college-level real estate courses and is a member of a local real estate board.

Real Estate Settlement Procedures Act (RESPA) A federal law requiring the disclosure to borrowers of settlement (closing) procedures and costs by means of a pamphlet and forms prescribed by the United States Department of Housing and Urban Development.

Real estate syndicate An organization of investors, usually in the form of a limited partnership, who have joined together for the purpose of pooling capital for the acquisition of real property interests.

Real estate trust A special arrangement under federal and state law whereby investors may pool funds for investments in real estate and mortgages and yet escape corporation taxes, profits being passed to individual investors who are taxed.

Real property In California, synonymous with real estate, meaning land and all that is attached thereto. In other states real property refers to the *Bundle of Rights* inherent in the ownership of real estate, including the right to sell, the right to enjoy, the right to lease, the right to give as a gift, the right to rent, the right to all profits.

Real Property Loan Law Article 7 of Chapter 3 of the Real Estate Law, under which a real estate licensee negotiating loans secured by real property within a specified range is required to give the borrower a statement disclosing the costs and terms of the loan and that also limits the amount of expenses and charges a borrower may pay with respect to the loan.

Real property sales contract An agreement to convey title to real property upon satisfaction of specified conditions; does not require conveyance within one year of formation of the contract.

Realtist A real estate broker holding active membership in a real estate board affiliated with the National Association of Real Estate Brokers.

Realtor A real estate broker holding active membership in a real estate board affiliated with the National Association of Realtors.

Recapture rate The rate of depreciation of the investment. It provides for the return of an investment over the period of its economic life.

Reconciliation   The process of interpreting the data and bringing the various value estimates into mutual relationship with one another in order to determine a final estimate of value. This process was formerly referred to as a correlation.

Recondition   To restore something worn to sound or original condition by readjustments and replacement of parts.

Reconstructed operating statement   A statement or accounting of the estimated income and expenses of an enterprise, made to determine the net income.

Reconveyance   This instrument of transfer is commonly used to transfer the legal title from the trustee to the trustor (borrower) after a trust deed debt has been paid in full.

Recorded   Listed as a matter of record.

Recorded map   A map recorded in the local county recorder's office.

Recorder   One who records specific information; for example, the county recorder.

Recording   The process of placing a document on file with a designated public official for public notice. This public official, usually a county officer known as the county recorder, designates the fact that a document has been presented for recording by placing a recording stamp upon it indicating the time of day and the date when it was officially placed on file. Documents filed with the recorder are considered to be placed on open notice to the general public of that county. Claims against property usually are given a priority on the basis of the time and the date they are recorded, with the most preferred claim going to the earliest one recorded and the next claim going to the next earliest one recorded, and so on. This type of notice is called constructive notice or legal notice.

Rectangular survey system   System for legal description of property based on principal meridians, base lines, and a grid system.

Redeem   To buy back; to repurchase; to recover.

Redemption   Buying back one's property after a judicial sale.

Redlining   A lending policy, illegal in California, of denying real estate loans on properties in older, changing urban areas, usually with large minority populations, because of alleged higher lending risks and without due consideration being given by the lending institution to the creditworthiness of the individual loan applicant.

Refinancing   The paying off of an existing obligation and assuming of a new obligation in its place; to finance anew, or extend or renew existing financing.

Reformation   An action to correct a mistake in a deed or other document.

Region   Generally a segment of the nation set apart from other areas by geographical boundaries.

Regression analysis   Statistical technique for calculating sales price or adjustments, or for estimating probable sales prices, or other variables.

Rehabilitation   The restoration of a property to satisfactory condition without drastically changing the plan, form, or style of architecture.

Reinforced concrete   *See* Concrete, reinforced.

Release clause   A stipulation that, upon the payment of a specific sum of money to the holder of a trust deed or mortgage, the lien of the instrument as to a specifically described lot or area shall be removed from the blanket lien on the whole area involved.

Release deed   An instrument, executed by the mortgagee or the trustee after the debt has been paid in full, that reconveys to the mortgagor or trustor the real estate that secured the loan.

Remainder An estate that takes effect after the termination of the prior estate, such as a life estate. A future possessory interest in real estate.

Remainder depreciation The possible future loss in value of an improvement to real property.

Remaining economic life An estimate of the remaining number of years of productivity of an economic unit such as an apartment house.

Remodeling To model anew, to reconstruct; especially, to reconstruct for adaptation to a new or higher and better use.

Renaissance Fourth phase in the cycle of a neighborhood; the transition to a new cycle through the demolition, relocation, or major renovation of existing buildings.

Renovation Restoration to life, vigor, activity; renewal, repair.

Rent A certain sum agreed on between a tenant and a landlord and paid at fixed intervals by the tenant to the landlord for the use of land or its appurtenances.

1. *Contract.* The rent established by agreement or contract.
2. *Economic.* The probable rent if the unit were offered for rent, that is, the reasonable expectancy in the market.
3. *Ground.* The rent imputable to the land only.

Rent multiplier *See* Gross rent multiplier

Rent roll Total of all scheduled rental amounts for tenant space, services, and parking.

Replacement Substitution.

Replacement cost The cost to replace a structure with one having utility equivalent to that being appraised but constructed with modern materials and according to current standards, design, and layout.

Reproduction cost The cost of replacing the subject improvement with one that is the exact replica, having the same quality of workmanship, design, and layout; or the cost to duplicate an asset.

Rescission of contract The abrogation or annulling of contract; the revocation or repealing of contract by mutual consent by parties to the contract, or for cause by either party to the contract.

Reservation A right retained by a grantor in conveying property.

Reserves for replacement Annual allowances set up for replacement of building components and equipment.

Residence *See* Single-family residence.

Residual A remainder.

Residual process A method of capitalizing income to estimate value.

1. *Building.* A method of value estimation by capitalizing the income remaining to the building.
2. *Land.* A method of value estimation by capitalizing the income remaining to the land.
3. *Property.* A method of value estimation by capitalizing the income to the whole property.

RESPA *See* Real Estate Settlement Procedures Act.

Restriction A limitation on the use of real property. Property restrictions fall into two general classifications—public and private. Zoning ordinances are examples of the former type. Restrictions may be created by private owners, typically by appropriate clauses in deeds, or in agreements, or in general plans of entire subdivisions. Usually they assume the form of a covenant, or promise to do or not to do a certain thing. They cover a multitude of matters including use for residential or business purposes, e.g., houses in a particular tract must contain at least 5,000 sq. feet of living area.

Retaining wall   A wall constructed to hold back earth.

Retrospective value   The value of the property as of a previous date.

Return   Profit from an investment; the yield.

Return of investment   Recapture or conversion of the investment in real estate to cash or other valuable assets.

Return on investment   Profits produced by the investment in real estate.

Reversion   The right to future possession or enjoyment by a person, or the person's heirs, creating the preceding estate (for example, at the end of a lease).

Reversionary interest   The interest a person has in lands or other property, upon the termination of the preceding estate. A future interest.

Reversionary rights   *See* Rights, reversionary.

Ridge   The horizontal line at the junction of the top edges of two sloping roof surfaces. The rafters at both slopes are nailed at the ridge.

Ridge board   The board placed on edge at the ridge of the roof to support the upper ends of the rafters; also called roof tree, ridge plate or ridgepole.

Right of survivorship   The right of a surviving tenant or tenants to succeed to the entire interest of the deceased tenant; the distinguishing feature of a joint tenancy.

Right-of-way   A right of passage on, over, or under another person's land; for example, for a gas line, power line, roadway, railroad, or water line.

Rights   A claim, interest, or title over anything, enforceable by law.

1. *Abutter's.* The reasonable right to light, air, and visibility that a property enjoys from another.
2. *Access.* The right of ingress to and egress from property that abuts an existing public road.
3. *Air rights.* Rights to the reasonable use of the air above a property.
4. *Power line.* A right to install and maintain a power line. *See* Right-of-way.
5. *Reversionary.* The right to the full possession, use, and enjoyment of a property upon the cessation of a lease, the expiration of the useful life of a building, or the like.
6. *Riparian.* The right to the use of water by the owner of land abutting a stream or water course. This use may not unreasonably interfere with riparian rights of others bordering the same water course.
7. *Squatter's.* The right of use and enjoyment by reason of a long and uncontested possession of a parcel of real property.
8. *Subsurface.* A right to the use of land underneath the surface; for example, an underground pipeline easement.
9. *Water.* The right to draw an amount or volume of water from a water course or reservoir.

Right, title and interest   A term used in deeds to denote that the grantor is conveying all of that to which the grantor held claim.

Riparian right   *See* Rights, riparian.

Riprap   A foundation or sustaining wall of stones thrown together without order, as in deep water or on a soft bottom; also, stones so used. Sometimes this term refers to dry-mix concrete in gunny sacks that are placed as a retaining wall and then watered to produce a rock-hard wall when dry.

Riser The upright board at the back of each step of a stairway. In heating, a riser is a duct slanted upward to carry hot air from the furnace to a room above.

Risk analysis A study made, usually by a lender, of the various factors that might affect the repayment of a loan.

Risk rating A process used by the lender to decide on the soundness of making a loan and to reduce all the various factors affecting the repayment of the loan to a qualified rating of some kind.

Roman brick Thin brick of slimmer proportions than standard building brick.

Roof The cover of any building (see Figure 9–34).
1. *A-frame.* A roof whose two sides slope upward at a steep pitch and meet at the top. From either end the roof looks like the capital letter *A*.
2. *Conical.* A cone-shaped roof.
3. *Double pitch.* A gable-type roof. *See* Roof, gable.
4. *Flat.* A roof with little or no pitch.
5. *Gable, double pitch.* A roof with two sides sloping upward and meeting at the top.
6. *Gambrel.* A gable roof with a lower, steeper slope and an upper, flatter one.
7. *Hip.* A roof with four sides sloping upward to meet at a ridge.
8. *Mansard.* A roof with four or more sides sloping upward but stopping short of meeting, so that the top of the roof is flat.
9. *Pyramid.* A roof resembling a pyramid, with four sides sloping upward to meet at a point.
10. *Shed.* A lean-to type roof with one sloping side and one vertical side meeting at a ridge. Also called single-pitch.
11. *Victorian.* A modified mansard roof usually found on towers in Victorian architecture.

Room Space that is enclosed or set apart by a partition.
1. *Bath.* A room that generally includes a toilet, wash basin, and tub or shower. A half bath has only a toilet and wash basin.
2. *Utility.* A room generally used as a laundry room, normally including a tub, washer, and dryer.

Row house *See* Townhouse.

Sale and leaseback A transaction in which, at the time of sale, the seller retains occupancy by concurrently agreeing to lease the property from the purchaser. The seller receives cash while the buyer is assured a tenant and a fixed return on buyer's investment.

Sale-leaseback-buyback A sale and leaseback transaction in which the leaseholder has the option to buy back the original property after a specified period of time.

Sales analysis grid Table of relevant data on comparable properties.

Sales comparison approach One of the three classic approaches to value, involving comparison of the subject property to similar properties which have recently sold.

Sales contract A contract by which buyer and seller agree to terms of a sale.

Sale value The market value.

Salvage value In computing depreciation for tax purposes, the reasonably anticipated fair market value of the property at the end of its useful life; must be considered with all but the declining balance methods of depreciation.

Sandwich lease A leasehold interest that lies between the primary lease and the operating lease.

Sash Wood or metal frames containing one or more window panes.

Satisfaction Discharge of a mortgage or trust deed from the records upon payment of the debt.

Satisfaction piece An instrument for recording and acknowledging payment of an indebtedness secured by a mortgage.

Scarcity A condition where demand exceeds supply; one of the four elements of value.

Scribing Fitting woodwork to an irregular surface.

Seal An impression made to attest the execution of an instrument.

Secondary financing A loan secured by a second mortgage or trust deed on real property. These can be third, fourth, fifth, sixth mortgages or trust deeds, on and on ad infinitum.

Second-growth lumber Lumber from trees that grow after removal or destruction of the old growth by cutting, fire, or other causes.

Section A part separated, a division; in government surveys, a section is one-thirty-sixth of a township, a standard one-mile square containing 640 acres.

Secured party The party having the security interest. Under the Uniform Commercial Code, the mortgagee, the conditional seller, the pledgee, etc., are all now referred to as the secured party.

Security agreement An agreement between the secured party and the debtor that creates the security interest.

Security interest A term designating the interest of the creditor in the property of the debtor in all types of credit transactions. It replaces such terms as chattel mortgage, pledge, trust receipt, chattel trust, equipment trust, conditional sale, and inventory lien.

Seisin (Seizin) Possession of real estate by one entitled thereto.

Seller's market The market condition that exists when a seller is in a more commanding position as to price and terms because demand exceeds supply.

Sentimental value An emotional attachment between a person and a property.

Separate property Property owned by a married person in his or her own right outside of the community interest including property acquired by the spouse (1) before marriage, (2) by gift or inheritance, (3) from rents and profits on separate property, and (4) with the proceeds from other separate property.

Septic tank An underground tank in which sewage from the house is reduced to liquid by bacterial action and then drained off.

Servicing loans Supervising and administering loans after they have been made. This involves such things as collecting payments, keeping accounting records, computing the interest and principal, foreclosure of defaulted loans, and so on.

Setback line A line set by an ordinance that determines how close to a property line a structure can be erected or installed.

Setback ordinance An ordinance requiring improvements built on property to be a specified distance from the property line, street, or curb.

Severalty ownership Owned by one person only; sole ownership.

Severance Act of severing, or state of being severed; partition.

Severance damage In eminent domain actions, the damage to the remainder of a property resulting from a part take of the whole property and the construction of the improvements as proposed.

Shake A hand-split shingle, usually edge-grained.

Sheathing Structural covering, usually boards, plywood, or wall-boards placed over exterior studding or rafters of a house.

Sheriff's deed   Deed given by court order in connection with sale of property to satisfy a judgment.

Shopping center, regional   A large shopping center with 250,000 to 1,000,000 square feet of store area and serving 200,000 or more people.

Sill   The lowest part of the frame of a house, resting on the foundation and supporting the uprights of the frame. The board or metal forming the lower side of an opening, as a door sill or window sill.

Simple interest   Interest computed on the principal amount of a loan only, as distinguished from compound interest, which is computed on both principal and accrued interest.

Single-family residence   Any improvement used as a dwelling for one related family group.

Sinking fund   A reserve accumulated to provide periodic payments to replace a wasting asset or to pay a debt.

SIR   Society of Industrial Realtors.

Site   A piece of land occupied by an improvement; land potentially so occupied.

Skeleton structure   The frame of a building, either wood or steel; also called bone structure.

Skylight   An opaque window in the roof.

Sky window   A transparent window in the roof.

Slander of title   False and malicious statements disparaging an owner's title to property and resulting in actual pecuniary damage to the owner.

Slope   An incline or slant.
1. Level to nearly level—0 to 3 percent.
2. Gently sloping—3 to 9 percent.

3. Moderately sloping or rolling—9 to 15 percent.
4. Strongly sloping or hilly—15 to 30 percent.
5. Steep—30 to 45 percent.
6. Very steep—Over 45 percent.

Slum area   An area of generally run-down, overcrowded residences, usually multiple-family, whose inhabitants are usually economically deprived.

Soil, adobe   *See* Adobe soil.

Soil pipe   Pipe carrying waste out from the house to the main sewer line.

Sole or sole plate   A member, usually a 2×4, on which wall and partition studs rest.

Span   The distance between structural support, such as walls, columns, piers, beams, girders, and trusses.

Special assessment   A charge against a parcel of real estate to meet the cost of a particular improvement, such as a sanitary sewer, road, water line, or storm drain.

Special benefits   Benefits to a particular property resulting from a public improvement. Where allowed, special benefits may be applied against claims for severance damage in the case of a part taken by a public body.

Special power of attorney   A written instrument whereby a principal confers limited authority upon an agent to perform certain prescribed acts on behalf of the principal.

Special warranty deed   A deed in which the grantor warrants or guarantees the title only against defects arising during the grantor's ownership of the property and not against defects existing before the time of the grantor's ownership.

Specific performance   An action to compel performance of an agreement, e.g., sale of land as an alternative to damages or rescission.

Split rate   A separate capitalization rate applied to land and improvements.

Square foot cost   The cost per square foot of area of land or a building or other structure; found by dividing the number of square feet of area into the total cost of the structure or land.

S.R.A.   Designates a person who is a member of the Society of Real Estate Appraisers.

SREA   Society of Real Estate Appraisers.

Stable phase   Second phase in the cycle of a neighborhood, marked by stability of the existing buildings and occupants.

Standard depth   Generally the most typical lot depth in the neighborhood.

Standard deviation   A measure of the extent of variability in a sample.

Standby commitment   The mortgage banker frequently protects a builder by a standby agreement, under which banker agrees to make mortgage loans at an agreed price for many months into the future. The builder deposits a standby fee with the mortgage banker for this service. Frequently, the mortgage broker protects self by securing a standby from a long-term investor for the same period of time, paying a fee for this privilege.

Statute of frauds   A state law, based on an old English statute, requiring certain contracts to be in writing and signed before they will be enforceable at law, for example, contracts for the sale of real property, contracts must be performed within one year.

Statutory warranty deed   A short-term warranty deed that warrants by inference that the seller is the undisputed owner, has the right to convey the property, and will defend the title if necessary. This type of deed protects the purchaser in that the conveyor covenants to defend all claims against the property. If conveyor fails to do so, the new owner can defend said claims and sue the former owner.

Step-up lease   *See* Graduated lease

Story   That portion of a house between a floor and the next floor above.

1. *Basement.* That space below the first floor that is full story height.
2. *Crawl space.* An unfinished accessible space below the first floor, usually less than full story height.
3. *First story.* (First floor.) The lowermost story accessible from outside the building at grade, with its floor closest to grade, and used as improved floor area.
4. *Half story.* A story finished as living accommodations located wholly or partly within the roof frame and having a floor area at least half as large as the story below. Space with less than 5 feet clear headroom is not considered floor area.

Straight lease   Lease agreement in which rent is fixed.

Straight-line depreciation   A method of measuring depreciation on the basis of equal annual amounts during the remaining economic life of the asset or structure.

Straight note   A note in which a borrower repays the principal in a lump sum at maturity while interest is paid in installments or at maturity. Also known as an *interest only* note.

Stringer   A timber or other support for cross members. In stairs, the support on which the stair treads rest.

Structural lumber   That lumber used as the skeletal members or framing of a structure or building.

Structure   Anything constructed or

erected from an assembly of materials. (For example, a single-family residence or garage.)

Studs   Uprights in lath-and-plaster partitions and in furring, upon which the laths are nailed or to which boards are nailed in frame buildings.

Subagent   A person upon whom the powers of an agent have been conferred, not by the principal, but by an agent as authorized by the agent's principal.

Subdivision   A legal definition of those divisions of real property for the purpose of sale, lease or financing that are regulated by law. For examples see California Business and Professions Code, Sections 11,000, 11,000.1, 11,000.5, 11,004.5; California Government Code, Section 66424; United States Code, Title 15, Section 1402(3).

Subjective value   Value in use and not in exchange.

Subject to a mortgage   When a grantee takes title to real property subject to a mortgage, the grantee is not responsible to the holder of the promissory note for the payment of any portion of the amount due. The most the grantee can lose in the event of a foreclosure is the grantee's equity in the property. In neither case is the original maker of the note released from primary responsibility. If liability is to be assumed, the agreement must so state. *See also* Assumption of mortgage.

Sublease   A lease given by a lessee.

Sub-marginal land   Land from which the return or income falls short of paying all expenses.

Subordinate   To make subject to, or junior or inferior to.

Subordination agreement   An agreement by the holder of an encumbrance against real property to permit that claim to take an inferior position to other encumbrances against the property.

Subpoena   A legal order to cause a witness to appear and give testimony.

Subrogation   Replacing one person with another in regard to a legal right or obligation. The substitution of another person in place of the creditor, to whose rights he or she succeeds in relation to the debt. The doctrine is used very often where one person agrees to stand surety for the performance of a contract by another person.

Subsoil   The bed or stratum of weathered material that underlies the surface soil.

Substitution   A replacement for a person or thing.

Substitution, principle of   The maximum value of a property tends to be set by the cost of acquiring an equally desirable and valuable substitute property, assuming no costly delay is encountered in making the substitution.

Subsurface   That which lies below the surface.

Subsurface rights   Rights in property below the surface; for example, an underground pipeline easement or oil, water, or mineral rights.

Sum of the years digits   An accelerated depreciation method.

Summation method   Another name for the cost approach to estimating value.

Superadequacy   *See* Over-improvement.

Supply and demand, principle of   Price or value varies directly with, but not necessarily proportionally to, demand—and inversely, but not necessarily proportionally, with supply.

Surety   One who guarantees the performance of another; guarantor.

Surplus productivity, theory of   A theory used to determine the value of land by subtracting from the effective gross income the cost of labor, management, and capital and capitalizing the remaining income imputable to the land. Also, the land residual process.

Survey   The process by which a parcel of land is measured and its area is ascertained.

Syndicate   A partnership organized for participation in a real estate venture. Partners may be limited or unlimited in their liability. *See also* Real estate syndicate.

Take-out loan   The loan arranged by the owner or builder developer for a buyer. The construction loan made for construction of the improvements is usually paid in full from the proceeds of this more permanent mortgage loan.

Tangible property   Physical objects and/or the rights thereto.

Tax   Enforced charge exacted of persons, corporations, and organizations by the government to be used to support government services and programs.

Taxable value   *See* Value, taxable.

Tax-free exchange   The trade or exchange of one real property for another without the need to pay income taxes on the gain at the time of trade.

Tax rate   The ratio of the tax to the tax base. The rate to be applied to assessed value of real property, which determines the amount of ad valorem tax to be paid.

Tax sale   Sale of property after a period of nonpayment of taxes.

Tenancy in common   Co-ownership of property by two or more persons who hold undivided interest, without right of survivorship; interests need not be equal.

Tenant   The party who has legal possession and use of real property belonging to another.

Tentative map   The Subdivision Map Act requires subdividers to submit initially a tentative map of their tract to the local planning commission for study. The approval or disapproval of the planning commission is noted on the map. Thereafter, a final *map of* the tract embodying any changes requested by the planning commission is required to be filed with the planning commission.

Tenure in land   The mode or manner by which an estate in lands is held. All rights and title rest with owner.

Termites   Ant-like insects that feed on wood.

Termite shield   A shield, usually of non-corrodible metal, placed on top of the foundation wall or around pipes to prevent passage of termites.

Testator   One who makes a will.

Theory   The analysis of a set of facts in their ideal relations to one another.

Third party   A person who is not a party to a contract that affects an interest he or she has in the object of the contract.

Threshold   A strip of wood or metal beveled on each edge and used above the finished floor under outside doors.

Tidelands   Lands that are covered and uncovered by the ebb and flow of the tide.

Tilt-up wall   A wall generally made of reinforced concrete that is poured horizontally and then, when dry, installed vertically on a structure.

Time of the essence   A condition of a contract expressing the essential nature of performance of the contract by a party in a specified period of time.

Time-share estate   A right of occupancy in a time-share project (subdivision) that is coupled with an estate in the real property.

Time-share project   A form of subdivision of real property into rights to the recurrent, exclusive use or occupancy of a lot, parcel, unit, or segment of real property on an annual, or some other periodic, basis for a specified period of time.

Time-share use   A license or contractual or membership right of occupancy in a time-share project that is not coupled with an estate in the real property.

Time value of money   The financial principle that a dollar in the present is worth more than a promised dollar in the future because of the present dollar's interest earning capability.

Title   Indicates the fee position of lawful ownership and right to property. The bundle of rights possessed by an owner. Combination of all elements constituting proof of ownership.

Title insurance   Insurance to protect a real property owner or lender up to a specified amount against certain types of loss, e.g., defective or unmarketable title.

Title report   A report that discloses condition of the title, made by a title company preliminary to issuance of title insurance policy.

Topography   The configuration of a surface, including its elevation and the position of its streams, lakes, roads, cities, etc.

Topsoil   Surface soil, as distinguished from subsoil.

Torrens title   System of title records provided by state law (no longer used in California).

Tort   Any wrongful act (not involving a breach of contract) for which a civil action will lie for the person wronged.

Townhouse   A living unit having a common wall with one or more other living units. It usually consists of two or more stories with ownership of the levels arranged so that one living unit does not occupy a space above or below another living unit.

Township   A primary unit of local government, of varying character in different localities. In government surveys, a division of territory containing 36 sections, or 36 square miles, or a square 6 miles by 6 miles.

Trade fixtures   Articles of personal property annexed by a business tenant to real property that are necessary to the carrying on of a trade and are removable by the tenant.

Trade-in   An increasingly popular method of guaranteeing an owner a minimum amount of cash on the sale of owner's present property to permit the owner to purchase another. If the property is not sold within a specified time at the listed price, the broker agrees to arrange financing to personally purchase the property at an agreed-upon discount.

Transferability   Capable of change in ownership or use. One of the four elements of value.

Transfer fee   A charge made by a lending institution holding or collecting on a real estate mortgage to change its records to reflect a different ownership.

Transition   Change in use, such as farm to residential to commercial.

Treads   Horizontal boards of a stairway.

Trend   A particular direction of movement; flow.

Trim   The finish materials in a building, such as moldings, that are applied around openings (window trim, door trim) or at the floor and ceiling (baseboard, cornice, picture molding).

Trust account   An account separate

and apart and physically segregated from broker's own funds, in which the broker is required by law to deposit all funds collected for clients.

Trust deed   A legal document by which a borrower pledges certain real property or collateral as guarantee for the repayment of a loan. It differs from the mortgage in a number of important respects. For example, instead of there being two parties to the transaction there are three. There is the borrower, who signs the trust deed and who is called the trustor. There is the third, neutral party, to whom the trustor deeds the property as security for the payment of the debt, who is called the trustee. And, finally, there is the lender who is called the beneficiary, the one who benefits from the pledge agreement in that in the event of a default the trustee can sell the property and transfer the money obtained at the sale to lender as payment of the debt.

Trustee   One who holds property in trust for another to secure the performance of an obligation. Third party under a deed of trust.

Trustor   One who borrows money from a trust deed lender, then deeds the real property securing the loan to a trustee to be held as security until the trustor has performed the obligation to the lender under terms of a deed of trust.

Truth in lending   The name given to the federal statutes and regulations (Regulation Z) that are designed primarily to ensure that prospective borrowers and purchasers on credit receive credit cost information before entering into a transaction.

Turnkey costs   Costs that include all of the charges to the consumer, not just the costs to the developer or builder.

Under-improvement   A structure, such as a house, that is too small or of such low quality that its placement on an expensive site is not justified.

Underwriting   Insuring something against loss; guaranteeing financially.

Undue influence   Use of a fiduciary or confidential relationship to obtain a fraudulent or unfair advantage over another because of that individual's weakness of mind, distress, or necessity.

Unearned increment   An increase in the value of real estate that requires no effort on the part of the owner; often due to increase in population.

Uneconomic   Financially unsound.

Uniform Commercial Code   Establishes a unified and comprehensive method for regulation of security transactions in personal property, superseded existing statutes on chattel mortgages, conditional sales, trust receipts, assignment of accounts receivable, and others in this field.

Uniform Standards of Professional Appraisal Practice (USPAP)   A set of standards and ethics developed to guide the appraiser in the development and reports of appraisals, maintained by the Appraisal Standards Board of The Appraisal Foundation.

Unimproved   Not improved, as not used or employed; land not tilled, cultivated, or built upon.

Unit   A single object; a standard of measure by which other quantities are evaluated.

Unit cost   The cost in money of a standard quantity (for example, a square foot or a cubic yard) of a particular item.

Unit cost-in-place method   A method of estimating the cost in money of a structure by breaking down the costs of the various units installed in the structure; for example, the cost per fireplace.

Unit price   *See* Unit cost.

Urban property   City property; closely settled property.

Urethane plastic   A manufactured material that can be made to resemble wood and is very durable and maintenance free; sometimes used for decorative purposes, such as paneling and molding.

Use, non-conforming   A use that is legal by reason of a use permit but does not conform to existing building codes.

Usury   On a loan, claiming a rate of interest greater than that permitted by law.

Utilities   Services rendered by public utility companies, for example, water, gas, electricity, telephone.

Utility   Condition of satisfying a need.

Utility room   *See* Room, utility.

Vacancy factor   The percentage of a building's space that is unrented over a given period.

Vacancy rate   A rate of unoccupancy, usually expressed as a percentage, that a property has or should experience over a given period of time.

Vacant land   Land that is unimproved; a site that does not have a structure on it.

Valid   Having force, or legally binding force; legally sufficient and authorized by law.

Valley   The internal angle formed by the junction of two sloping sides of a roof.

Valuation   Act of valuing, appraisal, as, the valuation of an estate; value set on a thing, appraised price.

Value   Worth; a fair return for money, goods, or services exchanged; monetary worth of a thing.

1.   *Amenity.* That value, difficult to measure in monetary terms, that is attributable to a property because of pleasant surroundings, such as a pretty view, quiet area, or ideal climate.

2.   *Appraised.* The value indicated by someone's estimate or opinion.

3.   *Assemblage.* Same as plottage.

4.   *Assessed.* A value placed on property for purposes of property taxation.

5.   *Book.* The value shown on the accounting books of an organization.

6.   *Capitalized.* The value indicated by the capitalization approach to valuation estimation.

7.   *Exchange.* The value indicated by a property's ability to command other properties in trade.

8.   *Insurable.* That portion of a property that can be covered under insurance to protect the owner against loss of a particular type.

9.   *Intangible.* That value attributable to a property that is difficult to determine precisely.

10.   *Intrinsic.* The value inherent in the property itself.

11.   *Market.* The estimated amount of money a property would normally be expected to bring in the open market over a reasonable length of time with a knowledgeable buyer and seller, neither of whom is under undue pressure.

12.   *Market value.* The most probable price which a property should bring in a competitive and open market under all conditions requisite to a fair sale, the buyer and seller, each acting prudently, knowledgeably and assuming the price is not affected by undue stimulus. Implicit in this definition is the consummation of a sale as of a specified date and the passing of title from seller to buyer under conditions whereby: (1) buyer and seller are typically

motivated; (2) both parties are well informed or well advised, and each acting in what he considers his own best interest; (3) a reasonable time is allowed for exposure in the open market; (4) payment is made in terms of cash in U.S. dollars or in terms of financial arrangements comparable thereto; and (5) the price represents the normal consideration for the property sold unaffected by special or creative financing or sales concessions* granted by anyone associated with the sale.

13. *Nuisance.* The value reflected in the price a buyer would be willing to pay to eliminate an objectionable situation.

14. *Plottage.* The increase in value brought about by the combining of two or more parcels of land with the result that the total value of the combined parcels in the "after" situation exceeds the value of the sum of the individual parcels in the "before" situation.

15. *Potential.* The value that can reasonably be foreseen in the future.

16. *Salvage.* The value imputable to a house, structure, or object if it

were to be moved to another location.

17. *Scrap.* The value imputable to components of a structure, such as lumber, copper, roofing materials, or bricks, if they are removed from the existing premises for use elsewhere.

18. *Sentimental.* The value imputable to a property because of a close personal interest or relationship by the owner or potential owner.

19. *Taxable.* Same as assessed value.

Vapor barrier   A means of preventing the moisture contained in the air within a house from seeping through the interior wall and condensing on the insulating material and destroying its thermal qualities. It also prevents condensation of moisture on the inner surface of exterior siding eliminating the probability of paint peeling or dry rot.

Variable expenses   Operating expenses that vary with occupancy level or intensity of use of a property, e.g., utility costs and maintenance.

Variable interest rate (VIRS)   An interest rate in a real estate loan that by the terms of the note varies upward and downward over the term of the loan depending on money market conditions. Also called variable mortgage rate (VMR).

Variance   In zoning, a legal exception to the use, type, density, or other allowable feature of the normal permitted development or use of a specific site.

Vendee   A purchaser; buyer.

Vendor   A seller; one who disposes of a thing in consideration of money.

Veneer   To overlay or plate, as a common sort of wood, with a thin layer of finer wood for outer finish or decoration; to cover with a veneer; to give an attractive appear-

*Adjustments to the comparables must be made for special or creative financing or sales concessions. No adjustments are necessary for those costs which are normally paid by sellers as a result of tradition or law in a market area; these costs are readily identifiable since the seller pays these costs in virtually all sales transactions. Special or creative financing adjustments can be made to the comparable property by comparisons to financing terms offered by a third party institutional lender that is not already involved in the property or transaction. Any adjustment should not be calculated on a mechanical dollar-for-dollar cost of the financing or concession but the dollar amount of any adjustment should approximate the market's reaction to the financing or concessions based on the appraiser's judgment.

ance to. Also, a brick or stone veneer.

Vent A pipe installed to provide a flow of air to or from a drainage system or to provide a circulation of air within such a system to protect trap seals from siphonage or back pressure.

Verification Sworn statement before a duly qualified officer to correctness of contents of an instrument.

Vested Bestowed upon someone; secured by someone, such as title to property.

Void To have no force or effect; that which is unenforceable.

Voidable That which is capable of being adjudged void but is not void unless action is taken to make it so.

Voluntary lien Any lien placed on property with consent of, or as a result of, the voluntary act of the owner.

Wainscoting Wood lining of an interior wall; lower section of a wall when finished differently from the upper part.

Waive To relinquish, or abandon; to forego a right to enforce or require anything.

Wall One of the upright enclosing parts of a building or a room.

Wall, bearing A wall that acts as a support for the roof or upper story of a house or structure.

Warranty deed A deed used to convey real property; contains warranties of title and quiet possession, and the grantor thus agrees to defend the premises against the lawful claims of third persons. In California the grant deed has supplanted it due to the modern practice of securing title insurance policies, which have reduced the importance of express and implied warranty in deeds.

Warranty of authority A represen-

tation by an agent to third persons that the agent has acted, and is acting, within the scope of authority conferred by his or her principal.

Waste The destruction, or material alteration of, or injury to, premises by a tenant.

Water rights The right to draw water from a water course; or the right to use water, as water on a lake, for recreation.

Water table The depth below the land surface at which water is found.

Wear and tear Depreciation of an asset due to ordinary usage.

Whole property The entire property, land, and improvements as one entity, as distinguished from the land parcel and the building structure being separate units.

Will A written, legal declaration of a person expressing his or her desires for the disposition of that person's property after his or her death.

Window An opening in the wall of a building for admission of light and air, usually enclosed by casements or sashes containing transparent material, such as glass, and usually capable of being opened and shut. *See* Figure 9–36.

1. *Bay.* A projecting window usually associated with Victorian or other traditional and conventional architectural styles.

2. *Bow.* A window similar to a bay window, but without quite the projection of the bay window.

3. *Bubble.* A projecting window in the shape of a half bubble.

4. *Casement, or swing-out.* A window with hinges on the side, that swings out.

5. *Dormer.* A window projecting horizontally from a pitched roof having its own wood frame extension with its own roof and sides.

6. *Double-hung.* A window contain-

ing two vertically moving (up and down) sashes.

7. *Fan.* A small half-circle window, usually above a door, used for ventilation in older apartment hallways; also, a decorative half-circle window in certain architectural styles.
8. *Fixed glass.* A window that can't be opened.
9. *Jalousie.* A window composed of several narrow, equal-length, rectangular pieces of glass, placed either vertically or horizontally, that open together. Also called *louvered* window.
10. *Louvered.* Same as jalousie.
11. *Sky.* A transparent window in the roof. Differs from a skylight in that it is not opaque.
12. *Sliding.* A window that opens by sliding horizontally.

Wraparound mortgage A financing device whereby a lender assumes payments on existing trust deeds of a borrower and takes from the borrower a junior trust deed with a face value in an amount equal to the amount outstanding on the old trust deeds and the additional amount of money borrowed.

X An individual who cannot write may execute a legal document by affixing an *X* (his or her mark) where the signature normally goes. Near the mark a witness then writes the person's name and signs his or her own name as witness.

Her

(X)
Mark

(Signature)

Bill Gray, Witness

Yard A unit of measurement 3 feet long.

Yield The interest earned by an investor on an investment (or by a bank on the money it has loaned). Also called *return* or *profit*.

Yield rate The yield expressed as a percentage of the total investment. Also called *rate of return*.

Yield capitalization Capitalization method that mathematically discounts future benefits at appropriate yield rates producing a value that explicitly reflects the income pattern, value change, and yield rate characterisitics of the investment.

Zero-lot-line home House built on the lot line, generally adjoining another home.

Zone The area set off by the proper authorities for specific use; subject to certain restrictions or restraints.

Zoning The public control of private land use by local police power that designates sections to be used for certain purposes, restricts heights and widths of structures, and imposes limitations on density of living units.

INDEX

A

Abstractive (extraction) valuation approach, 112
Access, 96, 361–362
Accrued depreciation:
   age-life measurement method, 219–220
   capitalization of rental loss measurement method, 223–224
   cost-to-cure depreciation method, 222–223
   economic obsolescence, 218–219
   functional obsolescence, 217–218
   observed condition measurement method, 221–222
   physical deterioration, 217
   sales data measurement method, 224–226
Age-life depreciation measurement method, 219–220
Air space, 23
Allocation site valuation approach, 111–112
Alquist-Priolo Special Studies Zone Act (1973), 101
Anticipation, 29
Appraisal Standards Board of Appraisal Foundation, 2
Appraisals:
   and computerization, 321–331
   comparative market analysis (CMA), 4–5
   cost approach, 200–227
   definition of, 3–4
   for a divorce or separation proceedings, 11
   for buying, 9–10
   for eminent domain, 10–11
   for financial statements, 11
   for inheritance tax, 7
   for insurance, 7
   for leases, 10
   for lending, 6–7
   for living trusts, 10
   for local tax assessment, 7–9
   for real estate brokerage, 11–12
   for selling, 9
   form reports, 5–6, 293–306
   history of, 1–2
   importance of, 2–3
   income approach, 73–74, 250–278
   letter reports, 6
   narrative report, 6
   process of, 62–76
   sales comparison approach, 231–247
   special-purpose, 355–366
   visual comparison, 4

Appraisers:
    liabilities of, 379–380
    licensing, 70–71, 375–378
    responsibilities of, 379
Architecture:
    functionality, 181–183, 193–197
    materials, 169–170
    multiple-family, 181
    roof styles, 175, 177
    windows, 177
Assemblage, 115, 358–359
Assessment value, 19
Assessors parcel number, 67–68

B

Band of investment method, 268–269
Boeckn Appraisal Manual, 210
Broker's net, 256–257
Brokerage, 11–12

C

Capital, 34
Capitalization approach, 73–74, 261–263
    band of investment method, 268–269
    comparative sales method, 266–268
    gross rent multiplier, 274–275
    rates, 263–266
    summation method, 270
    techniques, 271–274
Capitalization of rental loss depreciation measurement method, 223–224
Capitalizing, 114
Certificate and Statement of Limiting Conditions, 70
Certification. *See* Licensing
Change, 30–31
City analysis, 49–51
Climate, 50
Cluster homes, 344–345
Community apartment projects, 344
Compact homes, 348
Comparative (square foot) cost estimation method, 202–204
Comparative market analysis (CMA), 4–5
Comparative sales method, 266–268
Competition, 32
Computerization:
    DataQuick, 325–326
    digital imaging, 327, 331
    electronic data interchange (EDI), 331
    hardware, 321–324
    Metroscan, 325–326
    multiple-listing services, 324–325
    software, 326–327
Concept of agents in production, 34
Condemnation, 10–11
Condominiums, 341–343
Conformity, 31–32

Consistent use, 32–33
Construction. *See also* Architecture
  air conditioning, 148
  appliances, 151–152
  cabinets, doors, and windows, 140–141
  ceilings, 134, 136
  climate and materials, 120–121
  electrical system, 141–142
  energy efficiency, 151
  exterior walls, 128–130
  fencing and retaining walls, 156
  floor plan, 122
  floors, 131–133
  foundations, 122–123
  hardware, 152
  heat pumps, 145–146
  heating, 144
  insulation, 136, 138, 149–151
  interior sprinkler systems, 153
  interior walls, 133–134
  lawns, shrubs, and trees, 155
  lighting, 155–156
  of fair-quality residences, 160–162
  of high-quality residences, 157–160
  outdoor improvements, 156–157
  outdoor sprinkler systems, 155–156
  overview, 119–120
  patios and walks, 154–155
  plumbing, 143–144
  roofing, 123–128
  smoke detectors, 153
  solar energy, 146–147
  specialty equipment, 153
  swimming pools, 154
  vapor barriers, 139–140
  water, 142–143
  wind energy, 148–149
  yard improvements, 153–154
Continuing education requirements, 384
Contract rent, 251
Contribution, 32
Cooperative apartments, 343–344
Corner lot, 80–82
Cost estimation:
  accrued depreciation analysis, 216–228
  comparative (square foot) method, 202–204
  index method, 208
  indirect costs, 212–213
  limitations of, 226–227
  quantity survey method, 205, 207–208
  reproduction vs. replacement, 200–201
  site or yard improvements, 211
  sources of data for, 208–211
  unit-in-place method, 204–205
Cost, 19
Cost-to-cure depreciation measurement method, 222–223
Covenants and restrictions, 24
Cul-de-sac lot, 83–84

D

Data:
  analysis, 110, 240
  collection, 71–72, 232–236
  sources, 208–211
DataQuick, 53, 325–326
Deed restrictions, 101
Demand, 28
Depreciation. *See* Accrued depreciation
Deregulation, 2
Desirability, 78–79
Digital imaging, 327, 331
Direct capitalization, 261
Discount rate, 42
Divorce, 11
Dow Building Cost Calculator, 210
Drainage, 92
Duets, 347

E

E&O insurance, 385
Earthquake fault zones, 101
Easements, 101
Economic analysis:
  city, 49–51
  definition of economics, 38
  international real estate activity, 38–40
  national, 41–44
  neighborhood, 51–59
  regional, 44–49
Economic obsolescence, 218–219
Economic rent, 251
Effective gross income, 114
Electricity, 98
Electromagnetic Fields (EMFs), 102
Eminent domain, 10–11
Employment:
  appraisal corporations, 374
  government salaried opportunities, 370–372
  nonsalaried opportunities, 373–374
  private salaried opportunities, 369–370
  professional organizations, 375–378
Errors and omissions, 385–391
Escheat, 23
Expenses, 253–256
Exposure, 95

F

Fair Housing Amendments Act, 52
Federal Deposit Insurance Corporation (FDIC), 42
Federal Emergency Management Agency (FEMA), 102
Federal Home Loan Mortgage Corporation (FHLMC), 293
Federal National Mortgage Association (FNMA), 293

Federal Reserve System, 42–44
Fee ownership, 15
Fee simple absolute, 15
Final valuation, 285–287
Financial Institutions Reform and Recovery and Enforcement Act
    (FIRREA), 1, 392–401
Financial statements, 11
Fixed expenses, 253–254
Flag lot, 84
Flood hazard areas, 101–102
Foreign buying, 41
Form reports, 293–306
Functional obsolescence, 217–218

G

Going concern value, 20
Going rate, 114
Government National Mortgage Association (GNMA), 42
Government:
   survey, 64–66
   powers against private real estate, 22–23
Gross income, 251–252
Gross rent multiplier, 274–275
Ground rent capitalization, 115–116

H

Hazardous waste sites, 102
Highest and best use, 27–28

I

Income approach, 73–74
   broker's net, 256–257
   capitalization rates, 263–270
   capitalization techniques, 271–274
   expenses, 253–256
   gross income, 251–252
   gross rent multiplier, 274–275
   limitations of, 275–276
   reconstructed operating statement, 257
   vacancy and rent loss, 252–253
Increasing and decreasing returns, 33
Index cost estimation method, 208
Inheritance tax, 7
Insurable value, 19–20
Insurance, 7, 212
Interior lot, 82–83
Investment value, 19

K

Key lot, 84–85
Kit homes, 345–347

L

Labor, 34
Land development site valuation approach, 112–113
Land, 34–35
Land-residual valuation approach, 113–114
Landscaping, 211
Leaching lines, 100
Lease interests, 355–356
Leases, 10
Lender appraisal guidelines, 384–385
Letter reports, 6, 306–307
Licensing:
    continuing education requirements, 384
    education and experience requirements, 383
    levels, 70–71
    license term, 383
    master designations, 375–376
    professional organizations, 375–378
    state, 382
Limiting conditions, 70
Living trusts, 10
Lot and block, 67
Lots, 80–85

M

Management, 34
Market data approach, 73
Market value, 18–19
Marshall Valuation Service, 210
Mean, 286
Median, 286
Metes and bounds, 66–67
Metroscan, 325–326
Mobile homes, 333–335
Mode, 286
Modular home, 345
Multiple-family properties, 112
Multiple-listing services, 324–325

N

Narrative report, 6, 306–311
National Construction Estimator, 210
Natural gas, 98
Neighborhood analysis, 51–59
Nonmobile homes, 335–337
Nuclear facilities, 102

O

Observed condition depreciation measurement method, 221–222
Off-site improvements, 100–101
Office of Real Estate Appraisal (OREA), 381

Operating expenses, 254–255
Operating statement, 257
Opportunity cost, 35
Oral reports, 319
Overimprovement, 31

P

Part take, 359–361
Patio homes, 347
Personal property, 15–16
Physical approach, 72–73
Planned unit developments (PUDs), 350–351
Plottage, 115, 358
Police power, 22–23
Price, 19
Private deed restrictions, 24
Professional organizations, 375–378
Progression, 31–32
Property:
    definition of, 14
    description of, 78–103
    identification of, 64–68
    personal, 15–16
    types of ownership, 332–351
Property tax assessment, 7–9, 22
Property values, 1
Proposition 13, 7–9, 22
Public restriction. *See* Government
Public transportation, 101

Q

Quantity survey cost estimation method, 205, 207–208

R

Real estate, 14
Real Estate Appraisal Reform Amendments, 1–2
Real property:
    definition of, 14
    influences on, 20–21
    life cycle, 30
Reconciliation:
    data available, 281–282
    definition of, 28–281
    final value estimate, 285–286
    intended use of appraisal, 282
    statistical concepts, 286–287
    type of property being appraised, 281–285
Reconstructed operating statement, 257
Regional analysis, 44–49
Regression, 31
Regulation, 2
Rental property, 213
Replacement cost approach, 72

Reports:
  elements of, 292, 310–318
  form, 294–304
  letter, 306–307
  narrative, 306–311
  oral, 319
  types of, 289–291
Reproduction cost, 200–201
Reserve for replacements, 255–256
Reserve requirements, 42
Rights-of-way, 101
Rowhouses, 341

S

Sales comparison approach, 73
  adjusting for differences between sales and subject property, 240–246
  data analysis, 240
  data collection, 232–236
  fundamentals of, 106–111
  limitations of, 246
  processing data, 236–240
Sales data depreciation measurement method, 224–226
Sales price, 19
Sanitary sewers, 98–99
Septic system, 99–100
Severance damage, 361
Site analysis:
  access, 96
  deed restrictions, easements, rights-of-way, 101
  drainage, 92
  exposure, 95
  freeways, expressways, major city streets, 362–363
  off-site improvements, 100–101
  proximity to earthquake fault zones and flood hazard areas, 101–102
  proximity to electric and electromagnetic fields (EMFs), 102
  proximity to nuclear facilities or hazardous waste sites, 102
  proximity to other public facilities, 364–365
  proximity to shopping centers, 365
  public transportation, 101
  shape, 86
  size, 85
  slope, 86–92
  soil composition, 93
  trees, 93–95
  type of lot, 80–85
  utilities, 96–97
  view, 95
Site valuation:
  allocation approach, 111–112
  ground rent capitalization, 115–116
  land-residual approach, 113–114
  sales comparison (market data) approach, 106–111
Slope, 86–92
Soil composition, 93
Solar rights, 358
State licensing, 70–71

Substitution, 29
Summation approach, 72
Superadequacy, 3
Supply and demand, 28–29
Surplus productivity, 34

T

T-intersection lot, 83
Terminology, 441–500
Theory of surplus productivity, 114
Time shares, 351
Title by escheat, 23
Townhouses, 337–340
Tract restrictions, 24
Trees, 93–95, 155

U

U.S. Treasury Issues, 42
Uniform Residential Appraisal Report (URAR), 5–6
Uniform Standards of Professional Appraisal Practice (USPAP), 2, 402–410
Unit-in-place cost estimation method, 204–205
Utilities, 96–100
Utility, 78

V

Vacancy and rent loss, 252–253
Valuation process, 62–63
Value:
    principles controlling, 27–35
    types of, 16–18
Value in use, 20
View, 95
Visual comparison, 4

W

Water, 49–51
Watershed area, 100

Z

Zero lot line, 347
Zoning, 313